THE 250th ANNIVERSARY

HISTORY OF

ST. PAUL'S LUTHERAN CHURCH

OF WURTEMBURG,

RHINEBECK, NEW YORK

THE 250th ANNIVERSARY

HISTORY OF

ST. PAUL'S LUTHERAN CHURCH

OF WURTEMBURG,

RHINEBECK, NEW YORK

BY

MARK D. ISAACS

St. Paul's Lutheran Church of Wurtemburg

371 Wurtemburg Road

Rhinebeck, New York, 12572

www.bookstandpublishing.com

Published by
Bookstand Publishing
Morgan Hill, CA 95037
3353_2

ISBN 978-1-58909-937-1

Printed in the United States of America

To Mrs. Isaacs, my partner in life and in minstry.

With out her love and support you would not be reading this book!

—MDI

Foreword

Verstehen is an important technical term employed by German Sociologist and comparative religion scholar, Max Weber (1864-1920).[1] *Verstehen* means "interpretive or deep understanding."[2] This term is used by Weber to describe one vital aspect of his methodology. Weber wishes to understand the actions and beliefs of people in demarcated groups by reconstructing the *milieu* of values, traditions, interests, and emotions within which they live, thereby to understand how "subjective meaning" is formulated.[3] With *Verstehen,* the social scientist hopes to get into the mind and the life situation of the subjects he is attempting to study.

Percy L. Greaves explains that *Verstehen* "seeks the meaning of human action in intuition as a whole."[4] *Verstehen* "takes into account not only given [objective] facts, but also the reactions of other men, value judgments, the choice of ends and the means to attain such ends, and the valuation of the expected outcome of actions undertaken."[5]

Greaves adds that *Verstehen* "is the result of intellectual insight rather than factual knowledge, but it must always be in harmony with, that is, not in contradiction to, the valid teachings of all the branches of knowledge, including those of the natural sciences."[6]

While understanding is practiced by nearly everyone, deep understanding—*Verstehen*—is deliberate and systematic reflection conducted by scholars and social scientists. Greaves argues that *Verstehen* "is the only appropriate method for dealing with history, and the uncertainty of future conditions, or any other situation where our knowledge is incomplete."[7] In addition to history, Max Weber would include all social

---

[1] Dirk Käsler, *Max Weber: An Introduction to His Life and Work* (Chicago: The University of Chicago Press, 1979, 1988), p.178.

[2] Max Weber, translated by Stephen Kalberg, *The Protestant Ethic and the Spirit of Capitalism* (Los Angeles: Roxbury Publishing Company, 1904-1905, 2002). From the forward by Stephen Kalberg, p.lxxviii.

[3] Ibid.

[4] Percy L. Greaves, *Mises Made Easier: A Glossary for Ludwig von Mises' Human Action* (Irvington, New York: Free Market Books, 1990), p.141.

[5] Ibid.

[6] Ibid.

[7] Ibid.

sciences; i.e., economics, economic history, sociology, comparative religion, geography/geopolitics, and psychology.[8]

A Visit to the home of the late Max Weber in Heidelberg, Germany.
Photograph by Lane Tollefsen, July 14, 2007

Connection to St. Paul's Lutheran Church of Wurtemburg

I have had the privilege of serving as Pastor of St. Paul's Lutheran Church of Wurtemburg for the past fourteen years.[9]   And, I have lived in the historic 1870 Wurtemburg Parsonage since January 1, 2000. During this time, I have walked the cemeteries and studied the headstones. I have spent time alone in the church reading memorial plaques and culling through the well-ordered archives.[10]   I have spent many happy hours rummaging through the crevasses, corners, and cupboards of the old church seeking bits of information. I have also spent time listening to the stories and the recollections of lifelong members, as well as community leaders and local historians living in the Rhinebeck, New York area. During this time, I have sought *Verstehen*, a

---

[8] For more information on Max Weber see Mark D. Isaacs, *Centennial Rumination on Max Weber's "The Protestant Ethic and the Spirit of Capitalism"* (Boca Raton, FL: Dissertation.com, 2005).

[9] I was first assigned to St. Paul's (Wurtemburg) as an Interim Pastor effective June 29, 1996.

[10] This project would not have been possible without the work of the late Wurtemburg Parish Historian Barbara Frost. She has spent years lovingly assembling an archives numbered files protected by archival sheets in protective envelopes. These amazing files provide the raw data for this book.

deeper understanding of this special place, and of the people who lived, worshipped, and died here. Who were these people? And, why did they found, struggle, and support this special country church?

This book is a humble record of my findings and discoveries. For the past several years, I have endeavored to assemble bits of information, dates, old photographs, stories, and maps attempting to weave this material into a coherent narrative, so that these precious memories might help current members gain a deeper appreciation of this remarkable two-hundred-and-fifty-year-old congregation. I also hope that this work will contribute to the preservation of this material for future generations.

In my quest for *Verstehen,* I have intentionally included many extraneous details and tangents. In search of links and connections, I have explored many interesting side roads. Hence, I invite the reader, and the seeker, to join in my *Verstehen* quest.

Standing Silent Vigil in the Wurtemburg Cemetery
Photograph by the Rev. Mark D. Isaacs.

This book also includes nearly one-thousand two-hundred footnotes. These copious footnotes are both an aid to current readers and a gift to future researchers and historians. I invite future chroniclers to use, and to recheck, these sources in the next revision of this book—fifty or one hundred years from now.

Built on the Past Efforts

This book has been constructed on past telling—and retellings—of the Wurtemburg saga. On June 29, 1935, to commemorate the 175th anniversary of the founding of St.

Paul's Lutheran Church of Wurtemburg, Alvah G. Frost (1875-1954)[11] delivered an interesting historical address to the congregation.[12]

According to Alvah G. Frost, "The first historical sketch of the church, of which we have knowledge, was prepared under the authority of the Synod by the Rev. George Neff, D.D., (1813-1900)."[13] This handwritten historical sketch is preserved in the *1873 Church Record Book* in the archives of St. Paul's Lutheran Church of Wurtemburg.

Alvah G. Frost (1875-1954)
Photo: Archives of St. Paul's Lutheran Church of Wurtemburg

---

[11] Alvah George Frost was an active layperson and community leader. He attended Hartwick Seminary, and from 1896-1897 he served as an "Assistant in Mathematics" at the Seminary [Henry Hardy Heins, *Throughout All The Years: The Bicentennial Story of Hartwick in America, 1746-1946* (Oneonta, NY: Trustees of Hartwick College, 1946), p.166.]. He died in 1954, and is buried in the Wurtemburg Cemetery. See obituary clipping for Alvah G. Frost in *Mrs. Samuel S. Frost's (1819-1912) Scrapbook,* (St. Paul's Archives), p. 65.

[12] Alvah G. Frost, *An Address Given to Commemorate the 175th Anniversary of the Founding of St. Paul's Lutheran Church, Wurtemburg, New York, 1935*, pp.8-9. This outstanding pamphlet [also published as a long article in *The Rhinebeck Gazette*, June 28, 1935], is a transcription of an historical address delivered by Alvah G. Frost on June 29, 1935. It has also been preserved in the files of the Rhinebeck Historical Society at the Quitman House, and the Archives of St. Paul's Lutheran Church of Wurtemburg.

[13] "Shortly after" Pastor Neff's "settlement [1855] he preached altogether in the English language and ministered exclusively to the Wurtemburg church [Howard H. Morse, *Historic Old Rhinebeck* (Rhinebeck, New York, 1908), p.151]."

Pastor Neff, a Gettysburg Lutheran Seminary graduate (1842), served as pastor of St. Paul's from July 1855 to July 1876.[14] He also served as a professor at the Hartwick Seminary[15] and president of the New York and New Jersey Synod (1878-1886). Pastor Neff read his "Historical Sketch" at a meeting of the Conference held at the Wurtemburg Church in June 1872. Dr. Neff's paper was placed in the hands of the Rev. George U. Wenner,[16] the Synod historian. It was printed later in the *Lutheran Observer*.[17]

In his "Historical Sketch" Dr. Neff states, "The Church records of St. Paul's congregation at Wurtemburg give but little light upon it's early history, and the old members, who took an active part in its interests, having long ago gone to their reward, but [a] little [information] can be gathered from tradition."[18]

Another useful source for the preparation of this book was Rev. William Hull's important pamphlet, *History of the Lutheran Church in Dutchess County* (1881), a reprint from the July, 1881 *Lutheran Quarterly*.[19] The Rev. William Hull (1868-1939), an 1881 graduate of the Hartwick Seminary and a former attorney, served as pastor of St. John's Lutheran Church in Hudson, New York and Principal of Hartwick Seminary (1891-1893). "The versatile William Hull... an authority on local history... also served variously as a member of the theology faculty [of Hartwick Seminary], financial agent, fundraiser, and president of the Board of Trustees."[20] In his well-written pamphlet, Pastor Hull offers several valuable details concerning St. Paul's (Wurtemburg) during the nineteenth century.

The central challenge of the local church historian is to sift and cull often vague and imprecise records, random newspaper clippings, and obituaries preserved in scrapbooks, and fragments of oral tradition in an attempt to reconstruct and piece together an accurate historical record. Often, in small rural congregations, memories have been preserved via the oral tradition. As a result, there tends to be frustrating gaps and fragments of stories and details that have been forever lost with the deaths of the storytellers.

This history of St. Paul's Lutheran Church of Wurtemburg endeavors to pull and piece together as many of these scattered fragments of information as possible. At the same time, "gathering from the traditions," and attempting to reconstruct an accurate picture of the past two-hundred-and-fifty years at St. Paul's, will be part of an ongoing historical project. Readers are invited and encouraged to contribute additional materials and stories in an effort to accurately reconstruct and preserve the history and memories of St. Paul's. These materials will become a part of later editions of this work.

---

[14] Wentz, p.385.

[15] i.e., Assistant Professor in the Academic Department (1841-1844). Heins, p.163.

[16] George U. Wenner, D.D., L.H.D., *The Lutherans of New York (City): Their Story and Their Problems* (New York: The Petersfield Press, 1918).

[17] Rev. George Neff Manuscript, *1873 Church Record Book.*

[18] Ibid., p.8.

[19] William Hull, *History of the Lutheran Church in Dutchess County* (New York, J.E. Wible Printer: Gettysburg, PA, 1881), p.9.

[20] Ronald H. Bailey, *Hartwick College: A Bicentennial History: 1797-1997* (Oneonta, NY: Hartwick College), p.54.

A Communal Effort

This book is not the work of one researcher and writer. It is truly a group effort. In an effort to honor my predecessors, whenever possible, I have preserved the quaint words and phrases often employed by the original writers—copiously footnoting the primary sources. Many of these primary sources, including handwritten manuscripts, minutes from various groups that met at Wurtemburg over the years, clippings, receipts, contracts, and other ephemera have been preserved in the Wurtemburg Archives.

The Wurtemburg Church, Summer 1938
Photo by Charles F. Teed, St. Paul's Archives.

Indeed, this work would not have been possible without the assistance of the late Barbara Frost (1919-2009), historian of St. Paul's Lutheran Church of Wurtemburg whose outstanding archives, notes, manuscripts, and personal insights helped make this retelling accurate. The Archives of St. Paul's (Wurtemburg) are held in a locked filing cabinet in the church balcony. This material has been carefully and lovingly placed in numbered file envelopes and classified by topics. Barbara Frost also contributed her grandmother's [Mrs. Samuel S. Frost, *nee* Barbara Eliza Traver Frost, (1819-1912)] scrapbook containing an invaluable collection of obituaries and newspaper clippings about the Wurtemburg Church and community to the St. Paul's Archive. This scrapbook provided outstanding primary source information on many nineteenth-century dates, persons, and events.

Mrs. Samuel S. Frost's,
i.e., Barbara Eliza Traver Frost (1819-1912),
scrapbook was an invaluable research source for this book.
Photo: Archives of St. Paul's Lutheran Church of Wurtemburg

In addition to Barbara Frost, I wish to thank the late Mary Lown Traver Baas (1916-2007) for her wonderful recollections. Mary was a lifelong member of St. Paul's. Mary lived just south of the Church, attended Wurtemburg School No. 8 that was located on church grounds, and served as the church organist for years. Mary's father, Percy Lown, was also an active lay leader. Mary's mother Edna S. Hermans Lown (1877-1916) died within a few weeks of Mary's birth. The altar bears an inscription in her memory.

Special thanks are also extended to the late Craig Vogel and his wife Patsy Vogel who spent hours going through old maps, deeds, and charts in an effort to discover the precise location of "the Old Staatsburg Church;" and to Dr. Peter Dykeman for his assistance on researching the Esopus and Sepasco Indians; the Rev. Roy A, Steward, President of the Evangelical Lutheran Conference and Ministerium, a son of St. Paul's

(Wurtemburg); and Ruth Decker, historian of Christ Lutheran Church in Germantown, New York who provided valuable information and source material for this project.

In addition, I wish to thank Dr. Karl Krueger, my D.Min. Advisor and Librarian at the Lutheran Theological Seminary at Philadelphia, for his help with this manuscript, as well as suggestions for sources and assisting in researching. The resources and materials of the Krauth Library at the Lutheran Theological Seminary at Philadelphia provided invaluable information, especially with the effort of attempting to reconstruct the career records of the clergy who have served St. Paul's since 1760.

Another excellent resource for this project has been the Starr Library in Rhinebeck, New York. The Starr Library maintains an outstanding local history collection, including genealogical materials and *The Rhinebeck Gazette* on microfilm.

The Rhinebeck Historical Society and The Quitman House also provided valuable leads and source materials for this project.

Finally, I wish to thank the people of St. Paul's Lutheran Church of Wurtemburg. They deserve special credit for contributing pictures, stories, and support for this project. Without their love and support this project would not have been possible.

And above all, I wish to thank my wife and partner in ministry, Linda A. Isaacs. She made it possible for me to complete the course requirements for the D.Min degree, and she supported me during the long years, months, weeks, days, and hours it took to see this project to the end.

The Rev. Dr. Mark D. Isaacs,
M.Div., S.T.M., D.Min., Th.D., Ph.D.
Pastor, St. Paul's Lutheran Church of Wurtemburg
The Resurrection of Our Lord / Easter Sunday, April 24, 2011

Table of Contents

Chapter One: A Sense of Place: Geography and Location

When driving north from Hyde Park, New York, on highway 9-G, one and three-tenth miles after crossing into the town of Rhinebeck, Dutchess County,[21] New York,[22] we behold a large white church, set high on a hill, encircled by an impressive necropolis. For more than two centuries, this stately white church—located four miles east of the village of Rhinebeck, and seven miles from the Hudson River as the crow flies—has served as an area landmark reigning majestically over the Wurtemburg hills.[23]

Undoubtedly, practical Wurtemburg farmers selected this location for their church because the land was high and dry. At the same time, from the study of comparative religions we learn that nearly all world faiths believe that the gods dwell on high places, and to commune with these gods mortals must make an ascent toward the heavens.[24] For example, in Ancient Greek religion, Zeus reigns from Mt. Olympus.

We also recall that in Friedrich Nietzsche's *Thus Spake Zarathustra,* "Having attained the age of thirty [Zarathustra]… left his home and went into the mountains." After ten years, and "weary of wisdom," Zarathustra came down off the mountain to impart his teachings.[25]

In *The Holy Bible*, we recall five mountains that provided the setting for God's mighty acts: Mt. Ararat;[26] Mt. Sinai;[27] Mt. Carmel;[28] The Mount of Transfiguration;[29] and The Mount of Olives.[30] In *The Holy Bible*, we also recall the tower of Babel story, where humans sought to "build a city and a tower whose top may reach unto heaven."[31]

---

[21] Dutchess County was created November 1, 1683 when the Province of New York was divided into twelve counties. The English Crown was desirous of settling the lands in the various counties and granted large tracts of land to individuals, or groups, who would help populate them.

[22] Towns in New York State are like townships in Pennsylvania.

[23] Various eighteenth and early nineteenth century Dutch, English, and High and Low German spellings include: *Whitaberger Land*; *Wurttemberg*; *Wurtemburgh*; *Wertenbergh*; *Wertembergh*; *Wirtenburg*; *Wirtemberg*; *Wittenburgh*; and *Wittemburg.*

[24] Max Weber, *The Sociology of Religion* (Boston: Beacon Press, 1922), pp.22-23.

[25] Friedrich Nietzsche, *Thus Spake Zarathustra*, translated by Alexander Tille (New York: The Macmillan Company, 1896, 1924), p.1.

[26] Genesis 8:4.

[27] "And Moses went up unto God, and the LORD called unto him out of the mountain…" Exodus 19:3.

[28] Elijah confronts Queen Jezebel's four hundred and fifty prophets of Ba'al and the four hundred prophets of the groves (I Kings 18).

[29] Matthew 17:1-9.

[30] The Risen Lord ascends into heaven (Acts 1:9).

[31] Genesis 11:1-9.

The ancient Aztec's built their pyramids to offer their bloody human sacrifices close to the gods. Apparently, there is a cross-cultural urge to seek the gods on high places.

St. Paul's (Wurtemburg) is such a high place.[32] This location commands—and demands—respect and inspires a feeling of reverence and awe [*mysterium tremendum*].[33] From an aesthetic point of view, the building and church grounds are in harmony and in context with the area countryside.

St. Paul's (Wurtemburg) has been an area landmark since 1802.
Illustration by G. Poisman, 1973.

At the same time, St. Paul's Lutheran Church of Wurtemburg is—and always has been—a simple and plain country church. In recent years Rhinebeck, New York has become a trendy place for BMW driving New York City expatriates to reside in their

---

[32] Locally this area is known as "the Wurtemburg hills," GPS location: 41°53'45"N 73°52'3"W.

[33] Rudolf Otto, *The Idea of the Holy* (New York: Oxford University Press, 1923, 1969), p.12.

McMansions. It is difficult to imagine today, but these Wurtemburg hills were once dotted with dairy cattle and small farms that supported generations of area families.

Ancient stonewalls and an occasional old Dutch barn, bare silent testimony to bygone agrarian days. Hence, St. Paul's was built by practical area farmers who, because of distance and bad roads, found traveling nearly five miles west to the old Staatsburg Church, or four miles north along Pilgrim's Progress Road to worship at the Evangelical Lutheran Church of St. Peter the Apostle (The Old Stone Church), too difficult.[34]

The Evangelical Lutheran Church of St. Peter the Apostle,
"The Old Stone Church."
St. Peter's, founded in 1715, present structure built in 1786,
was "the mother Church" supplying pastors
for area Lutheran congregations including St. Paul's Wurtemburg.
St. Peter's disbanded during the Great Depression.
Photograph by the Rev. Mark D. Isaacs.

---

[34] Elizabeth McR. Frost (1884-1962), *The Men of Wurtemburg and Their House of God: 1760-1960: A Short History of St. Paul's Lutheran Church of Wurtemburg* (Rhinebeck New York, 1960), p.5. Elizabeth McRostie Frost (1884-1962) was the wife of Benson Frost, Sr. (1883-1970) [buried at the Wurtemburg Cemetery]. Benson Frost, Sr. was a prominent attorney, lay leader, and friend of President Franklin D. Roosevelt of Hyde Park, New York.

The Evangelical Lutheran Church of St. Peter the Apostle, "The Old Stone Church," was founded in 1715. The present landmark structure—still located on Highway 9 between Rhinebeck and Red Hook, New York—was built in 1786. St. Peter's was the mother church supplying pastors for area Lutheran congregations, including St. Paul's Wurtemburg. After years of decline, St. Peter's disbanded in 1938.[35] The official records of St. Peter's are on deposit in the Franklin D. Roosevelt Presidential Library in Hyde Park, New York.

From a distance, St. Paul's resembles a classic eighteenth century New England church or meetinghouse.[36] The windows, with the exception of the Good Shepherd stained glass window—added in 1921—are clear glass. The clear glass windows provide worshippers with the opportunity to gaze out into the cemetery and to peer out into the peaceful surrounding countryside. The basic style is Colonial Georgian; i.e., Neoclassical American Architecture (c.1780-1850).[37] The Colonial Georgian structure has been lovingly overlaid and embellished with generations of architectural improvements and add-ons. Today, the building stands as an eclectic conglomeration of styles reflecting various waves of changes and shifts in theological trends and liturgical styles.

From a purist's point of view, it would be easy to be critical of many of these "improvements." However, when we meditate upon the whole design—including the three cemeteries and the grounds—we come to appreciate this special sacred place as it has evolved, holding to a dynamic tension between a *domus dei* and a *domus ecclesiae*[38] style church. St. Paul's (Wurtemburg) is a true transgenerational family meetinghouse, with each generation leaving their own distinctive layer of architectural contributions.

---

[35] Thea Lawrence, *Unity Without Uniformity: The Rhinebeck Church Community, 1718-1918* (Monroe, NY: Library Research Association, 1992), p.98.

[36] Peter T. Mallary, *New England Churches & Meetinghouses: 1680-1830* (Secaucus, New Jersey: Chartell Books, Inc., 1985).

[37] See Harold Kirker, *The Architecture of Charles Bulfinch* (Cambridge, MA: Harvard University Press, 1969, 1998) and Asher Benjamin, *The Country Builder's Assistant* (Bedford, MA: Applewood Books, 1992 reprint of the 1797 edition).

[38] The *domus ecclesiae* "takes us right back to the beginning when the building for the Christian assembly was… the house of the church, the home of the assembly [Richard Giles, *Re-Pitching the Tent: Reordering the Church Building for Worship and Mission* (Collegeville, Minnesota: The Liturgical Press, 1999), p.87]."

Chapter Two: St. Paul's (Wurtemburg) in Context: A Brief Area History

Officially, St. Paul's Lutheran Church of Wurtemburg was founded in 1760. However, as we shall see, this date could be much earlier, probably prior to 1750—possibly even as early as 1734. It is important to note that, despite the fact that by most standards, 1760 is old, second and third generation settlers founded this Church.

The story of Rhinebeck and Wurtemburg begins in 1581 when the Dutch Republic was founded after winning independence from the Spanish Hapsburgs. Today, the areas of the Low Countries are divided between the Netherlands, Belgium, Luxembourg, and parts of France and Germany.[39] Prior to 1581, this region consisted of a number of independent bishoprics, duchies, and counties. Some of these lands were part of the Holy Roman Empire. Through marriage, conquest, or sale, these lands ended up in the hands of the Hapsburg Holy Roman Emperor Charles V (1500-1558) and his son, King Philip II of Spain (1527-1598).[40]

In 1568, the Netherlands, led by William of Orange (1533-1584), revolted against Hapsburg King Philip II.[41] The Dutch resented Philip's persecution of Calvinist Protestants, the imposition of higher taxes, and oppressive efforts by the Hapsburgs to centralize the devolving medieval government structures of the provinces.[42] Freed from Spanish Hapsburg political and economic domination, the free Dutch Republic grew to be a prosperous and powerful trading nation. The success of the Dutch Republic stunned many Europeans because it was a nation not based on a single royal dynasty or on the power of the Roman Catholic Church.

From an economic perspective, the Dutch Republic of the United Provinces completely out-performed all expectations. In Holland, this time period is known as "the Golden Age." Between 1590 and 1712, the Dutch maintained one of the strongest navies in the world, and they operated the largest fleet of merchantmen of all western nations. This allowed for their varied conquests, including breaking the Portuguese sphere of influence in the Indian Ocean and in the Orient. During the seventeenth century, the Dutch established a vast colonial empire and dominated world trade.[43]

---

[39] Michael Bradshaw, et al., *Contemporary World Regional Geography: Global Connections, Local Voices* (New York: McGraw Hill, 2007), pp.104-105.

[40] Harry Elmer Barnes, *The History of Western Civilization* (New York: Harcourt, Brace and Company, 1935), vol. II, pp.25-27.

[41] Ibid., p.87.

[42] Victor L. Tapie, *The Rise and Fall of the Habsburg Monarchy* (New York: Praeger Publishers, 1971).

[43] Ibid., p.25.

In 1609, as a part of this expanding Dutch hegemony, Henry Hudson (1565-1611), an Englishman, sailing under the Dutch flag, sailed West to the New World.[44] On his ship the *De Halve Maen*[45] he explored along the Atlantic coast from Virginia to Newfoundland. During this voyage, "he entered New York Bay and sailed up the great river which was to afterward be named the Hudson River in his honor."[46]

The natives called the river "Mahicanituck," meaning "river of the Mahicans."[47] It is vital to distinguish between the Mohegans, a tribe based in Eastern Connecticut,[48] and the Mahicans, a New York tribe based along the Hudson River north from the Dutchess County-Columbia County line, around Roeloff Jansen's Kill.[49]

Searching for the fabled Northwest Passage to China and the Orient, Henry Hudson pursued the river north beyond the present city of Albany. E. Clifford Nelson states that "although he did not find what he was looking for, Henry Hudson's explorations made Dutch merchants more aware of trade possibilities with the American Indians."[50]

The entrepreneurial Dutch were interested in beaver pelts and furs that only the Indians could provide.[51] In 1614, to protect the lucrative fur trade, the Dutch built Fort Orange where Albany now stands. At about the same time, an outpost was built in Manhattan. Hence, in the 1630s, the Dutch were the first Europeans to settle in the Middle Atlantic between New England and Virginia around their vital port of New Amsterdam.[52]

In 1621, the Dutch West India Company was established, and a charter outlining their powers and privileges was issued [The Dutch West India Company, like other companies of the Mercantilist period, was a true "monopoly," i.e., "a special privilege granted by the State"].[53] In 1624—only four years after the Pilgrims set foot on Plymouth Rock—the first permanent settlers arrived from the Netherlands. By 1664, the estimated total population of the New Netherlands was around ten thousand. By this time, there were also small settlements along the Hudson River in such present day places

---

[44] Will Durant, *The Story of Civilization, Part VII, The Age of Reason Begins* (New York: Simon and Schuster, 1961), p.478.

[45] *De Halve Maen* (The Half Moon) was the name of the ship in which Henry Hudson charted the river that now bears his name. It was an eighty-five foot, square-rigged, three-masted wooden sailing vessel, which carried a crew of fifteen to twenty men.

[46] E. Clifford Nelson, *Lutherans in North America* (Philadelphia: Fortress Press, 1975, 1980), p.5.

[47] Edward Manning Ruttenber, *Indian Tribes of Hudson's River: To 1700-1850* (Hope Farm Press, Country Books, 1872, facsimile reprint 1992), vol.1, p.99.

[48] Ibid., vol.1, p.44.

[49] Ibid., vol.1, p.51 and p.83.

[50] Nelson, p.5.

[51] Carl Waldman, *Atlas of the North American Indian* (New York: Checkmark Books, 2000), p.113.

[52] Bradshaw, p.504.

[53] Nelson, p.5, and Waldman, p.115.

as Fort Orange (Albany), Loonenberg (now Athens), Wiltwyck (now Kingston),[54] Hackensack, New Jersey and New York City.[55]

Most of the inhabitants of the New Netherlands were Dutch Reformed Christians— the State church of the Netherlands. Dutch colonial authorities had a marked preference for Calvinism, thus, in the Dutch colonies, Lutheranism was officially suppressed.[56] However, being pragmatic businessmen, in practice—more interested in profits than prophets—they were generally tolerant of other religions. The major challenge for New World promoters, politicians, and landowners was to attract and keep new immigrants. As a result, prior to the coming of the British in 1664, there was a minority population of Roman Catholics, English Puritans, Lutherans, Anabaptists, and even Jews in the Dutch colony.[57]

The British Take Control of New Amsterdam

In September of 1664, during *The Second Anglo-Dutch War*,[58] several English warships appeared at Manhattan and demanded the surrender of the Dutch colony of New Amsterdam. Peter Stuyvesant (1592-1672), the Dutch Governor at the time, lacked sufficient military might to offer efficient resistance "capitulated without an exchange of fire."[59] With this event, the Dutch tenure in North America came to an end.[60] At this point, the former Dutch colony was renamed "New York" in honor of the brother of King Charles II, the Duke of York.[61]

During the summer of 1686, three Dutch settlers from Kingston [across the Hudson River]—Gerrit Artsen (later the family known in the area as Van Wagenen[62]), Arie Roosa, and Jan Elting[63] (or Elton)—purchased land in Dutchess County from three

---

[54] In 1655 the Esopus Indians attacked Wiltwick [now Kinston, New York] and surrounding Dutch settlements in an attempt to drive the Europeans away once and for all. Bitter intermittent warfare was finally ended in May 1664 (Waldman, p.116).

[55] Nelson, p.5.

[56] Linda Koehler, *Dutchess County, New York Churches and Their Records: An Historical Directory* (Rhinebeck: Kinship, 1994), p.146.

[57] Nelson, p.6.

[58] In 1663, along the West Coast of Africa, British charter companies clashed with the forces of the Dutch West India Company over rights to slaves, ivory, and gold. *The Anglo-Dutch Wars* were Mercantilist economic clashes over trading privileges. These wars established who would be the dominant European naval power. The British emerged as the dominant world economic power.

[59] Nelson, p.6.

[60] Waldman, p.116.

[61] Bradshaw, p.504.

[62] Nancy Kelly, *A Brief History of Rhinebeck: The Living Past of a Hudson Valley Community* (New York: The Wise Family Trust, 2001), p.5

[63] Ibid.

Sepasco Indians. The deed for this transaction is dated June 8, 1686.[64] Their names, recorded on the deed, were "Aran Kee (also known as Ankony), Kreme Much, and Korra Kee."[65]

A few weeks later (i.e., July 28, 1686[66]), a fourth Dutchman named Hendrick Kip, also coming from across the Hudson River in Kingston, New York,[67] purchased additional land in the area from three Esopus Indians named "Anomaton, Calycoon, and Ankony."[68]

Edward Manning Ruttenber writes that, "The names and locations of the Indians tribes were not ascertained with clearness by the early Dutch writers."[69] Dr. Peter Dykeman, a member of St. Paul's who has extensively studied these aboriginal groups, uses terms such as "as far as we know" and "it has really never been ironed out"[70] when describing and identifying the Esopus and Sepasco Indians. Apparently the Sepasco Indians were an Eastern Algonquian speaking[71] band of the Wappinger tribe.[72] The Wappingers dominated the area from Manhattan to Poughkeepsie on the eastern shore of the Hudson River.[73]

Other sources state that the Sepasco Indians were a band or a group associated with the Mahicans. The Mahicans controlled the upper Hudson River north of the Roeloff Jansen Kill; i.e., around the present Columbia County-Dutchess County line. The border between the Wappingers and the Mahicans was fluid and murky, and the Sepasco Indians apparently lived between these two tribes.

The Esopus Indians, also an Eastern Algonquian speaking group, were a band of the Munsee Tribe that lived on the west side of the Hudson River across from present day Rhinebeck. Apparently, "they regularly came across the river to this area to hunt."[74]

---

[64] James H. Smith, *History of Dutchess County, New York: 1683-1882* (Interlaken, NY: Heart of the Lakes Publishing, 1882, 1980), p.252.

[65] Frank D. Blanchard, *History of the Reformed Dutch Church* (Albany: J.B. Lyon Company, 1921), p.12, Nancy Kelly, p.5, Tiejen, p.1.

[66] James H. Smith, p.252.

[67] The region in and around Kingston, New York was first settled by Europeans in the 1650's. Kingston was incorporated by patent May 19, 1667, recognized as a town May 1, 1702 and in 1827 Kingston City was incorporated.

[68] Nancy Kelly, p.5.

[69] Ruttenber, vol.1, p.34.

[70] Dr. Peter Dykeman, interview September 20, 2006.

[71] According to Russell, "there are at least thirteen different Algonquin language groups." Howard S. Russell, *Indian New England Before the Mayflower* (Hanover, NH: University Press of New England, 1980), p.21.

[72] Evan Pritchard, "The Major Algonquin Nations Throughout North America and What They Call Themselves," www.wilkesweb.us/algonquin/nations.htm <August 7, 2006>.

[73] Ruttenber, vol.1, p.51.

[74] Dykeman Interview.

Other sources claim that the Esopus Indians were a part of the Munsee (Wolf) band which was affiliated or related to the larger Lenni Lenape (Delaware) Tribe.[75] The Delaware (a European name) called themselves "Lenni Lenape" translated as "original people," "unmixed people," "the people," or "true men."[76] In the 1600s, the Lenni Lenapes were loosely organized bands of Native American people practicing small-scale agriculture and fishing to augment a largely mobile Hunter-Gatherer society in the region around the Delaware River, the lower Hudson River, and western Long Island Sound.

Henry Noble MacCracken writes that "it seems odd that Sopus [Esopus] Indians [also coming from across the Hudson River] should sell land in Dutchess [County].[77] Dykeman believes that the Esopus Indians "sold" these lands on the east side of the Hudson River to the naive Europeans even if the land did not belong to them.[78]

The net result was a total transfer of more than 2,220 acres of land along the east bank of the Hudson River to Gerrit Artsen, Arie Roosa, Jan Elting (Elton), Henrick and Jacob Kip. For the land, the Indians, from both the Sepascot and Esopus bands, received about $35 worth of goods—such as "six buffaloes [hides?], four blankets, five kettles, four guns, five horns, five axes, ten cans of powder, eight shirts, eight pairs of stockings, forty fathoms of wampum, two drawing knives, ten knives, rum, and one frying pan."[79]

The Native Americans, prior to the arrival of Europeans, were predominantly Hunter-Gatherers.[80] The "Woodland" tribes of the Northeast "supplemented their Hunter-Gatherer diet with fishing and farming."[81] They were primitive agriculturalists cultivating the crop trinity of "corn, squash, and beans."[82] However, as Jared Diamond argues, because corn [maize] had a low protein content, to get the required amount of calories to sustain life, this trinity of crops had to be supplemented by fishing, hunting, and gathering.[83] Hence, even sedentary native peoples were still committed to the traditional Hunter-Gatherer lifestyle.

Clashing Views of Land Use

Tragically, Native Americans and Europeans had radically different understandings of land and of land use. Native Americans believed that land was held in common by the family, clan, and tribe. From the Indian perspective, many of the early treaties and land

---

[75] Waldman, p.34.

[76] Ruttenber, vol.1, p.44.

[77] Henry Noble MacCracken, *Old Dutchess Forever! The Story of An American County* (New York: Hastings House, 1956), p.49.

[78] Dykeman Interview.

[79] James H. Smith, p.252., and E. Smith, *History of Kipsbergen* (New York: The Office of the Rhinebeck Gazette, 1894), and Sari B. Tiejen, *Rhinebeck: Portrait of a Town* (Rhinebeck: Phanter Press, 1990), p.1.

[80] Jared Diamond, *Guns, Germs and Steel: The Fates of Human Societies* (New York: W.W. Norton & Company, 1997), p.356.

[81] Waldman, p.34.

[82] Bradshaw, p.502.

[83] Ibid., p.357.

sales that were signed with the Europeans [the Dutch, and then the English] were more like leases. The early Wappingers, Munsees, Mahicans, and Lenni Lenapes had no idea that land was something that could be sold. From the Algonquian point of view the land belonged to the Creator, and the native peoples were only using it to shelter and feed their people. When the poor and bedraggled Europeans got off their ships after the long voyage, they needed a place to live. The Indians freely shared their land with them. Thus, from the Native American point of view, the Europeans were merely presenting them with a few token gifts in thanks for the kindness that they had been shown.

In contrast, in the minds of the Europeans, these "gifts" were actually meant as the purchase price of the land. Gold,[84] pelt, and land-hungry[85] Western Europeans held to a concept of private land ownership. In the Old World, lands were typically held by the aristocracy and by the Church. The New World was considered to be a place where land was both cheap and superabundant. While the Old World was densely populated, the New World appeared to the newly arrived Europeans to be largely uninhabited.[86] This relatively sparse population was due to the nature of Hunter-Gatherer societies. Charles Murray estimates that, depending on local conditions, a band of just twenty-five Hunter-Gatherers required more than a thousand square miles of hunting ground to sustain their clan.[87]

When Spanish, Dutch, and English Europeans encountered Native Americans, there was a true clash of cultures and worldviews. Between 1492 and 1890, due to "guns, germs, and steel" the estimated population of between sixteen-million and sixty-million Native Americans had been reduced to fewer than 250,000.[88] By 1640, epidemic diseases such as smallpox, measles, and typhus wiped out approximately ninety-five percent of the Native American population in the Hudson Valley. In addition, Dutch colonization and the fur trade caused major dislocations and conflicts within traditional Native American society. Demand for furs, and then land, lured the Indians from their traditional practices and customs, entrapping them in a system in which they became dependent on European luxury commodities. In addition, this toxic cultural and economic mix, created by contacts with the Europeans, triggered a series of sporadic wars between various rival tribal groups. These wars further weakened the disunified Indians and were typically followed by another wave of unfair treaties with the aggressive Europeans. Locally, this tragedy played out at the mid-nineteenth century. Local historian Nancy Kelly notes that "the last Sepasco Indian is said to have died in 1867 in a hut near Welsh's Cave and Lake Sepasco."[89]

Despite the fact that the lands in what were to become the Rhinebeck area were purchased in 1686, and that the stated founding date for the town of Rhinebeck is 1688,

---

[84] i.e., Spanish conquistadors after 1492.

[85] i.e., first the Dutch, then the British.

[86] Waldman, "British Land Use," pp.194-196.

[87] Charles Murray, *Human Accomplishment: The Pursuit of Excellence in the Arts and Sciences, 800 B.C. to 1950* (New York: HarperCollins Publishers, 2003), p.4.

[88] Waldman states that the exact population for 1492 is "a hypothetical and forever elusive number," p.31.

[89] Kelly, p.23.

James H. Smith states that "there is no evidence that the land conveyed by this patent was occupied by the owners before the year 1700."[90] He adds that "it is not certain that there was a single settler in the town of Rhinebeck anywhere before that year."[91]

The Dutch settlers Hendrick and Jacob Kip called their community "Kipsbergen." In 1697, Judge Henry Beekman (d. 1716) [father of Col. Henry Beekman, Jr. (d. 1776)] obtained a land grant from the English Crown and established the present village of Rhinebeck about four miles to the west of Wurtemburg. It was not until 1713 that the name "Ryn Beck" appeared as a reference to Judge Henry Beekman's accumulated landholdings.[92] In November, 1922, a bronze tablet, attached to a large boulder, was erected on the lawn of the Beekman Arms ["the oldest inn in America"] by the Chancellor Livingston Chapter, Daughters of the American Revolution, marking the crossing of the King's Highway [later the Albany Post Road, and now Route 9[93]] and the Sepasco Indian Trail, which ran from east to west to the Hudson River.

The Rev. Chester H. Traver, writes, "We think they brought along the name of Rheinbach, as Carl Neher, one of their members, a listmaster in 1710, came from Rheinbach, Germany, a small village about fifty miles south of Cologne and eight miles back from the Rhine River."[94] At the same time, Arthur Kelly "who has carefully researched the matter," finds that "no members of the great Palatine emigration came from Rheinbach."[95]

---

[90] James H. Smith, p.253.

[91] Ibid.

[92] Kelly, p.3.

[93] In 1703 the Colonial Assembly of New York Province provided for the building of Queen Anne's Highway. It was to be "a Publick and Common General Highway... to extend through the... County of Westchester, Dutchess County, and the County of Albany, the breadth of four rods (Kelly, p.7)."

[94] Chester Henry Traver, "Rev. Chester Traver's History of Wurttemburgh Church: Former Rhinebecker Writes Interesting Sketch of St. Paul's Lutheran Church" *The Rhinebeck Gazette*, September 18, 1915.

[95] Sari B. Tiejen, *Rhinebeck: Portrait of a Town* (Rhinebeck: Phanter Press, 1990), p.4.

Chapter Three: The Palatines Come to America

The road to 1760—and the founding of the church that became St. Paul's Lutheran Church of Wurtemburg—begins with the saga of the Palatines coming to America. The Palatines arrived in the Hudson River valley region in four great waves of migrations in 1709, 1710, 1722, and in 1737.

Generations of German-Americans, perhaps seeking to construct an historical parallel to the Pilgrim Myth foundational to Yankee historiography,[96] i.e., that our ancestors came to America seeking "religious liberty," or "freedom from persecution,"[97] have been taught that their Palatine ancestors were victims of French Roman Catholic atrocities and persecutions in their native Rhineland. For example, Henry Eyster Jacobs notes "These Palatines were the first Lutherans whom religious persecution drove to these shores."[98]

According to this heroic historical re-telling, seeking religious freedom, the Palatines made their way to Holland and then England. And, New York's "benevolent" governor Robert Hunter[99] "wanted to bring these poor people to his colony" for humanitarian reasons. According to these accounts, once they arrived in America, these Germans "were grateful refugees anxious to repay their debt to the British Crown."[100]

While this German-American parallel to the Pilgrim Myth is interesting, the reality is that "poverty and hunger fueled the migrations."[101] That is, it was hope for a better future and mundane economic opportunism—more than the lofty quest for religious liberty—that drove the Palatines to abandon their homeland and embark on the risky voyage to the wilds and hinterlands of America.[102]

In his important book, *Becoming German: The 1709 Palatine Migration to New York* (2004)*,* Philip Otterness sheds new light on this Palatine migration. He writes that "the so-called Palatine migration of 1709 originated in the western part of the Holy Roman

---

[96] e.g., Samuel Eliot Morison, Henry Steele Commager, and William E. Leuchtenburg, *The Growth of the American Republic* (New York: Oxford University Press, 1969), vol. I, p.52-55, and Thomas J. DiLorenzo, *How Capitalism Saved America: The Untold History of Our County from the Pilgrims to the Present* (New York: Crown Forum, 2004), p.58.

[97] Undoubtedly, the myth of "the poor Palatines" seeking religious liberty view was also fueled by anti-German sentiment that arose during the First World War.

[98] Henry Eyster Jacobs, *A History of the Evangelical Lutheran Church in the United States* (New York: The Christian Literature, 1893), p.175.

[99] Governor Robert Hunter (1664 -1734), a member of the [English] Whig party, served as colonial governor of New York and New Jersey from 1710 to 1720. Hunter was replaced by Peter Schuyler as acting governor from 1719 to 1720 and finally by William Burnet.

[100] Philip Otterness, *Becoming German: The 1709 Palatine Migration to New York* (Ithaca, NY: Cornell University Press, 2004)., p.1

[101] Ibid., p.23.

[102] Ibid.

Empire. This was a region composed of dozens of small German states, "of which the Palatinate was but one."[103]

According to E. Clifford Nelson, the term "Palatines" was a loose designation applied by contemporaries in England and America to emigrants from various German lands. Nelson explains that this confusion arose "partly because the geography of Germany was unfamiliar to outsiders who took 'Palatine' to be virtually synonymous with 'German." The people called 'Palatines' came not only from the Palatinate, but also from such adjacent German lands as Alsace, Baden, Württemberg, Nassau, Franconia, and even from more remote lands, such as Holstein and Silesia."[104]

The view that "the poor Palatines"[105] were merely seeking religious liberty apparently originated with the British Whig telling of the Palatine saga. In a debate before Parliament, in a bill to naturalize and aid Palatines refugees that had found their way to England, Sir John Knight painted the picture that many have retained; that is that "the Palatines came here [i.e., to England] to maintain the freedom and purity of their consciences, and their ingenuity and their diligence could not fail to enrich any land which should afford them asylum…"[106]

In support of the Whig cause, in his *Review of the State of the English Nation,* Daniel Defoe (1659-1731), dissenter journalist and author of *The Adventures of Robinson Crusoe* (1719), took up the cause alerting the public to the plight of the "poor inhabitants" of the Palatinate "fleeing Popish persecution."[107]

Ancient History

The German Lutheran congregations in the Colony of New York—including St. Paul's (Wurtemburg)—were made up of refugees from the Palatinate on the Rhine [*The Pfalz*] and from the Duchy of Wurtemburg [modern Baden-Württemberg].

The historical Electoral Palatinate was a much larger territory than that which later became known as the Rhenish Palatinate (*Rheinpfalz*), on the left bank of the Rhine. The Electoral Palatinate also included territory that lay on the right bank of the Rhine, containing the cities of Heidelberg and Mannheim. Heidelberg was the capital and leading city of the Palatinate.

The curious name "Palatinate" goes back to the days of the Roman Empire. Fifty years before the birth of Jesus Christ (c.7 B.C.), the Romans defeated the Gauls and established a stronghold in the strategic river and hill country of the Rhine River Valley, in what is now southwest Germany.[108] During the eighteenth century, this region featured a complex, mind-boggling, noncontiguous series of rump states and petty

---

[103] Ibid., p.2.

[104] E. Clifford Nelson, ed., *Lutherans in North America* (Philadelphia: Fortress Press, 1975, 1980), p.22.

[105] Ibid., p.1.

[106] James H. Smith, p.256.

[107] Otterness, p.53.

[108] Theodor Mommsen, *The Provinces of the Roman Empire* (New York: Barnes & Noble, 1885, 1996), p.120.

principalities. Collectively, these disconnected principalities were called "The Palatinate."[109]

The name "Palatinate" is derived via Latin *palatinus* from *palatium* "place," which was named after the Palatine Hill from the geography of Ancient Rome. Originally, Rome included seven small mountains along the Tiber River, and the hills were given the names "Palatine, Aventine, Caelian, Equiline, Viminal, Quirimal, and Capitoline."[110]

The term "Palatinate" or "Palatine" comes from the title bestowed upon the Roman official dispatched by Caesar to govern this region along the Rhine. Over time, this region was called a "Palatinate" and the wandering tribes who had settled in this region developed into civilized [*Civitas*] people of valor and integrity.[111] They were called "Palatinates," later shortened to "Palatines."

A series of Roman officials and German emperors governed the Palatinate for hundreds of years. The populace was a mixture of Gauls, Celtic, Germanic, and Roman peoples.[112] After the fall of Rome (410-476 A.D.), the Rhine Valley and the surrounding countryside was ruthlessly ruled by a series of petty warlords who built mountain-top castles and fortresses to protect their lands. While these various armed camps fought to dominate the region, the farmers, craftsmen and tradesmen living in the fertile countryside labored to create productive farms, orchards, vineyards, and towns in the valley and surrounding hills.

A Center of Commerce and Prosperity

Gradually, as power was consolidated and fiefdoms grew larger, the Palatinate emerged from this period of constant internal warfare during the Middle Ages. Cities such as Mainz, Mannheim, Worms, Oppenheim, and Heidelberg slowly became centers of religion, education, government, and commerce.

Thus, the Palatine immigrants to the Hudson River valley came from the area of the Palatinate on the Rhine River in the general area of the German southwest,[113] a fertile land of beautiful fields of barley and wheat, orchards, and vineyards. The valleys and hillsides of the region produced some of the finest crops in Europe.[114] These immigrants were craftsmen, vinedressers, artisans, masons, weavers, and farmers who were distinguished by their industry and thrift.[115]

However, during the seventeenth century, because of a seemingly endless series of devastating religious and political wars, the land and people living in this European garden spot along the Rhine were reduced to poverty and destitution.

---

[109] Otterness, pp.9-10.

[110] John F. Walvoord and Roy B. Zuck, *The Bible Knowledge Commentary: An Exposition of the Scriptures* (Wheaton, IL: Victor Books, 1983).

[111] The Romans divided all people into two categories; i.e., *Civitas* and pagans/barbarians.

[112] Mommsen, p.129.

[113] Otterness, p.4.

[114] Ibid., p.9.

[115] Ibid., pp.20-21.

On *The Thirty Years' War*

Due to its central and strategic location between the Spanish Hapsburgs, the Bourbons in France, the Spanish Netherlands, the Holy Roman Empire, and Saxony, the Palatinate was devastated during *The Thirty Years' War* (1618-1648).[116] The disastrous *Thirty Years War*[117] was the true First World War, and the last great war fought in Europe over religion.[118]

This horrific conflict began in Bohemia as a religious struggle with political overtones, and ended as a purely political struggle; i.e., Bourbon France attempting to undermine Spanish Hapsburg hegemony, using religion as an excuse for mass murder and plunder.[119] It pitted Lutheran and Calvinist Protestants against Roman Catholics, except for Roman Catholic France, which supported—first clandestinely, then openly—the Protestant cause against the Hapsburgs.[120]

The build–up of tension between Protestants and Roman Catholics in the Holy Roman Empire during the period from *The Peace of Augsburg* (1555) to the outbreak of *The Thirty Years' War*[121] in 1618, reflects in part the vitality of both the later Reformation and of the Catholic Counter-Reformation.

On the theological right, Ignatius of Loyola (1491-1556) and the militant Jesuits—the shock troops of the Counter-Reformation—radicalized Roman Catholic ideology and theology.[122] On the Reformation left, the remarkable John Calvin (1509-1564) systematized and "hard-boiled" the Protestant position.[123] The end result was no possibility of compromise, reconciliation, or a synthesizing of theological views on either side of the Western Christian spectrum.

The Thirty Years' War began as a conflict between Calvinists and Roman Catholics. Unlike Lutheranism, Calvinism had not been recognized as a licit religion in the Holy Roman Empire in *The Peace of Augsburg* (1555). This posed a continuing problem for German princes who became Calvinists after 1555. Calvinism, due to its intellectual rigor and logical consistency, was an attractive option to many Protestants; i.e., militant anti-Roman Catholics.

When the Jesuit educated Ferdinand II (1578-1637)—who had a deep and bitter hatred for Protestantism—became Emperor and King of Bohemia, these religious

---

[116] C.V. Wedgwood, *The Thirty Years War* (London: The Folio Society, 1938, 1999).

[117] Robert G. Clouse, *The Church in the Age of Orthodoxy and the Enlightenment: Consolidation and Challenge from 1600 to 1800* (St. Louis: Concordia Press, 1980), pp.23-28.

[118] Richard Bonney, *Essential Histories: The Thirty Year's War: 1618-1648* (Oxford, U.K.: Osprey Publishing, 2002).

[119] Ibid., p.29.

[120] Tapie, pp.84-111, and Eric W. Gritsch, *Fortress Introduction to Lutheranism* (Minneapolis: Fortress Press, 1994), p.30.

[121] The great German legal scholar Samuel Puffendorf (1632-1694) coined the phrase, "*The Thirty Years' War*."

[122] The Jesuits dominated *The Council of Trent* (1546-1564).

[123] John Calvin, *Institutes of the Christian Religion,* translation by F. L. Battles, edited by J. T. McNeill. (Philadelphia: Westminster Press, 1559, 1960).

tensions came to a head.[124]   Anti–Protestant religious violence broke out in 1618, and Protestant Hussite Bohemian nobles appealed to the Holy Roman Emperor for protection and a guarantee of their religious liberties.   Receiving no satisfaction, the Hussite Bohemians revolted.

Bohemian nobles deposed King Ferdinand II, and offered the Bohemian crown to Fredrick V, the Calvinist ruler of the Palatinate (1596-1632). Upon his acceptance of the crown of Bohemia—and with the famous *Second Defenestration of Prague* (May 23, 1618)[125]—fighting broke out between Calvinists and Roman Catholics.   Finally, the German Lutherans, Danes, Swedes, and even the French became involved in the warfare on German lands.

The Four Phases

Historians typically divide *The Thirty Years' War* into four phases; i.e., The Bohemian Phase (1618-1625); The Danish Phase (1625-1629); The Swedish Phase (1630-1635); and The French Phase (1636-1648).   Major battles of the war included *White Mountain* (1620); *Breitenfeld* (1631);[126] *Lützen* (1632); and *Nördlingen* (1634).

The Catholic League, fighting to preserve Hapsburg hegemony, was led by Imperial Generalissimo Albrecht von Waldstein (1583-1634) and Field Marshall Johannes Tserklaes, the Count of Tilly (1559-1632).

The Protestant side was led by King Christian IV of Denmark (1577-1648) and King Gustavus Adolphus "the Lion of the North" of Sweden (1594-1632),[127] supported by the Machiavellian diplomatic intrigues of French First Minister Cardinal Richelieu (1585-1642).

The massive armies of *The Thirty Years' War* featured mercenary troops, professional soldiers, and men seeking glory and booty.   They became pikemen,[128] dragoons,[129] cuirassiers,[130] musketeers,[131] artillerymen, and cavaliers.   As disillusionment

---

[124] Bonney, p.12.

[125] Tapie, p.87.

[126] *The First Battle of Breitenfeld*, just north of Leipzig, (September 17, 1631) was the largest set-piece battle of the war. A united Swedish-Saxon army of 40,000 to 42,000 troops under the command of King Gustavus Adolphus defeated a force of 31,000 Hapsburg-Catholic League troops under the command of Count Tilly (Bonney, p.44).

[127] Gustavus Adolphus is considered by historians to be "the Father of Modern Warfare." Among other innovations, Gustavus introduced combined arms techniques mixing highly disciplined light and heavy cavalry, pikemen, musketeers, and a heavy reliance on rapid aimed fire by light field artillery, linear defenses, and the exploitation of enemy weaknesses by rapid battlefield maneuvers. Napoléon Bonaparte, and Carl von Clausewitz, idolized Gustavus Adolphus as one of the greatest generals of all time.

[128] A pike is a two-handed pole weapon, ten to fourteen feet long, that was used extensively by infantry during the war as a counter-measure against cavalry assaults (Bonney, pp.30-31).

[129] During the seventeenth and early eighteenth centuries a dragoon was a soldier trained to fight on foot, but transport himself to the battlefield on horseback. In other words, he moved as cavalry but fought as infantry. The extreme mobility of the dragoons gave commanders the

set in and discipline broke down, many soldiers deserted their units and became "free booters (*Freireuter*)," joining gangs of unruly desperados preying on the helpless civilian population.

At the time, Germany was merely a cultural identity and a geographic designation not a unified political entity. Hence, it lacked the ability to prevent foreign armies from maneuvering in German lands. During this seemingly endless war, geographic Germany became the "involuntary battlefield on which militarily superior nations settled their conflicts and increased their assets."[132] It is important to remember that at this time there was not a unified nation-state of Germany. Germany was merely "a loose collection of hundreds of principalities and city-states."[133] Germany remained a disunited patchwork of duchies, fiefdoms, free cities, and small independent kingdoms until 1871. Steven Ozment states that "with its population approaching twenty million, the empire [a loose confederation] [134] contained 2,500 independent political entities, depending on how far down the political scale, from electoral prince to lowly *Schenk* (a noble servant to higher royalty) one counted."[135]

Plundering the Germans

Thus, during the duration of the war, hordes of often undisciplined foreign troops and mercenary armies crisscrossed German territories plundering and slaughtering the defenseless civilian population. Typically, these marauding armies of professional soldiers, mercenaries, deserters and criminal gangs—from both the Protestant and the Roman Catholic side—lived off the land. Famine and plagues followed the plundering armies. Multitudes of refugees fled before hordes of pillaging armies who, when their employer was unable to pay for their mercenary services, sustained and enriched themselves by begging, robbing, raping, and destroying anything that stood in their way.[136] Innocent German civilians were arbitrarily slaughtered, burned out of their homes, raped, and plundered as huge armies sought booty.[137] And worse, "the principal

---

ability to rapidly redeploy these troops as needed. The name derives from the dragoon's primary weapon, a carbine or short musket called the *dragon*.

[130] *Cuirassiers* were heavy cavalry units. They originally developed out of the men-at-arms forming the heavy cavalry of feudal armies. Their special characteristic was the wearing of full armor, which they retained long after other troops had abandoned it (Bonney, p.29).

[131] Gustavus Adolphus pioneered the use of the musket volley or "salvo" as an offensive tactic for Swedish infantry. Due to the slow reloading time of the musket, until c. 1700 it was necessary to use pikemen to defend the musketeers from cavalry.

[132] Otterness, p.12, and Steven Ozment, *A Mighty Fortress: A New History of the German People* (New York: HarperCollins Publishers, 2004), p.108.

[133] Otterness, p.3.

[134] i.e., The Holy Roman Empire. Since 1438 Germany's overlord had been the Hapsburg dynasty and the Holy Roman Empire.

[135] Ozment, pp.108-109.

[136] Bonney, pp.68-71.

[137] Ibid., pp.72-73.

18

beneficiary of the plundering [of German cities and towns] were often not soldiers but the citizens of neighboring towns who bought up stolen goods for a fraction of their value from plunderers who were mainly interested in cash."[138]

The Thirty Years' War also included an attempt to wipe out Protestantism in the Rhine Palatinate. The inhabitants of the Palatinate were subjected to wave after wave of brutal plunder campaigns. The total extermination of the population was prevented because the residents learned to flee from the armies at the rumor of approach, taking a few necessary belongings and what animals could be hastily driven away. The anguished population returned—sometimes years later—to their burned and pillaged farms and villages to eke out a wretched subsistence until the next campaign came their way.

In the wake of the marauding armies came famine, poverty, economic chaos, civil unrest, and disease. This, in turn, led to further decimation of the German population. Weakened by malnutrition, various diseases—such as influenza, typhus, and dysentery—ravaged the civilian population. Indeed, during the war, more civilians may have died of various diseases and plagues than by direct military action.[139]

In May, 1631, during the sack of Magdeburg, in perhaps the single worst atrocity—in a war marked by atrocities and horrors—an estimated 24,000 people, mostly civilians, were killed by fire and military action.[140]

In some places entire villages were simply wiped out. For example, the walled city of Rothenburg was sacked, plundered, and burned four times during the war. In 1650, when soldiers finally evacuated the once prosperous and now ruined city, "it was reduced to an insignificant small country town and development was suspended for centuries."[141] Rothenburg only began to recover during the early nineteenth century when German Romantic poets and artists re-discovered this picturesque city that had literally been frozen in time two centuries before.[142]

The War Finally Ends with *The Peace of Westphalia*

The war dragged on sporadically for nearly thirty years. Finally, a peace was hammered out between the belligerents in a series of conferences held in the German province of Westphalia in the years 1643–1648.[143] The warring parties negotiated a series of agreements known as *The Peace of Westphalia*. *The Peace of Westphalia* signaled the end of religious wars in Europe and it redrew the map. These political boundaries basically held until the outbreak of the Napoleonic Wars (1789-1815)[144] and *The Congress of Vienna* (1815),[145] which established new national boundaries.

---

[138] Ibid., p.74.

[139] Ibid., p.75.

[140] Ibid., p.72.

[141] Wolfgang Kootz, *Rothenburg ob der Tauber* (Kraichgau Verlag GmbH), p.7.

[142] In December 2004 I had the privilege of spending several days in the now beautiful walled city of Rothenburg ob der Tauber.

[143] Wedgwood, pp.405-441.

[144] Bonney, pp.88-91.

[145] Ozment, p.162.

The tragic irony of *The Peace of Westphalia* is that it merely provided for a return to the religious and political situation as it was in 1529. In 1529, at *The Diet of Speyer,* certain German princes and representatives of various imperial free cities made their first famous "protestation" on behalf of the Lutheran faith. All the bloodshed and misery had brought the religious settlement full circle in that tormented land. In 1648, the religious lines were in general the same as they were in 1529—and much as they remain to this day.[146]

By the close of the *Thirty Years War,* in addition to losing an estimated one third to one half of its total population,[147] Germany was economically devastated, and politically divided into more than three hundred territories or states, each governed by an absolutist prince or other ruler.[148] This horrific war left Germany culturally, politically, economically and physically ruined. Ozment writes that, "The greatest devastation occurred in the Palatine, Mecklenburg, Pomerania, Brandenburg and the Duchy of Württemberg."[149]

It took Germany more than two hundred years to recover from the trauma of *The Thirty Years' War.* Some historians have argued that because of *The Thirty Years' War* Germany was crippled as a nation until at least the rise of Otto von Bismarck (1815-1898) in the 1860s, and that this perceived weakness; i.e., trying to catch-up to France (1648-1789) and England (1815-1914) politically and economically, helped trigger the Great War (1914-1918). The question of "catching up to England and France," and of making high German culture and Germany a leading European nation, was one of Sociologist Max Weber's (1864-1920) life-long intellectual concerns.[150]

Enter Louis XIV

The net effect of *The Thirty Years' War* was to weaken the Spanish Hapsburgs and to increase the power and influence of Bourbon France.[151] This shift in the power structure of Europe led to what Will Durant called, "the French zenith (1648-1815)."[152] In the same way, it could be said that 1492 to 1648 was the golden era of Spanish Hapsburg hegemony, and that 1815 to 1918 [some historians have argued a terminus date of c. 1945] was the era of the global domination of the British Empire.

---

[146] Tim Dowley, J. H. Y. Briggs, Robert Dean Linder, and David F. Wright, *Introduction to the History of Christianity* (Minneapolis: Fortress Press, 1995, 2002), p.427.

[147] Ozment, p.121.

[148] Philip Jacob Spener, *Pia Desideria*, translated by Theodore G. Tappert (Philadelphia: Fortress Press, 1675, 1964), p.3.

[149] Ozment, p.121.

[150] See Mark D. Isaacs, *Centennial Rumination on Max Weber's The Protestant Ethic and the Spirit of Capitalism* (Boca Raton, FL: Dissertation.com, 2005).

[151] Judith G. Coffin, et al., *Western Civilizations: Their History and Their Culture* (New York: W.W. Norton, 2002), vol. II, p.530.

[152] Will Durant, *The Story of Civilization: Part VII, The Age of Louis XIV* (Simon and Schuster, 1963), p.2.

In France, striving toward the Absolutist ideal of "one king, one law, one faith," Louis XIV (1643-1715)—the "Sun King"[153]—attempted to impose religious uniformity upon his own people.

Louis XIV, "The Sun King"
set the standard for Absolutist European Monarchs

Louis XIV's extravagant spending led to the construction of the remarkable Chateau of Versailles outside Paris.[154] Originally a hunting lodge built by his father, Louis XIV officially removed to this spectacular royal palace along with his court on May 6, 1682.[155] Ashley states that the construction of the Chateau of Versailles "cost millions of pounds and killed thousands of workmen."[156]

Louis XIV had several reasons for shifting the seat of the monarchy out of Paris and for erecting this massive symbol of extravagant opulence. Versailles, like an elaborate stage set, served as a dazzling and awe-inspiring backdrop for State affairs and for the reception of foreign dignitaries. At Versailles, attention was not shared with the capital of Paris or the French people, instead the focus was on the glorious Sun King. Court life at Versailles centered on opulence, with courtiers living out lives of expensive luxury.

---

[153] Ibid.

[154] Coffin, vol. II, p.598.

[155] Ibid. p.95.

[156] Maurice Ashley, *The Age of Absolutism: 1648-1775* (Springfield, MA: G. & C. Merriam Company, 1974) p.74.

Like planets and celestial bodies orbiting around the Sun, courtiers and nobles dressed with suitable magnificence and constantly attended festive balls, gala performances, extravagant dinners, and endless celebrations.[157] At Louis XIV's Versailles, many French noblemen had the choice of either surrendering all privileges and influence, or to depend entirely on the king for monopoly grants and subsidies. Instead of exercising their power and potentially triggering conflict with their powerful king, the nobles shamelessly vied for the honor of dining at the king's table or the privilege of carrying a candlestick as the king retired to his bedroom.[158]

With the help of the Jesuits, and with his "one king, one law, one faith" policy, the flamboyant Louis XIV waged an aggressive and protracted campaign in France against the Quietists,[159] the Jansenists[160] as well as the Huguenots [French Calvinists].

In France, thousands of Huguenots [French Calvinists] were shamelessly massacred in cold blood on St. Bartholomew's Day, August 24, 1572.[161] This shattered, but did not destroy, Protestantism in France. In 1589, when Protestant Henry IV (1589-1610)[162] succeeded to the French throne, Protestant hopes ran high. To prevent this, French Roman Catholics formed an alliance with Hapsburg Spain that threatened war if Henry IV remained a Protestant. For the sake of peace, and to preserve his throne, Henry IV yielded and gave up his Protestantism. However, in 1598, with *The Edict of Nantes,* he had Protestantism legally recognized, and granted the freedom to practice Reformed Christianity.[163] In 1610, Henry IV was assassinated by a dagger wielding Roman Catholic fanatic.[164] Despite this tragedy, *The Edict of Nantes* continued to successfully provide legal and religious tolerance for the Huguenot minority.

The Edict of Nantes Revoked

In October 1685, Louis XIV issued *The Edict of Fontainebleau. The Edict of Fontainebleau* revoked *The Edict of Nantes* which had protected Huguenot freedoms for more than eighty-five years.[165] "Seeking a fierce monopolistic national Roman

---

[157] Coffin, vol.II, p.597.

[158] Ashley.

[159] The term *Quietism* refers to a seventeenth century Christian mystical movement that taught that spiritual exaltation can be reached by self-abnegation and by withdrawing the soul from all outward activities, and by focusing on passive religious contemplation. Thus, God works in the heart of a person whose whole being is passive and quiet.

[160] Louis XIV offered the Quietists and the Jansenists a choice between recanting, imprisonment, or exile.

[161] Earle E. Cairns, *Christianity Through the Centuries: A History of the Christian Church* (Grand Rapids: Zondervan Publishing House, 1996), p.309.

[162] Henry IV initiated the Bourbon dynasty which ruled France until 1789 (Coffin, p.523).

[163] Cairns, p.309.

[164] Coffin, p.523.

[165] Ashley, p.72.

Catholicism of the Spanish style,"[166] the public practice of any religion except Roman Catholicism was prohibited. Louis XIV believed that in order to achieve national unity and personal glory, he had to first achieve a religiously unified nation—specifically a Roman Catholic State. This was enshrined in the principle of *"cuius regio, eius religio,"* which defined religious policy throughout Europe since its establishment, by *The Peace of Augsburg*, in 1555.[167]

The Edict of Fontainebleau banished from the realm any Protestant minister who refused to convert to Roman Catholicism. Protestant schools and institutions were banned. Children born into Protestant families were to be forcibly baptized by Roman Catholic priests, and Protestant places of worship were demolished. *The Edict* also expelled all Protestants and Jews from French colonies, and precluded individuals from publicly practicing or exercising their religion, but not from merely believing in it.[168] Thus, *The Edict* provided "liberty is granted to the said persons of the Pretended Reformed Religion [Protestantism]… on condition of not engaging in the exercise of the said religion, or of meeting under pretext of prayers or religious services."[169]

The Edict of Fontainebleau triggered a bitter new round of State sanctioned persecution of French Protestants. Louis XIV began the persecution of the Huguenots by quartering soldiers in their homes. Theoretically, this was within his feudal rights, and hence, legal. But, the practice had fallen into disuse until revived by Louis XIV.[170]

Many historians hold the Jesuits partly responsible for *The Edict of Fontainebleau*. Other historians argue that in the years leading up to 1685 the Huguenots were very unpopular with their Roman Catholic neighbors. The Huguenots tended to be middle class. Traditionalist Roman Catholic French peasants tended to be resentful of the Huguenots' upward social mobility, and many French aristocrats felt threatened by the Huguenots' increased economic and political power. The Huguenots were thought to be "too rich, too successful, and too clannish."[171]

Although *The Edict of Fontainebleau* formally denied Huguenots permission to leave France, lacking basic civil rights, thousands of Huguenots found ways to flee France. With their professional, artistic, and business skills, the predominantly middle-class Huguenots fled to England, the Palatinate, various German states, Holland, and America.[172] In the end, an estimated 200,000 Huguenots fled France taking with them their capital as well as their skills in commerce and trade. Others fled to the mountains of central France. Most of the Protestants who left France in this period were professional

---

[166] W.R. Ward, *Christianity Under the Ancien Regime: 1648-1789* (New York: Cambridge University Press, 1999), p.14.

[167] Otterness, p.14.

[168] Coffin, p.599.

[169] Ashley, pp.72-73.

[170] Cairns, p.310.

[171] Nancy Mitford, *The Sun King: Louis VIV at Versailles* (New York: Harper & Row Publishers, 1966), p.143.

[172] Robert E. Lerner, Standish Meacham, and Edward McNall Burns, *Western Civilizations: Their History and Their Culture* (New York, W.W. Norton, 1993), p.576.

people or skilled craftsmen. Their exodus caused both a capital and a "brain drain" that helped cripple the French economy for generations.[173]

In the end, *The Edict of Fontainebleau,* and the departure of the industrious Huguenots, proved to be a major blow to long-term French economic development.[174] Indeed, one of the causes of the French Revolution (1789-1799) was that the exodus of the middle-class Huguenots led to the institution of rigid class divisions in France. Thus, the famous "Three Estates of the *Ancien Regime* [i.e., the First Estate (the clergy, about ten percent of the population); the Second Estate (the nobility, about two percent of the population); and Third Estate (the commoners and peasants)]." As a result of this act of religious intolerance, France lost many of its most intelligent and hardworking citizens.[175] Hence, this exodus helped set the stage for the crushing class conflict, dismal economic conditions, and hopeless poverty that helped trigger the French Revolution and the rise of Napoléon Bonaparte (1789-1799-1815).

Fleeing to the Palatinate

Being on the border with France, the Lower Palatinate formed an easy asylum for a great number of Calvinist refugees from both Holland and France. And, because the Rhine region was on the border with France, it also became a common battlefield on which the hostile armies supporting Roman Catholic and Protestant rulers fought to settle their territorial, political, and religious disputes.

For example, in 1674, as the French army retreated across the Palatinate, they inflicted terrible devastation. The Rhineland was systematically reduced to a wasteland by the French in an effort to prevent the enemy's army, if they attempted to counterattack in force, from finding supplies to provision and sustain their army.

The Palatinate was again devastated in *The War of the Grand Alliance* (1689-1697). This war, in which both sides once again plundered the region, was precipitated by Louis XIV when his armies marched into the Palatinate. This provocation triggered a war between France and the Allied Nations of Spain, England, and various German states.[176] Once again, as the French army moved into the Palatinate, in order to prevent the region from becoming a source of supply for the allied armies, nearly every hamlet, town, and marketplace was looted and burned. In addition, grain fields were plowed under, vineyards were destroyed, and orchards were cut down. Important castles, fortifications [potential decentralized centers for opposition to central power], and churches in the region were also destroyed.[177]

The notorious French General Comte de Melac (c.1630-1704) was a career soldier under Louis XIV. He became infamous for brutally and mercilessly executing the French

---

[173] Coffin, p.599.

[174] Max Weber, translated by Stephen Kalberg, *The Protestant Ethic and the Spirit of Capitalism* (Los Angeles: Roxbury Publishing Company, 1904-1905, 2002). *The Protestant Ethic and the Spirit of Capitalism* (New York: Charles Scribner's Sons, 1930), pp.41-45.

[175] Tim Dowley, J. H. Y. Briggs, Robert Dean Linder, and David F. Wright, *Introduction to the History of Christianity* (Minneapolis: Fortress Press, 1995, 2002), p.426 and Coffin, p.685.

[176] Ashley, p.83.

[177] Ibid.

policy of terrorizing civilians, and for destroying the enemy's infrastructure and economic base, rather than engaging in major set piece military battles. Under his command, numerous towns and villages in southwestern Germany were systematically burned, and the livelihood of the population was destroyed. To this day, in the Palatinate, Melac's name is a synonym for war criminal, mass murderer, and arsonist.

Damage inflicted by Louis XIV's troops
can still be seen in the ruins of Heidelberg Castle.
Photograph by Lane Tollefsen taken during the author's visit on July 15, 2007.

For example, in February, 1689, General Melac destroyed the walls of Heidelberg and its castle towers, and burned more than half of the city. Inhabitants who tried to rescue their goods were slain in the streets. Everywhere were found the corpses of Heidelberg's civilians that had frozen to death. In the same campaign, the citizens of Manheim were compelled to assist in destroying their own fortifications. They were then driven out, hungry and naked, into the winter cold, and their city was burned.[178]

At *The Peace of Ryswick*, October 30, 1697, the infamous Ryswick clause was included, by which the churches were to stand as they had been during the hostile occupation. Thus, the Protestants lost their churches, and the Roman Catholic service was restored in entirely Reformed communities.[179]

---

[178] Otterness, p.12.

[179] Charlton T. Lewis, *A History of Germany* (New York: Harper & Brothers, 1883), pp.462-463.

Thus, the people of the Rhenish Palatinate were repeatedly caught in the fury and crossfire of *The War of the League of Augsburg* (1689-1696); *The War of Spanish Succession* (1702-1713); and *The War of Austrian Succession* (1740-1748).[180]

Like Johann Wolfgang von Goethe (1749-1832), who also visited these ruins, the author inspects the "Romantic ruins" of Heidelberg Castle on July 15, 2007.
Photograph by Lane Tollefsen.

In 1704, during *The War of the Spanish Succession*, the First Duke of Marlborough (Captain General John Churchill[181]), and Prince Eugène of Savoy led the English, Dutch, Danes, and various German states, including Prussia through the Rhineland, to fight the French at the *Battle of Blenheim* (August 13, 1704). *The Battle of Blenheim* was the first major French defeat in over forty years, and one of the first major English victories on the continent since *The Battle of Agincourt*[182] nearly three hundred years before. *The Battle of Blenheim* destroyed the myth that the armies of Louis XIV were invincible.

Despite this decisive victory, three years later the French, under Marshall Villars, drove their opponents up the Rhine and once again occupied the country as conquerors.[183]

---

[180] Hajo Holborn, *A History of Modern Germany: 1648-1840* (Princeton: Princeton University Press, 1964, 1982), pp.101-122.

[181] The famous ancestor of Sir Winston Churchill.

[182] *The Battle of Agincourt*, fought on St. Crispin's Day (October 25, 1415), was immortalized in William Shakespeare's play *Henry V*.

[183] Otterness, p.22.

Louis XIV's purpose was to gain plunder to support his extravagant royal spending and to establish a vast buffer zone between the German territories and the French border. [184] In order to expand the hegemony of France, Louis XIV ordered the Protestant inhabitants of the Palatinate to leave their homes. At this time, a estimated thirty thousand Palatines were displaced.[185]

Louis XIV died on September 1, 1715 of gangrene, a few days before his seventy-seventh birthday. He had reigned for seventy-two years, making his the longest reign in the recorded history of Europe.[186] His body lies in the famous Basilica of Saint Denis, a suburb of Paris.

A Deeper Understanding of "The Poor Palatines"

By 1708-1709, the Lower Palatinate—caught in the geopolitical struggle between the French Bourbons, and the Spanish and Austrian Hapsburgs—had been ravaged by almost a century of uninterrupted war and plundering. The Palatines were part of a major migration of Germans that opted to leave their homeland in the face of continued economic deprivation, relentless political upheaval, and warfare in the area of the Rhine Valley and southwest Germany.

At the same time, historian Philip Otterness argues that due to the fluidity of the religious and political boundaries in "the Palatinate," the precise identity of these immigrants "was more malleable than might be expected—Roman Catholics could call themselves Protestants, Hessians could call themselves Palatines, people who emigrated freely [for economic reasons] could call themselves religious refugees."[187]

Who were these folk? Otterness writes, "the 1710 immigrants to New York may have settled farther north than later waves of German-speaking immigrants to British North America, but they shared many characteristics with them."[188]

Otterness writes:

> The 1710 immigrants came from the German southwest, often from the Palatinate, but also from other territories along the Rhine, Main, and Neckar rivers. They were primarily members of the Lutheran and Reformed Churches. Most were farmers, craftsmen, and rural artisans. They emigrated from small villages not cities. They came as families. They were drawn to America by dreams of prosperity on the promise of abundant and inexpensive land free from feudal encumbrance.[189]

---

[184] Nelson, p.22.

[185] *The 1743 Palatine House* (*The Old Lutheran Parsonage): 250 Years; 1743-1993: The Oldest Building in Schoharie County* (Schoharie, New York: Schoharie Colonial Heritage Association, 1993), p.2.

[186] Mitford.

[187] Otterness, p.3.

[188] Ibid., p.4.

[189] Ibid.

Otterness makes several important points here. First, "the Palatines" came from a wider geographic area in Germany than is commonly assumed.[190]

Second, "the Palatines" tended to be vinedressers, carpenters, weavers, tailors, blacksmiths, farmers and artisans from small towns and villages.[191] That is, they were not illiterate and unskilled people.

Third, religiously speaking they were a "mixed multitude." Otterness states that they were thirty-one percent Lutheran, thirty-nine percent Reformed, and twenty-nine percent Roman Catholic.[192] The British shipped Roman Catholic Palatines, who were unwilling to convert to Protestantism, back to Germany.[193] Their common bond was that they all spoke German—with a host of regional dialects.

Fourth, "they came as families." Otterness notes that very few single men, widowers, or widows were found among the manifests and in the records. He found that, "eighty percent were married, and most had children with them. On the average, each family had 4.7 members… [and of that] …less than seven percent of the adult emigrants were single men or women."[194] On the other hand, the Portuguese, the Spanish, and the French tended to colonize their New World possessions with single men seeking a quick fortune. In contrast, the British—and the Germans—tended to come to the New World as whole families intending to settle and build a new society.[195]

Fifth, this mass exodus from the southwest part of Germany was a part of a greater emigration from the region. Otterness explains, "during the eighteenth century, North and South America drew about 125,000 German immigrants, while almost 700,000 Germans emigrated to Prussia and areas to the east." Thus, most Palatines headed east, not west! Otterness concludes that in many ways the 1710 emigration was unusual.[196]

Finally, "the Palatines" apparently came to America for economic reasons. As we have argued above, in the past those who have told the Palatine saga tended to stress the idea of religious persecution. Otterness argues, and Nelson concurs, that reports of religious persecution of the Protestant Palatines were probably "exaggerated in order to secure the sympathy and [to gain political] support of other Protestants [primarily in the Netherlands and England].

Nelson adds, "that a fair number of Roman Catholics joined the Protestants in leaving the Palatinate and adjacent territories suggests that religious persecution was not as important as a cause of emigration as the war, [dismal economic conditions] and severe weather."[197]

---

[190] Ibid., p.9.

[191] Ibid., p.20.

[192] Ibid., p.21.

[193] Ibid., p.69.

[194] Ibid., p.19.

[195] Ibid., p.21.

[196] Ibid., p.25.

[197] Nelson, p.23.

In his research, Otterness discovered that greater economic opportunities, the promise of cheap land, and dreams of prosperity led the majority to leave their troubled homeland in search of a better life.

During this time, German speaking peoples had few, if any, political rights and freedoms. Serfdom was not officially abolished in the Palatinate until 1803.[198] Since they were still living under a system of virtual serfdom, potential emigrants were required to petition local officials stating why they chose to leave. According to Otterness, these petitions indicate that "poverty and hunger fueled the migration."[199] The Palatines saw little hope of escaping poverty under present political and economic conditions. Conditions forced them, in the words of one petitioner, "to look for [their] bread elsewhere." To add insult to injury, once they received government permission to depart, "they had to pay a departure tax."[200]

To add to the misery, the winter of 1708 to 1709 was one of the worst on record. Record cold temperatures destroyed the few fruit trees and vineyards that had escaped destruction by the marauding French armies. Nelson writes that, "during the unprecedented severity of the winter of 1708 to 1709... wine reportedly froze solid in casks and bottles and... spit was said to have congealed during its fall from lips to the ground." For many Palatines this additional hardship caused many of them to lose all hope for a future in their homeland.

Around that same time, agents and representatives from the American colonies, most notably the Carolinas and Pennsylvania, had traveled throughout the region promoting immigration to America, stressing the availability of rich farmlands and religious freedom.

Pastor or "Promoter" Joshua Kocherthal?

The majority of traditional and conventional American Lutheran histories depict Rev. Joshua de Kocherthal (c. 1669/1670–December 27, 1719) as a heroic pioneer Lutheran pastor who led his flock up the Hudson River to, what is now, Newburgh, New York. The *truth* is far more interesting.

First, there is the intriguing question of the name "Joshua de Kocherthal."[201] Writing in 1985, Ruth Decker states that, "genealogical research in the past twenty years, as reported by Pastor Heinz Schuchmann of Karlsruhe, Germany, reveals that Kocherthal's name was really Harrsch."[202] She adds that, "no record of Kocherthal can be found in Landau or in the Palatine Archives at Speyer, [Germany]."[203] Apparently, Joshua

---

[198] Ironically, thanks to Napoléon Bonaparte! Otterness, p.17.

[199] Ibid., p.23.

[200] Ibid., p.22.

[201] Nelson, p.22.

[202] Ruth Decker, *275 Years of Lutheran Witness in the Central Hudson Valley: Christ Lutheran Church of Germantown, New York: 1710-1985* (Germantown, New York: Christ Lutheran Church, 1985), p.3.

[203] Ibid.

Harrsch adopted the Kocherthal name indicating that he "came from Fachenfeld in the Kocher River Valley."[204]

Otterness also sheds new light on one of the best known leaders of the 1710 Palatine immigration. Joshua Harrsch [Kocherthal] was born near Bretten, Germany. He served as a Lutheran pastor in Landau, Palatinate and at several small parishes south of Heidelberg. In 1704, following the French invasion of 1703, he visited London to investigate the feasibility of emigration to America.

According to Otterness, Kocherthal was much more than just a spiritual leader. He was also a promoter and an effective propagandist for the New World. Today he would be called a real estate promoter.

In 1706, the Rev. Joshua Kocherthal, a Palatine Lutheran clergyman, made a trip to England to educate himself about the conditions in the English-American Colonies. Upon his return to the Palatinate, he wrote a book stressing the attractive settlement possibilities in America.

Kocherthal's book was entitled *A Complete and Detailed Report of the Renowned District of Carolina Located in English America*.[205] This book was designed to appeal to a semi-literate audience, and was intended to be read aloud.[206] In this book, Kocherthal praised the colony's fertile soil and low taxes. He also stressed the favorable climate where tobacco, various fruits such as grapes, apples, and pears could be grown.[207] For good measure, the cover was embossed with a gold imprint of Queen Anne of England. The book, which ran through several editions, implied that Queen Anne would give free land in America to those willing to become settlers. He even raised the possibility that the Queen would be willing to provide free transportation for those willing to resettle in the colonies.[208]

At this point Kocherthal had not set foot in the Americas. Apparently, he based his book on English records and claims of land agents. His book stressed the advantages of settlement in the Carolinas. To the poor, war-weary, and hopeless Palatines, Kocherthal's book must have been an answer to prayer.

In 1708, an advance party from the Rhenish Palatine accompanied Kocherthal to investigate the situation in New York. Here, they made contact with a local Lutheran pastor, Justus Falckner (1672-1723).[209] Falckner was the first Lutheran pastor ordained in America.[210]

---

[204] Ibid.

[205] In his book Otterness includes a copy of the title page of Kocherthal's book which "spurred the 1709 German emigration." A copy of Kocherthal's book is held in the Rare Book Collection at Duke University, p.28.

[206] Otterness, p.27.

[207] Ibid.

[208] Ibid., p.25.

[209] Kim-Eric Williams, *The Journey of Justus Falckner* (Delhi, NY: ALPB Books, 2003).

[210] Koehler, p.146.

30

In the same year, Rev. Kocherthal and fifty-four Palatines visited England and petitioned Queen Anne for their settlement in America. With support from the Queen, they sailed for New York in October, 1708, on the ship *Globe*, arriving in New York City after nine weeks at sea.

The first Palatine settlement in New York was at the mouth of the Quassaick Creek, near present Newburgh, New York. Governor Lovelace, on behalf of the Queen, allotted 500 acres of land for church purposes, two hundred acres for Rev. Kocherthal's family, and fifty acres to each additional person. However, no contract was signed before the Governor died on May 6, 1709. In order to secure permanent provision and financial aid to the colony, Rev. Kocherthal sailed back to London in August, 1709. When Kocherthal arrived in London in December, 1709, he learned that thousands of his countrymen were fleeing the devastation along the Rhine.

In 1709, he returned to Europe and, in 1710, led about ten shiploads of Palatines to America. He settled them along the Hudson in East Camp and West Camp.[211]

Pastor Kocherthal died in 1719.[212] Kocherthal and his wife are buried *under* St. Paul's Lutheran Church in West Camp. His grave marker is embedded in the wall of the vestibule, and can still be seen today.[213]

The Palatines in England

As a result of dismal economic prospects—and promotional books such as Kocherthal's—thousands of "Palatines" began to leave their homeland. E. Theodore Bachman writes, "From sheer economic hardship, thousands of Palatines looked elsewhere. England, the leading Protestant colonial power, received a massive influx from the Palatinate and South Germany. Clotted in and around London, they taxed the resources as well as strained the bounds of hospitality of Queen Anne (1702-1714)."[214]

On a geopolitical level, it was to England's benefit to use the Palatine sojourners as a buffer to protect its American frontier from the French and the Indians. Queen Anne's assistance to the Palatines was also humanitarian in nature. Queen Anne was personally concerned about the distressed Protestants of Germany. The Queen felt that it was her Christian duty to aid the oppressed Palatines because they were of the same Lutheran faith as her late husband, Prince George of Denmark, who died in October, 1708. The Palatine cause was also a popular issue in England's Whig dominated Parliament. Against the aggressive, intolerant, and tyrannical "one king, one religion" policies of Louis XIV, many in England came to regard themselves as champions of the Protestant cause in Europe.

Queen Anne's agents had agreed that all who wished to leave the Palatinate and find their way down the Rhine to Rotterdam would be transported to England by English ships. Seeking a better life, in the spring of 1709, thousands of Palatines journeyed up

---

[211] Erwin L. Lueker, ed., *Lutheran Cyclopedia*. (St. Louis: Concordia Publishing House, 1954, 1985).

[212] Koehler, p.146.

[213] *The Lutheran*, George H. Straley, "Take a Tour of Lutheran Landmarks," June 4, 1975, p.6.

[214] E. Theodore Bachman, *The United Lutheran Church in America: 1918-1962* (Minneapolis: Augsburg-Fortress, 1997), p.30.

the Rhine toward Rotterdam. It took about a month to make the trip from the barren Palatinate. Some maneuvered through the darkness in small open boats while others walked north toward Holland. Soon the roads and fields, which lay deep in snow, were blackened by numerable men, women, and children fleeing from their homes. Along the route to Rotterdam, many sympathetic Hollanders provided the refugees with food, clothing, and money. Despite this, many Palatines died along the way. By June 1, 1709, about a thousand a week were arriving at Rotterdam. From Rotterdam they made their way to London.[215] Eventually, more than fifteen thousand people had arrived in London.[216]

By October, 1709, because both the Dutch and English authorities were unable to accommodate any more, the rush of Palatine refugees had nearly ceased. Otterness states that "sources vary." One reports that 32,468 Palatines went to England for transport to America; another says that 13,000 reached London by mid-summer. With discrepancies and despite specifics, all sources agree that the numbers reached proportions never dreamed of by the planners of the exodus. *The Palatine London Census of 1709,* a valuable source of information, records only about 6,300 names, less than half of the Palatines that reached London in the spring and summer of 1709.[217]

Thus, an estimated 30,000 Palatine refugees poured into London. The refugees were temporarily settled in three main camps: Deptford, Camberwell, and Blackheath. The Palatine families were herded into an encampment of vacant buildings, warehouses, barns and sixteen-hundred tents at Blackheath on the south side of the Thames River. Here they waited for more than six months for possible transport to America.[218] Their existence in this refugee camp was probably worse than anything they had experienced in their homeland.

At first, explains Otterness, "the English provided public charity, but this was not enough to sustain them."[219] Private charitable groups were overwhelmed. Bread prices rose to astronomical levels. Over-crowding led to unsanitary conditions and the crude temporary shelters made the refugees prone to disease. Nearly all of the refugee families were destitute. The arrangements for their passage were delayed many months and continued support by the English government caused discontent among the English working classes.[220]

As their numbers increased, they became both "a practical and a political problem,"[221] Queen Anne's advisors suggested that these people could be relocated. To increase the total Protestant population some of the Palatines were dispatched to

---

[215] Abdel Ross Wentz, *History of Gettysburg Seminary: 1826-1926* (Philadelphia: The United Lutheran Publication House, 1926), p.20.

[216] Otterness, p.2.

[217] Ibid., p.45.

[218] Ibid., p.47.

[219] Ibid.

[220] Ibid.

[221] Ibid., p.70.

Ireland.[222] Others were sent to America. In America, the Palatines were dispersed in three main areas, "Pennsylvania, around New Berne, North Carolina, and in the Hudson River valley in New York."[223]

The government believed that "the Germans would increase Britain's riches by turning some of New York's [frontier] wastelands into [productive] farms."[224] As a result, Queen Anne and the government arranged for their transportation to the American colonies.[225]

The New York Option

New York became a viable option when, on September 9, 1709, Robert Hunter, a Whig and a Scottish officer who had served as the Duke of Marlborough's *aide-de-camp* on the Continent, and "thus had some familiarity with the situation in the German principalities," was appointed governor of New York.[226]

Hunter proposed relocating 3,000 Germans to the hinterlands of upstate New York—perhaps in the Schoharie River valley—in return for several years' labor to produce naval stores; i.e., hemp, shipmasts, tar, and pitch.[227] It was hoped that the Palatines might help develop a great tar and pitch industry for British naval and commercial purposes.[228] Previously, naval stores had to be imported from Scandinavia[229] [Sweden had long monopolized the trade in naval stores[230]], and during the prior decade the world market price of tar had more than doubled.[231] At the time, the British navy—composed entirely of wooden ships in constant need of pitch caulking—was the largest naval force in the world. Following the precepts of Mercantilist economics, the naval stores project was conceived so that Britain would be economically self-sufficient and be able to maintain a positive trade balance. With this scheme, American tar and pitch could be traded for English woolens.[232]

---

[222] Ibid., p.87.

[223] Henry Eyster Jacobs, *A History of the Evangelical Lutheran Church in the United States* (New York: The Christian Literature, 1893), p.184.

[224] Otterness, p.71.

[225] W.E. Lunt, *History of England* (New York: Harper and Row, 1928, 1957), p.477ff.

[226] Otterness, p.72.

[227] Nelson, p.24 and Otterness, p.2.

[228] Robert F. Scholz, *Press Toward the Mark: History of the United Lutheran Synod of New York and New England: 1830-1930* (Metuchen, New Jersey: The Scarecrow Press, 1995), pp.18-19.

[229] Otterness, p.103.

[230] Ibid., p.72.

[231] Ibid.

[232] Ibid.

Hunter viewed the Palatines not as suffering refugees, but as assets in an ambitious commercial venture.[233] He hoped to not only produce naval stores for the Crown, but also to reap a handsome personal fortune from the enterprise.[234]

On the other hand, the Palatines came to America seeking economic opportunity, freedom, and new lands. Thus, they viewed the tar-making scheme as a "means to an end."[235]

The Palatines were also brought to New York by the English Crown to curb a potential French-Canadian invasion of the province of New York, and to provide a strategic frontier buffer against the French and Iroquois Indians.[236] Earlier, the Dutch and then British settlers, had seized the best land.[237] By 1710, the only available land was on the sparsely populated fringes of the frontier. The Palatines provided a solution to this problem. In addition, in the long-run, it was hoped that the Palatines would inter-marry with the Indians on the frontier and their off-spring would be loyal to the Crown. The relocation of the Palatines appeared to provide a "win-win solution" for the British government.

The Crossing

In mid-April, 1710, Governor Robert Hunter, and 3,300 Palatines in a convoy of ten ships, left England.[238] Like most trans-Atlantic crossings in the early eighteen century, the voyage to America in 1710 was a long and deadly experience. Once the voyage to the New World began, conditions on board the ships quickly became unbearable. The Palatines were in a weakened condition after more than a year living in refugee camps in the London area. Prior to departing from England, a hundred were reported sick on one ship. Soon, all of the Palatine ships became ravaged with fever, typhus, and other ailments. Since there was no provision for even elementary sanitation, unsanitary drinking water, vermin, wormy biscuits, foul air, little sunlight and exercise caused sickness and death for a great number of immigrants. Eighty deaths were reported in one ship alone. It is recorded that four-hundred and forty-six out of the original 2,814 died enroute, and another two-hundred and fifty died shortly after arrival in New York.[239]

One of the ships, *The Herbert*, ran aground and burned off of Block Island at the eastern end of Long Island Sound. Most of its supplies and many lives were lost in the wreck. John Greenleaf Whittier (1807-1892) immortalized the wreck of *The Herbert* in a poem, "The Palatine." The Palatine cemetery can still be found on Block Island, Rhode Island.

---

[233] Ibid., p.81.

[234] Ibid, p.72 and p.94.

[235] Ibid., p.82.

[236] Ibid., p.73.

[237] Nelson, p.24.

[238] Otterness, p.75.

[239] Ibid., pp.78-79.

Once they arrived in New York, their problems did not diminish. Gov. Robert Hunter's original plan to set up his naval stores project on land in the Schoharie River Valley fell through when the land reverted back to the Mohawks.[240]

Instead, on October 3, 1710, Governor Robert Hunter decided—or was persuaded by Robert Livingston (1654-1725)—to purchase a 6,000 acre tract of land in "Livingston Manor" on the Hudson River.[241] At the same time, Livingston signed a contract to provide the Palatine tar-makers with "bread and beer."[242] Earlier, Livingston had established a flourmill, a sawmill, a gristmill, and a brewery on his manor that could easily provide these products.[243] With the prospect of "spurring development of his yet unproductive manor," the transaction "had obvious advantages for Livingston."[244]

The problem with the British colonies in America was that large land holders were having trouble attracting settlers who were willing and able to immigrate and become tenants on their newly acquired lands. For example, Robert Livingston, a quarter of a century after becoming proprietor of Livingston Manor, "had been able to attract only a dozen or so tenant families."[245] In fact, notes Clare Brant, prior to the arrival of the Palatines, Robert Livingston was the "proprietor of nothing but a vast undeveloped tract, lord over virtually no one—a situation that he was desperate to remedy."[246]

The Lord of the Manor

Robert Livingston, first "Lord of the Manor" of Livingston in New York, was one of seven children of the Rev. John Livingston. He was a lineal descendent of the fifth Lord Livingston, ancestor of the earls of Linlithgow and Callendar,[247] an energetic preacher of the Reformed Church in Scotland, who was banished for his nonconformity,[248] and took refuge in Rotterdam, where he died in 1672.[249] From his father's banishment, Robert Livingston gained a practical understanding of Dutch culture and business methods. This knowledge served him well when he arrived in New York.

In the autumn of 1674, at the age of twenty-four, Robert Livingston came to New York.[250] Livingston has been described as "a perfect type of those disreputable men who came to America only to get rich quickly." He was part businessman, part con-man, part political operative, and always a charming self-promoter. Politically, he was "a

---

[240] Ibid., p.86.

[241] Ibid., p.80.

[242] Ibid., p.90.

[243] Clare Brant, *An American Aristocracy: The Livingstons* (New York: Doubleday & Co., 1986, 1990), p.60.

[244] Otterness, p.80.

[245] Brant, p.59.

[246] Ibid.

[247] Ibid., p.13.

[248] Ibid., pp.12-13.

[249] Ibid., p.14.

[250] Ibid., p.10.

committed Tory" who freely and frequently became a Whig when it was necessary to promote his own cause. A born grafter, later in his career Livingston was a business associate of the infamous pirate Captain William Kidd (1645-1701), and thereby added greatly to his fortune.[251] According to Brandt, "rumor has it that [prior to Kidd's capture] Robert Livingston spirited the gold off of one of Captain Kidd's ships in Long Island Sound and buried it at various locations at his [Colombia County] manor."[252]

The enterprising young Livingston soon found his way to the settlement of Albany. At the time, "Albany was a primitive Dutch trading outpost on the edge of a savage wilderness."[253] Within a year he had been made Town Clerk and Secretary for Indian Affairs. To these offices were added those of Collector of Excise and Quitrents, Clerk of Peace, and Clerk of the Court of Common Pleas.[254]

Livingston also became a clerk for Nicholas Van Rensselaer, the director of Rensselaerwyck, "the greatest of the Dutch patroonships" in America.[255] Patroonships—which were later called "manors" after the English takeover of 1664—were mammoth land grants given on easy terms by both the Dutch and the British provincial governments in order to promote quick settlement of New York's vast open territory. Patroons received land in return for an nominal annual quitrent paid to the Crown. In turn, patroons were to collect rents from settlers who would clear and develop the land. Under this system tenants—like serfs in Europe—could not buy their lands. Land title remained perpetually with the lord. Tenants were forced to pay in gold, produce, and services. These contracts were signed for life, and were often multigenerational.[256] Indeed, this system was a kind of New World form of feudalism and serfdom.

Nicholas Van Rensselaer conveniently died in 1678.[257] Alida, who was twenty years younger than her late husband, inherited his entire estate. Less than eight months later, Livingston, who had been described by his foes in Albany as "a recently arrived Scottish opportunist, land speculator, and former clerk of her deceased husband" married the widow Alida Schuyler Van Rensselaer. Alida was the daughter of Colonel Philip Pieterse Schuyler of Albany.[258]

Robert Livingston and Alida had three sons, Philip, Robert, and Gilbert. They are the founding ancestors of the Livingston dynasty in America.

In 1686, because of his political connections, Robert Livingston received from Gov. Dongan a large tract of land—nearly 160,000 acres—which was confirmed in 1715 by a royal charter issued by King George I, creating the manor and lordship of Livingston.[259]

---

[251] Ibid., p.42, and pp.45-47.

[252] Ibid., p.49.

[253] Ibid., p.18.

[254] Ibid., p. 12.

[255] Ibid., p.20.

[256] Ibid., p.18.

[257] Ibid., p.21.

[258] Ibid.

[259] Ibid., p.27 and p.66.

This tract embraced large portions of what are now Dutchess and Columbia counties in the State of New York.

Perceiving a windfall, and a chance to enhance his own "proprietorship and sovereignty," Livingston cut a deal with Governor Robert Hunter. In exchange for selling back to the Crown a 6,000 acre plot of land from Livingston Manor, "whose pine trees he vouched were suitable for tar-making" he undertook the provisioning and supervision of the Palatine refugees.[260]

Life in The Tar Camps

In October, 1710, more than nineteen-hundred able-bodied Palatines were moved ninety-two miles up the Hudson River, to Livingston Manor on the east side of the Hudson River. They were eventually settled in a series of "camps" or *Dorfs* along the shores of the Hudson, where Germantown and Saugerties are now located. The settlers hastily built rough huts and cabins to stave off the winter months. Here, it was said, "there were great numbers of pines fit for the production of turpentine and tar, out of which rosin and pitch could be made. In addition to manufacturing tar and pitch, they were also forced to raise hemp for cordage [ships cords and ropes].[261] To preserve these cords and ropes against the corrosive salt air, they needed to be soaked in a diluted tar mixture.

For the unfortunate Palatines, and "for all parties involved in the tar-making enterprise, things quickly turned sour."[262] The project failed for several reasons.

First, in England, in late 1710, the Whig party was voted out of power, and the Tories were not interested in supporting either the naval stores scheme or the Palatines. Hence, political support—and funding—for the project disappeared in London.

Second, the native pine trees in the Hudson River Valley were unsuitable for making turpentine, tar, or pitch.[263] The white pines of New York did not produce the levels of pitch and tar as expected. Despite felling and barking about 100,000 trees during the summer of 1711, only 200 barrels of tar were extracted. For such a large number of pine trees, the yield of tar was poor, and the tar itself was of poor quality.

Third, the entire project was grossly mismanaged by Governor Robert Hunter.[264] In his haste to make quick money, he failed to clearly define the task or provide for specifications and necessary supplies to accomplish the task of producing naval stores. Governor Hunter, a former military man, did not know anything about tar and pitch making, and he certainly did not know the Palatines.[265] Governor Hunter expected to make a fast fortune via the naval stores project, while the Palatines expected to receive fertile land and freedom in America. The entire project was ill-supervised and poorly managed.

---

[260] Ibid., p.60.

[261] Ibid.

[262] Ibid.

[263] *The 1743 Palatine House*, p.3.

[264] Brandt, p.60.

[265] Bachmann, p. 31.

Fourth, the Palatines were farmers, vinedressers, and craftsmen, not loggers. The Germans, who dreamed of freedom from feudal domination by owning land of their own were "unhappy with their new tasks."[266] The Palatines came from village communities that had been ravaged during *The Thirty Years' War*. From this bitter experience Rhineland peasants had learned that "petty local rulers were utterly incapable of protecting peasant communities." They developed a strong and deep distrust for outside authority. "Such authority," explains Otterness, "seemed to be the source of war and taxes, religious persecution, and economic instability." As a result, the Palatine peasants developed a strong sense of "self-reliance and disregard for authority."[267] Their brief experience with both Gov. Hunter and Robert Livingston merely confirmed these long held feelings. In addition, the Palatines felt that they had been both taken advantage of and deceived. They quickly came to resent both Livingston and Hunter. As a result, when the project began to go bad, "they soon refused to make naval stores and [the governor] was forced to abandon the project."[268]

During the winter of 1710-1711 the Palatines were ill-housed on forty-foot by fifty-foot lots[269] in temporary huts they had hastily constructed. Corrupt local officials had "redirected" funds Parliament had appropriated for the project, and the Palatines were given "spoiled meat and short rations." In the chaos, Robert Livingston was unable to provide promised food supplies and had a falling out with Gov. Robert Hunter.[270] As a result, the Palatines almost starved to death.

By the spring of 1712, it was apparent that the tar-making project was a total failure. In the fall of 1712, just before the killing frost, Gov. Hunter publicly announced that the subsidization of the Palatines had come to an end, and that "the hapless refuges were left to their own."[271] Thus, their meager provisions were cut off. However, in the same proclamation, Hunter stated that the Palatines were still under obligation to Her Majesty's navy to resume tar making in the spring. Thus, they were "forbidden to leave their settlements and to take up freeholding on the west bank of the Hudson River."[272]

Facing a winter of starvation, many of the independent Palatines defied Gov. Hunter's order and moved northward, southward, eastward, and westward.[273] Some "set out upon a long trek to the Schoharie Valley" and settled on land purchased from the Mohawks.[274] Others "crossed the Hudson River and never returned."[275] A few families

---

[266] Nelson, p.24.

[267] Otterness, p.93.

[268] Ibid.

[269] Otterness explains that "for their efforts they were given a mere two thousand square feet of desolate land for each family and a contract to produce naval stores (p.92)."

[270] Brandt, p.62.

[271] Ibid.

[272] Ibid.

[273] William Hull, *History of the Lutheran Church in Dutchess County* (New York, J.E. Wible Printer: Gettysburg, PA, 1881), p.9.

[274] Decker, p.14.

crossed into Livingston Manor and signed themselves into tenancy under Robert and Alida Livingston. Others stayed where they were, and eventually assumed title to their own land creating the settlement of Germantown.[276] Those who stayed at Livingston Manor and East Camp suffered to the point of boiling grass and eating leaves from the trees to survive the winter of 1712-1713.

The remainder, "thirty-five Palatine families, containing one hundred and forty persons besides widows and children,"[277] moved south into Dutchess County, where there was no tenant system, and became independent farmers on land belonging to the Beekman family. These families purchased land from Henry Beekman. This area, near present day Rhinebeck, New York was then called "Beekman's Landing." Within a few years they prospered.

For the next forty years, several waves of German-speaking settlers arrived in the area. Additional ships containing immigrants from the German southwest arrived in 1717, 1722, and 1726.[278] The German settlers who arrived after 1730 "settled south and east of the village of Rhinebeck, in an area referred to on a map of 1802 as the 'Wittemburgh tract.'"[279]

1743 Palatine House

To visualize how the first Palatine Colonists may have lived in the New World, it is only necessary to take a short drive from Rhinebeck up to Schoharie, New York—fifty miles north and west of Rhinebeck. In the village of Schoharie, New York, the old Lutheran Parsonage [*The 1743 Palatine House*], the home of the Rev. Peter Nicholas Sommer (January 9, 1709-October 27, 1795) and his wife Marie, has been beautifully restored and preserved by the local historical society.[280]

Pastor Sommer came to Schoharie, New York from Hamburg, Germany in 1743.[281] From the Lutheran church in Schoharie, he served Lutheran congregations in Stone Arabia, Palatine Bridge, Cobleskill, and other places in the area during his long forty-six-year ministry. In the early days of Lutheranism in America, clergy were in short supply and the faithful were scattered in remote outlying settlements. The Dutch and the English—who arrived in New York first—seized the best land, leaving the dangerous hinterlands open for the Germans. Again, both the Dutch and the English tended to regard German settlers as useful buffers between themselves and often hostile native peoples. Hence, the first Lutheran pastors were circuit riders preaching and teaching over

[275] Brandt, p.62.

[276] Ibid.

[277] Alvah G. Frost, p.5.

[278] Otterness, p.145.

[279] Nancy V. Kelly, *A Brief History of Rhinebeck* (Rhinebeck: The Wise Family Trust in Cooperation with the Historical Society of Rhinebeck, 2001), p.15.

[280] In 1971, with the aid of the Presbyterian Church and a matching grant from the New York State Historic Trust, the Schoharie Colonial Heritage Association restored the 1743 Palatine House and created a "Living Museum."

[281] Nelson, p.17.

vast territories. It is hard to imagine traveling these distances without the benefit of either modern roads or automobiles. Imagine riding a horse from preaching point to preaching point in the dead of an Upstate New York winter! Indeed, in those days, there were "giants in the earth!"[282]

The 1743 Palatine House
Photo by the Rev. Mark D. Isaacs

Sommer received his theological education at the University of Jena.[283] On May 16, 1744, he was married to Maria Kayser of Stone Arabia, New York.[284] She was the daughter of Orthodox Lutheran leader, the Rev. Wilhelm Christoph Berkenmeyer (1687-1751)[285] of Loonenberg (i.e., now Athens, New York). Pastor Berkenmeyer presided at the wedding.[286] The couple had eleven children—including two sets of twins.

In 1743, the Palatine colonists living near Schoharie built a medieval German peasant-style Parsonage for their new minister. The walls of the post-and-beam cottage are constructed with a matrix of woven green sticks covered with plaster and daub. The

---

[282] Genesis 6:4a

[283] *The 1743 Palatine House*, p.5.

[284] Pastor Sommer turned over the congregation at Stone Arabia, New York on December 1, 1751 to Rev. Johannes Fredrick Ries who became the first resident pastor of that congregation (Ibid., p.7). From 1760-1791 Pastor Ries served as pastor of St. Paul's (Wurtemburg).

[285] Wilhelm Christoph Berkenmeyer arrived in America in 1715. He served fourteen congregations scattered along the length of the Hudson River Valley [E. Clifford Nelson, p.14.]. See also Wilhelm Christoph Berkenmeyer, translation by Simon Hart, translation initiated by Harry J. Kreider, and edited by John P. Dern, *The Albany Protocol: Wilhelm Christoph Berkenmeyer's Chronicle of Lutheran Affairs in New York Colony, 1731-1750* (Ann Arbor, MI, 1971).

[286] Berkenmeyer was a bitter theological and personal opponent of the Pietist J.C. Hartwick. Berkenmeyer accused Hartwick of being a "crypto-*Herrnhutter.*" Ronald H. Bailey, *Hartwick College: A Bicentennial History: 1797-1997* (Oneonta, NY: Hartwick College), p.7 and p.21.

post-modern visitor is struck by how difficult life must have been in those early days. Pastor Sommer, his wife, and their eleven children lived in three small rooms; i.e., a kitchen and workroom, a great room/ "master" bedroom where church services were once held, and an unfinished upstairs loft where the children slept. The entire house was heated by two great "jamless" or open-brick fireplaces. Visitors can literally stand inside the fireplace chimney and look up to see the sky above! Cooking was done on one of the open fireplaces usually with one heavy cast-iron pot suspended over the fire. The house must have been constantly filled with smoke, dirt, insects, and foul odors.

As was the custom of the day, the entire family [and visitors!] drank out of a three-handled common cup, and they ate from a large common rectangle-shaped wooden bowl with their own spoon stored on a "spoon board." The first pastors of the Evangelical Lutheran Church of St. Peter the Apostle who served the people of the Staatsburg mission must have lived under similar primitive conditions. Seeing these rustic conditions, we recall the famous quote from Thomas Hobbes (1588-1679), that in the state of nature there are, "no arts, no letters, no society, and which is worst of all, continual fear and danger of violent death, and that the life of man is solitary, poor, brutish and short."[287]

The Palatines and Their Dutch and English Neighbors

During this time, the Dutch and English establishment erroneously regarded these German settlers as ignorant. This was doubtless due to the fact that for three generations after settlement, the Palatines refused to use the English language and tended to keep to themselves. The English language, and the English legal procedure, remained obstacles to their relations for years. Virtually, from the time that they had left the Rhineland, in almost every business transaction that they had engaged in with the English and Dutch, they felt they had been deceived and treated unjustly. As a result, they tended to avoid dealings with them. In addition, the government continued to try to force the Palatines out into the frontier as a first line of defense against the French and the Indians. The Palatines accepted their roll as a front-line defense in order to hold title to land so that they would be able to support themselves and own land to leave to their children.

In 1766, Benjamin Franklin (1706-1790) said of the Palatines, "They brought with them the greatest wealth, industry, integrity, and character that have been developed by years of suffering and persecution."[288]

Through a strange irony of fate, the Palatines, who had emigrated from Germany to escape the continued brutalities of the French, were compelled to again face the same enemies in America. It was during the years 1754 to 1763, that the French, assisted by their Indian allies, the Ottawas, Hurons, Miamis, Shawnees, and Illinois, made frequent raids from Canada and the Ohio Valley on the settlements of the Palatines.

In 1715, the Palatine settlers built a log church where today's Wey's Crossing Road meets Route 9.[289] This location was called "Pink's Corner."[290] Today, only "an ancient

---

[287] Thomas Hobbs, *Leviathan* (1652).

[288] Alvah G. Frost, *An Address Given to Commemorate the 175th Anniversary of the Founding of St. Paul's Lutheran Church, Wurtemburg, New York, 1935.*

[289] Edward M. Smith, *Documentary History of Rhinebeck, in Dutchess County, New York* (Rhinebeck, 1881, 1974 reprint edition), p.92.

cemetery remains."[291] This church, "likely the first church in Dutchess County, "served as a place of worship for both the Lutheran and German Reformed congregations."[292] In 1729, with "contentions arising between them, they thought best for both parties to separate, and to have each a church for themselves."[293] The Lutherans sold out to the "Reformed Protestants." Thus, this humble union log church became *The Evangelical Lutheran Church of St. Peter the Apostle*. This Church, in turn, became the mother church to "the Staatsburg Church," the forerunner of the present day St. Paul's Lutheran Church of Wurtemburg.

---

[290] Ibid., p.98.

[291] Ibid.

[292] Nancy V. Kelly, p.12.

[293] Edward M. Smith, *Documentary History of Rhinebeck, in Dutchess County, New York* (Rhinebeck, 1881, 1974 reprint edition), p.98.

Chapter Four: Theological Perspectives

"The good of the Kingdom of God is the policy of this Church."
                                                    –The Wurtemburgh Motto[294]

In a 1990 speech recorded at St. Paul's during a meeting of the Rhinebeck Historical Society, the late Parish Historian Barbara Frost (1919-2009) explained that, "St. Paul's has always been a community church. This is one of the reasons we have trouble with 'Lutheranism' here in this congregation, because so many people were not brought up as Lutherans."[295]

Barbara Frost's statement that "St. Paul's has always been a community church [and] … this is one of the reasons we have trouble with 'Lutheranism'" is vital to note.

From the start, the Palatines were "a mixed multitude" influenced by at least three major streams of Protestant thought. These were, Lutheranism [in a weakened and diluted form!], Calvinism, and Pietism. We also must recall that in 1710, the British forced Roman Catholic Palatine refugees to either convert to Protestantism, or be returned to Germany.[296] Rather than convert, several thousand returned to Germany.

The Palatines included many Lutherans with strong Pietist leanings. In addition, in America, the Palatines tended to live in "mixed" communities, living among like-minded adherents of the German and Dutch Reformed Church. The common bond among these immigrants was that they were Protestant, they spoke German, they could not afford to support a minister of their own particular denomination, and they wanted to hear the Word of God preached in their native tongue.

Wilhelm Christoph Berkenmeyer (1687-1751), an old-line autocratic Hannover Orthodox Lutheran pastor from Loonenberg (now Athens, New York), and Johann Christoph Hartwick (1714-1796), a Pietist from Halle University, serving in the Rhinebeck-East Camp area—including "the Staatsburg Church"—disagreed on nearly every theological issue. However, Berkenmeyer and Hartwick both agreed that marriages between the Reformed, and their often nominal Lutheran congregants, posed a serious problem.

In his writings, Berkenmeyer repeatedly complained about the problem. Meanwhile, Bailey notes that Hartwick's frequent injunctions against the practice of Lutherans marrying Calvinists "antagonized many people in an area dense with mixed marriages

---

[294] *The Holiday [Wurtemburgh] Messenger*, St. Paul's Lutheran Church, Wurtemburgh, Rev. William G. Boomhower, Pastor, December, 1914. [In the archives of St. Paul's (Wurtemburg)].

[295] Barbara Frost, audio tape lecture on "The History of St. Paul's Lutheran Church of Wurtemburg" delivered to the Rhinebeck Historical Society, December 1990. St. Paul's archives.

[296] According to Henry Noble MacCracken, "at least 3,500 Roman Catholic Palatines were returned to Germany." Henry Noble MacCracken, *Old Dutchess Forever! The Story of An American County* (New York: Hastings House, 1956), p.103.

and heavily populated by followers of the French theologian and reformer John Calvin."[297]

Blended Lutheranism

Even those Palatines that claimed to be Lutheran tended to be influenced by Calvinist thinking. Church Historian Philip Schaff notes:

> Martin Luther regarded ceremonies, the use of clerical robes, candles on the altar, the attitude of the minister in prayer, as matters of indifference [i.e., *adiaphoria*] which may be retained or abolished. In the revision of the baptismal service, 1526, Luther abolished the use of salt, spittle, and oil, but retained the exorcism in an abridged form. He also retained the public confession and absolution, and recommended private confession of sin to the minister.[298]

Schaff adds, "The [more conservative] Lutheran churches in Northern Germany, and in Scandinavia, adopted the [traditional Lutheran] order of Wittenberg with sundry modifications; but the Lutheran churches in Southern Germany (Württemberg, Baden, the Palatinate, and Alsace) tended to follow the simpler type of the Swiss [Reformed] service."[299]

In addition, within the Lutheran Church in Germany, according to Schaff:

> The Lutheran order of worship underwent radical changes during the seventeenth and eighteenth centuries under the influence of [both Lutheran Orthodoxy and Pietism and then] Rationalism; the spirit of worship cooled down; weekly communion was abolished; the sermon degenerated into a barren moral discourse; and new liturgies and hymnbooks with all sorts of misimprovements were introduced.[300]

In Germany, this problem was compounded because "each Lutheran State Church had its own liturgy and hymnbook, and there was no uniform Lutheran liturgy, such as *The Common Prayer Book* of the Church of England."[301]

By 1817, during the three hundredth anniversary of the Reformation, "there was a gradual revival of the liturgical spirit in different parts of Germany, with a restoration of many devotional treasures of past ages."[302] Thus, after 1817, there was a deliberate effort by many Lutherans in Germany to repristinate Lutheranism. Leaders of this movement included Klaus Harms (1778-1855) and Johann Konrad Wilhelm Löhe (1808-1872).[303]

---

[297] Ronald H. Bailey, p.20.

[298] Philip Schaff and David Schley Schaff, *History of the Christian Church* (Oak Harbor, WA: Logos Research Systems, Inc., 1997).

[299] Ibid.

[300] Ibid.

[301] Ibid.

[302] Ibid.

[303] Eric W. Gritsch, *Fortress Introduction to Lutheranism* (Minneapolis: Fortress Press, 1994), p.44.

The problem was, the first wave of Palatines arrived in America in 1710, prior to these liturgical reforms. Hence, it was common during the nineteenth and early twentieth century for fiercely independent Hudson River Lutheran congregations, including Wurtemburg, to resist liturgical reforms and "improvements." This would include changes such as giving up the common cup in favor of individual glasses (a c.1900 dispute), then returning to the option of a common cup (a c.2005 discussion), the going from quarterly, to monthly, and then to weekly communion. In the early 1980s, there was a serious dispute at St. Paul's (Wurtemburg) over the issue of adopting weekly communion.

Thus, Schaff writes, "waves of German settlers introduced a new element into American Christianity, which hitherto had been dominated by the Calvinist tradition. Other Reformation streams made their contribution." He adds that "German groups had already been touched by the Pietist movement which itself directly fed the fires of the Revival in England."[304]

Practical Calvinism

The Heidelberg [or Palatinate] Catechism,[305] modeled after Luther's *Small Catechism* (1529), is a document taking the form of a series of questions and answers, for use in teaching Reformed Christian doctrine. *The Heidelberg Catechism* (1563), originally written in German, has been translated into many languages, and is regarded as one of the most influential of the Reformed catechisms.[306]

Commissioned by Elector Frederick III, sovereign of the Palatinate from 1559 to 1576, it is sometimes referred to as "the Palatinate Catechism." Elector Frederick III appointed Zacharius Ursinus and Caspar Olevianus to write a catechism based on input from leading Reformed scholars of the time.[307] Zacharius Ursinus, who had been trained by Philip Melanchthon (1497-1560), was professor of theology at Heidelberg University.[308] One of its aims was to counteract the teachings of the Roman Catholic Church by basing each of its theological assertions on texts from *The Holy Bible*. It is said that *The Palatinate Catechism* combined "the intimacy of Martin Luther, the charity of Philip Melanchthon, and the fire of John Calvin."[309]

The Catechism is divided into fifty-two sections, each to be taught one Sunday of the year. In its current form, *The Heidelberg Catechism* consists of 129 questions and answers. Alister E. McGrath states "the text shows the traditional Reformed emphasis

---

[304] Dowley, p.438.

[305] Allen O. Miller and Eugene Osterhaven, translators, *The Heidelberg [or Palatine] Catechism* (Cleveland: United Church Press, 1962).

[306] Alister E. McGrath, *The Christian Theology Reader* (Malden, MA: Blackwell Publishers, 1995, 2001), p.27-28 and Philip Schaff, *The Creeds of Christendom with A History and Critical Notes* (New York: Harper & Brothers, 1877), vol. III, pp.307-355.

[307] Allen O. Miller and Eugene Osterhaven, p.5.

[308] Ibid., p.6.

[309] Frank L. Cross, ed., *The Oxford Dictionary of the Christian Church* (New York: Oxford University Press, 1958, 1983), p.629.

which gives priority to Word over image."[310] The Synod of Heidelberg approved the catechism in 1563. In the Netherlands, the National Synods of the sixteenth century adopted it as one of the "Three Forms of Unity," making it requisite for Elders and Deacons to subscribe to, and ministers to teach. The influence of *The Heidelberg Catechism* extended to the Westminster Assembly of Divines who, in part, used it as the basis for *The Westminster Catechism* (1648).

Martin Luther's *Small Catechism* (1529)*, The Heidelberg [or Palatinate] Catechism,* and other catechisms, are important because they reflect the practical theology of the common lay people. There is no doubt that the Protestant Palatines who settled in the Hudson River Valley were deeply influenced by these catechisms. Hence, much to the chagrin of many of the Lutheran clergy who have served congregations in the region over the years, many Palatine "Lutherans" that settled in the Hudson River Valley were *de facto* or "cultural" Calvinists.

The Rise of Pietism

Rooted in the tradition of Rhenish mysticism, the Palatinate and Württemberg also provided fertile soil for the growth of Lutheran Pietism. The German Theology [*Theologia Germania*[311]] and the "*Devotio Moderna*" of the Brethren of the Common Life originated in the region. In Württemberg, "Pietism gained and retained a large popular basis."[312]

Prior to the rise of Pietism (c.1675), Christian faith and morals in German lands were at a low ebb. Dismal spiritual, political, social, and economic conditions were the result of two major factors. First, was the disastrous *Thirty Years War* (1618-1648). Second, was a negative reaction by both clergy and lay folk to the age of Protestant Scholastic Orthodoxy.

The horrors of *The Thirty Years War* triggered a profound faith crisis for many German-speaking people. Indeed, after the slaughter, the plundering, and social upheavals of the seemingly endless *Thirty Years War* there was a crisis of faith and a total breakdown in moral sensitivity. One evangelical pastor at the time complained, "old and young alike can no longer tell what is of God or of the devil, poor widows and orphans are counted for dung, like dogs they are pushed into the street, there to perish of hunger and cold."[313]

The gains of the Reformation, and Christian *praxis* and morals in general, degenerated. Paul Tillich writes that in the wake of this catastrophic war, "life became extremely brutal, unrefined and uneducated." And, "the [Establishment] Orthodox Lutheran theologians did not do much about it."[314]

---

[310] Ibid., p.28.

[311] See Martin Luther, ed., *The Theologia Germanica of Martin Luther,* translated by Bengt Hoffman (New York: Paulist Press; The Classics of Western Spirituality, 1980).

[312] Holborn, p.141.

[313] Robert G. Clouse, *The Church in the Age of Orthodoxy and the Enlightenment: Consolidation and Challenge from 1600 to 1800* (St. Louis: Concordia Press, 1980), p.75.

[314] Paul Tillich, *A History of Christian Thought: From Its Judaic and Hellenistic Origins to Existentialism* (New York: Simon & Schuster, 1968), p.285.

In the history of Lutheranism, the period of 1580-1675, "the Age of Orthodoxy,"[315] leaves much to be desired with respect to effective preaching, pastoral care, moral guidance, and spiritual support of its suffering people.

In the face of this national spiritual crisis, Orthodox Lutheran clergy remained aloof, self-satisfied and inattentive to the spiritual needs of the people. During the age of Protestant Scholasticism, Lutheranism degenerated into a religion of the mind that had little relevance for the common folk. During the period, partially to refute the theological and philosophical arguments of the Counter-Reformation, the liberating theological insights of Reformers, such as Martin Luther and Philip Melanchthon, had been ossified into a complex matrix of rigid Neo-Aristotelian formulas.[316]

Johann Gerhard (1582-1637), the foremost dogmatician of Lutheran Orthodoxy, laid the foundation for much of the theological activity that followed. Building on the foundation of Martin Chemnitz' earlier work and on the Reformation tradition, Gerhard is best known for his massive *Loci theologici* (1610–1625). This multi-volume *opus*, written in Latin for his fellow academics, was a comprehensive treatment of the evangelical doctrinal position, based on a particularly wide range of material.[317]

Abraham Calov (1612-1686), professor in Wittenberg University, perpetuated the tradition associated with Gerhard, but also accentuated these ideas in a doctrinaire and polemical manner. His polemical attacks were aimed not just at Roman Catholic theology, but also at Calvinists and other non-Lutheran Protestants.[318] His *magnum opus* was the voluminous *Systema locorum theologicorum* (1655–1677).[319] Calov enjoys the distinction of having produced the most thorough discussions on dogmatic prolegomena ever offered by a Lutheran during the period of Orthodoxy.[320]

Gritsch notes that "these scholastic theologians appealed to the authority of Martin Luther, yet used Aristotelian means—even though Luther had been convinced that Aristotelian logic transformed Christian theology into pagan philosophy."[321]

The rigorous, systematic, and profound tomes of Orthodox Lutheran theologians tended to create a chasm between the clergy and the lay folk. This movement fostered the notion that the Christian faith was merely a function of the mind; i.e., right doctrine and right thinking.

Johann Arndt and Philip Jacob Spener

Pietism traces its roots to the writings of Johann Arndt (1555-1621). In his most famous book, *True Christianity* (1606-1609),[322] Arndt asserted that orthodox Lutheran

---

[315] Gritsch, *Fortress Introduction to Lutheranism*, pp.28-29.

[316] Tim Dowley, J. H. Y. Briggs, Robert Dean Linder, and David F. Wright, *Introduction to the History of Christianity* (Minneapolis: Fortress Press, 2002), p.444.

[317] Bengt Hagglund, *History of Theology* (St. Louis: Concordia Publishing House, 1968), p.304.

[318] Gritsch, *Fortress Introduction to Lutheranism*, p.29.

[319] Hagglund, p.305.

[320] Robert D. Preus, *The Theology of Post-Reformation Lutheranism* (St. Louis: Concordia Publishing House, 1970, 1999), vol. I, p.226.

[321] Gritsch, *Fortress Introduction to Lutheranism*, p.29.

doctrine was not enough to produce Christian life. Arndt, who was regarded by later Pietists as a *Luther redivivus*,[323] advocated a mysticism which he borrowed largely from the late Middle Ages; i.e., Bernard of Clairvaux (1091-1153) and Johannes Tauler (1300-1361).[324] For Pietists in Germany, Scandinavia, and the American colonies, next to *The Holy Bible,* Arndt's *True Christianity* was their most significant devotional influence.

Philip Jacob Spener (1635-1705),
was the leader of "the Second Reformation,"
a movement popularly known as "Pietism."

Pietists were also inspired by Philip Jacob Spener's great call to reform; i.e., *Pia Desideria,* "Pious or Heartfelt Desires" (1675).[325] Spener, a prolific writer and preacher at Strasbourg [on the southern border of France and Germany], and as pastor and senior of the ministerium in Frankfurt-am-Main, emerged as the leader of the Pietist movement in Germany. He studied history and theology at the University of Strasbourg, and, in 1688, was appointed a senior member of the Lutheran clergy in Frankfurt. In his writings and sermons, Spener stressed the value of a life of devotion rather than mere correct dogma. He began to hold devotional meetings known as *Collegia pietatis.* With these

---

[322] Johann Arndt, *True Christianity,* translation and Introduction by Peter Erb (New York: Paulist Press, 1979).

[323] *True Christianity,* Introduction by Peter Erb, p.xv.

[324] Ibid.

[325] Philip Jacob Spener, *Pia Desideria,* translated by Theodore G. Tappert (Philadelphia: Fortress Press, 1675, 1964), p.29.

48

small groups, pastors and laymen met together for Bible study and prayer. [326] The popular and effective *Collegia pietatis* quickly multiplied and formed a basis for the Pietist movement. [327]

Spener believed that spiritual life was more important than "correct" doctrine and he felt that preaching should call its hearers to more pious living rather, than deeper philosophical thinking. Spener's approach offered a radical critique of the sterile Orthodox and Neo-Scholastic ministerial training of his day. He also called the laity to a pious and active faith. [328] His visionary program did much to reform the standard religious instruction of his day.

Spener also advocated a contextual approach to biblical preaching. He worked to restore the rite of Confirmation, set aside days of fasting and prayer, and argued for the necessity of *Busskampf;* i.e., conversion followed by holy living. No wonder that many Church historians consider Philip Jacob Spener to be the founder of the "Second Reformation."

Despite this, unable to refute Spener, the Orthodox University of Wittenberg charged that he was guilty of two-hundred-and-sixty-four theological errors!

August Herman Francke

After Philip Jacob Spener, the Pietist movement manifested itself in three basic forms. The first was led by Spener's great successor August Herman Francke (1663-1727). At the University of Leipzig, August Herman Francke and two other professors formed the *collegium philobiblicum* for the exegetical study of *The Holy Bible*. [329] Francke soon was forced out of the University for his Pietist views.

Spener helped Francke secure an academic appointment at the University of Halle. [330] Through the influence and labors of Francke, Halle University became the academic citadel of the Pietist movement. [331] Through Francke's organizational genius, Halle became more than an academic center for Pietism. Rather, it became a literal "New Jerusalem" a seedbed for the new piety.

Francke began with the establishment of a school for the poor in 1695. Three years later, he founded the Halle orphanage. This orphanage was the first such institution in Germany devoted exclusively to the education of orphans. Later on, additional schools and enterprises were joined to Francke's numerous institutions. This included an apothecary shop and a print shop devoted to the mass production of religious literature and the publication of Bibles for distribution in Germany and abroad. In addition to "internal missions," Francke also supported foreign missions. [332]

---

[326] Ibid.

[327] Dowley, Briggs, Linder, and Wright, p.446.

[328] J.D. Douglas, *Who's Who in Christian History* (Wheaton, IL: Tyndale House, 1992).

[329] Tappert. p.21.

[330] The author briefly visited Halle Univeristy while on a trip to Germany in December 2004.

[331] Ibid., p.23.

[332] Hajo Holborn, *A History of Modern Germany: 1648-1840* (Princeton: Princeton University Press, 1964, 1982), p.138.

The author with a bronze bust of Lutheran philosopher and jurist
Christian Thomasius (1655-1728) at Halle University.
Professor Thomasius was an early champion of the Enlightenment.
Among other things, he opposed punishment for witchcraft
and the application of torture.
Photo: Linda A. Isaacs.

Pietism also manifested itself in a more radical form. This form followed the teachings of Gottfried Arnold (1666-1714)[333] and Count Nikolaus Ludwig von Zinzendorf (1700-1760).[334] Unlike mainstream Pietism, the radicals tended to be mystics

---

[333] Gottfried Arnold, who for a number of years was professor at the Pietist University of Giessen, was deeply moved by pantheistic mysticism. This made him skeptical and critical of the State-Church and institutionalized religion. In his famous book *Nonpartisan History of the Church and Heretics* (*Unparteiische Kirchen und Ketzer-Historie*), (1699-1700), Arnold argued that only the original Church of the Apostles can be recognized as the true Christian Church. According to Arnold, thereafter all church history becomes the story of desertion from the Christian ideal (Holborn, p.143.).

[334] Zinzendorf, educated in Halle, created a home for the displaced Moravian Brethren at *Herrnhutt*. A.J. Lewis notes that Zinzendorf was indifferent to the Lutheran Confessions, and that he was willing to accept any Lutheran, Calvinist, and Protestant—even Roman Catholics—as long as they worshipped Jesus Christ. See A.J. Lewis. *Zinzendorf: The Ecumenical Pioneer: A Study in the Moravian Contribution to Christian Mission and Unity* (Philadelphia: The Westminster Press, 1962).

with no interest in internal reform of the Church. Rather, they cultivated the experience of "the inner word" and "the inner light."[335]

The Rev. Dr. Johann Albrecht Bengel (1687-1752)

Bengel and Württemberg Pietism

A more conservative and orthodox form was known as "Württemberg Pietism."[336] The best example of "Württemberg Pietism" is the great Johann Albrecht Bengel (1687-1752).[337] Bengel, a second generation Pietist, was the son of a Lutheran minister. He was born on June 24, 1687 in Winnenden, Württemberg, a small town located twelve miles northeast of Stuttgart.[338] Interestingly, Bengel was an exact contemporary of the famed German Lutheran composer Johann Sebastian Bach (1685-1750).

---

[335] Conrad Bergendoff, *The Church of the Lutheran Reformation: A Historical Survey of Lutheranism* (St. Louis: Concordia Publishing House, 1967), p.167.

[336] *Pietism: A Much-Maligned Movement Re-examined*: Christian History, Issue 10 (Carol Stream, IL: Christianity Today, Inc.) 1997.

[337] See, Mark D. Isaacs, *THE END? Textual Criticism and Apocalyptic Speculation in Johann Albrecht Bengel (1687-1752)* (Phoenix, AZ: Robert Welsh University Classical Press, 2010).

[338] John Christian Frederic Burk, *A Memoir of the Life and Writings of John Albert Bengel, Prelate of Wurtemberg, Compiled Principally from Original Manuscripts* (London: William Ball, 1837), p.1.

In 1693, only four months after his father died, during a French invasion of Swabia under Louis XIV,[339] the town—including his widowed mother's house—was "miserably destroyed and burnt to ashes by the French." This tragic fire not only caused the loss of their humble home, but also lost to the young Bengel was his dead father's precious theological library. Later in life—and typical of his deep faith in God—Bengel thanked God for this tragedy, stating, "the providence of God had removed from him the temptation of reading too great a variety of books."[340] Instead of "a variety of books" Bengel was left with *The Holy Bible* alone to study.

Bengel became "the exegete of Pietism."[341] Orthodox Lutheran theologians tended to view *The Holy Bible* as a fragmented arsenal of proof-texts to be employed in theological disputations. In contrast, Bengel saw the New Testament as an organic whole, "a revelation in which each part was to be considered."[342] As one of the foremost New Testament scholars of his day he was the author of the famous *Gnomon,*[343] which became a standard of Biblical interpretation for generations of preachers.

He is remembered as the father of textual criticism, a scholar, an independent thinker, and a chiliast. Bengel meticulously calculated the return of Christ in 1836 and hoped for "the glorious church of the millennium." While his June 18, 1836 prediction did not materialize, "his exposition of the book [of Revelation] left abiding results."[344]

Pietists in Colonial America

Many of the pastors who ministered to Lutherans in colonial America were commissioned and sent out from the remarkable Halle Institution located in present day Halle, Saxony-Anhalt, Germany. Their reports; i.e., *Hallische Nachrichten [Halle Reports]*, represent the most complete record of early Lutheran church life in America.

For example, the Rev. Justus Falckner (1672-1723), "the first Lutheran minister ordained in this country," was educated at Halle University under August Herman Francke.[345] He matriculated at Halle on June 20, 1692, just as the new university was starting up its first classes."[346] Falckner came to America in 1700. He was ordained in Philadelphia in 1703, and served many Lutheran churches in Upstate New York.[347]

---

[339] The same wave of French invasions that drove the Palatines to New York.

[340] Burk, p. xxxiii.

[341] Donald K. McKim, *Handbook of Major Biblical Interpreters* (Downers Grove:, Illinois: InterVarsity Press, 2000), p.289.

[342] Conrad Bergendoff, p.158.

[343] Johann Albrecht Bengel, *Bengel's New Testament Commentary: Gnomon Novi Testamenti,* translation by Charlton T. Lewis and Marvin R. Vincent (Grand Rapids: Kregel Publications, 1742, 1860-1861, 1981).

[344] Ibid., p.158.

[345] Henry Eyster Jacobs, *A History of the Evangelical Lutheran Church in the United States* (New York: The Christian Literature, 1893), p.172.

[346] Kim-Eric Williams, p.9

[347] Nelson, p.14.

Otterness writes that, "Books and pamphlets describing Britain's North American colonies, particularly Pennsylvania, had been circulating in the Rhineland since the 1680s. William Penn wrote or commissioned several such pamphlets to promote his colony. In 1700, Daniel Pastorius, who had helped found Germantown, Pennsylvania, in 1683, wrote a book describing the colony and its geography that circulated widely in the German territories.

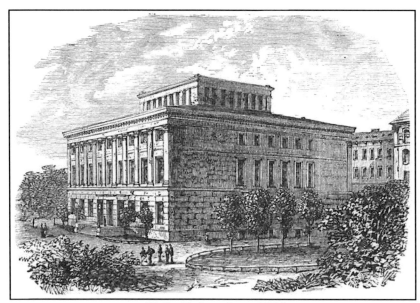

Halle University c. 1836

Two years later Daniel Falckner [the older brother of Justus Falckner], also a Pietist with close ties to Halle, wrote a promotional book entitled *Curieuse Nachricht von Pennsylvania* (Interesting News of Pennsylvania). In 1694, Falckner had accompanied a group of Pietists who had settled in Pennsylvania. He returned home in late 1698 or early 1699. At the request of August Hermann Francke, he wrote this book describing Pennsylvania, its people, and its economy. He also provided details on the passage overseas. The book consisted of a series of questions written by Francke, who was interested in Pennsylvania as a place of settlement for Pietists, and of answers supplied by Daniel Falckner.

In this book, "Falckner described Pennsylvania as a fertile land that lacked little except settlers. In response to the question 'What is there a deficiency of in America?' Falckner wrote: 'The chief deficiency consists in people and craftsmen. The other deficiencies will be easily supplied.'"[348]

In 1704, Daniel Falckner's popular book was combined with Pastorius's book, and the two were reprinted and issued as one volume.

The congregations in the Central Hudson cluster, including St. Paul's (Wurtemberg) were also served by at least two very important Halle former students. These were the Rev. Johann Christoph Hartwick and the Rev. Dr. Frederick Henry Quitman.

---

[348] Otterness, p.26.

Francke's son, Gotthilf August Francke (1696-1769), sent Henry Melchior Mühlenberg (1711-1787) to America to become the organizer of the colonial Lutheran Church. Mühlenberg, though not the first on the scene, has been called the patriarch of American Lutheranism. His theology was profoundly shaped by Hallensian Pietism.

In 1750, Mühlenberg, a friend of Hartwick's, came to Rhinebeck in an attempt to settle a dispute within the Rhinebeck and East Camp parish. Apparently this dispute had been orchestrated by the heavy-handed and controlling Rev. William Berkenmeyer of Loonenburg (now Athens), New York.[349] Berkenmeyer, who studied at the University of Altdorf, was an Orthodox Lutheran. He considered himself to be the supreme clerical leader of Lutheranism in the Hudson Valley. He "was a staunch adherent of the old line Lutheran Orthodoxy, and he would have nothing to do with Pietism in any form."[350]

Conclusion

For the early Palatine settlers in the Hudson River Valley, their worshipping communities often began as union churches of German-speaking Protestants, consisting of both Reformed and Lutherans. These union churches tended to last until sufficient immigration of Lutherans and Reformed permitted division into separate, self-sustaining congregations.[351]

Thus, the common bond for these early congregations was the German language, not abstract theological distinctions. For example, the first Protestant church in the Rhinebeck area was built in 1715. It was located at Pinck's Corner, or Wey's Crossing; i.e., just north of the present intersection of State Highways 9 and 9-G. This was a union church which served both German speaking Lutheran and Reformed Protestants. MacCracken adds that "here our first Palatines are buried."[352] From this beginning, *The Evangelical Lutheran Church of St. Peter the Apostle* became the mother church and hub of a cluster of area Lutheran churches.[353]

Hence, for practical and for historical reasons, in worship and practice, Pietistic Lutheran theology—with an infusion of Reformed theology from friends and neighbors—would have been the dominant theological form at Wurtemburg.

---

[349] Ruth Decker, *275 Years of Lutheran Witness in the Central Hudson Valley: Christ Lutheran Church of Germantown, New York: 1710-1985* (Germantown, New York: Christ Lutheran Church, 1985), p.19.

[350] Ibid.

[351] Scholz, p.19.

[352] MacCracken, p.102.

[353] William Hull, *History of the Lutheran Church in Dutchess County* (New York, J.E. Wible Printer: Gettysburg, PA, 1881), p.3.

Chapter Five: "The Staatsburg Church" Becomes St. Paul's (Wurtemburg)

S t. Paul's Lutheran Church of Wurtemburg was first known as "the Staatsburg Church," then "the Wirtemburg Church," and then "St. Paul's" sometime after the American Revolution.[354] According to the Rev. William Hull (1868-1939),[355] the first organization from which St. Paul's Lutheran Church of Wurtemburg grew was located near Staatsburg.[356]

In a September 18, 1915 *Rhinebeck Gazette* article, the Rev. Chester H. Traver, D.D., wrote that according to "a letter written by the pastor [i.e., the Rev. Johannes Christopher Hartwick] while absent in Pennsylvania in 1750-1751... services [at this time] were held in a church in, or near, Staatsburg."[357]

Alvah G. Frost, quoting Dr. George Neff[358] states that, "this had been called 'the Staatsburg Church.'" Apparently, the Staatsburg Church was a humble "missionary station on [or near?] the Hudson River"[359] that was "served by different preachers, the famous Johannes Christopher Hartwick, among them."[360]

"Here," according to Dr. Neff, "a few [High] German families resided. A small building was erected for divine worship and one of the early missionaries preached to them. In time, it was discovered that in the interior of the town a few honest, upright, and industrious families from the Kingdom of Württemberg had left the comforts of home in

---

[354] James H. Smith, *History of Dutchess County, New York: 1683-1882* (Interlaken NY: Heart of the Lakes Publishing, 1882, 1980), p.272, and Edward M. Smith, *Documentary History of Rhinebeck, in Dutchess County, New York* (Rhinebeck, 1881, 1974 reprint edition), p.120, explain that the earliest deeds and records do not refer to "the Staatsburg Church" as either "St. Paul's" or "Lutheran." Apparently, it was not until sometime after the American Revolution that these names were applied.

[355] The Rev. William Hull, author of *History of the Lutheran Church in Dutchess County* (New York, J.E. Wible Printer: Gettysburg, PA, 1881), served as Pastor of St. John's Lutheran Church in Hudson and Principal of Hartwick Seminary from 1891-1893. He was interested in the history of the Lutheran Church in the Hudson River Valley, and, c. 1880, he wrote several important historical sketches of area churches.

[356] Ibid., p.9.

[357] Chester Henry Traver, "Rev. Chester Traver's History of Wurttemburgh Church: Former Rhinebecker Writes Interesting Sketch of St. Paul's Lutheran Church" *The Rhinebeck Gazette*, September 18, 1915. A similar article was published in *The Lutheran Quarterly*, July 1916, pp.382-398.

[358] The Rev. George Neff's handwritten "*Historical Sketch*" is preserved in the *1873 Wurtemburg Church Record Book*.

[359] Hull, p.9.

[360] Chester Henry Traver, *The Rhinebeck Gazette* (1915), p.6, and Elizabeth McR. Frost, *The Men of Wurtemburg and Their House of God: 1760-1960: A Short History of St. Paul's Lutheran Church of Wurtemburg,* Rhinebeck New York, 1960, p.5.

the Fatherland and had pitched their tents in a section that was then a dreary wilderness but which had great facilities for farming purposes. These families were always distinguished from the Hollanders [Low Dutch folk who tended to be Reformed[361]] who were numerous around them, as 'Württembergers' from whence the settlement and the church received and still retain their historical title "Wurtemburg."[362]

This map—with modern road names appended—shows the relationship between "The Staatsburg Church (c.1760-c.1800)" and the present location of St. Paul's.
Source: Section of map of Rhinebeck published in
The New Historical Atlas of Dutchess County, New York.
(Reading, PA: Reading Publishing House, 1876)

Alvah G. Frost gives the location of that first "missionary station and church" as "on the farm then occupied by Stephanus Fraleigh and family at the foot of Primrose Hill

<hr />

[361] The Rhinebeck Dutch Reformed Church, founded in 1731, was "the Establishment Church" and the home church of the Livingstons, the Beekmans, the Kips, and many other influential early Rhinebeck families [Frank D.Blanchard, *History of the Reformed Dutch Church of Rhinebeck Flatts, New York.* (Albany, New York: J.B. Lyon Company, 1921.)]

[362] The Rev, George Neff manuscript, *1873 Wurtemburg Church Record Book.*

56

Road." Frost adds that the Stephanus Fraleigh [also spelled "Frohlich"[363]] farm was located at the south end of the Beekman Patent[364] on the King's Highway, "at the foot of Primrose Hill Road, stood a small wooden building, with a cemetery across the road."[365] He adds, "on the south end of the [Beekman] patent, Stephanus Fraleigh, under a lease dated 1719, had a farm, in later years (c.1935) the property of Guertner Fraleigh, a descendent of the sixth generation."[366]

Edward M. Smith provides more information on the identity of Stephanus Fraleigh. He writes, "Stephanus Frolich, with a wife, two daughters over nine and one under eight years of age, were among the Palatines that settled in the West Camp in Ulster County in 1710."[367]

Smith adds, "Stephen Froelick was a freeholder, and the only one of this name in what is now the town of Rhinebeck, in 1723. He obtained a lease from Henry Beekman for the farm on the Albany Post Road, now [i.e., 1881] the property of Guertner Fraleigh, a descendant in the sixth generation, in 1719."[368]

Smith states that "we have no doubt that Stephanus Fraleigh was the person found in the West Camp in 1710, and the ancestor of all the Froelicks and Fraleighs who have lived and died and are now living in Dutchess County."[369]

According to Smith, "Stephanus Fraleigh made his will in 1749, in which he released two children, without naming them, of all their obligations to his estate, and left his property to his wife, Barbara."[370]

In a list of members of St. Peter the Apostle Lutheran Church[371] compiled c.1734 and attributed to Christopher Hagedorn, "Stephan Frohlich, daughter Anna Catharine; Eva, and John Peter" are listed as members in "Staatsburg."[372] At the time, "the Staatsburg Church" was one of the preaching points served by Lutheran pastors based in

---

[363] Much to the consternation of post-modern readers eighteenth century spellings of places and names, particularly German and Dutch names transliterated into English, often varied from document to document.

[364] The Beekman Patent was originally granted to Henry Beekman (1688-1776) on April 22, 1697. This first patent did not adequately describe the bounds of the property and Beekman applied for another patent in 1703 which gave a better description.

[365] Alvah G. Frost, p.6, and Elizabeth McR. Frost, p.4, Hull, p.9.

[366] Alvah G. Frost, p.5.

[367] Edward M. Smith (1881), p.216.

[368] Ibid.

[369] Ibid.

[370] Ibid.

[371] Arthur C. Kelly notes that "the records of St. Peter's Lutheran Church (disbanded in 1938) were transcribed by the compiler in 1968… Since that time, the original records of that Church burned in a house fire of a trustee of the Church." [Arthur C. Kelly, *Records of Lutheran Churches of Rhinebeck, Dutchess County, New York Area: Members, Confirmands, and Family Lists: 1734-1889* (Rhinebeck, NY: Kinship Books, 2000), p.iii.]

[372] Ibid., p.1.

St. Peter the Apostle Lutheran Church. This Hagedorn compilation is the earliest [surviving] recorded reference to what became St. Paul's (Wurtemburg).

We also find in the old German Reformed Church, records that Catharine Frolich was the wife of Johannes Weist in 1741; Ursula Frolich, the wife of Marden Burger in 1745; Martinus Frolich, the husband of Anna Maria Hagedorn in 1756; Petrus Frolich, of Margaretha Flegeler in 1766; Maria Frolech, the wife of Gerhard Dederick in 1766; Henry Frolich, the husband of Margaret Van Lowen in 1768; and George Frolich, the husband of Gertrude Pultz in 1770.[373]

Smith states, "The Staatsburgh in which Dominie Hartwick preached and baptized the children was near the Frolich homestead, and his records are in the Rhinebeck Lutheran book."[374]

"A family record," writes Smith, states that "Peter Fraleigh was born August 15, 1720, died January 26, 1792. Margaret, his wife, born August 25, 1724, died June 2, 1805. This is not the beginning of the record. We have placed it first because it was the first in date. It is preceded by the record of Stephen which follows, and we are left in doubt whether Peter was father or elder brother to Stephen."[375]

Stephen Fraleigh was born July 28, 1742, married, October 23, 1764, Maria Van Benschoten. They had issue as follows: Maria, born April 13, 1765; Margaret, born July 22, 1767; Solomon, born December 18, 1768; Peter, born November 10, 1770; Elsjen, born January 26, 1775; Lanne, born January 26, 1781, died March 28, 1794. Maria Fraleigh died August 11, 1812 at the age of sixty-six years. Stephen Fraleigh died on April 11, 1820 at the age of seventy-seven years.[376]

Solomon Fraleigh married Christina, daughter of Conrad Laslief, born March 28, 1770, married, September 5, 1789. They had issue as follows: Maria, born October 5, 1790; Conrad, born May 27, 1792; Peter, born April 25, 1794; Stephen, born November 12, 1796; and Lydia, born April 12, 1799.

Smith notes that "Peter Fraleigh became the owner of the farm at the death of his father, and the graveyard known as Peter Frolich's took its name from him."[377] Peter Fraleigh [son of Solomon and Christina Fraleigh, and a grandson of Stephanus Fraleigh] and his wife, Elizabeth Felder, appear in the records of the German Reformed Church for the first time on July, 9, 1780. On this day, their son, Johannes, was baptized by Dominie Cock, the sponsors being Johan Felder and Anna Maria Streit.[378]

A Stephen Fraleigh [son of Solomon and Christina Fraleigh, and a grandson of the original Stephanus Fraleigh] died January 11, 1879 at the age of 83. Thus, he was born November 12, 1796. He was buried at the Rhinebeck Cemetery. A note states that "he

---

[373] Ibid.

[374] Ibid. p.216.

[375] Ibid.

[376] Ibid.

[377] Ibid., p.216.

[378] Ibid., p.217.

lived south of the village."[379] This would be consistent with Fraleigh land in the general area of the Staatsburg Church.

Alvah G. Frost adds that "The Fraleigh farm was near the Staatsburg-Hyde Park line and the Staatsburg Church," to which "was doubtless on that farm near the Fraleigh homestead [on the west side of the Albany Post Road[380]] and the graveyard was on the opposite side of the road from the house."[381] Frost supports this location by adding that, "the missionary station [was located] on the main road leading from New York to Albany [i.e., the Old Albany Post Road, now bypassed by Route 9], about five miles from the present location of the church."[382] Driving on current roads, this location is 3.8 miles due west of the present Wurtemburg Church.[383]

Adding to the mystery, Evangelical Lutheran Conference and Ministerium [ELCM] President, the Rev. Roy Steward recalls that as a young boy he took the school bus down Primrose Hill Road, turning north on the Old Albany Post Road [the purported location of the Staatsburg Church.] A few yards from this intersection, he recalls an old marker which stated something like, "the original location of the Lutheran Church."[384] To date there is no record of this highway marker. Continued research needs to be conducted to ascertain the specific location of the Staatsburg Church.

The 1743 Letter

"The Staatsburg Church" is mentioned in a September 12, 1743 letter from "the leaders and elders *pro tempore* of the Evangelical Lutheran German congregations at Queensbury [Germantown], Tarbush [Manorton] and Ancram in the manor of Livingston and county of Albany, as also at Rhinebeck, Beekman's Mills and at Staatsburg all on the east side to the Hudson River" to the Consistory of Holy Trinity Lutheran Church in London.[385] Wilhelm Christoph Berkenmeyer, Lutheran Pastor at Loonenburg [Athens, New York] also signed the letter dated September 18, 1743.[386]

The next mention of "the Staatsburg Church" in the St. Peter's records occurs in 1747, with a listing of fourteen confirmands.[387] On May 22, 1748, Johannes and David Schreiber (born May19, 1748), twin sons of Peter and Anna Barbara Schreiber, were

---

[379] Arthur C. Kelly, *Deaths, Marriages and Much Miscellaneous from Rhinebeck, New York Newspapers: 1846-1899* (Rhinebeck, NY: Kinship Books, 1978), p.50.

[380] Barbara Frost states that her uncle Alvah G. Frost gave this more specific location.

[381] Newspaper clipping from *The Rhinebeck Gazette*, on the 175th Anniversary history by Alvah G. Frost. Also, *1873 Wurtemburg Church Record Book*.

[382] Alvah G. Frost, p.6.

[383] As of 2010, there remains no evidence of the original building or the "cemetery across the road." Further investigation into this specific location is required!

[384] Interview with the Rev. Roy Steward, Jr., September 3, 2006.

[385] Simon Hart and Harry J. Kreider, translators, *Lutheran Churches in New York and New Jersey, 1722-1760: Lutheran Recorded in the Ministerial Archives of the Staatsarchiv, Hamburg, Germany* (United Lutheran Synod of New York and New England, 1962), pp.217-222.

[386] Ibid., p.222.

[387] Ibid., p.15.

baptized at the Staatsburg Church.[388] Presumably, this baptism was conducted by Berkenmeyer. Spahler served from 1733 until 1748, and Hartwick arrived 1748.[389]

Michael Boltz [also "Pultz"] and wife Anna Barbara are listed as members of the Staatsburg Church in 1750.[390] Michael Pultz, who died on December 30, 1823, at the age of 84, is buried in the old St. Paul's Churchyard.[391] Hence, we have a link back to the Staatsburg Church.

Peter Fralick's Burying Yard: The Lost Cemetery

In 1881, Edward M. Smith wrote, "Peter Fraleigh became the owner of the farm at the death of his father, and the graveyard known as 'Peter Frolich's' took its name from him, and was on the opposite side of the road from his house. The Bergs, Burgers (Burckhards in the old records), Frolichs and Van Benschotens and Schryvers were buried in this ground, and generally without tombstones."[392]

In another part of his book, while providing genealogical information on the Bergh family, Smith writes, "Christian Bergh died August 9, 1780; his wife, Anna Margretta Wolleben, died December 5, 1782. They were both buried in Peter Fralick's burying yard. John Bergh, son of Christian, the first, died August 14, 1794, and was also buried in Peter Fralick's burying yard."[393]

Smith adds, "We have no knowledge of [the exact location of] Peter Fralick's burying yard. It was somewhere in the precinct of Rhinebeck. Peter Fralick resided on the [Albany] Post Road, between Beekman's Mill at the Rhinebeck Flatts, and Peter Schryver's, in 1753; and Christian Bergh, between Peter Schryver's and the south end of the precinct."[394]

Alvah G. Frost's phrase "a small wooden building [with] a cemetery across the road"[395] is also intriguing. In the present Wurtemburg Cemetery, near the east side of the present church building, constructed in 1802, there is a row of eighteen ancient headstones located four and one-half to six feet from the foundation of the church. These graves are clearly too close to the foundation wall to contain actual human remains.[396] It is intriguing that many of the headstones along the east wall of the church predate 1802. For example, one of these ancient stones reads, "Michael Seeger, died 1763." Another reads "David Marquart, 1769-1776." Could it have been possible that when they

---

[388] Arthur C. Kelly, *Baptismal Records of St. Peter's Lutheran Church, Rhinebeck, New York: 1733-1899* (Rhinebeck, NY: Kinship Books, 1968), p.13.

[389] Ibid., p.11.

[390] Ibid., p.27.

[391] Arthur C. Kelly, *Rhinebeck, New York: Death Records of the 18th and 19th Centuries* (Rhinebeck, NY: Kinship Books, 1992), p.53.

[392] Edward M. Smith, pp.216-217.

[393] Ibid., p.178.

[394] Ibid.

[395] Alvah G. Frost, p.6.

[396] At the same time, these stones may have been removed over the decades. With ancient rural churchyards one never knows!

relocated their Church they abandoned "the cemetery across the road"[397] and moved these headstones to the new church location? Could it be possible that these graves are merely cenotaphs?

Adding to this mystery, Barbara Frost spoke of unsubstantiated rumors that there are old barns and buildings in the area surrounding the old Staatsburg Church, with tombstones mortared into their foundations. She adds that her Uncle Alvah G. Frost could never prove these rumors.[398] Could these rumors be true? Is there an unmarked and forgotten cemetery, containing the mortal remains of the Staatsburg Church dead in Christ, buried from c.1735 to 1800? The question remains open for future investigators.[399]

A Log Cabin or a Barn Church?

After years of reading, and often frustrating research, Barbara Frost believes that "the Staatsburg Church" was not a formal building, but rather a group of people which gathered on the Stephen Fraleigh farm, perhaps in a barn or in a simple log structure.[400]

Lutheran historian Abdel Ross Wentz helps us to visualize what the Staatsburg Church might have looked like. Wentz writes that "the meager church buildings of the seventeenth century, usually small structures built of logs, were gradually replaced in the eighteenth century by larger and more substantial buildings, usually of stone."[401]

Henry Melchior Mühlenberg's Visit

In 1750, the great patriarch of Lutheranism in America Henry Melchior Mühlenberg (1711-1787), visited Rhinebeck to settle a dispute between the Rev. John Christopher Hartwick and his congregations.[402]

"The Staatsburg Church" is mentioned in Mühlenberg's journal entry for September 17, 1750. It reads, "We visited the fourth small congregation at the place called Staatsburg, about eight miles from Rhinebeck, held divine services there and took leave."

The next day, adds Mühlenberg:

> …we had our baggage transported to the house of a member of the congregation on the Hudson River, there to wait for a boat to take us to New York. During the time which I spent in Mr. Hartwick's congregations I sought, so

---

[397] Ibid.

[398] Interview with Barbara Frost, September 15, 2006.

[399] Despite tantalizing references from Neff, Hull, Traver, and Frost, after years of frustrating searches of deeds, maps, and historical records I was unable to find extant evidence of the precise location of "the Staatsburg Church." If this location could ever be discovered it would be an appropriate site for a New York State Historical Marker.

[400] Barbara Frost interviewed September 15, 2006.

[401] Abdel Ross Wentz, *A Basic History of Lutheranism in America* (Philadelphia: Mühlenberg Press, 1955), p. 27.

[402] William J. Mann, *The Life and Times of Henry Melchior Mühlenberg* (Philadelphia: G.W. Frederick, 1888), p.253.

far as possible with my meager ability and God's grace, to contribute my part toward general pacification and the best interests of all; otherwise I did not concern myself at all with the personal circumstances of their quarrels or enter into any investigation of them.[403]

Henry Melchior Mühlenberg (1711-1787)

"The Staatsburg Church" is mentioned in Mühlenberg's journal entry for September 17, 1750. It reads, "We visited the fourth small congregation at the place called Staatsburg, about eight miles from Rhinebeck, held divine services there and took leave."

The next day, adds Mühlenberg:

...we had our baggage transported to the house of a member of the congregation on the Hudson River, there to wait for a boat to take us to New York. During the time which I spent in Mr. Hartwick's congregations I sought, so far as possible with my meager ability and God's grace, to contribute my part toward general pacification and the best interests of all; otherwise I did not concern myself at all with the personal circumstances of their quarrels or enter into any investigation of them.[404]

Mühlenberg's journal entry is important for two reasons. First, the "official" founding date for St. Paul's Lutheran Church of Wurtemburg has been listed for years

---

[403] Henry Melchior Mühlenberg, translated by Theodore G. Tappert and John W. Doberstein, *The Journals of Henry Melchior Mühlenberg In Three Volumes* (Philadelphia: The Evangelical Lutheran Ministerium of Pennsylvania and Adjacent Parts and the Mühlenberg Press MCMXLII), vol. I, p.252.

[404] Ibid.

and years as "1760." This entry indicates that there was at least a missionary station, or a preaching point, or at most a small congregation meeting in a barn or a home prior to September 17, 1750, when Mühlenberg visited.

Second, it appears that the eccentric Pastor Hartwick also had issues with the people of the Staatsburg Church as well as St. Peter the Apostle Church in Rhinebeck. Mühlenberg, as a Pietist trained at Halle University, sought to avoid needless controversies and conflicts.[405] He apparently took the high road and preached the Gospel to the people of the Staatsburg Church.

Evidently, as time passed, these "Palatine families found better farm lands further back from the Hudson river and they moved thither."[406] The Rev. Roy Steward, who grew up in the area and has extensively studied the issue, is of the opinion that as the threat of local Indian tribes receded, the "Wurtemburgers," as they were called by their Dutch neighbors, began to move to the east seeking better farm lands.[407]

Dr. Neff refers to the communication sent Col. Henry Beekman,[408] and his permission given under the date of April 27, 1759, for the erection of the first church.

On March 20, 1759, Leonard Wager (Weger) and (Johann) Michael Pultz[409] (1739-December 12, 1823)[410] applied to Col. Henry Beekman, a large land-owner in that section, and the father-in-law of General Morgan Lewis (d.1844), the fourth Governor of the State and "the father of public education [in New York],"[411] for a grant of land to build a church.[412] He replied on April, 17, 1759, granting their request for the privilege of building.

---

[405] Philip Jacob Spener, *Pia Desideria* (Philadelphia: Fortress Press, 1675, 1964), pp.97-102.

[406] Hull, p.10.

[407] Interview, September 2, 2006.

[408] Col. Henry Beekman (1688-January 3, 1776), the patentee, was the son of William Beekman who had come to New Amsterdam in 1647 with Governor Peter Stuyvesant (1612-1672). William Beekman had been born in Holland, of German ancestry, on April 28, 1623 and married Catherine, daughter of Frederick Hendricks DeBough of New Amsterdam on September 25, 1649. The couple had seven children, three sons and four daughters. He was an assistant alderman of New Amsterdam, vice-governor of the Delaware, and in 1664 the sheriff of Ulster County. He was reportedly a brewer, and he died in 1707. [Philip L. White, *The Beekmans of New York*, 1956.] Judge Henry Beekman, the oldest son of William, was baptized March 9, 1652 and m. June 5, 1681 to Joanna DeLopes, the widow of Joris Davidszen and the daughter of Capt. Luyt Jacob Loper of Stockholm and Cornelia Molyn of Amsterdam. Henry settled in Ulster County where he became a county judge, member of the legislature, colonel of the militia, deacon, and elder of the Reformed Dutch Church. He died in late 1716 and possibly never set foot on the Beekman Patent that he had established. Henry Beekman had four children, and after his death, the Beekman Patent was divided three ways among his three surviving heirs. His widow Joanna was still alive in September 1728, but deceased by 1736.

[409] Pultz was originally spelled "Boltz," and in various old documents [typical of the eighteenth century], the name is sometimes spelled "Poltz" and "Bultz."

[410] Buried in the old section of the Wurtemburg Cemetery.

[411] Alvah G. Frost, p.8.

[412] Morse, p.146.

Col. Henry Beekman's sent the following reply:

New York, April 17, 1759 "Messrs. [Leonard] Wager & Boltz [Michael Pultz]:- Having received your letter of the twentieth, concerning leave to build a church, etc., which reasonable request I willingly grant, and give you what further assurance that shall be adjudged for such purpose necessary, wishing you good prosperity in the meanwhile, am and remain,

Your well-wishing friend, HENRY BEEKMAN[413]

Johann Michael Pultz and Leonard Weger and his son Michael each gave an acre of land for "*ein Gottes Haus und ein Gottes acker.*"[414] The text reads:

In the year of Our Lord, 1758, December 27th, at this time, we had called our congregation together and we came together to build church (*Gottes Haus*) where the Lord should bless the place [translators notation, *it is not quite clear here*] and to confirm the agreement Leonard Wager and Michael Wager, his son, on the building, and Leonard Wager and Michael Wager generously gave a field which was an acre of land to build a Church (*Gottes Haus*) and a cemetery (*Gottes Acker*) and permitted it here with the condition before the congregation that neither they nor their descendents (children and children's children) should ever have possession of the land again, with the condition, however, that of the church should come to poverty and no service of God might ever more be held here Leonard Wager and Michael Wager might have each his own again as before. And so we accept it as declared above." This document was signed by eight individuals, including Leonard Wager and Michael Wager.[415]

The first officially recorded baptism at St. Paul's, dated October 23, 1760,[416] was the baptism of Salome Geiger (born November 22, 1759), the daughter of Wilhelm Geiger.[417] The first recorded confirmations at St. Paul's occurred on September 16, 1763. This

---

[413] Edward M. Smith, *Documentary History of Rhinebeck in Dutchess County* (Rhinebeck, NY, a Palatine Reprint, 1881, 1974), p.119. Edward M. Smith was the founder of *The Rhinebeck Gazette*.

[414] *St. Paul's Lutheran Church of Wurtemburg*, c. 1996 brochure.

[415] Wurtemburg Archive File #72. This document, originally written in an archaic cursive German script, was translated into English. A handwritten and undated copy of the translation is preserved in the Archives on the stationary of "Frost & Frost, Counselors at Law [i.e., Benson R. Frost, and Benson R. Frost, Jr.]." The text is presented here.

[416] James H. Smith, p.275 and Alvah G. Frost, p.7.

[417] *Baptism Records of St. Paul's Lutheran Church of Wurtemburg*, transcribed and indexed by Arthur C.M. Kelly, Rhinebeck, New York: Kinship, 1969), p.1.

included twenty-eight people, including seven married couples, such as "Jacob Kling and wife Margar."[418]

Fifteen years later, on November 5, 1774, Col. Henry Beekman also conveyed to the trustees of the church nineteen and three-quarters acres [i.e., a wood lot] about a mile west from the present location.[419] Edward M. Smith explains that to conduct a church in those days a government license and special charter was required to receive and collect subscriptions. On September 5, 1774, "for the sole and only proper use, benefit and behoof (sic) of the Protestant Church now erected on the southeast part of Rhinebeck, commonly called the 'Whitaberger Land.'"[420]

In this connection, Dr. Neff adds: "They (the congregation) having selected the commanding site on which the Church now stands, beautiful for situation and one of the finest on the line of the Hudson River and their church building becoming somewhat dilapidated, they decided to build a new Church, and in 1802 the present building was erected."[421]

The Rev. Chester H. Traver notes that, "Owing to some unrecorded cause, services were no longer held at Staatsburg, and the building, in 1802, was taken down and the lumber, used in remodeling this Church."[422]

In 1802, a new building was erected.[423] Barbara Frost questions the accuracy of Dr. Traver's often repeated claim that the Staatsburg Church was taken down, and some of the lumber was used in the construction of the new Wurtemburg Church. She argues that "the boys who would have taken part in the 1802 project of dismantling the Staatsburg Church, and transporting heavy timbers with teams of horses up Primrose Rose Hill Road to the present Wurtemburg location, would have recalled details of this major project. There is no historical evidence of these recollections."[424]

At the same time, in the belfry of the present building [and perhaps within the finished walls of the rest of the building] it appears that the building has been constructed of ancient hand-hewn colonial timbers. Could these ancient timbers have been recycled from the original Staatsburg location?

In 1807, the nineteen and three-quarters acres obtained from Henry Beekman in 1774 were sold and the proceeds were used to pay for the new building.[425]

---

[418] *Records of Lutheran Churches of Rhinebeck, Duchess County, NY Area: Members, Confirmands, & Family Lists*, 1734-1889, transcribed and indexed by Arthur C.M. Kelly, Rhinebeck, New York: Kinship, 2000), p.103.

[419] Frost, p.8.

[420] Edward M. Smith, p.120.

[421] Neff, *1872 Historical Sketch.*

[422] Chester H. Traver, *Lutheran Quarterly* (1916).

[423] The 1802 date is supported by Rev. William Hull (1881), p.120; Edward M. Smith (1881), p.120; James H. Smith (1882), p.275; Howard H. Morse (1908), p. 148; Alvah G. Frost (1935), p.9; Elizabeth McRostie Frost (1960), p.6. Sari B. Tiejen (1990) gives the date as "1803."

[424] Barbara Frost interviewed September 15, 2006.

[425] James H. Smith, p.275.

June 1, 1785, George (1741-January 1, 1821)[426] and Sebastian Pultz and Paul and Sebastian Wager deeded two acres of ground, one acre each.[427]

Early Wurtemburg Recollections

For a picture of what worship was like in those early days, we have an interesting recollection from *The Diary and Ledger of William H. Traver*. He wrote:

> I recollect when Domeny [i.e., Dominie, "Pastor" in Dutch] Quitman died…. I recollect Dominy [the Rev. Dr. Frederick Henry] Quitman when he used to preach in Wertenbergh [*sic*]. At them times they used to go to Church there without fire and the way they used to keep warm, every family had a foot stove. It was a square box ten or twelve inches square and about the same width with a door on one side and in that box there was an iron cup and that they would fill full of live coal and that would last and if it wasn't warm enough, they would go in the sexton's room. He always had a big fire. It was built with a great big fireplace.[428]

William H. Traver adds that "the sexton's room was built against the schoolhouse on the east side [of the schoolhouse] so he was [both] sexton and School Master."[429]

1832 Repairs

In 1832, the Wurtemburg Church was repaired and improved and a distinctive octagonal steeple was added. The belfry builder and architect was Stephen McCarty.[430] Stephen McCarty was a well-known local "joiner" who also built the octagonal belfry at The Evangelical Lutheran Church of St. Peter the Apostle Church [the Old Stone Church] in 1824.[431] McCarty also built the octagonal belfry on the Rhinebeck Dutch Reformed Church.[432] From this 1832 job, we have preserved *The Day Book Of LeGrand Curtis*[433] dated September 26, 1831:

---

[426] Buried in the Old Wurtemburg Cemetery.

[427] Smith, p.121.

[428] William H. Traver, *Diary and Ledger of William H. Traver* (Rhinebeck: DAR Collection). William H. Traver (1802-1873) is buried in the old section of the Wurtemburg Cemetery. See also, *A Rhinebeck Album: 1776-1876-1976* (Rhinebeck: Rhinebeck Historical Society and Moran Printing, Inc., 1976), p.25.

[429] Ibid.

[430] *Building Structure Inventory For*—with a handwritten sheet—completed by Connie Fowle, Rhinebeck Historical Society for the Division for Historic Preservation New York State Parks and Recreation, August 27, 1980 (on file at the Quitman House, Rhinebeck New York).

[431] Morse, p.120.

[432] In a document, dated November 18, 1818, Stephen McCarty is listed as pledging $10.00 to help pay the expenses for the building of a steeple at the Dutch Reform Church in Rhinebeck [Frank D. Blanchard, *History of the Reformed Dutch Church of Rhinebeck Flatts, New York* (Albany, New York: J.B. Lyon Company, 1921), p.179.]

"Job $875
Wirtemburg Church Commence New roof, pews,
Pulpit & ceiling
find all to work in Old stuff that will do
painting outside & in paint & painting $125
New steeple by Job $275
Partion in front of church $25
for laying lower floor $20
                                                      $125 paint
                              job $875
                                                      $1320

        515 days   Carpenters work
          painting out $125
                Whole job $1195"[434]

The Major Renovation of 1861

From October 6, 1860 until January 15, 1861—just prior to the outbreak of the American Civil War—a major renovation was undertaken at St. Paul's (Wurtemburg). This renovation is significant because it established the basic form and layout of the present worship space.

Barbara Frost writes that, "the motivation for the renovations of 1861 was provided by the need for a Church Hall. In 1859 the Church held, under a tent, a most successful Fall Festival. This Festival was the beginning of the famous Wurtemburg Turkey Supper.[435] It was held in November in conjunction with the full moon to provide light for rural farmers and their families so that they could find their way home at night. It was so successful that it was repeated."[436] As plans grew more elaborate, it was apparent that a Church Hall was needed.

In 1860, the basement was dug under St. Paul's and, "in 1861 the church was enlarged and remodeled."[437] The Wurtemburg Archives hold a marvelous collection of detailed specifications and documents relating to this major renovation.

According to these documents, during this renovation the north gallery [balcony] was removed, the pulpit was put in the recess,[438] the Narthex was added on the south side,[439] the belfry was moved from the north end of the building to the south side, the old

---

[433] A subcontractor working with Stephen McCarty?

[434] This page, from *The Day Book Of LeGrand Curtis,* has been reproduced in Sari B. Tiejen, *Rhinebeck: Portrait of a Town* (Rhinebeck: Phanter Press, 1990).

[435] In October, 2011 we will hold our 150th Annual Turkey Supper.

[436] "Barbara Frost Manuscript," Wurtemburg Archive File Folder #44.

[437] Hull, p.10 and Morse, p. 148.

[438] Also, Chester Henry Traver, *The Rhinebeck Gazette* (1915).

[439] In 2008, when the lift elevator was added, we could clearly see how the siding was tied into the older building when the Narthex was added in 1861.

bell was hung in the new tower, and the pews were reversed [a 180 degree turn!]. [440] That is, prior to this renovation the pews faced south. The specifications for this renovation also included detailed instruction for reusing the doors, windows, and siding from the old building. [441]

During this renovation a forty-by-fifty-eight-foot basement was also dug under the old church. The 1860 specs state that:

> The dirt [is] to be removed to the depth of eight feet so as to a seven foot in the clear when floor is in and lathed and plaster overhead. The walls are to be made of [field] stone furnished by the trustees of the Church and delivered at the Church to be twenty-two inches thick laid up dry and pointed on the outside with an aperture in the southeast part and an airy therein for putting up a stairway—also airys [window wells] for windows. [442]

The specifications continue, "four register holes [are] to be put in the ceiling [of the basement] for the use of heaters. Three chimneys two to start from the foundation of the basement and to be carried to such heights as their uses may require." One of these chimneys—in the northwest corner—is still used to vent the oil burner. The plastered frame of a second chimney that is no longer used can still be seen in the northeast corner of the worship space.

Upstairs, "the old pulpit of the church [is] to be removed to the basement and their put as advised by committee." And, "a reading desk to be arranged with screws for lowering or raising"[443] was also to be provided.

The specs add that "seats [pews] in present audience room [nave] to be reversed facing north and remaining space of audience room [nave] to be filled with new seats [pews]."[444] With these pews, "an entrance from each aisle or ends" was to be provided. During this same renovation, fifty-eight plated pew numbers were added at the cost of $14.00 [these numbers are still on the pews].

The specs also stated that "the north galley [was] to be removed and a side gallery [was] to be continued to the north end."[445] Also, a "recess [is] to be cut into the north gable of church sixteen feet in length more or less width sixteen or eighteen feet more or less in height and have a platform four feet high more or less."[446] "The pulpit [is] to be put in recess and the recess pulpit and altar to be modeled after the Reformed Dutch

---

[440] Alvah G. Frost, p.9.

[441] St. Paul's Lutheran Church of Wurtemburg [Evangelical Lutheran Conference and Ministerium] brochure printed by the Church in 2000 based on information taken from Wurtemburg Archive File Folder #91.

[442] Wurtemburg Archive File Folder #91.

[443] Ibid.

[444] Ibid.

[445] Ibid.

[446] Ibid.

Church of Rhinebeck."[447]   Once again, it is interesting to note the influence of Reformed worship practice and theology on this Lutheran church.

In the Wurtemburg archives, there is a copy of the final receipt dated January 15, 1861, indicating that the builder Peter M. Fulton was paid in full for his work.[448]   This receipt was signed by Trustees Hiram A. Pultz, Samuel L. Frost, and Jacob A. Ackert. The total cost of the renovation was $2500 including $275.00 for new pews and $50.00 for wainscoting and ornamental windows on the north end.

Various Renovations

During the summer of 1892, the interior of the Wurtemburg Church was repapered and painted, the pulpit platform was lowered, and a new pulpit—still in use—placed upon it. The organ and choir were moved from the gallery and relocated to the right side of the pulpit. The officers also presented a new pulpit Bible. The re-opening ceremonies were held on August 22, 1892.[449]

In 1999, a $13,000 project to repair and restore the belfry was undertaken by the congregation. During this process, the distinctive comet weathervane was removed, restored, repainted, and replaced. In the summer of 2000, the lightning rod was also repaired and reinstalled. Also in 1999, vinyl siding was placed over the ancient Wurtemburg clapboards. After serious discussion and long debate, the congregation agreed to go ahead with the vinyl siding because it was not "a terminal decision." At some future date, if funds are available, the vinyl could be removed and the original clapboards could be painted.

During the Summer of 2002, the old ceiling in the basement Social Hall, which had been installed in 1916, was removed and replaced. The opportunity was taken to rewire the downstairs with updated electrical service. New stronger lights were also installed.

During the reconstruction, when the old ceiling was removed, massive beams made from huge logs shaved on one side leaving the bark on the other were exposed. The ancient bark is still visible on these timbers. Other supporting beams appear to be recycled hand-hewn barn beams with the notches still visible. Over the years these ancient beams have dried, cured, and hardened so that it is difficult to drive a nail into them. Perhaps the old rumors were correct. Perhaps these ancient beams were taken from the original Staatsburg Church.

In 2008, a lift elevator was installed at the cost of $125,000. During this project, the east stairway into the Social Hall was turned to accommodate the lift shaft. Upstairs two pews were removed, and a new door and sidewalk was also installed to provide access. A major portion of the funds for the project were provided by a gift from Henry and Mary Lown Traver Baas. During the winter of 2010, a major plaster restoration and paint project was executed inside the sanctuary of St. Paul's. During this process, the plaster and lath work in the ceiling was expertly restored and reinforced with fiberglass mesh and several hundred screws with large washers [now hidden by layers of plaster].

---

[447] Ibid.

[448] Wurtemburg Archive File Folder #91.

[449] *The Rhinebeck Gazette*, July 26, 1890.

Chapter Six: Worship Life at Wurtemburg

Liturgy has been defined as "the work of the people." For two-hundred-and-fifty years, the old Wurtemburg Church has been the center of both the spiritual and social life of faithful Christian families living in the area.

What was the Service like in the earliest years of the Staatsburg Church (c.1760-1800), and then the Wurtemburg Church during the nineteenth century? While none of these early liturgies have survived, a few hints can be gleaned by referring to the overall history and evolution of the Lutheran liturgy in America.

First, it must be remembered that the first Lutheran communities in the New World were scattered over a wide and sparsely populated territory. They lacked both pastoral care and spiritual leadership. In the early days, there were few—if any—pastors to lead worship and to administer the Sacraments.

Second, as we have stated above, they were also a "mixed multitude" living in "divided homes."[450] The Palatines that settled in the Rhinebeck area were both Reformed and Lutheran. Orthodox Lutheran Pastor Wilhelm Christoph Berkenmeyer and Pietist Lutheran Pastor John Christopher Hartwick [they had a strong antipathy toward each other] both complained bitterly in their letters about the Palatines tendency to inter-marry among the Reformed.[451]

Hence, from the start, the Lutheran Christians of this area were influenced by Calvinist theology and by Reformed worship styles; i.e., a minimalist liturgy with the focus on the preached Word [**Word > Sacrament**]. This tendency was compounded by the Pietist movement (c.1675) that profoundly influenced faith and praxis in the Palatinate.

Early pastors, including John Christopher Hartwick (1746-1758) and Dr. Frederick Henry Quitman (1760-1832) [and possibly Johannes Frederick Ries (1760-1791)], were graduates of the Pietist Mecca of Halle University. Thus, it is highly likely that these pastors would have used an order of service which reflected the theological views of the Pietist movement.

Henry Melchior Mühlenberg, the patriarch of Lutheranism in America, "was sent out by Dr. Gotthilf August Francke (1696-1769)[452] of Halle and Dr. Ziegenhagen of London to labor among the scattered Lutherans in Pennsylvania and the other colonies [including

---

[450] Wilhelm Christoph Berkenmeyer, *The Albany Protocol: Wilhelm Christoph Berkenmeyer's Chronicle of Lutheran Affairs in New York Colony, 1731-1750, translation* by Simon Hart, translation initiated by Harry J. Kreider, and edited by John P. Dern (Ann Arbor, MI, 1971), p.169.

[451] Ibid.

[452] Son and successor of August Herman Francke.

New York]."[453] Liturgical scholar Luther Reed adds that, "his diaries, correspondence, and catechetical methods all indicate Pietist strains and influences."[454]

Mühlenberg, who proclaimed the ideal of "one Church, one Book,"[455] prepared a liturgy which was adopted by the Ministerium of Pennsylvania in 1748.[456] Mühlenberg's *German Order for the Service and the Holy Communion*, together with English forms for Baptism and Marriage, "This first American liturgy," writes Luther Reed, "was the only one authorized for nearly forty years [i.e., covering the period of 1748-1788]."[457]

Reed states:

> When we remember Henry Melchior Mühlenberg's association with the Pietists at Halle, and the fact that he labored in America under primitive conditions with scattered groups on the frontiers of civilization, it is astonishing that he should have concerned himself greatly about the preparation of a liturgy. His sense of historical and devotional values, his appreciation of church order, and his statesmanlike insight led him there almost at once.[458]

Thus, Mühlenberg, the church planter and organizer, used the liturgy to bring order out of chaos.

Reed writes that "the Mühlenberg Liturgy… was little more than an outline."[459] In 1762, Christopher Sauer printed an American edition of the Mühlenberg Liturgy in Germantown, Pennsylvania. The hymnal contained the historic Gospels and Epistles for the Church Year and a series of Collects published by Veit Dietrich in his Nuremberg *Agend-büchlein* (1543).[460] Reed states that, in general, this early liturgy reflected the historic conservative type of service found in the Saxon, north German, and Scandinavian Lutheran churches at the time. The typical order of Service was:

> A Hymn of invocation of the Holy Spirit.
> Confession of Sins-Exhortation, Confession, Kyrie.
> Gloria in Excelsis Deo, in metrical form.
> Collect-Salutation and Response with Collect for the Day.
> Epistle for the Day.
> Hymn.
> Gospel for the Day.

---

[453] Luther Reed, *The Lutheran Liturgy: The Story of the Common Liturgy of the Lutheran Church in America* (Philadelphia: Mühlenberg Press, 1947), p.162.

[454] Ibid., p.164.

[455] Luther Reed, *Worship: A Study of Corporate Devotion* (Philadelphia: Mühlenberg Press, 1959), p.61.

[456] Luther Reed, *The Lutheran Liturgy*, p.164.

[457] Ibid., p.165.

[458] Ibid., p.163.

[459] Ibid., p.166.

[460] Ibid., p.167.

Nicene Creed.
Hymn.
Sermon.
The General Prayer.
The prayer concluded with the Lord's Prayer.
Hymn.
Salutation, responses, and closing collect.
Aaronic Benediction.[461]

In the early decades of the nineteenth century, the liturgy was thought of simply as a minor feature of the hymnal. Dr. Frederick Henry Quitman appended a minimalist liturgy to the *New York Synod Hymnbook of 1814*.[462] The General Synod in 1837 also appended this English language liturgy of the New York Synod to its own hymnbook.[463]

According to Reed;

The English hymnbooks in general use at the time were *The General Synod's Hymnal of 1828*, with an appendix of 1852, and *The New York Synod Hymnbook of 1814*, with an appendix of 1834. The first of these was thoroughly impregnated with Calvinistic and Arminian material of highly subjective character. It was arranged in accordance with a dogmatic scheme which practically ignored the church year. The *New York Hymnbook* [due to Dr. Quitman's influence], while of higher literary and intellectual quality, had a strong infusion of Rationalistic thought. Its emphasis upon the ethical, rather than the devotional, was in agreement with the point of view and the practice of New England Unitarianism.[464]

Reed adds:

The Ministerium of New York… at first probably used the Mühlenberg Liturgy in manuscript and later the printed form of 1786. The Synod, however, was affected by the English movement earlier than was the Ministerium of Pennsylvania. Dr. J. C. Kunze published a *Hymn and Prayer Book* in 1795, which contained an English translation of the Liturgy of 1786 and a considerable number of very unsatisfactory translations of hymns from the German.[465]

Hence, it can be safely assumed that during the period between c.1760 and 1800 those that attended the gatherings at the Staatsburg Church used a liturgy similar to Mühlenberg's *German Order for the Service and the Holy Communion*. And, after 1814, they must have used Dr. Quitman's *New York Hymnbook*, with the 1834 appendix. These

---

[461] Ibid.

[462] Ibid., p.171.

[463] Ibid.

[464] Ibid.

[465] Ibid., p.174.

early liturgies would have been totally foreign to post-modern Lutherans accustomed to the *Lutheran Book of Worship* and contemporary variations.

The oldest hymn books to be discovered in the extensive archives of St. Paul's (Wurtemburg) are copies of *The Book of Worship of the General Synod* (1870). The little hymnal [a pocket edition] was only four-and-one-half inches by six inches. And, it contains only the words—with no music!

"This is my body give for you..."
Photo: Linda A. Isaacs

The worship service in the 1870 *Book of Worship* is interesting to read. It is minimalist to say the least. The entire Service is only five pages long. It contains a call to worship, a long confession of sins, and the Apostles' Creed. The 1870 *Book of Worship* also includes the *Augsburg Confession*.

In 2005, Church Council member Joseph Dahlem, using memorial funds, headed up a committee that refurbished the hymnbook racks on the back of the pews. Evidently, these pew racks had originally been designed to hold the six-inch pocket edition of the 1870 *Book of Worship*. For one hundred and thirty five years, generations of Wurtemburgers have worshipped in pews with newer larger hymnals protruding above the back of the pews. The refurbished hymnbook racks now perfectly accommodate the *Lutheran Book of Worship*.

Hymn Books Used at St. Paul's Lutheran Church of Wurtemburg[466]

> *Book of Worship of the General Synod* (1870)
> *Common Service Book* (1888)
> *Book of Worship with Hymns and Tunes* (1899) [General Synod]
> *Common Service Book and Hymnal* (1917) [United Lutheran Church]
> *Service Book and Hymnal* (1957) [Lutheran Church in America]
> *Lutheran Book of Worship* (1978)
> *With One Voice: A Lutheran Resource for Worship* (1995)[467]

Multiple well-worn copies of *The Book of Worship of the General Synod* (1899) edition can also be found stacked on the high shelves in the balcony at St. Paul's. This hymnal also contains the full text of the *Augsburg Confession;*[468] a model church constitution;[469] and, the Constitution of the General Synod.[470]" This is an outstanding feature. We wonder how many generations of old Wurtemburgers perused *The Augsburg Confession* (1530) and learned the precepts to Lutheranism when they were supposed to be listening to some endless dry nineteenth-century sermon. This hymnal is also interesting in that it contains the familiar *SBH* and *LBW* style of "little numbers in the front" with big hymn numbers in the back. Apart from the "King James" English, post-modern Lutherans would certainly have little difficulty navigating in this old hymnal.

Also, found among the archives, and stacked in the corners at St. Paul's, are multiple well-worn copies of *The Common Service Book* (1888). The 1888 *Common Service Book* is a truly beautiful hymnbook. The title page and the typesetting throughout the hymnbook is high Gothic. It reeks of respectability, and it looks like a serious Church book. At the same time, it is unclear how, or when, the 1899 *Book of Worship of the General Synod* and the 1888 *Common Service Book* were used at St. Paul's.

---

[466] Copies of these books a can be found in the archives at Wurtemburg.

[467] Hymnal supplement.

[468] *The Book of Worship of the General Synod* (Philadelphia: United Lutheran Publications House, 1899), pp.207-233.

[469] Ibid., pp.245-258.

[470] Ibid., pp.259-262.

Luther Reed wrote:

> *The Book of Worship of the General Synod* (eighth edition, 1880) contained only sixteen pages of liturgical material. This was overshadowed by a lengthy collection of family prayers for the morning and evening of each day of the week. The morning service included a confession lifted bodily from *The Prayer Book of the Episcopal Church.* It contained some historical elements, but they were at times in unhistorical order. There was no provision whatever for the historical Introits, Collects, Epistles, and Gospels of the Church Year, nor was any liturgical order provided for the Holy Communion. The hymns were largely subjective and frequently Calvinistic in character. The only recognition accorded the Church year was the inclusion of twenty hymns for Church festivals.[471]

Multiple copies of the next generation *Common Service Book and Hymnal* of 1917-1918[472] are also found stacked in the corners of St. Paul's. This hymnbook was the product of the newly created United Lutheran Church, in 1918.

The 1918 hymnbook was apparently used until 1957, when the new *Service Book and Hymnal* was introduced. During the 1960s and 1970s, St. Paul's (Wurtemburg) used the red *Service Book and Hymnal* (1957).

During the summer of 2001, we attempted to reintroduce the *Service Book and Hymnal* for both historical interest and for variety's sake. We did the Second Setting for ten weeks in a row. The experiment proved to be a dismal failure. Since 1996, to the present, St. Paul's has experienced phenomenal growth in membership. The vast majority of these new members are not from traditional Lutheran backgrounds. The old *S.B.H.* that was familiar to a few longtime Lutherans proved to be a truly foreign worship experience for the majority of our newest members. It was in interesting experience!

Communion Practice

Thea Lawrence notes that "in 1907, Third Lutheran Church [in the village of Rhinebeck] adopted individual communion cups and was considered to be much in advance of the other churches [in the area]."[473] An editorial in *The Rhinebeck Gazette* stated, "there can be no longer any uncertainty in the minds of sensible persons as the unhealthful, unsanitary and unclean conditions existing in the old method [i.e., the common cup]"[474]

Boldly resisting the winds of change, Wurtemburg held to the traditional common cup. In the early 1930s, one writer noted the conservative Wurtemburgers continued to maintain the quaint custom of using the common cup.

On the First Sunday in Advent, December 3, 1989, Pastor Richard Mowery—with Council approval—introduced weekly communion to St. Paul's. Prior to this time,

---

[471] Luther Reed, *The Lutheran Liturgy,* p.193.

[472] *The Common Service Book and Hymnal* (Philadelphia: The Board of Publication of the United Lutheran Church in America, 1917-1918).

[473] Lawrence, p.77.

[474] *The Rhinebeck Gazette,* April 6, 1907.

communion was offered on "the first Sunday of the month and the first Sunday of the six Church seasons and on festivals."[475]

At the time, this decision was considered to be very controversial. On March 4, 1990, St. Paul's held a congregational meeting to discuss the possibility of adopting the practice of weekly communion. At the March 4 meeting, "fifty percent spoke [in favor] of weekly communion and fifty percent [opposed]."[476] At the meeting the congregation decided that "for those wishing to receive communion, it was suggested that the time could be used in prayerful meditation. All are encouraged to exercise their choice and to be comfortable with it."[477]

Apparently, this did not settle the issue. Communion practice continued to divide the congregation. A letter from Pastor Richard Mowery dated August 27, 1990 stated, "After much discussion at Council and in the Pastoral Relations Committee and in consultation with our Bishop, and because of division over the question of weekly communion, I have asked the Council… to return to the previous pattern of frequency of Holy Communion for the time being."[478] At the same time the letter stated that "we… support the goal of weekly communion."[479] Within a year or two of this communion controversy the issue was settled and the practice of weekly communion was adopted.

In 2010—and since June 29, 1996, when Pastor Mark D. Isaacs was appointed to serve at St. Paul's—weekly communion is considered to be the norm and standard. At this point, older members have generally adapted and accepted the practice, while newer members—many from non-Lutheran backgrounds, and many are former Roman Catholics—would probably be shocked to learn that weekly communion was ever an issue.

The 1960 Conn Organ

An undated *Poughkeepsie Journal* newspaper column (c. 1979?) states that "to celebrate its 200th anniversary, in 1960, the church installed indoor bathrooms and an electric pipe organ to replace the old pump organ." At a Congregational Meeting held on May 22, 1960, approval was given to the Memorial Organ Committee to purchase a new organ. The new organ, "a Conn Artist Model with a #123 C speaker in Walnut finish" was purchased on April 14, 1960, from the Poughkeepsie Music Shop and Studios for $2,500 "with the old [pump] organ" given in trade. The organ was formally dedicated on Sunday, May 29, 1960, at a special "Memorial Sunday Service."[480]

The following are the names given to the Memorial Organ Committee to be memorialized:

---

[475] Undated page from an article written by the Rev. Richard Mowry published in the parish newsletter in fall of 1989? (Archive Folder #29).

[476] March 12, 1990 letter to the members of St. Paul's from Congregational President Norman F. Craft (Archive Folder #29).

[477] Ibid.

[478] August 27, 1990 letter to the members of St. Paul's from Congregational President Norman F. Craft (Archive Folder #29).

[479] Ibid.

[480] "The Memorial Organ," St. Paul's Lutheran Church of Wurtemburg archives.

The Rev. Dr. George Neff Family; Austin Frost, Jr.; The Ackert Family; Mildred von der Lieth Tompkins; Edna Hermans Lown; Charles M. Frost; J. Alden Andrew; Mr. and Mrs. George Formen; Austin S. Frost; Ethel Forman Tompkins; Virginia Washburn Finch; Alvah G. Frost; Mr. & Mrs. Irving J. Burger; Mr. & Mrs. Joseph Greenhalgh; Mr. & Mrs. Dewitt Ayres; The Rev. Elder J. Himes; Minda Thompson; Ralph Haver; Cecil and Millard Boomhower; Harry H. Hill, Sr.; Lewis and Alice Markle; Mr. and Mrs,. Alverson C. Marquet; Jacob and Agnes Closs; The Moore Family; H. Caroline Ackert; Lilly P. Pultz; Mr. and Mrs. Joseph Arnett; Bertha Cure; Warren H. Closs; Lee E. Sempson; Nillett R. and Lizzie Schultz Traver; Mr. and Mrs. Charles R. Traver; Frank and Nellie Crapser; Mr. and Mrs. Fred Traver; Virtus L. Haines; The Rev. Dr. and Mrs. John G. Traver; Emma Hamilton Kilmer; Philip M. Rossman; The Rev. Dr. and Mrs. Chester H. Traver; The Dr. Rev. Henry H. Wahl; Mr. and Mrs. Byron Traver: John and Kathleen Wager; Percy M. and Lottie Lown; Edward Cookingham; Lillian Wilsey Traver; Barbara Leona Traver Closs; Mr. and Mrs. Henry G. Traver; Frank and Elizabeth Bonham; and Louis Naber.

The 1989 Rogers Organ

Starting in 1985, when it was apparent that the 1960 Conn organ needed to be replaced, the people of St. Paul's began an effort to raise more than $22,000 for the purchase of a new organ. In 1989, the congregation selected and had installed a Roger's Classic 205 organ. It was installed by Rick Tripodi of the Altenburg Piano House in Elizabeth, New Jersey. John Stokes voiced the pipes.[481]

---

[481] "American's Lutheran Churches Choose Rogers," *Heraldings From Rogers* (a publication from the Rogers Organ Company, c.1990), p.3.

Chapter Seven: Organizations, Associations, and Traditions

For most of its past two-hundred-and-fifty years, St. Paul's Lutheran Church of Wurtemburg was a tightly knit rural congregation. For many years, the Wurtemburg Church was a center for community life. During the late nineteenth and early twentieth centuries, many interesting organizations were formed in conjunction with the ministry at St. Paul's.

This remarkable picture was taken on April 13, 1889. It shows the cast of a "Church entertainment" held at Wurtemburg featuring Alice Markle, William S. Ackert, Charles R. Traver, Mary Traver, Mary Schultz, Elmer Schultz, and Marian Schultz.
Photo: St. Paul's Archives.

The Wurtemburg Archives are replete with an astonishing array of associations, organizations, drama societies, and groups complete with constitutions, lists of officers, detailed minutes, and meticulous treasurer's books.[482] It is truly impressive how organized, formal, and intentional these Wurtemburgers were when they created those many groups.

In 1960, Elizabeth McR. Frost recalled that it was a long custom that, for twenty weeks each winter, a *Singing School* was held at Wurtemburg. At this school, in addition to "the pleasure of the music, instruction was given in singing by note."[483] Imagine what

---

[482] Archives of St. Paul's Lutheran Church of Wurtemburg.

[483] Elizabeth McR. Frost, *The Men of Wurtemburg and Their House of God: 1760-1960: A Short History of St. Paul's Lutheran Church of Wurtemburg* (Rhinebeck New York, 1960), p.7.

an annual twenty-week singing school would do for the present quality of our congregational singing!

The Rev. John Kling taught Wurtemburg Union Lyceum members
"to advance to the stage deliberately, stand erect,
throw your shoulders back, and take a full breath."
Photo: Archives of St. Paul's Lutheran Church of Wurtemburg.

The Wurtemburg Union Lyceum

During the late nineteenth and early twentieth century, an organization called *The Wurtemburg Union Lyceum* also held regular meetings. The Lyceum programs included "declamations, essays, debates, and complete dramas."[484]

An example of the *Wurtemburg Union Lyceum's* programs and activities comes from a typed manuscript found in the archives. At the December 15, 1886, meeting of the *Lyceum,* the Rev. John L. Kling gave an introductory talk on "how members should proceed when taking part in reading or singing." Pastor Kling suggested that, when asked to speak, members should "advance to the stage deliberately, stand erect, throw your shoulders back, and take a full breath."[485] He added that "you should not clear your throat, which you do because of nervousness, but take a shallow breath or two, which will

---

[484] *The Constitution of the Wurtemburg Union Lyceum* (Archive Folder #105) is dated 1883-1884.

[485] Typed minutes of *Wurtemburg Union Lyceum* meeting, December 15, 1886 by F. E. Traver (Archive Folder #105).

clear your throat." Then, "look over your audience, announce the name of your selection and proceed."[486]

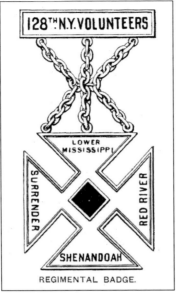

*The 128th New York Volunteer
Regiment Veterans Medal*

At the same meeting, William B. Brown (1840-1916)[487] of the Hillside section of Rhinebeck delivered an address to the *Wurtemburg Union Lyceum* on "The Hardship of War." "The war" was the American Civil War (1861-1865). In 1886, twenty years after the war, William B. Brown, the son of John (1803-1865) and Catherine Van Nosdall Brown (1812-1861), discussed his wartime experiences, and the experiences of his four brothers [Joseph H. Brown; Derrick Brown; James K. Brown; Benjamin H. Brown[488]], who all enlisted to support the Union cause. All five of the Brown brothers were mustered into Company C of the 128th Regiment, New York Volunteers (U.S. Infantry) on the same day; i.e., September 4, 1862.[489] Understating this action, *Wurtemburg Union Lyceum* minutes reported that "the Browns were very patriotic."[490]

---

[486] Ibid.

[487] William B. Brown (1840-1916) is buried in the Rhinebeck Cemetery near the veterans section.

[488] Edward M. Smith, p.220.

[489] Colonel David S. Cowles received authority, July 19, 1862, to raise a regiment in the counties of Columbia and Dutchess; it was organized at Hudson, New York, and there mustered in the service of the United States for three years on September 4, 1862.

The companies were recruited principally: A at Hudson, Ghent, Chatham, Austerlitz, New Lebanon, Canaan, Germantown and Claverack; B at Washington, Amenia, Dover, Pawling, North East, Stanford, and Pine Plains; C at Rhinebeck, Milan, Red Hook, Clinton, Stanford, and Hyde Park; D at Poughkeepsie, Hyde Park, Beekman, Fishkill, Pine Plains, Pleasant Valley, Clinton, Livingston, Greenport, and LaGrange; E at Kinderhook, Chatham, Valatie, Hillsdale, and Austerlitz; F at Fishkill, Pawling, Pine Plains, North East, Washington, Amenia, and Hudson; G at Stuyvesant, Hudson, Ancram, Clermont, Taghkanick, Gallatin, Claverack, New Lebanon,

Joe was the oldest, and Bennie[491] was too young to carry a musket, so they took him as a Drummer Boy. Another brother, John H. Brown (1850-1914), "cried because he was too young to go off to war with his brothers [he was only twelve at the time!]."[492]

William B. Brown stated "Joe was killed in the first battle in which he was engaged." He added that during the course of the battle, "we marched over his body three times."[493] Records indicate that Joseph H. Brown (born in Rhinebeck on August 26, 1837), Company K, 128th New York State Volunteer Infantry, was killed in action on September 19, 1864 at the Third Battle of Winchester, Virginia.[494] At this time, the 128th Regiment was a part of the XIX Corps was under to comment of General William Henley Emory (1811-1887). In this battle, Union forces, under Brigadier General Philip Sheridan (1831-1888), campaigning in the Shenandoah Valley, fought CSA General Jubal Early (1816-1894). During the battle, 749 Union troops were killed, and 4,440 were wounded.

As the war dragged on, the brothers were separated. On October 19, 1864, William— along with eighty-one other men from the 128th Regiment—was taken prisoner during the Battle of Cedar Creek in the Shenandoah Valley near Middletown,

---

Stockport, Ghent, and Hillsdale; H at Fishkill, Poughkeepsie, Hyde Park, and Beekman; I at Poughkeepsie; and K at Chatham, Hudson, Claverack, Greenport, Hyde Park, Clinton, Germantown, Red Hook, and Copake.

The regiment left New York State on September 5, 1862. It served in the Middle Department, VIII Corps, at and near Baltimore, Maryland, from September, 1862; at New Orleans, Louisiana, from December, 1862; in the 1st Brigade, Sherman's Division, Department of the Gulf, from January, 1863; in 1st Brigade, 1st Division, XIX Corps, from March, 1863; in the 3rd Brigade, 3rd Division, XIX Corps, from June, 1863; in 2nd Brigade, 1st Division, XIX Corps, from July, 1863; in 3rd Brigade, 1st Division, XIX Corps, from November, 1863; in 3rd Brigade, 2nd Division, XIX Corps, from February, 1864; in 3rd Brigade, 1st Division, X Corps, from April 2, 1865; and it was honorably discharged and mustered out, under Capt. Thomas N. Davis, July 12, 1865, at Savannah, Ga. [The regiment took a gallant and conspicuous part in the long siege of Port Hudson, Louisiana, (May 21-July 9, 1863), fighting desperately during the assaults of May 27 and June 14. The splendid service rendered by the 128th is well attested by its casualties during the siege, which amounted to 22 killed, 100 wounded and 6 missing, a total of 128. Colonel David S. Cowles fell while gallantly leading his regiment during the assault of May 27, 1863 the command suffering its heaviest losses on this occasion.]

During its service, the 128th Regiment lost by death, killed in action, 2 officers, 41 enlisted men; of wounds received in action, 20 enlisted men; of disease and other causes, 3 officers, 203 enlisted men; total, 5 officers, 264 enlisted men; aggregate, 269; of whom 41 enlisted men died in the hands of the enemy. [Frederick Phisterer, *New York in the War of the Rebellion* (Albany: J. B. Lyon Company, 1912.)]

[490] *Wurtemburg Union Lyceum* minutes.

[491] In 1863, Benjamin H. Brown transferred to the Infantry Corps and served as a Hospital Steward.

[492] *Wurtemburg Union Lyceum* minutes.

[493] Ibid.

[494] David H. Hanaburgh, *History of the 128th Regiment, New York Volunteers (U.S. Infantry) in the Late Civil War* (Poughkeepsie, N.Y.: 1894), p. 236, and Arthur C.M. Kelly, *Rhinebeck, New York: Death Records of the 18th and 19th Century*, p. 4.

Virginia. D.H. Hanaburgh,[495] a member of the 128th Regiment, also taken prisoner at this time, writes that on the morning of October 19, 1864, elements of the 128th Regiment, XIX Corps, were posted "to the left of the pike and in a hollow at the foot of a hill." The battlefield was covered with smoke and fog. In the confusion, "we knew that the Rebels had broken in on our right along the pike."[496]

D.H. Hanaburgh adds:

> ...deploying, we began to retreat to the rear and up a hill... We supposed we heard our picket line officer ordering us to fall back and did so in good order. Soon we saw a line of [Confederate] skirmishers, dressed for the most part in Union blue, moving back. We were soon made aware of our mistake by hearing the orders, accompanied with an oath, to throw down our arms. Surrounded as we were by the heavy Rebel skirmish line which had broken in on our right, and knowing for the heavy fire on our left that the enemy must be in that direction, we saw no possible chance of escape and chose the only course to save our lives and unconditionally surrendered. The first words from the Confederate Provost Guards were "where is your pocket-book?"[497]

Cedar Creek is remembered as a great victory for Brigadier General Philip Sheridan. While losing more than 5,500 of his 31,000-man army, the VI, VIII, and the XIX Federal Corps devastated CSA General Jubal Early's Army of the Valley by inflicting almost 3,000 casualties and destroying nearly all of its artillery in the headlong fight. Cedar Creek "provided telling omens for the collapsing Confederacy."[498]

First, the eighty-two captured men of the 128th Regiment, including Frank W. Rikert also from Rhinebeck,[499] were taken to Libby Prison. William Brown told the *Wurtemburg Union Lyceum* that they "nearly starved to death in Libby Prison."[500] Libby Prison, located in Richmond, Virginia, was one of the best known, and most notorious, Confederate facilities, used to incarcerate Federal prisoners-of-war. After the Battle of First Bull Run (July 21, 1861), a former three-story tobacco warehouse was converted into a prison to hold thousands of captured Union soldiers.[501]

Describing the inhumane conditions in Libby Prison, William Brown told the *Lyceum* audience his fellow suffering prisoners were so hungry that "even rats made a tempting morsel." He also recalled being held in a crowded room. The prisoners were so

---

[495] After the war, David H. Hanaburgh became a Methodist minister.

[496] Hanaburgh, p.183.

[497] Ibid.

[498] David S. Heidler and Jeanne T. Heidler, editors, *Encyclopedia of the American Civil War: A Political, Social, and Military History* (New York: W.W. Norton & Co., 2000), p.385.

[499] Edward M. Smith, p.220.

[500] *Wurtemburg Union Lyceum* minutes.

[501] Heidler and Heidler, pp.1179-1180.

tightly packed together that when they lay down and wanted to turn over "someone gave the signal and they all had to roll over at the same time."[502]

William Traver and James K. Brown (seated)
Photo: Archives of St. Paul's (Wurtemburg)

After a time at Libby Prison, they were transferred to "the Rebel Prison" at Salisbury, North Carolina.[503] David and Jeanne T. Heidler state that, "along with Andersonville and Florence, Salisbury ranked among the worst prison camps in the Confederacy."[504] Until this prison was liberated and emptied in late February 1865, more than 3,708 Union prisoners had either been killed by their captors or died because of the unspeakable conditions.

At the end of his discourse, the modest William B. Brown apologized "for not being a speaker, and said that one of the other Browns could have done better, referring to his

---

[502] *Wurtemburg Union Lyceum* minutes.

[503] Hanaburgh.

[504] Heidler and Heidler, p.1698.

84

brother Derrick, who was a newspaper correspondent."[505] The *Lyceum* then sang a well-known Civil War song, *Tenting on the Old Camp Ground*, led by James K. Brown (1841-1924), "one of our members and a brother." This song was greeted with "great applause."[506]

Derrick Brown (1838-1914)

Derrick Brown (1838-1914), who also served in Company C of the 128th Regiment, along with twenty-three other men, transferred to the *Corps d'Afrique*[507] on July 25, 1864.[508] After the war Derrick lived in Poughkeepsie, New York and became active in veterans affairs. Derrick Brown served as president of the 128th Regimental Association. Derrick Brown was also an active Freemason. He died on August 31, 1914, and he is remembered to this day with a large bronze plaque in the Poughkeepsie Masonic Temple.[509] He was buried in the family plot[510] with full Masonic full ceremonies in the Rhinebeck Cemetery.

---

[505] Ibid.

[506] *Wurtemburg Union Lyceum* minutes.

[507] A unit of African-American soldiers, Heidler and Heidler, p.52. On May 1, 1863, XIX Corps General Orders No. 40 proclaimed that, "The Major General commanding the Department proposes the organization of a *corps d'armee* of colored troops, to be designated as the *Corps d'Afrique*. It will consist ultimately of eighteen regiments, representing all arms: Infantry, Artillery, and Cavalry, organized in three Divisions of three Brigades each, with appropriate corps of Engineers and field Hospitals for each Division ..."

[508] Hanaburgh, p.233.

[509] Derrick Brown was Past Master of Triune Lodge, No.782, Free and Accepted Masons [the Rev. Dr. Henry Lafayette Ziegenfuss was a charter member of Triune Lodge]; District Deputy Grand Master for the 14th Masonic District, State of New York; Past High Priest, Poughkeepsie Chapter, No.172, Royal Arch Masons; Past Thrice Illustrious Master, King Solomon Council,

Like his brother, James K. Brown served in Company C, 128th New York State Volunteer Infantry Regiment. After the war he returned to Rhinebeck and he married Mary Arnett. The couple had one child. They farmed near Wurtemburg. He was active in the Hamilton Sleight G.A.R. of Poughkeepsie, and the Armstrong G.A.R. Post in Rhinebeck. James K. Brown is buried in the Wurtemburg Cemetery. The Rev. E.L. Davison of Wurtemburg officiated at his funeral.[511]

The Wurtemburg grave of James K. Brown.
Photo by the Rev. Mark D. Isaacs

In 2007, his granite tombstone, which had fallen over, was reset on a new deep concrete foundation by the Wurtemburg Cemetery Association. Each Memorial Day his grave—along with the graves of his fellow veterans—is marked with an American flag.

No. 31, Royal and Select Masters; and Past Grand High Priest of Royal Arch Masons, State of New York.

[510] The Brown family plot, located just up the hill from the Rhinebeck G.A.R. Civil War monument, contains the remains of his wife and parents. In the grave next to Derrick Brown, there is a cenotaph marker for Joseph H. Brown.

[511] "James K. Brown," *The Rhinebeck Gazette*, January 26, 1924.

The Zelosophic Society of Wurtemburg

During the winter of 1868, the men of the congregation formed *"The Zelosophic Society of Wurtemburg."* The curious name "Zelosophic" can be roughly translated from the Greek as "endowed with a zeal for learning or wisdom." Perhaps modeled after The Zelosophic Society founded at the University of Pennsylvania in October 1829 [Pastor George Neff attended the University of Pennsylvania], the purpose of the Wurtemburg version was to provide a forum for young men to discuss literature and to conduct formal debates.

Mrs. Elizabeth Rugan Neff (1818-1883)[512]
Photo: Archives of St. Paul's Lutheran Church of Wurtemburg.

At the University of Pennsylvania, the Zelosophic Society engaged in debates against their archrival Philomathean Society. Beginning in 1847, these debates drew huge crowds to various Philadelphia auditoriums. On the eve of the Civil War, a Zelo verses Philo debate on slavery took place while pistols lay atop the lectern between the debaters. In 1862, a committee of Zelo members formed a union with similar literary

---

[512] See obituary clipping for "Mrs. Elizabeth Rugan Neff" in *Mrs. Samuel S. Frost's (1819-1912) Scrapbook,* (St. Paul's Archives), pp. 21-22.

organizations in other American colleges, including Columbia, Brown, and Lafayette. The umbrella group, called the United States Literary League, was the first cooperative group of its kind in America, but it seems to have only lasted through 1866. For a short time the two groups organized opposing football teams, with the Zelos often emerging victorious. By 1876, the Zelosophic Society discontinued.

In a fine Spenserian hand, in a seven by eight-and one-half-inch black notebook, *The Constitution and Minutes of the Zelosophic Society of Wurtemburg,* proclaims:

> We, whose names are hereunto annexed, desirous of forming ourselves into a literary association, for the improvement of our minds in declamation and debate, do here by agree to form such an association, under the name and style of the Zelosophic Society of Wurtemburg...[513]

The Society's constitution was signed by Mandeville S. Frost, John Rugan Neff [son of Pastor George Neff who was named after John Rugan, a colleague and brother or relation of Mrs. Elizabeth Neff?], who taught with Pastor Neff at Hartwick Seminary (1844-1845)[514]]; Theodore Traver; Ervington Dedrick; A.C. Marquart; J.C. Ackert; Chester H. Traver [future Lutheran pastor]; William E. Traver [future Lutheran pastor]; George E. Moody; Edwin Traver; Joseph Arnet, Jr. and William Burger.[515] "The Roll Call" of the Society lists fourteen members. J. Rugan Neff, the son of Pastor George and Elizabeth Neff, was elected as the first President.

The first meeting was held at the Wurtemburg School House [on the ground of the St. Paul's Church] on December 8, 1868. **NOTE:** Here we see that the Wurtemburg School House was used by the Church as a sort of community room and social hall.

The Society Minutes meticulously record their debate questions. The debate questions provide an interesting window into the times. Debate questions included: "Resolved, that the pleasures of winter are greater than those of summer;"[516] "Resolved, that intemperance causes more misery than war;"[517] "Resolved, that city life is preferable to that of the country;" "Resolved, that woman exert greater influence in Society than men;"[518] "Resolved, that wealth causes more misery than poverty;"[519] "Resolved, that Christopher Columbus deserves more praise for discovering America than George Washington for defending it;"[520] "Resolved, that married life is productive of more

---

[513] *Minutes of the Zelosophic Society of Wurtemburg,* in the archives of St. Paul's Lutheran Church of Wurtemburg, p.1.

[514] Henry Hardy Heins, *Throughout All The Years: The Bicentennial Story of Hartwick in America, 1746-1946* (Oneonta, NY: Trustees of Hartwick College, 1946), p.163.

[515] *Minutes of the Zelosophic Society of Wurtemburg,* p.15.

[516] Ibid., December 8, 1868, p.20.

[517] Ibid., December 17, 1868, p.22.

[518] Ibid., January 6, 1869, p.28.

[519] Ibid., January 13, 1869, p.32.

[520] Ibid., January 20, 1869, p.34.

happiness than single life;"[521] and "Resolved, that the whites were justified in driving the Indians from their settlements."[522]

J. Rugan Neff, President of
the Wurtemburg Zelosophic Society
Photo: Archives of St. Paul's Lutheran Church of Wurtemburg.

At the October 6, 1869, meeting the issue to be debated at the Zelosophic Society was, "Resolved, that the present fashions ought not to be encouraged."[523] The minutes state that "a few of the members became very much excited by the difference of opinion on a few minor points and got in no small combat of words. After relieving their minds they were called to order by the President and motion of adjournment proposed."[524] Here, the minutes of the Wurtemburg Zelosophic Society suddenly and mysteriously come to an end, with many blank pages remaining in the minutes book. Apparently, the discussion of the controversial topic of post-Civil War men's fashion preferences broke the Wurtemburg Zelos! Perhaps in the interest of harmony within the community the members of the Wurtemburg Zelosophic Society felt it prudent and wise to disband!

The Mission Society
The Woman's Home and Foreign Missionary Society of Wurtemburg was formed on August 30, 1879. At the first meeting, the opening prayer was given by Rev. Joseph G. Griffith and officers were elected. The President was Mrs. Hiram Pultz; Vice President, Mrs. Ambrose Pultz; Recording Secretary, Miss Marietta Traver; Corresponding Secretary, Mrs. Joseph G. Griffith; Treasurer, Mrs. Philmore Burger.

---

[521] Ibid., January 28, 1869, p.36.

[522] Ibid., February 11, 1869, p.38.

[523] Ibid., p.52.

[524] Ibid., p.53.

In 1934, for the Fifty-Fifth Anniversary of the Woman's Missionary Society, Mrs. Joseph G. Griffith—the eighty-three year old widow of Pastor Griffith, then living in Montoursville, Pennsylvania—wrote:

> As I look back through more than a half a century, how many incidents and memories of dear old Wurtemburg crowded in upon me. First there was dear, kind, old Rev. William D. Strobel, D.D. (1808-1884),[525] then pastor of Third Evangelical Lutheran Church in the village, who first planted the missionary seed. Dr. Strobel had just returned from the General Synod in Ohio where the formation of a Woman's Synodical Society had been discussed and sanctioned. He came out to the Wurtemburg Parsonage and talked it over, and so enthused the Dominie [Griffith] and his wife that we, in turn, passed it on to the women of the church and the seed took root. Accordingly, a call was made for the women to meet at the Parsonage to organize a Missionary Society. In answer to that call, a few came together (the pastor's wife among them) and then and there the Society was launched, with many misgivings, but the effort had God's blessing resting upon it and today you are numbered among that army of loyal women who are supporting mission projects in India, Africa, China, Japan, South America and in our own homeland.[526]

Ettie Tompkins Traver,[527] the wife and co-worker of the Rev. Dr. John Gideon Traver, Principal and Professor at Hartwick Seminary,[528] shared her recollections about the early days of the Missionary Society. She wrote, "I well remember my mother's [i.e., Mrs. Amos Tompkins[529]] going out day after day canvassing for new members. Sometimes she came home very happy because of new names added. One day she came home quite discouraged, for when she asked one woman to join she received the reply, "I was at church and heard all about it, and when I get ready, I will join."[530] Later, that woman did join and became an active member.

---

[525] See obituary clipping for "The Rev. William D. Strobel, D.D." in *Mrs. Samuel S. Frost's (1819-1912) Scrapbook* (St. Paul's Archives), pp.1-2.

[526] Sarah F. Frost [Mrs. Alvah G. Frost] "Missionary Society History Given On 75th Anniversary," *The Rhinebeck Gazette*, December 1954. Wurtemburg Archives #43.

[527] Hartwick Seminary students affectionately called the faithful couple "Uncle John and Aunt Ettie."

[528] See interesting biographical tribute to Dr. John Gideon Traver written by their son the Rev. Amos John Traver, D.D. Henry Hardy Heins, *Throughout All The Years: The Bicentennial Story of Hartwick in America, 1746-1946* (Oneonta, NY: Trustees of Hartwick College, 1946), pp.134-139. During his career, Dr. Amos John Traver wrote nearly twenty books dealing with Lutheran evangelism, youth work, and stewardship.

[529] "When Dr. John Gideon Traver became Principal of Hartwick in 1893 "Grandma Tompkins" became "chief cook, baker, and dispenser of patent medicines" for students [Ronald H. Bailey, *Hartwick College: A Bicentennial History: 1797-1997* (Oneonta, NY: Hartwick College), p.69].

[530] Sarah F. Frost, *The Rhinebeck Gazette*, December 1954.

Ettie Tompkins Traver added, "I also vividly remember my mother's writing essays for the public meetings. How did she do it with no *Woman's Work* [magazine], no tracts, no other missionary magazines? How did she get her help? There was a worn Bible ever near and the *New York Weekly Witness*, but her greatest inspiration was her prayer life, for she lived close to the Master."[531]

Ettie Tompkins Traver
Photo: Archives of St. Paul's Lutheran Church of Wurtemburg.

Ettie Tompkins Traver continued:

> I do not know how old I was when I joined the Missionary Society, but I am sure I attended the Convention when it met in Wurtemburg Church in 1884. And, I was a delegate to the convention in German Valley in 1886. 'Aunt Meal' Schultz took me under her wing and saw me safe there and home again. I had been asked to give an essay on 'The Spreading of the Gospel' and believe me, I did some hard work on it. I remember sitting out on the old stone wall on the farm, trying to get ideas. My hair had been 'shingled' during an attack of measles so I looked younger than my age and we heard someone comment 'that child never wrote that essay!' How grateful I am for that early training.[532]

Sarah F. Frost comments that, "and very effective it surely proved in her case." Ettie Tompkins Traver later became the first President of the Woman's Missionary Society of the United Lutheran Church of America, as well as being Synodical Woman's

---

[531] Ibid.

[532] Ibid.

Missionary Society President for New York and New Jersey, and holding other responsible offices for the Lutheran Church.[533]

Ettie Tompkins Traver
and the Rev. Dr. John Gideon Traver (1938)
Photo: Archives of St. Paul's Lutheran Church of Wurtemburg.

To commemorate the Fortieth Anniversary of the Woman's Missionary Society Mrs. G. R. Haines delivered a speech at the September 1919 meeting. In this formal address, she stated that according to Society Treasurer Mary Marquet, during the past forty years the Woman's Missionary Society of Wurtemburg had raised $4,238.08 for foreign missions. Adjusted for inflation, this would equal an incredible $52,105.83 (2010)![534]

In 1960, Elizabeth McR. Frost wrote, "[the Woman's Missionary Society] has always been very active and is still active today. Regular meetings are held, there is a great deal of study, and there are constant contributions to all missionary work."[535]

While the Woman's Missionary Society focused on foreign missions, in 1890, The Ladies' Aid Society was also formed to support local efforts.. Elizabeth McR. Frost wrote, "A good deal of money for the Church expenses have been earned by this group."[536]

In 1957, these two societies were united under the name, The United Lutheran Church Women, each organization having its own officers. Recently, a complete union has been effected, with one set of officers.[537]

---

[533] Ibid.

[534] Handwritten Manuscript, p.5. Wurtemburg Archives #43.

[535] Elizabeth McR. Frost, *The Men of Wurtemburg and Their House of God: 1760-1960: A Short History of St. Paul's Lutheran Church of Wurtemburg* (Rhinebeck New York, 1960), p.7.

[536] Ibid.

[537] Ibid.

Wurtemburg Woman Today

In 2002, the women of St. Paul's formed WELCM [i.e., "welcome'], the Women of the Evangelical Lutheran Conference and Ministerium. Unlike the wonderful old nineteenth-century style Woman's Home and Foreign Missionary Society and The Ladies' Aid Society, this group meets bimonthly—often in retreat formats—and focuses on the spiritual needs and concerns of working women.

"20,000 Clams!"
baked at a Wurtemburg Dinner on August 15, 1905.
Original Document in the Archives of St. Paul's.

Linda A. Isaacs, wife and co-worker of the Rev. Dr. Mark D. Isaacs, leads the current generation of Wurtemburg women. At their meetings, typically held in the Social Hall on Saturday mornings, the Women of the Evangelical Lutheran Conference and Ministerium [WELCM] engages in discussions relevant to current issues, as well as contributing to various causes and projects at St. Paul's, including annual Confirmation Camp scholarships and world missions. Since 2002, WELCM has also held very successful retreats at Mt. St. Alphosus in Esopus, New York, and other locations. Scheduled events include guest speakers, musical performances, in depth studies on women in the Bible, and planning more effective methods of community outreach for the coming year.

The Young Men's Association and the Lutheran Brotherhood

In 1879, the young men of St. Paul's also formed an association. This group met at the church monthly on Sunday afternoons. Upon marriage, members became "associate members." According to Elizabeth McR. Frost, "this Young Men's Association came to an end about 1900, because there were no more bachelors."[538] Thus, the beautiful farm girls of Wurtemburg must be held responsible for the demise of this fine Christian organization!

Famous Evangelist Rodney "Gipsy" Smith (1860-1947)
conducted a series of successful
revival tent meetings in Rhinebeck in 1915.

In 1915, The Men's Brotherhood [i.e., the Lutheran Brotherhood] was formed, holding a business and social meeting once a month. Elizabeth McR. Frost reports that "there was always a program, a speaker, or pictures; and once in a while, when something especially delightful was planned, the ladies were invited to attend. This organization was extremely beneficial in many ways and, in particular, it sponsored the restaurant booth at the Dutchess County Fair."[539]

Pastor Robert P. Ingersoll of the First Baptist Church in the village spoke at the Brotherhood meeting of March 17, 1915. Area historian Thea Lawrence notes that "the remarkable Rev. Robert P. Ingersoll arrived in Rhinebeck in July 1911." [540] She adds that "he was a man of many talents, chiefly musical, and many concerts were presented at the church. He also brought evangelists to preach both in the Baptist and Methodist churches… [and] he was director of the music committee for the tent revival meeting

---

[538] Ibid., p.8.

[539] Ibid.

[540] Thea Lawrence, *Unity Without Uniformity: The Rhinebeck Church Community, 1718-1918* (Monroe, NY: Library Research Association, 1992), p.130.

[held in Rhinebeck] conducted by [the then famous and beloved] evangelist Rodney "Gipsy" Smith (1860-1947) in the summer of 1915."[541]

__The Union Tent Meeting of 1915 featuring Evangelist Rodney "Gipsy" Smith (far left); the Rev. William Boomhower from Wurtemburg; Rev. Walter D. Miller from Third Lutheran; Rev. Bennett for the Methodist Church and Rev. Ingersoll from the First Baptist Church. The young boy is the grandson of Gipsy Smith.__
Photo: Thea Lawrence, *Unity Without Uniformity: The Rhinebeck Church Community, 1718-1918*, (Monroe, NY: Library Research Association, 1992).

During this 1915 revival meeting, on an average evening, more than a thousand people gathered together in the tent near the Methodist Church as Gipsy Smith spoke about the difference between an intellectual faith and a saving faith. The Rev. William Boomhower of Wurtemburg arranged for the Sunday School Rally to be held in the Gipsy Smith Tabernacle.

On August 28, *The Rhinebeck Gazette* reported that the revival was nearing its end. They stated, "The Campaign has been conducted in as close an imitation of Billy Sunday's methods as possible. Revival has made Rhinebeck the Mecca of the surrounding country for three weeks."[542]

As the revival ended, *The Rhinebeck Gazette* printed a letter from Rev. William Boomhower regarding the event. He wrote:

> As a Lutheran, and unused to this form of religious work I have been able to enjoy a religious forward movement absolutely void of anything freakish, extreme, unreasonable or objectionable... It is a victory for the thinking people of Rhinebeck that Smith was supported enthusiastically in all his positions on the religious and moral questions of the day... Personally, I feel that one reason for

---

[541] Ibid.

[542] *The Rhinebeck Gazette*, August 28, 1915.

the success of the meeting lies in the use of Scripture in the preaching... The strong, safe point of Gipsy Smith's preaching is its foundation in the Word of God. The huge blazing banner which said 'Rhinebeck for Christ' has been taken down, but its memory remains.[543]

In 1915, a men's group known as the Lutheran Brotherhood was formed at St. Paul's. According to the detailed minutes, seventeen to thirty-eight "brothers" regularly attended their monthly meetings. Typically, these meetings would include a Scripture reading, a hymn—such as *The Church in the Wildwood*, or *When the Roll is Called up Yonder*—and a speaker or a discussion of issues of the day, followed by refreshments. The wide use of these and other evangelistic hymns help us to understand not the liturgically correct hymns or the formal theology taught in Hartwick, Gettysburg, or Philadelphia Seminary, but the popular faith held by the folks in the pews during the early twentieth century. Perhaps one of the problems with the Church of the post-modern era is that we, the clergy, have arrogantly stopped listening to the needs and desires of the people in our congregations!

The Lutheran Brotherhood provided a time of fellowship for the men of the congregation, but they were also an active group that did things around the Church, such as painting, renovation, purchase of additional chairs for the social hall, etc. They held an annual "Brotherhood Banquet," usually in December.

Topics and speakers at their meetings were diverse and wide ranging. For example, on August 16, 1920, the Rev. Walter D. Miller, from Third Evangelical Lutheran Church in the village gave an address on "Christian Socialism."[544]

At another meeting, according to *The Brotherhood Minutes*:

Pastor Robert P. Ingersoll [of First Baptist Church in Rhinebeck] told us of the wonderful work of the famous evangelist Billy Sunday[545] and the work of his followers when they hit the sawdust trail and his advancement in the Christian work from the time he was converted, and how he turned down positions which would have paid him thousands a year to take up the calling of Christ, and become one of his disciples. Mr. Ingersoll also explained the style and delivery of Billy Sunday's sermons [Billy Sunday was known for his "down-home style and his backwoods vocabulary" and for his "flamboyant antics, theatrical poses, and impassioned gestures."[546]]. We all agreed that Pastor Ingersoll was one of the

---

[543] *The Rhinebeck Gazette*, September 4, 1915.

[544] *Minutes of the Lutheran Brotherhood* (1915-1927), p.115.

[545] William (Billy) Sunday (1862-1935) was known in his lifetime as "the baseball evangelist." He had little formal education and he began his career as a professional baseball player in 1883. He had a conversion experience in 1886 at Chicago's Pacific Garden Rescue Mission. In 1891, he walked away from his sports career to devote himself to full-time ministry. By the time of his death in 1935, Billy Sunday had preached thousands of sermons reaching millions of Americans in approximately two hundred campaigns.

[546] Daniel G. Reid, ed. *Dictionary of Christianity in America* (Downers Grove, IL: 1990), p.1046.

best speakers that Wurtemburg has had for a long time with all due respect to our pastor.[547]

At the same meeting, there was a one line note that "we enjoyed an interesting talk on ancient aerial navigation."[548] Unfortunately, *The Brotherhood Minutes* do not reveal the meaning of the cryptic phrase "ancient aerial navigation!"

The Brotherhood Minutes for July 21, 1915, state that Alvah G. Frost "gave us one of the most interesting talks we have had on what we can learn from Germany and the advancement of the German people in the past forty years; i.e., their schools and government." And, "how the government is working constantly for the public betterment."[549]

From the perspective of the First and Second World War, it is sometimes forgotten that prior to President Woodrow Wilson's Declaration of War against Imperial Germany April 6, 1917, most Americans favored isolationism and neutrality.[550] Many Irish-Americans had a strong antipathy toward Great Britain [e.g., the Easter Uprising of 1916], and many German-Americans admired Germany's remarkable social, economic, political, and cultural advancement following the 1866 to 1871 unification of Germany led by Iron Chancellor Otto von Bismarck.[551]

For example, at this time, the great H.L. Mencken of Baltimore (1880-1956) "heaped praise on the New Germany dreamed of by Nietzsche and founded by Bismarck, a country that, though nominally democratic, was in practice 'a delimited, aristocratic democracy in the Athenian sense—a democracy of intelligence, of strength, of superior fitness… a new aristocracy of the laboratory, the study, and the shop.'"[552]

However, once war was declared, Wurtemburgers joined the Army and the Navy and fully supported the war effort. To this day, the American flag, displayed in the sanctuary is a statement to our English-speaking neighbors that German-Americans are loyal and patriotic Americans.

On April 18, 1921, there was a discussion of the question, "of what the farmers owe to the merchants of Rhinebeck and what the merchants owe to the farmers."[553]

On May 28, 1921, the Brotherhood took up the question of "what is the trouble with our rural schools?"[554] Prior to the consolidated school district movement of the 1930s and 1940s [after the Prussian model!], the families of the Wurtemburg area were served by the one-room schoolhouse located next to the church [Wurtemburg School District

---

[547] *Minutes of the [Wurtemburg] Lutheran Brotherhood* (1915-1927), pp.7-8

[548] Ibid., p.7.

[549] Ibid., p.13.

[550] Clarence B. Carson, *A Basic History of the United States: The Growth of America: 1878-1928* (Phenix City, AL: American Textbook Committee, 1985, 2001), pp.185-191.

[551] Michael Stürmer, *The German Empire: A Short History* (New York: The Modern Library, 2002).

[552] Terry Teachout, *The Skeptic: A Life of H.L. Mencken* (New York: HarperCollins, 2002), p.124.

[553] *Minutes of the [Wurtemburg] Lutheran Brotherhood* (1915-1927), p.128.

[554] Ibid., p.139.

No. 8.]. Prior to the rise of the Progressive Education movement in America, the ancients believed that children and education needed to be kept close to home and close to the Church.[555]

The minutes report that on February 20, 1922, "Mr. Lacy, of the Farm Bureau, gave us a very interesting speech on Farmer's Week at the college [Cornell?] and what he heard discussed. There were also a few words along the line of seed, oats, and potatoes."[556]

On April 17, 1922, there was "a very interesting talk by Brother Smith J. Hermans on his recent trip to Nova Scotia."[557]

On December 17, 1923, Charles R. Traver (1863-1928) "gave an interesting talk on the gypsy moth."[558] It is interesting to note that gypsy moths were a problem in the Wurtemburg area way back then! The gypsy moth was accidentally introduced into the United States in 1868 by French scientist, E. Leopold Trouvelot (1827–1895), who was living in Medford, Massachusetts. Trouvelot enjoyed raising many types of caterpillars, including silkworms. Trouvelot hoped to crossbreed the Eurasian gypsy moth with silkworms in order to create an American silk industry. A few of his subjects escaped, and now the gypsy moth is one of the most notorious pests of hardwood trees in the Eastern United States. The first gypsy moth outbreak occurred in Massachusetts in 1889. By 1898, the Gypsy Moth was considered to be a serious pest in the Northeast.

At the meeting of January 21, 1924, the was a "literary program" presented by "The Rev. Douglass of Rhinebeck, who gave us an very interesting and instructive stereopticon view of *Ben Hur*."[559] We wonder about the origin of these stereopticon slides. Were they taken from the stage play adaptation of *Ben-Hur* that opened at the Broadway Theater in New York City in 1899?[560] Or, were these slides related to the 1907 fifteen minute short silent film based on the novel?[561] Or, were these slides somehow related to the promotion of the first full-length motion picture of *Ben-Hur* starring Ramon Navarro, which opened on December 30, 1925?

---

[555] See Samuel L. Blumenfeld, *Is Public Education Necessary?* (Boise, ID: Paradigm Company, 1985) and Samuel L. Blumenfeld, *N.E.A.: Trojan Horse in American Education* (Boise, ID: Paradigm Company, 1984) and Thomas Sowell, *Education: Assumptions verses History: Collected Papers* (Stanford, CA: Hoover Institution Press, 1986).

[556] *Minutes of the [Wurtemburg] Lutheran Brotherhood* (1915-1927), p.143.

[557] Ibid., p.146.

[558] Ibid., p.186.

[559] Ibid., p.188.

[560] *Ben-Hur* took to the road, and often held two-week engagements at American cities. The production was also taken overseas, and appeared in Europe and Australia. It is estimated that there were over six-thousand performances given and over twenty-million people saw *Ben-Hur* during its twenty-one year run. The final performance of *Ben-Hur* was delivered in April of 1921.

[561] This film was an unauthorized work, and the producers were sued by Lew Wallace's son Henry on behalf of the estate. The estate won the case, and because of Henry Wallace's foresight, he is ultimately responsible for securing the intellectual property of authors from copyright infringement by film and theatrical productions.

After the Dan Brown, Harry Potter, or *Twilight* craze we tend to forget that Lew Wallace's "novel of Christ" was one of the best-selling books of the nineteenth century.[562] By 1912, the book sold more than one-million copies in America.[563] And, in 1913, Sears and Roebuck ordered one-million copies of an edition of *Ben-Hur* that they sold via their catalogs for 39 cents each.[564] This is the largest book order ever placed.

Major General Lew Wallace (1827-1905)

This powerful tale grew out of a discussion on a train that Lew Wallace[565] had with the famous Col. Robert G. Ingersoll (1833-1899).[566] In 1876, on the way to the Republican National Convention, Lew Wallace had a conversation with the famous orator and flamboyant freethinking agnostic Robert G. Ingersoll. After a conversation with Ingersoll about the weaknesses, contradictions, and flaws of the Christian religion Wallace realized that he did not know as much as he would like to about his own faith.

---

[562] Robert Morris, "Lew Wallace," *The Short Talk Bulletin* (Silver Spring, MD: The Masonic Service Association of North America, May 2005), vol. 83, No.5.

[563] Lew Wallace, *Ben-Hur: A Tale of Christ* (Pleasantville, N.Y. The World's Best Reading Edition, 1880, 1992), p.553.

[564] Ibid.

[565] Lewis "Lew" Wallace, a West Point graduate, was a lawyer, Union general in the American Civil War [he commanded troops at Shiloh and Monocacy], governor, American statesman, Freemason, and author. Wallace participated in the military commission trial of the Lincoln assassination conspirators, and the court-martial of Henry Wirz (1823-hanged November 25, 1865), commandant of the notorious Andersonville Prison Camp. During the 1870s and 1880s Wallace held a number of important political posts. He served as governor of New Mexico Territory from 1878 to 1881, and as U.S. Minister to the Ottoman Empire from 1881 to 1885.

[566] Col. Robert Green Ingersoll was born in Dresden, New York (on the West Shore of Seneca Lake) on August 11, 1833, and he died suddenly in Dobbs Ferry, New York on July 21, 1899. Ingersoll was buried with full military honors in Arlington National Cemetery.

He attended the Methodist Church off and on throughout his life, but considered himself indifferent to religion.

Wallace thought that the idea of doing research for a book he could write would be the best motivation for him to tackle reading *The Holy Bible*. He had already written a short story describing the journey of the wise men to Bethlehem—a subject which had fascinated him since he was very young. This became the first book of *Ben-Hur*, with the rest of the novel describing the "religious and political conditions of the world at the time of the coming," as he says in his *Autobiography*. Although he may have been indifferent to religion before writing the book, he says in the preface to *The First Christmas*, 1899, that the act of writing resulted in "a conviction amounting to absolute belief in God and the divinity of Christ."

At another Lutheran Brotherhood meeting the discussion topic was, "what benefit does the Weather Bureau do for us?"[567] Alvah G. Frost, who taught for a time at the Wurtemburg School, No.8, gave a talk on "the job of a schoolmaster."[568] At the March 16, 1925, Brotherhood meeting "Carlton Traver gave a very interesting account of his recent trip to Indiana."[569]

On November 16, 1925, in a tantalizing and frustrating tid-bit for a local church historian, "Brother Homer Burtis Kipp (d. October 24, 1926) spoke about some of the former years of this Church…" Imagine if a text of this talk had be preserved in the archives!

According to *The Minutes*, "Rev. Elder Jay Himes entertained us during the evening with his radio."[570] And, at the August 16, 1926, Brotherhood meeting, Charles R. Traver gave a talk "on the political situation and law enforcement."[571]

In 1927, the Brotherhood contributed money for the purchase of new hymnals.[572]

At the July 18, 1927, meeting, "Mr. Wilber of Poughkeepsie gave us a very interesting talk on his experiences as a police officer and detective for twenty-five years in the New York City Police Department."[573] Imagine hearing eyewitness police tales from the streets of New York City c.1910!

The Lutheran Brotherhood held regular meetings until at least 1953. The official minutes abruptly end with the meeting of March 16, 1953.

The Luther League

In 1913, The Luther League was organized. In 1960, Elizabeth McR. Frost reported that "this is now one of the most active societies of the Church. Devotional and social meetings are held, money is being raised, and a great deal is being done for the Church

---

[567] *Minutes of the [Wurtemburg] Lutheran Brotherhood* (1915-1927), p.195.

[568] Ibid., p.194.

[569] Ibid., p.203.

[570] Ibid., p.223.

[571] Ibid., p.229.

[572] Ibid., p.238.

[573] Ibid., p.248.

by these young people. The beautiful red silk altar linens are their latest gift."[574] These paraments are still in use at St. Paul's.

The Rev. Roy Steward, who grew up in the Wurtemburg Church during the late 1950s and early 1960s, fondly recalls many Luther League meetings, both at St. Paul's and on the district level. He attributes many of his leadership skills to his early experiences serving as president of the Wurtemburg Luther League.[575]

In 2002, after many years, The Luther League was revived for a few years. The League met in conjunction with Confirmation Class on alternate Sunday evenings. At this time, the highlight of the youth group year was the annual Confirmation Camp experience at Camp Son-Rise on Schroon Lake, New York. At camp, during the first week in August, our young people sang, worshipped, swam, hiked in the Adirondack Mountains, and went white-water rafting. This week was a truly memorable experience for our young people.

Camp Son-Rise is an outstanding camp run by the Lutheran Church-Missouri Synod. The camp counselors are students from the various Concordia colleges across the nation. They provide Lutheran role models for our younger members, many of whom have never known a fellow Lutheran! For several years, St. Paul's (Wurtemburg) has financially supported this worthy ministry.

The Famous Turkey Supper

In Rhinebeck, St. Paul's (Wurtemburg) is synonymous with the annual Turkey Supper. In 1859, the first annual Turkey Supper —a great Wurtemburg institution—was held. According to Barbara Frost, the first Turkey Supper was an outdoor Fall Festival. The Festival proved to be such a success that it prompted the congregation to renovate the Church. This renovation included digging out the basement to provide a Social Hall for future events.[576] The Turkey Supper has been held every year since, except 1918, and one year during the Second World War.

Alvah G. Frost explains that, "The records would indicate that it has missed but one year during that entire period; that year was during the last Great War when certain supplies were obtained with difficulty [provisions were rationed, and turkeys were difficult to obtain]."[577] For the same reason, during the Second World War, the supper was not held for a year.[578] For decades, before the appearance of the automobile, the supper was held in November, and it was invariably held on the first moonlit Wednesday and Thursday evenings in November. In recent decades, the Turkey Supper has been held on the third Saturday in October.

The Turkey Supper was held prior to Election Day so that area politicians could electioneer among the Wurtembergers. Barbara Frost tells an amusing story about how, at one of these suppers, a Republican candidate schmoozing for votes mistakenly took the

---

[574] Elizabeth McR. Frost.

[575] Interview ELCM President the Rev. Roy Steward, September 2006.

[576] Barbara Frost handwritten manuscript, Archive #48.

[577] Alvah G. Frost, p.9.

[578] Specifically, during the Second World War, area turkeys were canned and shipped to the Soviet Union to aid the Red Army in their brutal struggle with the National Socialists.

new hat of his Democrat rival. Needless to say, when that story got around it cost the Republican the election.[579]

In 1935, Alvah G. Frost wrote that, "This annual event has been widely known, and during all these years it has been a great homecoming event for the community and former residents."[580]

The annual Turkey Supper is a great tradition that still continues. On October 22, 2011, keeping this great tradition alive, Wurtemburg will hold its One Hundred and Fiftieth Annual Turkey Supper. We serve three settings, and workers from the congregation enthusiastically volunteer to help prepare needed foods. Each year, nearly four-hundred guests are served. In a typical year more than twenty fresh turkeys are prepared for the feast.

The Turkey Supper draws people from the surrounding community. In 2005, a woman in her late eighties recalled attending the Turkey Supper when she was a child of four (this would be c.1930!). This is a great event and over the years it has helped build relationships and social bonds within the congregation. As Psalm 133:1 reminds us, "Behold, how good and how pleasant it is for brethren to dwell together in unity!"

For the past six years, longtime Wurtemburg member Shirley Swenson has headed up a group of faithful women who make a beautiful quilt that is raffled off during the Turkey Supper's final setting.

A few years ago, as the dramatic moment for the drawing approached, the always impartial Pastor Mark was invited to preside over the quilt raffle drawing. At random he selected one of the Turkey Supper workers, a young confirmation-age girl named Lia Michos, to draw the name of the lucky winner. As the tension increased, and as the crowd grew silent she drew a ticket from the box—it was *HER NAME*!!! Despite good-hearted howls of protest—and a three-hour lecture from Pastor Mark on the evils of gambling—Lia won the quilt. And, despite this "amazing coincidence," Rhinebeck area residents continue to purchase tickets for this fun event.

The Shed Society

In 1860, the Wurtemburg [Carriage] Shed Association was incorporated. The Wurtemburg Sheds were intended to provide shelter for the horses during worship services and other church events. The Rev. Chester H. Traver explained the need for the sheds, writing, "the merciful man is merciful to his beast."[581] The Shed Association issued stock and purchased land west of the church.[582] Fifty sheds were constructed by Society members.[583]

Several years ago, while on vacation in Lancaster County, Pennsylvania, I happened to drive by an Old Order Mennonite Church. This quaint country church had a row of sheds complete with horses and carriages. It is difficult to imagine, but prior to the

---

[579] Barbara Frost December 1990 lecture to the Rhinebeck Historical Society.

[580] Ibid.

[581] Chester Henry Traver, *The Rhinebeck Gazette* (1915).

[582] Alvah G. Frost, p.9; Elizabeth McR. Frost, p.7.

[583] *Poughkeepsie Sunday New Yorker*, "Old Country Church Stands As Monument to Immigrant Germans' Work Back in 1760", May 29, 1960, p.1-A.

advent of the automobile, this scene would have been a common weekly occurrence at the Wurtemburg Church. In 1935, Alvah G. Frost noted that, "it was not uncommon in those days to find that there was insufficient shed room for those who drove to Sunday morning services."[584]

"The Wurtemburg Sheds"
This outstanding water color
was commissioned by the First National Bank of Rhinebeck in the 1960s,
and illustrates the approximate location of the landmark Wurtemburg Sheds.
Illustration by Richard King. Archives of St. Paul's Lutheran Church of Wurtemburg.

Mary Lown Traver Baas, who, as a child attended Wurtemburg School District, No. 8, fondly recalled that during school recesses the children would often play in and among the old sheds.[585] She added that the Church Sexton used one of the sheds to store his tools and equipment.[586]

The church archives contain stock certificates and detailed minutes of annual Shed Society meetings over the years. Ownership of the sheds were passed down from father to sons for generations.[587]

---

[584] Alvah G. Frost, p.9.

[585] Interview with Mary Lown Traver Baas, September 21, 2006.

[586] Ibid.

[587] *Poughkeepsie Sunday New Yorker*, Sunday, May 29, 1960, p.1-A.

*Benson Frost, Sr. was a prominent Rhinebeck attorney, lay leader,
and friend of President Franklin D. Roosevelt of Hyde Park, New York.*
Photo: Archives of St. Paul's Lutheran Church of Wurtemburg

Again, a post-modern investigator is impressed with the high level of formal organization for all of the societies and corollary groups associated with St. Paul's over the years. By the early-1960s, it was apparent to all that the landmark Wurtemburg Sheds, which had fallen into disrepair, had to be torn down. They had become a hazard and a temptation for area children. However, before this could be done, Attorney Benson Frost, Sr. had to meticulously track down the shed owners to get their titles donated back to the Wurtemburg Church. Interestingly, a few older members still lament the decision—at the time there was no other choice—to tear down the old Wurtemburg Sheds.

Ziegenfuss University

Since 1996, on Monday evenings, an adult Bible study and discussion group led by Pastor Mark, and affectionately known as "Ziegenfuss University," has met. Topics discussed include: Dan Brown's *The Da Vinci Code*; Biblical Archeology; the Book of Revelation; the Dead Sea Scrolls; *The Book of Concord*; the works of Martin Luther; *The Apocrypha*; Church, Sect and Cult; Paul's Epistles; Reformation History; and Dietrich Bonheoffer; Islam and *The Koran*, etc. This freewheeling forum provides interested adult learners with an opportunity to ask hard questions and to receive college level teaching on vital issues and topics of the day.

Ziegenfuss means "goat-foot" in German. "Ziegenfuss University" was founded in September 1992, by the Rev. Mark D. Isaacs while he served as pastor of Third Evangelical Lutheran Church in the village of Rhinebeck. From 1996 to December 1999, while Third and St. Paul's were a part of a two-point parish, "Z.U." met in joint session for all interested parties. After Pastor Mark resigned from Third Lutheran and the ELCA on December 31, 1999, Ziegenfuss University continued to meet at St. Paul's.

"Ziegenfuss University" is named in honor of the Venerable Rev. Henry Lafayette Ziegenfuss, D.D., (November 3, 1844–February 8, 1894), the First Archdeacon of Dutchess County. The Rev. Dr. Henry L. Ziegenfuss was born at Kresgeville, Monroe County, Pennsylvania. His parents were Lutheran. In 1862 he was matriculated at Pennsylvania College [now Gettysburg College].

In June 1863—with the invasion threat of Gen. Robert E. Lee's Confederate Army— he enlisted in an emergency militia unit; i.e., the 26th Pennsylvania Volunteers—a special regiment under the command of Col. W. W. Jennings, made up of Pennsylvania College students.

On June 30, 1863, Ziegenfuss and the fellow members of his pick-me-up regiment of one-hundred fellow farm boys and college students "fought" in a strange encounter on the Chambersburg Pike, a few miles west of Gettysburg. The 26th met advanced units of the battle-hardened Army of Northern Virginia. The Confederate veterans, fresh from their triumphs at Fredericksburg[588] and Chancellorsville,[589] were apparently amused by the ill-equipped rag tag mob of college boys sent out to defend the town. The boys were armed with antique Revolutionary War era muskets, hunting rifles, a few old pistols, and shotguns. A few were wounded, a few were captured, and their shoes and boots were confiscated by the Rebels. All were disarmed, and a few of the lads fled as far as Harrisburg, where they sat out the Battle of Gettysburg [July 1-3, 1863].[590]

Young Henry L. Ziegenfuss was among those taken prisoner by the Confederates. According to his obituary, published in *The New York Times*, "he was taken prisoner and acted as an assistant to surgeons at a Confederate hospital [during the battle of Gettysburg.]"[591] Imagine the human suffering, misery, and death that young Henry L. Ziegenfuss must have witnessed during his captivity in these primitive field hospitals

---

[588] December 13, 1862. James M. McPherson, *Battle Cry of Freedom* (New York: Oxford University Press, 1988), pp.571-575.

[589] May 2-6, 1863. Ibid., pp.638-645.

[590] Ibid., p.658.

[591] Obituary of the Rev. Dr. Henry L. Ziegenfuss, *The New York Times*, February 11, 1894.

where limbs were amputated without anesthesia, and where antibiotics and modern sterile conditions were unheard of!

A small granite marker along Highway 30 [the Chambersburg Pike] commemorates the spot where this historic misadventure took place.[592] Ziegenfuss survived the battle and his captivity, and graduated with honors from Pennsylvania College in 1866.

Additional Details on the 26th Pennsylvania Volunteer Militia

In the days and weeks prior to the Battle of Gettysburg, Pennsylvania [Gettysburg] College, the Lutheran Seminary, and the surrounding countryside, raised an emergency company of men more than one-hundred strong to protect the region. This was Co. A of the 26th Pennsylvania Volunteer Militia. This regiment was under the command of Col. William Wesley Jennings. Jennings, who lived in nearby Harrisburg, had just returned from nine months of active service as colonel of the 127th Regiment.[593] He had a solid reputation for being an officer who was both brave and tactful.

On June 25, 1863, the 26th Pennsylvania Volunteer Militia under Col. W.W. Jennings arrived at Gettysburg. Thus, the 26th Regiment was the first to arrive on the field at Gettysburg. At this point, the exact location of General Robert E. Lee's Confederate forces were not known by the Federals. There were rumors that Lee had launched an invasion of the North. The 26th Regiment was to be used as a guard unit in one of the mountain passes near Gettysburg [out along the Chambersburg Pike west of Gettysburg].

Since Company A was largely composed of students from the Lutheran College and Theological Seminary at Gettysburg it was therefore a pleasure for them to come home to Gettysburg. However, their joy was of short duration. At about 8:00 AM on June 26, their colonel was ordered by Major Granville O. Haller of the U. S. Regular Army, to march his men out on the Chambersburg Pike, with Company A, in the front.[594]

Col. Jennings learned that General Jubal A. Early's Division was moving in force toward Gettysburg. Jennings—as the commander of the green militia regiment of college students and farm boys—protested. However, since there was apparently no other option [the bulk of Federal forces were still marching up from the South and the East], the 26th was ordered into action.

Three miles west of Gettysburg, on the Chambersburg Pike, the militia came upon the enemy. According to reports, "when they tried to load their guns, they had to bite all the paper off the bullets to get them down. After being discharged a few times, it was

---

[592] Several years ago, when I enquired to a National Park Ranger about the 26th Pennsylvania Volunteers he laughed so hard at my question that he was barely able to give his answer!

[593] 127th Regiment, Pennsylvania Volunteer Infantry, Col. W. W. Jennings, Commanding, Lieut. Col. H. C. Alleman; Major G. Rohner, 3rd Brigade, 2nd Division, 2nd Corps. The 127th Pennsylvania Volunteer Infantry Regiment participated in the Battle of Fredericksburg, Virginia, December 13, 1862 and the Battle of Marye's Heights, Virginia, May 3-4, 1863.

[594] D.B. Shuey, *History of the Shuey Family in America from 1732 to 1919* (Galion, Ohio: self-published, 1919), pp. 106-108.

impossible to reload their guns. The militia were soon outflanked, and forced to retreat to Harrisburg, during which retreat about two hundred were captured."[595]

C.S.A. General Jubal Anderson Early
(1816-1894)

Among the captured were many college boys from Co. A. This included Henry L. Ziegenfuss. They were later corralled on the steps of Christ Lutheran Church in Gettysburg. C.S.A. General Jubal A. Early rode up to inspect the humiliated members of the Pennsylvania militia. He grinned and said: "Hi, you little boys must have slipped out of your mothers' band-boxes, you look so nice. Now be off home to your mothers. If I catch you again I'll spank you all."[596] Thus, many were released.

About Colonel W.W. Jennings
Colonel William Wesley Jennings (1838-1894), second son of William and Elmina E. (Boas) Jennings, was born in Harrisburg, Pennsylvania on July 22, 1838. He was educated in the public schools of that city. At the age of fifteen, he entered his father's foundry business and learned the trade of a moulder, He became well skilled in the art of iron making. He followed his trade until 1860, when he purchased his father's plant and successfully engaged in the iron business on his own account. The business continued until 1877. Jennings was active in the organization of the Harrisburg Board of Trade and acted as its first president. In 1880, he was elected president of the First National Bank of Harrisburg. He held this position until his death. He was also president of the Commonwealth Guarantee Trust and Safe Deposit Company; president of the Harrisburg

---

[595] Ibid.

[596] William A. Scott, *The Battle of Gettysburg* (Gettysburg, Pennsylvania: self published, 1905).

Steam Heat and Power Company; a director of the Cumberland Valley Railroad Company, and held interests in other large corporations.[597]

Colonel William Wesley Jennings

William W. Jennings distinguished himself during the Civil War as a volunteer soldier and officer. When President Abraham Lincoln called for men, he enlisted as a private in the "Lochiel Greys." He was chosen as first lieutenant of his company, and served as such through the three month campaign of 1861. Upon the return from the front, Lieutenant Jennings was appointed by the governor of Pennsylvania to the position of past adjutant and drill master at Camp Curtin. He accepted and filled this position until July, 1862. However, Jennings was anxious to be actively engaged on the field. Thus, he applied for and obtained permission to raise a regiment. As a result, he was placed in command of the 127th Pennsylvania Regiment at the rank of colonel. He was in command of this regiment until the expiration of his term of service in May, 1863.

Colonel Jennings then returned to private life. During General Lee's invasion of Pennsylvania, he was again called to the field and placed in command of the 26th Emergency Regiment.

Politically Colonel Jennings was a Republican. He held numerous offices, including serving as sheriff of Dauphin county. He served from 1864 to 1856 and from 1876 to

[597] Luther Reily Kelker, *History of Dauphin County, Pennsylvania* (Lewis Publishing Company, 1907), pp. 10-11.

1879. In the capacity of sheriff, on the night of July 23, 1877—during the Great Railroad Strike of 1877—an armed mob of strikers took possession of the city of Harrisburg. As High Sheriff, Colonel Jennings was able to suppress the deadly riot, and soon peace and good order were restored to the city.

W.W. Jennings was an active and honored member of Robert Burns Lodge, No. 464, Free and Accepted Masons, at Harrisburg, and also of Pilgrim Commandery, Knights Templar. He was one of the organizers of Post No. 58, Grand Army of the Republic. Colonel Jennings died on February 28, 1894.[598]

On to the Philadelphia Lutheran Seminary

After the Civil War, and after college, Henry L. Ziegenfuss went to Mt. Airy Lutheran Theological Seminary in Philadelphia. He graduated and was ordained on Trinity Sunday in 1869. Rev. Ziegenfuss was called to Third Evangelical Lutheran in Rhinebeck, New York in 1869. While serving Third he was also Professor of Chemistry in the DeGarmo Institute which stood at the present site of the Third Lutheran Parish Hall on Livingston Street, in the village of Rhinebeck.

On August 29, 1872, *The Rhinebeck Gazette* [599] reported that, "Rev. H. L. Ziegenfuss, pastor of the Lutheran Church in this village, will return from his play-spell [vacation?] on Friday or Saturday. Services will be held at his church on Sunday at the usual hours 10:30 AM and 7:00 PM." During this "play-spell" he must have been praying about an important decision. In the early fall of 1872, Rev. Ziegenfuss resigned his pastorate at Third Evangelical Lutheran Church.

On October 3, 1872, he became a candidate for Orders in the Protestant Episcopal Church. From Rhinebeck, he went on to serve as a lay reader, then Deacon at St. Margaret's in Staatsburg. For six months, after his ordination to the Priesthood—April 20, 1874, he served as Rector of historic St. James Episcopal Church in Hyde Park.[600] In his book *Historic Old Rhinebeck* (1905), Howard H. Morse states that, "Two ... [Third Lutheran] pastors selected Rhinebeck girls for wives."[601] The "two" included Rev. Ziegenfuss and "Rev. Archibald E. Deitz who married a daughter of H. N. Secor." On June 11, 1874, Rev. Ziegenfuss married Ella Van Vliet—the only daughter of Isaac F. Van Vliet, M.D. (1822 - February 23, 1876). The ceremony was held at the Church of the Messiah, with the Rev. Dr. A. F. Olmsted officiating.

Edward M. Smith reports that Rev. Reuben Hill (who served Third Evangelical Lutheran Church from 1866-1868) "was succeeded by the Rev. Henry L. Ziegenfuss, who left the Lutherans for the Episcopalians, after a very short Lutheran pastorate, and is now the pastor of a strong Episcopalian church in the city of Poughkeepsie."[602]

In 1875, at the age of thirty, Rev. Henry L. Ziegenfuss became Rector of Christ Church in Poughkeepsie, New York. In 1888, Pastor Ziegenfuss presided over the construction of the magnificent—and current—Christ Church building. He faithfully

---

[598] Ibid.

[599] *The Rhinebeck Gazette,* August 29, 1872.

[600] President Franklin D. Roosevelt (1882-1945) was baptized at St. James Church in Hyde Park.

[601] Howard H. Morse, *Historic Old Rhinebeck* (Rhinebeck, New York, 1908), p.186.

[602] Edward M. Smith, *History of Rhinebeck* (1881).

served Christ Church until his sudden death in 1894. During this time Rev. Ziegenfuss also served as the first Archdeacon of Dutchess. Hence the title: "The Venerable Henry Lafayette Ziegenfuss." In addition, during his tenure the people of Christ Church built their present building. He was awarded an honorary Doctor of Sacred Theology [S.T.D.] degree by Hobart College in 1890.

The Venerable Rev. Henry Lafayette Ziegenfuss, S.T.D.
Photo: Archives of St. Paul's Lutheran Church of Wurtemburg

Among other things, in 1882, Rev. Ziegenfuss organized the Christ Church Guild. The purpose of this Guild was for "social and literary gatherings." At Guild meetings Rev. Ziegenfuss led discussions and directed readings on such topics as theology, philosophy, and astronomy. Dr. Ziegenfuss's "Guild" is not unlike our own "Ziegenfuss University."

Rev. Ziegenfuss was well qualified to head such an eclectic "Guild." According to *The Records of Christ Church Poughkeepsie*, edited by Helen W. Reynolds, in addition to theology, Rev. Ziegenfuss had a strong "interest in science," ranging from chemistry to biology. In addition, he "read and spoke German with ease and fluency, which gave him direct and early access to the world of thought in the foreign universities."[603] When Rev. Ziegenfuss died he had a library of over 3,000 books.[604]

---

[603] Helen W. Reynolds, editor, *The Records of Christ Church Poughkeepsie* (Poughkeepsie, NY: 1911), p.220.

[604] A few years ago I visited Christ Church in Poughkeepsie. The building still stands, however Dr. Ziegenfuss's library has long since been dispersed.

110

The Record reports that during his career Dr. Ziegenfuss became, "one of the best known of the clergy of the Diocese of New York, honored and esteemed by his associates in the ministry ... and widely loved by the laity."[605]

This high opinion was seconded by another book called *The Eagle's History of Poughkeepsie"1683-1905* by Edmond Platt. This book states that Dr. Ziegenfuss, "was greatly beloved by his parishioners."[606]

Dr. Ziegenfuss is described as an author [he wrote at least two books 1874 and 1882 and a host of articles on topics such as fly fishing!]. According to his *New York Times* obituary, "Dr. Ziegenfuss was one of the original members of the National Rod and Reel Association. And, for several years, he acted as one of the judges at their annual tournament [held in Central Park in Manhattan]."[607]

He was a "distinguished student of theology," an "able preacher," an "indefatigable worker" and a friend and pastor to all including, "high and low, rich and poor, Episcopalian, non-Episcopalian, in Poughkeepsie, throughout Dutchess County."[608]

They add, "there has probably never been a minister in Poughkeepsie more generally popular, among all Churches, and all classes, than he; but it was not for his learning that this esteem was accorded, nor was it by the exercise of any tact or diplomacy that it was won. The essence of the great power of his personality might be defined as its humanness."[609]

According to *The Record* "the circumstances of his death were peculiarly touching."[610] Mrs. Ellen Ziegenfuss was "for many years an invalid and unable to bear the care of a home." During this time the couple lived in the Hanson House. This landmark Poughkeepsie hotel was later used by Gov. Franklin D. Roosevelt during his various political campaigns.[611]

In the winter of 1894, her illness grew worse. She died on January 23, 1894. "Fatigued by the unceasing care he had given her, Dr. Ziegenfuss became ill with grip, and, a few days after his wife's funeral, he was removed to Vassar Hospital. A heart weakness, the knowledge of which he had long kept to himself, proved the bar to his recovery, and in his sleep, on Thursday evening, February 8, 1894, he died."[612]

---

[605] Reynolds, p.218.

[606] Edmond Platt, *The Eagle's History of Poughkeepsie"1683-1905* (Poughkeepsie, NY: Poughkeepsie] Eagle, 1905).

[607] Obituary of the Rev. Dr. Henry L. Ziegenfuss, *The New York Times*, February 11, 1894.

[608] Reynolds, p.294.

[609] Ibid., p.295.

[610] Ibid.

[611] The late Barbara Frost—whose father Benson Frost, Sr. was a personal friend of Franklin D. Roosevelt—recalls that has a little girl she attended a political rally at the Hanson House. She vividly recounted looking up to see F.D.R.'s astonishing efforts to walk to the podium with the assistance of his braces. This is something that FDR's handlers successfully hide from the American public.

[612] Ibid.

***The Venerable Dr. Henry Lafayette Ziegenfuss
is buried next to his wife in
the Van Vliet Family Plot Rhinebeck Cemetery.***
Photo: Photograph by the Rev. Mark D. Isaacs.

In addition to being a great pastor and churchman, Henry Lafayette Ziegenfuss was an active Freemason. He was raised in Rhinebeck Lodge in 1869, and he was a charter member of Triune Lodge in Poughkeepsie, New York. His memory was honored by his Masonic brothers with a beautiful stained glass window which can still been seen in the lodge room in the Poughkeepsie Masonic Temple. A few years ago the Rev. Dr. Mark D. Isaacs delivered an address to the Royal Arch Masons in Poughkeepsie on the life of Henry Lafayette Ziegenfuss.

Clearly, Henry Lafayette Ziegenfuss was an outstanding Christian man and a great pastor. The question is, would Dr. Ziegenfuss have approved of us calling our Monday night adult Bible Study "Ziegenfuss University?" I think he would have smiled and said, "That sounds like my own 'Christ Church Guild of 1882!'" Thus, in the spirit of Dr. Henry Lafayette Ziegenfuss, we gather on Monday evenings at St. Paul's to discuss, to read, and to study important topics and issues.

"The coming of moving pictures, radio, and television," wrote Elizabeth McR. Frost in 1960, "in a sense crowded these activities out, and stopped the constant gathering of the church members.[613] Despite these many distractions, St. Paul's (Wurtemburg) continues to offer a wide range of programs and organizations that are tailored to minister to the wants and the needs of today's members.

---

[613] Elizabeth McR. Frost, p.7.

Chapter Eight: Wurtemburg School, No. 8

Martin Luther urged parents to prepare their children for a useful life in this world by giving them a basic broad education.[614] Thus, over the years, showing traditional strong Lutheran support for education, at least four "one-room" schoolhouses stood on the grounds of St. Paul's Lutheran Church of Wurtemburg.

Wurtemburg School, No. 8, c. 1900
Photo: Archives of St. Paul's Lutheran Church of Wurtemburg.

About the year 1785, the officers and members of the Wurtemburg Church felt the need for a school and applied to George and Sebastian Bastian Pultz for leave to build a schoolhouse on the land deeded to the church. The request was granted.[615] Thus, the first school, a simple two-room structure, was built in 1796.

In his diary and ledger, William H. Traver states that, "The [first] schoolhouse stood about where the [second] schoolhouse now stands and the sexton's room was built against the schoolhouse on the east side so he was sexton and School Master."[616]

---

[614] Ewald M. Plass, editor, *What Luther Says: A Practical In-Home Anthology for the Active Christian* (St. Louis: Concordia Publishing House, 1959), pp.446-453.

[615] *The Rhinebeck Gazette*, February 12, 1881.

[616] *Diary and Ledger of William H. Traver*, DAR Collection. William H. Traver (1802-1873) is buried in the old section of the Wurtemburg Cemetery.

Both schools occupied the site south and east of the Church, where the 1870 Parsonage now stands. One-room was used as a schoolroom, and the other room housed "the man who combined the duties of school teacher and church sexton."[617]

Barbara Frost, whose grandfather Mandeville Frost (1845-1922) taught at the Wurtemburg School for several years,[618] confirms that in the early days, "the functions of schoolmaster and church sexton were performed by the same person."[619]

According to an 1881 handwritten document written by the Trustees of the Wurtemburg Church, "In 1796, or about that time, the Church established a parochial school and built a schoolhouse on the Church lot. When the State of New York instituted the Common School System, and the State was divided into County School Districts, 'Wurtemburg District No. 8' was organized."[620]

About the year 1835, this original schoolhouse had become so dilapidated that it needed repairs. It was taken down and a second schoolhouse was built where the 1870 Wurtemburg Parsonage now stands.[621]

Later, Wurtemburg District No. 8 put a third schoolhouse on the west side of Wurtemburg Road, partially on land belonging to a neighboring farmer.[622] This building stood across the street from the 1802 Church near the Wurtemburg Sheds.

Halving the Schoolhouse

Sometime between 1876 and 1878,[623] there was an interesting controversy involving this third schoolhouse. Half of this third school building was located on a piece of land owned by George Pultz [is this George Griffin Pultz 1818-1892?] and the other half was on land belonging to Adam Progue.

For several years, George Pultz requested that the school district move the schoolhouse off of his property to another location. His request was ignored. Finally, in a bold and provocative move, Pultz ordered the school district to get its building off of his land by noon on a certain date.

Barbara Frost states that at this point in the controversy, Pultz said, "get the school off my property, or I'll cut off the part that is trespassing!"[624]

When the School Trustees refused to comply with his order, Pultz said there "would be no more school there, as he would saw the schoolhouse in two and apply the part which stood on his land."[625]

---

[617] Ibid.

[618] Barbara Frost interviewed September 15, 2006.

[619] Barbara Frost, *St. Paul's Epistle* [parish newsletter], June 4, 1978, pp.3-4. Archives #44.

[620] "Your Trustees take this opportunity…" Archive Document Folder #44.

[621] *The Poughkeepsie [Sunday] New York*, October 2, 1955.

[622] "There is a story…" handwritten notes and manuscript by Barbara Frost c.1979-1980. Archives #44.

[623] Barbara Frost, "The School of Wurtemburg," *St. Paul's Epistle* [parish newsletter], June 4, 1978, p.3. Archives #44.

[624] "There is a story…" handwritten notes and manuscript by Barbara Frost c.1979-1980. Archives #44.

Even then, the Trustees refused to take him seriously until Pultz, and some helpers, appeared with saws late the morning of the appointed day. Armed with saws and tools they were prepared to cut the building in half.[626]

Wurtemburg Schools kids dressed up for Halloween, c. 1900
Photo: Archives of St. Paul's Lutheran Church of Wurtemburg.

Seeing George Pultz' determination, the School Trustees then hastily loaded the building onto rollers and had oxen pull the building onto the Wurtemburg Road. At this point, they still had no idea where to take their school.

Since practically all of the residents of the school district were also members of the Church, the School Trustees finally decided to place the school near the back of the church property for the time being. It remained there for at least two years, until the school district decided to build a new and larger school on the same site.[627] George Marquet then hauled the old third schoolhouse about a mile south to his farm, where it was used as an outbuilding.[628]

In 1955, *The Poughkeepsie New Yorker* noted that this building, apparently still standing, "became a woodshed on the farm of Harry Marquet."[629]

The fourth Wurtemburg School was built in the spring of 1878.[630] This was a solid one-room schoolhouse lined with wainscoting and a vestibule. It was built on church property.[631] It was said to have been one of the finest one-room schoolhouses in the area.

---

[625] *The Poughkeepsie New Yorker*, Sunday, October 2, 1955.

[626] "There is a story…" handwritten notes and manuscript by Barbara Frost c.1979-1980. Archives #44.

[627] Ibid.

[628] Ibid.

[629] *The Poughkeepsie New Yorker*, Sunday, October 2, 1955.

[630] *The Rhinebeck Gazette,* "Wurttemburgh Church," February 19, 1881.

[631] "There is a story…"

The building measured twenty-four feet by thirty feet and was located on the south side of the Church building.

The Great Wurtemburg School Tax Fight

Wurtemburg Parish Historian, Barbara Frost, wrote, "In 1880, and 1881, there was a terrible tax fight." The School District Trustees, most who were also Church members, noted that the school was standing on two acres of ground (see Church deeds from Poltz [Pultz] and Weger [Wager]) and proceeded to levy a school tax on the Church for these two acres of land. The Wurtemburg Church Trustees, also many of whom lived in that school district, fought back. To cover the school tax, the School Trustees threatened to seize and sell Church furniture, including, "the Church pews, books, and altar furniture."[632] Eventually, the Church Trustees prevailed. After all, the school stood on their two acres with their permission and the permission of the Pultz family, who gave that particular part of the Church property.[633]

Two of our now deceased older members, Mary Lown Traver Baas and Eda Steward recalled with affection their years as students in the old Wurtemburg School. Mary Baas, who attended the Wurtemburg School until she went to school in town in the eighth grade, said that she preferred going to the one-room schoolhouse. She explained that she really liked going to the Wurtemburg School because students worked at their own pace at their desk, and in the one-room school there was never any homework.[634]

Mary Baas also explained that students were taught that two fingers meant that you wanted to speak, and one finger meant that you needed to use the outhouse. This historic outhouse can still be seen just north of the present Church.[635]

In the same interview, Mary Baas reported that if one broke the rules, a student would have to stand in the corner as punishment. When asked if she had direct knowledge of this form of punishment, Mary smiled and laughed.

The End of the Wurtemburg School

Marcella Clarke explains that early one-room "schools were built with walking distance in mind. This assured farmers and homeowners that their children would have a limited number of miles to walk to and from school each day."[636]

Clarke adds, "These school buildings were often plain, with outhouses to serve necessity. Boys typically were charged with the task of carrying in the firewood provided by parents to heat the building in the winter. School taxes were raised in each district to pay for general supplies. Districts were under the loose control of county supervisors. Rhinebeck was part of Dutchess County District No.4."[637]

---

[632] "There is a story…" handwritten notes and manuscript by Barbara Frost c.1979-1980. Archives #44.

[633] Barbara Frost, *St. Paul's Epistle* [parish newsletter], June 4, 1978, p.3. Archives #44.

[634] Interviewed September 24, 2006.

[635] Ibid.

[636] Marcella Clarke, *Diary of a Central School: The Story of Rhinebeck Central School* (Lowell, MA: King Publishing, 2004), p.37.

[637] Ibid.

In the town of Rhinebeck, prior to 1941, there were twelve local school districts. These were:

No. 1,	Morton School
No. 2,	Rhinecliff School
No. 3,	Hook School Hillside
No. 4,	Hillside School
No. 5,	Rhinebeck School
No. 6,	Stone Church School
No. 7,	Ackert Hook School
No. 8,	Wurtemburg School
No. 9,	Eighmyville School
No. 10,	White Schoolhouse
No. 11,	Miller School
No. 12,	Flat Rock School

Clarke writes in January 30, 1941, "the districts that expressed approval by their majority [i.e., in favor of consolidation] through their petitions were: "No.2, Rhinecliff; No.5, Rhinebeck; No.6, Stone Church; No.8, Wurtemburg; No.10, White Schoolhouse; and No.12, Flat Rock."[638] In May 8, 1941, she adds, "Wurtemburg… opted to send their pupils to Rhinebeck. [At the time] there were only four students in that district."[639]

Through the tireless efforts of local groups such as, "The Citizen's School Committee, headed by Miss Albertina T.B. Traver, and their whirlwind campaign,"[640] the movement toward consolidated school districts meant the end for one-room schoolhouses all across America. Gradually, these schools closed, and the children were bused to central schools. In Rhinebeck, this occurred between 1941 and 1949.

About One-Room Schoolhouses

For post-modern Americans, one-room schoolhouses, such as Wurtemburg School District, No. 8, seem to be quaint, archaic, primitive, and thoroughly passé. One-room schoolhouses tend to conjure up images of Laura Ingalls Wilder's famous *Little House on the Prairie* series. Laura Ingalls Wilder (1867-1957) was both a student and a teacher in a one-room schoolhouse. Her teaching career ended in 1885, when she got married. At that time, married women were not permitted to teach.

One-room schoolhouses reflected the twin Jeffersonian ideals of agrarian democracy and local control via decentralization.[641] These neighborhood schools were intended to aid in the process of Americanizing the children of immigrant families so that they could be assimilated into the mainstream of American society. These schools were to teach basic literacy and respect for duly constituted authority. These schools also were given the task of supporting the moral and religious values of home and community. As a

---

[638] Ibid., p.42.

[639] Ibid., p.47.

[640] Ibid., p.42.

[641] Wayne Urban and Jennings Wagoner, Jr., *American Education: A History* (New York: McGraw-Hill, 1996), p.74.

result, during the nineteenth and early twentieth centuries, one-room schools dotted the landscape throughout rural portions of the United States.

New York State passed legislation establishing school districts in 1812. This legislation provided money for the construction of "common schools." Parents were required to pay for each child they sent to school, depending on the number of days each child attended. This was called the "rate bill." Despite the fact that fees for poor students were generally provided for by local charitable benefactors, the rate bill system was considered to be unfair.

New York State authorities abolished the "rate bill" system in 1867, and established so-called "free elementary school education."[642] Since schools were already supported by local school taxes the term "free" is an interesting political euphemism.

In 1874, the New York State legislature passed the nation's first compulsory education law. It required that all children between the ages of eight and fourteen attend school for at least fourteen weeks per year. Typically, the school year began in November and ran through the first week in March. Students were required to receive instruction in spelling, reading, writing, English grammar, geography, and arithmetic.[643]

The compulsory education law was amended in 1894 to include children up to the age of sixteen, and the school year was extended from October until June.[644] One of the "hidden" motivations for expanding compulsory education laws was to deal with the social problem of child labor. Social Progressives and Reformers united with labor union leaders, whose motive was to eliminate competition in the labor market by excluding child labor.[645]

Before the rise of the Normal School system designed to train public school teachers, most one-room school teachers were young men—and then almost exclusively young women—who had done well in the district schools. After graduation, they decided to become teachers.

Teacher's wages were low "averaging one to two dollars per day for a nine-month term." However, teachers often received room and board as a part of their compensation package. Often, female teachers—who were required to be single—would receive room and board at a nearby home.[646] As we have previously stated, prior to 1878, at Wurtemburg, the schoolteacher doubled as the Church Sexton and lived in a room adjoining the school.

The Three Rs

In most rural areas, such as Wurtemburg, students met in a single room. There, a single teacher taught "the three Rs" (reading, 'riting, and 'rithmetic) to seven or eight

---

[642] Lori VanDeValk, *The Oliver Schoolhouse: An Exhibit at the Old Stone Fort Museum Complex, Schoharie, New York* (Schoharie, NY: Schoharie Historical Society, 2000), p.2.

[643] Ibid.

[644] Ibid.

[645] Forest Chester Ensign, *Compulsory School Attendance and Child Labor* (Iowa City: Athens Press, 1921) and Murray N. Rothbard, *Education Free & Compulsory* (Auburn, AL: Ludwig von Mises Institute, 1971, 1999), pp.37-55.

[646] VanDeValk, p.4.

different grade levels of elementary-age boys and girls. Rather than the one-size fits all graded system found in public schools today, instruction and individual assignments were given to each pupil according to their level of understanding and progress. Students freely progressed at their own individual pace. In this system, older students helped younger students, and younger students benefited from overhearing the lessons being presented to the older students. Thus, the mixing of students of various ages was more natural than the current regimented grade system.

The Old Wurtemburg Schoolhouse stood just north of the Church.
Photo: Archives of St. Paul's Lutheran Church of Wurtemburg.

In contrast to the current system of mammoth, consolidated public schools one-room schoolhouses were on a more human scale. In addition to encouraging children of different ages to interact and learn from each other, one-room schoolhouses had another tremendous advantage; i.e., these decentralized schools were under the local control of parents and families. Today, with massive public schools, with thousands of students and multi-million dollar budgets, and with legions of educational administrators and bureaucrats pursuing their own agendas and protecting their own special interests, many parents tend to feel that they lack a voice and that their opinion has no impact. In turn, teachers and concerned educational professionals are often frustrated, as discipline problems abound, and as parents appear apathetic.

In his revisionist history of the origins of the public school monopoly in America, Samuel L. Blumenfeld systematically traced the theological, philosophical, and historical evolution of education in the United States, as it was transformed from the near-total *laissez-faire* system of our nation's first fifty years, to the troubled centrally controlled bureaucracy that it has become today.[647]

---

[647] Mark D. Isaacs, "Book Review: 'Is Public Education Necessary?'" *The New American*, December 9, 1985.

In his 1981, book *Is Public Education Necessary?*[648] Blumenfeld chronicled the career of Horace Mann (1797-1859), who has been called "the father of American public education." Blumenfeld writes, "If Mann was the father of anything, it was of centralized, state-controlled public education, governed by a State bureaucracy, and financed by taxes on property."[649] After visiting Prussia, Mann used its educational system as a model for the creation of what became an American network of compulsory primary and secondary government run schools.[650]

The Father of American Public Education
Horace Mann (1797-1859)

To accomplish this end, Mann founded a series of State-supported "Normal Schools," or State teachers colleges, designed to train teachers in the latest methods of molding young minds.[651] Normal Schools were intended to be "secular seminaries for training public school teachers."[652] Blumenfeld argues that "once a nation's teachers colleges became the primary vehicle through which the philosophy of Statism was advanced, this philosophy soon infected every other quarter of society...."[653]

According to Blumenfeld, prior to the 1830s, and the education reforms of Horace Mann, no schools in the U.S. were state supported or state controlled. They were local, decentralized, parent-teacher enterprises, supported without taxes [or with minimum

[648] Samuel L. Blumenfeld, *Is Public Education Necessary?* (Boise, Idaho: Paradigm Company, 1981).

[649] Ibid., p.184.

[650] Ibid., p.233.

[651] I hold a B.A. degree in economics from Westfield State College in Westfield, Massachusetts. Westfield State was founded in 1833 by Horace Mann as a "Normal School."

[652] Blumenfeld, p.213.

[653] Mark D. Isaacs, "Book Review: '*Is Public Education Necessary?*'"

taxes], and taking care of all children. They were remarkably high in standards and were Christian. From Mann to the present, the state has used education to socialize the child. The school's basic purpose, according to its own philosophers, is not education in the traditional sense of the 3 Rs.[654]

Inside the Wurtemburg School, 1890-1891
Anita Traver, ClaraBell Pultz, Lillian Marquet, Fannie Traver, Edith Frost, Ardelle Frost
"Queen" Gertrude Marquet, Verna Pultz, and Florence Frost
Photo: Archives of St. Paul's Lutheran Church of Wurtemburg.

A Typical Day

The typical school day was 9:00 AM to 4:00 PM, with a morning and an afternoon recess of fifteen minutes each and an hour period for lunch.[655] Students often walked home for a noon day family meal. The older students were given the responsibility of bringing in water, and carrying in coal or wood for the stove. The younger students would be given responsibilities according to their size and gender, such as cleaning the blackboard, taking the erasers outside for dusting, plus other duties that they were

---

[654] Ibid.

[655] VanDeValk, p.5.

capable of doing. In this way, students, rather than being pampered and waited on, participated in their own education.

In an interview, Mary Baas recalled that, when she was a child attending the old Wurtemburg School, every day the children were responsible for carrying a bucket of water from the pump behind the 1870 Parsonage down to the schoolhouse. Then, during the day, the students had drinking water. Mary laughed when she stated that "everyone drank out of the same dipper, and no one died!"[656]

During the nineteenth century, because paper was relatively expensive, students used slates and slate pencils for their lessons.[657] In addition, students did extensive memory work. The traditional hallmark of a well-educated person was one who could "recite their lessons."

Thea Lawrence, quoting Howard H. Morse,[658] writes that early one-room schools in the Rhinebeck area:

> …offered a general nonsectarian type of religious teaching along with the three Rs. *The King James Bible* (1611) was used, and the Lord's Prayer was recited at the beginning and end of each day. *The New England Primer*, which was religious in tone, was the basic textbook. The "book learning" acquired in the public school enabled each child to reckon with money, the write a simple letter, and to repeat the catechism.[659]

The McGuffey Eclectic Readers

In New York State, early schools used mostly Noah Webster's *Blue Backed Spelling Book* (1782)[660] and *McGuffey Eclectic Readers.*[661] Most of today's educational professionals, if they are aware at all of *McGuffey's Readers,*[662] tend to regard them as quaint and primitive pedagogical relics of the nineteenth century.[663]

First published in 1836, *McGuffey's Eclectic Readers* dominated the market until the 1920s, and were among America's most influential works of popular literature. During *The Readers'* heyday, approximately half of all American children learned to read the McGuffey way. Between 1836 and 1850, at a time when the population of the United States was less than twenty-three million, seven-million copies of *The McGuffey Readers* were sold. Altogether, between 1837 and 1920, an estimated 122 million copies were

---

[656] Mary Baas interview July 22, 2006.

[657] VanDeValk, p.5.

[658] Morse, p.200.

[659] Lawrence, p.43.

[660] See Mark D. Isaacs, "The Origin of Webster's Dictionary," *The New American*, November 11, 1985.

[661] VanDeValk, p.4.

[662] *McGuffey's Eclectic Readers* (John Wiley & Sons; 6th Rev. edition, 1989).

[663] Mark D. Isaacs, "Classics Revisited: McGuffey's Remarkable Readers," *The New American*, October 10, 1988, p. 57.

published.[664]   This figure is even more remarkable considering that each book was probably used by five or six students before being retired.

The McGuffey Eclectic Readers did more than teach millions of children to read. They were so widely used that they became a unifying force in American culture. Historian Henry Steele Commager correctly observed that *The McGuffey Readers* "gave to the American child of the nineteenth century what he so conspicuously lacks today—a common body of allusions, a sense of common experience, and of common possession."[665]

An example of the fruits of this "common experience" was President Teddy Roosevelt. When he explained to the nation that he did not wish to be a "Meddlesome Matty" about some lofty affair of state, the people knew precisely what he was talking about. T.R. was referring to a character named "Matilda" who appeared in a humorous poem in the *Fourth McGuffey Reader*.[666] "Matty" was a curious little girl who, among other things, could not keep her nose out of her Grandmother's snuffbox.

Another example of how the contents of *The McGuffey Readers* became part of American culture is the famous children's poem "Mary's Lamb." This poem first appeared in the September 1830 issue of *The Juvenile Miscellany*. It was written by Sarah Josepha Hale (1788-1879). This charming poem has nearly attained the status of a Mother Goose rhyme because it was incorporated—without credit to the author—into the 1844 edition of *The McGuffey Readers*. In 1877, a McGuffey alum named Thomas A. Edison made history when he recorded the immortal line "Mary had a little lamb" on his first phonograph.

The McGuffey Readers were popular for many reasons. Above all, children liked *The Readers*. They included simple, yet charming stories, with pictures and rural settings, with which they could identify. Other readers of the time, published mainly in Unitarian New England, were written by Boston Brahman urban types. Unlike *The McGuffey Readers*, the New England readers were pretentiously aimed at gifted students from privileged families. *The McGuffey Readers* were created specifically for the growing number of new European emigrants, and for the rural American middle class.

Unlike their pompous New England rivals, *The McGuffey Readers* were basically free from the endless haranguing of social reformers on inflammatory issues such as slavery and temperance. Instead of a frontal assault demanding radical social reform, *The McGuffey Readers* employed a more tempered—and more effective—method to teach children the evils of slavery.

In a famous lesson called "The Birds Set Free," a rich man approaches a boy in a park who is selling caged birds for fifty cents apiece. The man proceeds to buy the entire cageful from the lad. No sooner is the deal transacted than the man turns the entire stock loose, explaining to the boy: "I was shut up for three years in a French prison, as a prisoner of war, and I am resolved to never see any creature in prison which I can make

---

[664] Richard A Bartlett, *The New Country: A Social History of the American Frontier*, 1776-1890 (New York: Oxford University Press, 1974), p.390.

[665] Henry Steele Commager, *"McGuffey and His Readers," Saturday Review*, June 16, 1962, pp. 50-51, pp.69-70.

[666] *Fourth McGuffey Reader*, pp.42-43.

free."[667] Thus, under the guise of teaching kindness to animals, a powerful yet gentle anti-slavery message is taught.

Using a McGuffey Reader

When post-modern readers first pick up a set of *The McGuffey Readers*, they are often stunned by the high level of reading in *The Fifth* and *Sixth Readers*. Many of today's college students would probably have difficulty digesting the contents of these two wonderful volumes.

It is important to note that the seven-volume McGuffey graded series (*Primer* to *Sixth Reader*) does not correspond to our twenty-first century concept of grade levels. *The McGuffey Readers* were designed to be used in one-room schoolhouses. In these schools, children from age six to late teens shared the same classroom and the same teacher. Again, in a one-room school, learning was natural, not forced. Each student progressed at their own individual pace. There was no rigid collectivist educational structure with "social promotions." Instead, each student used *The First McGuffey Reader* until he was able to move on to *The Second Reader*, and so on. Needless to say, this individualized system benefited "slow learners" as well as "gifted" students—without multi-million dollar special education programs!

Children as an Asset

In addition, students in these country schools often attended school sporadically. In rural America, children were not only members of a family, they were an economic asset. They were expected to work alongside their parents on the farm. During Spring planting and at harvest time, many children would be forced to miss school. As a result, it was not uncommon for a wide range of ages to be working in *The First* or *Second Reader*.

According to Stanley W. Lindberg, author of the book, *The Annotated McGuffey*, "[M]ost nineteenth century students finished at least *The Second Reader*, but many left school permanently before completing *The Third*." Lindberg adds that, "for many years, anyone who finished *The Fourth Reader* was considered very well educated indeed."[668]

McGuffey Methodology

McGuffey Readers are progressive. Each lesson in a *McGuffey Reader* lays the foundation for the next, just as each *Reader* lays the foundation for the next volume. As the readers progress, phonics and accenting are introduced to further assist young readers. New words are broken up into bite-size syllables, so that students can attack unfamiliar words one piece at a time.

For those who came through the public school system during the 1950s, 1960s and 1970s, reading *The McGuffey Readers* today makes us wish that we were children again. Rather than the mindless Dick-and-Jane, "see-Spot-run," look-say method readers, McGuffey gave youngsters real meat-and-potatoes reading. Rather than accepting lower standards—as many of today's educators and parents do—McGuffey kept the challenge before his young readers. He expected a lot from his little ones, and he got it.

---

[667] *Third McGuffey Reader*, pp.54-56.

[668] William Holmes McGuffey, Stanley W. Lindberg, editor, *The Annotated McGuffey: Selections from the McGuffey Eclectic Readers, 1836-1920* (Florence, KT: Van Nostrand Reinhold, 1976).

Instead of busy work and pointless fluff, McGuffey gave his readers an astonishing anthology of the greatest English and American literature. *The Readers* featured Bible selections, and poems by writers such as William Wordsworth, Lord Byron, John Milton, John Greenleaf Whittier, Edgar Allan Poe, Ralph Waldo Emerson, and William Shakespeare. In addition, *The Readers* include prose selections from the works of Addison and Steele, Lord Macaulay, Parson Weems, James Fennimore Cooper, William Blackstone, Nathaniel Hawthorne, William Makepeace Thackeray, and the great Samuel Johnson. With all the writers included, it is interesting to note that Washington Irving was the most featured writer.

The publishers of *The McGuffey Readers* were able to include a plethora of great writers because, during the nineteenth century, there was not an international copyright law. And the texts did not have to be cleared through bureaucratic and politically correct textbook committees on the state and local level. When McGuffey and others compiled the *Readers*, they were able to select from the best of American and British literature.

The McGuffey Readers did not shrink from teaching morals and traditional values to the children. Beginning with *The Primer*, *McGuffey Readers* are laced with brief, simple tales and lessons that taught students solid values, such as the importance of thrift, charity, hard work, honesty, and temperance. It is no accident that today's public schools are plagued with violence, cheating, drug abuse, gangs, and a host of social problems. Many of today's students act like Philistines because they were the victims of a progressive, "values-neutral" education. As the Scripture teaches, "you reap what you sow!"

It is also notable that the original *McGuffey Readers* were very Protestant. In later editions, as the usage of *The McGuffey Readers* expanded into non-Protestant areas, the Calvinist theological polemics were toned down in later editions. The originals included lessons such as, "The Character of Martin Luther." The Luther lesson was dropped in the 1843 edition because, among other things, it included biased statements such as, "Luther's death filled the Roman Catholic party with excessive as well as indecent joy...."[669]

Meet The Rev. McGuffey

By most accounts, William Holmes McGuffey (1800-1873), the creator of the original *McGuffey Readers,* and the man who became known as "the schoolmaster to the nation," was a dour, strict, and humorless career educator. He was born in western Pennsylvania into a Scotch-Irish Presbyterian family. His family moved to Ohio when he was very young. By 1826, after graduating from college, and having held several teaching positions, he had risen to the rank of Professor of Ancient languages at the new Miami University in Oxford, Ohio. This later enabled his shrewd publishers to boast that McGuffey was a "former professor at Oxford."

In the mid-1830s, the Cincinnati publishing firm of Truman and Smith approached Catherine Beecher—the sister of the famous Reverend Lyman Beecher (1775-1863)—with a request to do a series of "western" reading texts.[670] Beecher declined, but

---

[669] pp. 58-59.

[670] Milton Rugoff, *The Beechers: An American Family in the Nineteenth Century* (New York: Harper and Row, 1981), p.182.

recommended William Holmes McGuffey for the task. He agreed to compile four "graded" readers for a flat fee of $1,000. McGuffey completed the task in just two years. All four Readers, plus *The Primer*, were published in 1836 and 1837.

***William Holmes McGuffey (September 23, 1800 – May 4, 1873)
was the American professor and college president
who is best known for compiling "The McGuffey Readers."***

William Holmes McGuffey went on to be ordained as a Presbyterian minister, and to serve as president of two colleges in Ohio. In 1845, he became a professor of moral philosophy at the University of Virginia. He remained in Virginia until his death in 1873. By this time, nearly fifty-million copies of his *Readers* had been sold. Despite this astonishing publishing success, all of the royalties that McGuffey ever received for his work was the original $1,000. However, each Christmas, to show their "gratitude," his publishers presented McGuffey with a barrel of "choice smoked hams."

The Fifth and *Sixth Readers* were the products of William's younger brother, Alexander Hamilton McGuffey (1816-1896). Alexander was a scholar in his own right. In addition to his work on the *McGuffey Readers*, he did a majority of the work on the popular *McGuffey Eclectic Speller*. Alexander taught for several years, but later shifted careers, opting for the practice of law.

The basic *McGuffey Readers* were revised many times throughout the years. Neither of the McGuffeys was directly involved with these revisions. New, revised editions were published in 1841, 1844, 1857, 1866, and 1879. Major changes included a gradual mellowing of the overt religious content of many of the lessons. Still, in sharp contrast to the totally secular anti-God readers in common use today, even the much revised 1879 edition presented God as the Father and the Creator.

The McGuffey Readers were used widely in America until just after the end of the First World War. During this time, John Dewey (1859-1952), the philosopher head of the Teachers College at Columbia University from 1904 to 1930,[671] and his disciples began an all-out assault on traditional American education. Dewey was a militant secular humanist, a socialist, a Statist, and an atheist[672] who believed that "the State can do no wrong, for right is determined by what the State does."[673]

Dewey's classic credo can be found in his influential book, *Democracy and Education* (1916) in which he argued that "education was a process of growth through the continuous reconstruction of experiencing."[674] He looked with contempt at the decentralized family-controlled, nineteenth-century American educational system [i.e., the one-room schoolhouse], because it stressed "fixed" traditional values such as patriotism and reverence to God. John Dewey, and the Progressive Education Movement, began to promote "democracy" and "equality," not in their legal or civic sense, but in terms of the engineering of a socialized citizenry [social engineering]. Dewey's most basic educational idea was that a greater emphasis should be placed on the broadening of intellect and development of problem solving and critical thinking skills, rather than simply on the memorization of lessons. Public education became the means of creating a new social order of the educators' design. Such men saw themselves and the school in messianic terms.[675]

Dewey believed that a public school should be "more than a school." He argued that the public education system should become "the new secular State established church." He viewed the public school as a vehicle for social salvation. Toward this end, Dewey wrote, "[T]he teacher is always the prophet of the true God, and the usherer in of the true kingdom of God." The purpose of public education in the Deweyist scheme was to create a new faith, a new socialist man, a member in a single one-world family.[676]

Since a primary goal of progressive education is to stamp out individuality and to foster "absorption into the collective mass," *The McGuffey Readers* and the one-room schoolhouse became the chief targets of the movement. Reformers, allied with Dewey's new faith, attacked *The McGuffey Readers*, calling them "old-fashioned" and "outmoded." By the mid-1920s, they had succeeded in their efforts, and American public education began its long decline.

---

[671] Urban and Wagoner, p.206.

[672] Ronald Nash quotes Dewey writing, "Faith in the prayer-hearing God is an unproved and outmoded faith. There is not God and there is not soul. Hence, there are not needs for the props of traditional religion." *The Closing of the American Heart* (Dallas, TX: Probe Books, 1990), p.91.

[673] David A. Noebel, *Understanding the Times: The Religious Worldviews of Our Day and the Search for Truth* (Eugene, OR: Harvest House Publishers, 1991), p.55.

[674] Sidney Hook, *John Dewey: Philosopher of Science and Freedom* (New York: Barnes & Noble, 1959), p.155.

[675] Rousas John Rushdoony, *The Messianic Character of American Education: Studies in the History of the Philosophy of Education* (Nutley, NJ: The Craig Press).

[676] David A. Noebel, *Understating the Times: The Religious Worldviews of Our Day and The Search for Truth* (Eugene, OR: Harvest House Publisher, 1991).

The Demise of the One-Room Schoolhouse

At least two key factors led to the demise of one-room schoolhouses such as Wurtemburg School, No. 8.

First, motorized school buses in the 1920s made longer distances possible, and one-room schools were soon consolidated in most portions of the United States into multiple classroom schools, where classes could be held separately for various grade levels. As a rule, rather than ten to fifteen children grouped from the ages of six through fifteen, children were grouped in classes of twenty to twenty-five by their age.

And second, the one-room school was also killed by an alliance of progressive education advocates, the consolidated school movement, and teachers' unions such as the NEA. The National Education Association, the largest labor union in the United States, preferred consolidated schools because larger, centrally controlled public schools made collective bargaining feasible.[677] In the end, a combination of these forces led to the demise of the one-room school.

In 1955, Wurtemburg School, No. 8
was sold for $300, relocated, and converted into a private home.
Photo: *The Poughkeepsie New Yorker*, Sunday, October 2, 1955.

According to Barbara Frost, from c. 1941 until 1954, the old schoolhouse, which stood north of the Church, was used by the congregation for storage.[678] In April 1954, the old schoolhouse was purchased at auction by Mr. and Mrs. John H. Dorrer for $300.00 and moved to the west side of 9G. After extensive remodeling, the old schoolhouse was converted into a home.

During the renovations of the old school, John Dorrer discovered a block of wood pushed between the studs under a window. On this block of wood, written in pencil, there was an inscription which read, "John H. Van Etten trimmed these windows

---

[677] Samuel L. Blumenfeld, *NEA: Trojan Horse in American Education* (Boise, ID: Paradigm Company, 1984).

[678] Barbara Frost cassette tape of speech to the Rhinebeck Historical Society delivered on December 1990. The tape is in the Wurtemburg Archives.

February 25, 1878 and Reuben Ackert...” Unfortunately Ackert's contribution was illegible.[679]

The 1955 article in *The Poughkeepsie New Yorker* goes on to describe in great detail the old schoolhouse. They reported:

> It was twenty-four feet wide, thirty feet deep. It faced the south, with an ornate front door and an even more ornate louver frame above. That front door, still on the house [c.1955] has four panels, each edged with a wide molding and a round wooden ornament, shaped like an electric door bell at each corner of the molding, a total of sixteen. A scrolled ornamental plaque is between each upper and lower door panel. The louver over the door has a frame reminiscent of that of a cuckoo clock. The little sloping roof over the doorway has sawtooth trim at the sides, and is supported by ornamental brackets.[680]

The article adds:

> There were two windows on the front, two on either side, two in the back, all with wide frames inside. Wainscoting ran around all four inside walls, and there was a platform at the back of the building for the teacher. The wainscoting and plaster walls were all covered with a faded yellow paint when the Dorres bought the building.[681]

They add, "when all that white paint outside, and the yellow inside were fresh, that school must have been attractive in a thoroughly mid-Victorian fashion.”[682]

Today, one-room school houses are considered to be quaint and charming, a reminder of a bygone era. Many have been converted into museums. A neighboring one-room schoolhouse can still be seen at the Old Stone Church. The building is used as a Sunday school classroom for the congregation that currently meets in the Old Stone Church building.

---

[679] *The Poughkeepsie New Yorker*, Sunday, October 2, 1955.

[680] Ibid.

[681] Ibid.

[682] Ibid.

Chapter Nine: The Church Triumphant: Wurtemburg Cemeteries

uneral industry historians Robert W. Habenstein and William M. Lamers state that typically, "Early American burial was in the churchyard"[683] or in a decentralized family plot located on private land. For example, in the case of the first cemetery associated with this congregation, this would include "Peter Fraleigh's burial yard" somewhere in the vicinity of Primrose Hill Road and the Old Albany Post Road.[684]

The second burial place at Wurtemburg is a churchyard-style graveyard reflecting the European and New England practice of placing the graves of the departed in rows, in and around the yard of the church. Hence, from 1802,[685] "the ground east and south of St. Paul's church at Wurtemburgh was used for burial purposes."[686]

In May 1913, Dr. J. Wilson Poucher counted and recorded 326 inscriptions from the stones in the old Wurtemburg churchyard. Over the years, many of these old stones have become badly weathered, broken, or even stolen by vandals. Today, because there are no written records for the churchyard, many of these old graves are unmarked and the dead are known only to God.[687]

This old country churchyard is more than a quaint memory of the past, it is a powerful theological statement. Unlike the modern and post-modern "American way of death,"[688] which centers on denial of death and sterile euphemisms, such as "passed away," early rural New Yorkers and New Englanders "recognized death as a natural, inevitable, and commonplace reality."[689] The people of old Wurtemburg would agree with their New England neighbors of the time[690] that "the grave was as familiar as the

---

[683] Robert W. Habenstein and William M. Lamers, *The History of American Funeral Directing* (Milwaukee, Wisconsin, 1955), p.198.

[684] Edward M. Smith, *Documentary History of Rhinebeck, in Dutchess County, New York* (Rhinebeck, 1881, 1974 reprint edition), p.178.

[685] As we have stated above, the present church and cemetery were located at their current location in 1802. From 1760 until 1802 [a 42 year period], St. Paul's and a cemetery was apparently located at the end of Primrose Hill Road [3.8 miles from the present location]. It is likely that many of the oldest tombstones recording deaths during this early period, now in the present churchyard [in a row near the east side of the church], were relocated from the first Primrose Hill / "Staatsburg" St. Paul's location sometime after 1802.

[686] J. Wilson Poucher, M.D., and Helen Wilkinson Reynolds, *Old Gravestones of Dutchess County, New York: Nineteen Thousand Inscriptions* (Poughkeepsie, New York: Dutchess County Historical Society, 1924), p.311.

[687] Ibid.

[688] Jessica Mitford, *The American Way of Death* (New York: Simon and Schuster, 1963).

[689] Habenstein and Lamers, p.200.

[690] Melvin G. Williams, *The Last Word: The Lure and Lore of Early New England Graveyards* (Boston: Oldstone Enterprises, 1973), pp.1-2.

cradle, and they never saw any reason to ignore or disguise it."[691] To this day, when the doors of St. Paul's are open, worshippers feel a strong connection with the *Church Triumphant*, that "great cloud of witnesses"[692] that surrounds and embraces the *Church Militant*.[693]

During the mid-nineteenth century, a combination of over-crowding in urban areas, and public health concerns, led to the creation of a movement which called for interment of the dead outside of the corporate limits of towns and cities. An 1806 report from the New York City Board of Health advised the removal of all graveyards from the city.

In the United States, inspired by London's beautiful garden-style Highgate Cemetery, Mt. Auburn Cemetery near Boston (the first garden cemetery in the U.S. was founded in 1831); Laurel Hill Cemetery near Philadelphia;[694] and Greenwood Cemetery in New York City (1837) were founded.

As a part of this movement, New York State passed the *Rural Cemetery Act of 1847*. This act provided for the legal establishment of cemetery associations. It granted these associations certain privileges such as tax exemption, the right to make their own rules and regulations, and to distribute payments for land purchase for cemetery uses over the life of the cemetery.[695]

Thus, reflecting "the rural cemetery movement," the Wurtemburg Cemetery Association was formed on October 2, 1852. Dr. Poucher states that Wurtemburg, "in 1852 and 1866, [additional] land south of the church was acquired for burial uses."[696] From this point on, "the old graveyard… remained the only repository for the dead up to 1852, when increased facilities for burial purposes was apparent to the then large and prosperous congregation."[697]

On October 2, 1852, a Wurtemburg Cemetery Association was formed with Jacob G. Lambert, President and Gideon A. Traver, secretary. The association was incorporated on January 6, 1855.[698] At the time of its organization, it bought one acre of ground to the south of the church and since then, at least two additions have been made.[699]

The Church Records of St. Paul's Lutheran Church of Wurtemburg present a vivid picture of life and death in Upstate New York during the nineteenth century. Some of the

---

[691] Zephine Humphrey, *A Book of New England* (Howell Sosken, 1947), p.211.

[692] Hebrews 12:1.

[693] All Saints' Day takes on a new and deeper meaning when we consider the mute witness of those sleeping in the churchyard.

[694] Thomas H. Keels, *Images of America: Philadelphia Graveyard and Cemeteries* (Charleston, SC: Arcadia Publishing, 2003), pp.21-34.

[695] Robert W. Habenstein and William M. Lamers, *The History of American Funeral Directing* (Milwaukee, Wisconsin, 1955), p.423.

[696] J. Wilson Poucher, p.311.

[697] *A Brief History of Church with By-Laws, Rules and Regulations of Wurtemberg Cemetery Association* (Rhinebeck: Wurtemburg Cemetery Association, 1897), p.5.

[698] *Brief History* (1897), p.8 states that the Cemetery Association's incorporate was recorded in Poughkeepsie, New York, book number 1, of Church Deeds, p.205 and p.206.

[699] Alvah G. Frost, p.9.

pastors that served St. Paul's buried their people without making notes and comments in the Church Records. However, some pastors—such as Rev. John L. Kling and the Rev. George W. Fortney—made detailed entries as to the cause of death.

Shocking and Remarkable Deaths

Some of these entries listing the cause of death state: "sick a few days;" "died suddenly;" "congestion of the bowels;" "cholera inflammation;" "measles;" "consumption [tuberculosis];" "paralysis;" "blood poisoning;" "dropsy [an unnatural accumulation of serous fluid in any cavity of the body, or in the subcutaneous cellular tissue]; "Edema [swelling often caused by kidney or heart disease];" *La Grippe;*" "typhoid fever;" "softening of the brain;" "Bright's disease [chronic inflammatory disease of the kidneys];" "bilious fever;" "dysentery;" "dyspepsia;" "apoplexy;" "arm cancer;" "peritonitis;" "killed in New York (age sixty-two);" "found dead in bed, heart disease (age seventy-seven);" "found dead where cutting a tree (age fifty);" and "suicide by drowning."[700]

Children died of "an abscess;" "cholera *infantium* [a disease of infants prevailing in summer and characterized by vomiting, uncontrollable diarrhea, and collapse. The predisposing cause appears to be the hot weather. It is especially fatal in large cities] (age nine, and age six months);" "regurgitation (age four days);" "croup [croup pneumonia] (age three);" "spinal meningitis (age two);" "inflammation of the brain (age eight months) [encephalitis];" "appendicitis (age ten);" and "accidental shooting (age fifteen)." Between February 21, and March 1, 1869, three children of congregational members ages three, two, and two died. No cause of death is listed in *The Church Records*.

Between January 16 and 18, 1892, four members of the church ranging from age fifty-three to eighty-five died of *"La Grippe* [influenza like symptoms]." On April 13, 1892, a fifth church member died of *La Grippe.*[701]

Frederick Marquart was killed by a horse on August 14, 1832, "that was being run by Wilber Sleight while going home from church."[702] Egbert Crouse "drowned while fishing" on August 10, 1833.[703] George Crusius died January 7, 1840 of a "pitch fork wound," and he "leaves a wife and six children."[704] Ruben A. Pultz died on March 29, 1888, at the age of twenty-nine, of "excessive vomiting occasioned by an overdose of ipecac."

Mrs. William Traver (d. November 25, 1868 at the age of sixth-eight), "died suddenly in Church." A "Mr. Soper," buried at Wurtemburg, was found dead "at his hen house near Esopus"[705] on September 26, 1869, at the age of 60 after being "shot by

---

[700] *1873 Wurtemburg Church Record Book.*

[701] Arthur C.M. Kelly, *Rhinebeck, New York; Death Records of the 18th and 19th Centuries*, p.110.

[702] Ibid., p.101.

[703] Ibid., p.102.

[704] Ibid.

[705] Ibid., p.105.

robbers on his farm."[706] We are left to wonder if the murderer of Mr. Soper was ever apprehended. And, John P. Fatel died on June 14, 1878, after being "kicked by a horse."

Honored Veterans

Each Memorial Day the cemeteries at Wurtemburg are faithfully visited by members of the American Legion Post in Rhinebeck. The veterans lovingly and respectfully place American flags on the graves of every known veteran buried in the cemetery.

Among the veterans buried in Wurtemburg are: David P. Traver, Revolutionary War Veteran, died July 9, 1835, at the age of seventy-six years and thirteen days; Henry M. Ackert, Civil War Veteran from the 150th Regiment, New York (Dutchess County) Volunteer Infantry. The 150th fought at the Battle of Gettysburg on July 1, 2, and 3, 1863. Their valor is remembered with an impressive monument on Culp's Hill.

Spanish American War Corporal William J. Bradley of the 8th Regiment NY Volunteers, Company C (October 10, 1877-September 1907); Private Roy T. Crucius served in the Medical Corps. He died on June 8, 1918, of "pleuro-pneumonia." He is remembered in the framed Honor Roll of the Great War posted in the narthex. Roy T. Crucius, son of George H. Crucius and Mary L. Traver, was born May 21, 1898. He as baptized on July 2, 1899, by the Rev. Chauncey Diefendorf.

Sgt. George Monsees

Sgt. George Monsees, U.S. Army (July 7, 1903 - June 20, 1944), was killed in action in France during the Second World War. He is buried at the Normandy American Cemetery in St. Laurent-sur-Mer, France.[707] As a part of the 313th Infantry Regiment, 79th Infantry Division, Sgt. Monsees landed on Utah Beach on June 14, 1944. The 79th Division entered combat on June 19, 1944, as a part of the drive for Cherbourg, France. He was killed in action in fighting along the Valognes-Cherbourg Highway on June 20, 1944. Cherbourg was liberated from the Nazis on June 29, 1944. Sgt. George Monsees was awarded the Silver Star and Purple Heart. He was awarded the Silver Star after pulling several of his wounded men to safety before being killed by enemy fire. His memory is honored by a cenotaph marker at the Wurtemburg Cemetery.

In 2005, sixty one years after his death, congregation member Matt Moran and his two children, Harry and Rebecca, visited the Normandy American Cemetery. In an act of love and respect they poured a container of Wurtemburg soil on the grave of Sgt. Monsees.

Private Austin S. Frost, Jr.

Private Austin S. Frost, Jr. [Service # 32852019] 26th Infantry Regiment, 1st Infantry Division died on January 31, 1945 of wounds received on January 24, 1945 while administering first aid to a wounded soldier.[708] A letter to his mother from his

---

[706] Ibid., p.106. Andrew J. Soper [the only Soper buried in a marked grave at Wurtemburg], who died on June 11, 1864, at the age of thirty, is buried in a grave in the northwest corner of the 1853 cemetery. Is this the son of the murdered "Mr. Soper (age 60)?"

[707] Plot F, Row 12, Grave 43.

[708] Killed in action in Belgium during World War Two. See Pvt. Austin Frost, Jr.'s obituary in *Mrs. Samuel S. Frost's (1819-1912) Scrapbook,* (St. Paul's Archives), p.68.

commander stated that "he was an inspiration to his fellow comrades and the dies a soldier." Buried at: Henri-Chapelle American Cemetery, Henri-Chapelle, Belgium [Plot D Row 16 Grave 8]. He was awarded the Purple Heart.

Private Austin Frost, Jr. was killed in action in Belgium .
He is buried in Henri-Chapelle American Cemetery, Henri-Chapelle, Belgium,
and there is a cenotaph in the Wurtemburg Cemetery.
Photo: Archives of St. Paul's Wurtemburg

In 2000, the Wurtemburg Cemetery Association acquired a tract of land for a new cemetery across the street to the west of the church. Raymond Rhodes (2000) was the first burial in this cemetery.

Chapter Ten: Synods, Ministeriums, and Affiliations

Since 1760, venerable old St. Paul's Lutheran Church of Wurtemburg has been a part of many different Lutheran synods, ministeriums, and regional and national Lutheran organizations. These would include:

The New York Ministerium (1786-1929)
The General Synod (1820-1918)
The New York Synod (1908-1929)
The New York and New Jersey Synod (1872-1908)
The Synod of New York Synod (1867-1872)
The United Lutheran Church in America (1918-1962)
The Lutheran Church in America (1962-1988)
The Evangelical Lutheran Church in America (1988-2000)
The Evangelical Lutheran Conference and Ministerium (2000-present)

General Synod-General Council

In the middle of the nineteenth century, Lutherans in America were involved in a series of internal personal, political, and theological struggles and controversies that played themselves out on the national level with the formation of two rival Lutheran organizations; i.e., *The General Synod* and *The General Council*. From the perspective of a post-modern reader, the whole topic is *generally* confusing. Hence, it requires further details.

The General Synod of the Evangelical Lutheran Church—the first of the national Lutheran synods in America—was organized at a convention held in Hagerstown, Maryland on October 22-24, 1820. The first regional synods participating in the organization of the general body included the Maryland-Virginia Synod; the New York Ministerium; the North Carolina Synod;, and the Pennsylvania Ministerium.[709]

Apparently, the idea of a general body on a national level was first suggested in 1807 by the Rev. Justus Henry Christian Helmuth (1745–1825). The idea was also promoted after 1812 by members of the North Carolina Synod. It took definite shape in the *Plan Entwurf*, adopted in 1819, in Baltimore by the Pennsylvania Ministerium and representatives from other synods.[710]

Almost from the beginning, national Lutheran unity was nearly impossible to achieve. For example, the more conservative Tennessee Synod objected to the organization on doctrinal grounds, and the Ohio Synod did not join for practical and geographic reasons. At the time Ohio was on the western frontier. The New York

---

[709] Erwin L. Lueker, *Christian Cyclopedia*. "General Synod," (St. Louis: Concordia Publishing House, 1954), p. 326.

[710] W. Kent Gilbert, *Commitment to Unity: A History of the Lutheran Church in America* (Philadelphia: Fortress Press, 1988), p.9.

Ministerium withdrew after the first meeting because of lack of interest. In addition, the Pennsylvania Ministerium withdrew from the General Synod in 1823 because it feared centralized authority, and because some of its congregations feared infringement on their liberties. Seeking to avoid the authoritarian bureaucratic State-Church model found in the Old World, the idea of congregational polity, local control, and decentralization was an important issue for many Lutherans in America.[711] When the Pennsylvania Ministerium withdrew, a new Synod was formed west of the Susquehanna River; i.e., the Synod of Western Pennsylvania. In 1825, the Western Pennsylvania Synod rejoined the General Synod.

Samuel Simon Schmucker

The General Synod survived its critical initial years chiefly through the organizational and leadership skills of the remarkable Samuel Simon Schmucker.

Samuel Simon Schmucker (February 28, 1799–July 26, 1873) was the son of the Rev. John George Schmucker and the father of eleven children, including: the Rev. Beale Melanchthon Schmucker; the Rev. George William Spener Schmucker (1836-1904) [who served as pastor of the Evangelical Lutheran Church of St. Peter the Apostle in Rhinebeck (1862-1869)]; and the prolific Philadelphia author Samuel Mosheim Smucker [for some reason, Samuel changed his name from "Schmucker" to "Smucker"].[712]

Samuel Simon Schmucker was born in Hagerstown, Maryland, and educated at the University of Pennsylvania and at Princeton Theological Seminary. During his two years at the University of Pennsylvania, he received a solid basic theological education from the veteran Lutheran clergyman, the Rev. Dr. Justus Henry Christian Helmuth (1745–1825).[713] With Helmuth's gentle Pietistic influence, Schmucker developed a life-long "aversion for sharp theological definitions" and for petty denominational distinctions.[714]

At Princeton Theological Seminary one of his professors was Archibald Alexander (1772-1851) and one of his fellow students was Charles Hodge (1797-1878). From 1812 to 1929, the theological dynasty of Archibald Alexander, Charles Hodge, A.A. Hodge, and B.B. Warfield—Princeton Theology—combined the rigorous Calvinism of Francis Turrentin (1623-1687) with Scottish Common Sense Realism, to become the standard of historic Reformed orthodoxy in North America.[715] As a leader of "the Old Princeton

---

[711] Lueker, p. 326.

[712] W. Ken Gilbert, p.10.

[713] Simon Samuel Schmucker, *Fraternal Appeal to the American Churches with a Plan for Catholic Union with Apostolic Principles*, edited with an introduction by Frederick K. Wentz (Philadelphia: Fortress Press, 1838, 1965), p.1.

[714] Abdel Ross Wentz, *The Lutheran Church in American History* (Philadelphia: United Lutheran Publications House, 1923, 1933), p.201.

[715] M. James Sawyer, *Survivor's Guide to Theology* (Grand Rapids: Zondervan, 2006), pp.324-325.

School," Charles Hodge's three volume *Systematic Theology* (1872) is an American theological classic.[716]

The Rev. Samuel Simon Schmucker, D.D. (1799 – 1873)
Founder of the Gettysburg Lutheran Theological Seminary and
Pennsylvania (Gettysburg) College.
Photo: Lutheran Theological Seminary at Gettysburg.

Schmucker was ordained in 1821 by the Evangelical Lutheran Synod of Maryland. For six years he served five churches in the parish in and around New Market, Virginia.[717] While serving these congregations, and perceiving a need for trained Lutheran pastors, he began preparing students for the ministry in the early 1820s. In the days prior to formal Lutheran seminary education, experienced pastors would often individually tutor pastoral candidates. In 1826, he founded and became the first professor at the Lutheran Theological Seminary at Gettysburg, Pennsylvania.[718] He was also instrumental in founding Pennsylvania (now Gettysburg) College in 1832.[719]

---

[716] Charles Hodge, *Systematic Theology* (Grand Rapids: William B. Eerdmans Publishing, 1872, 1982).

[717] Schmucker, Frederick K. Wentz, ed., Introduction, *Fraternal Appeal,* p.2.

[718] Erwin L. Lueker, *Christian Cyclopedia.* "Samuel Simon Schmucker," (St. Louis: Concordia Publishing House, 1954), p.703.

[719] Abdel Ross Wentz, *Pioneer in Christian Unity: Samuel Simon Schmucker* (Philadelphia, 1967).

In addition, seeing the need for some national Lutheran ecclesiastical organization, in 1820, Schmucker became one of the driving forces in the formation of the General Synod. From 1820 until 1918, the General Synod served as a rallying point for American Christians who sought to be Lutheran. While the platform of the General Synod was broadly "evangelical," it fostered a Lutheran self-consciousness that helped to avoid the general submergence of Lutheranism into a generic American sectarianism.

The General Synod also stood in opposition to Rationalism. In the years following the American Revolution, and in the wake of the French Revolution (1789-1799), a wave of Deism, Rationalism, and "infidelity" swept all churches in America into a period of low morale and flagging zeal.[720] For example, in the New York Ministerium, Dr. Fredrick H. Quitman of Rhinebeck was one of the best-educated and most influential Rationalists in America.[721] In the face of this theological trend, the General Synod confessed Jesus Christ as "the Son of God, and ground of our faith and hope," thus acting as a check on inroads of Socinianism [i.e., Unitarianism]. Frederick K. Wentz writes that gradually, "sober Rationalism's hold upon American culture was replaced with a warm-blooded and often extravagant Romanticism that had an unbound enthusiasm for the future greatness and leadership of the young nation."[722]

Dr. Schmucker was also an advocate of direct social and political action by evangelical citizens. Schmucker vehemently opposed the Mexican-American War (1846-1848), stating that the war was both unconstitutional and contrary to Christianity itself. He was also an outspoken abolitionist. Like Henry Clay and Abraham Lincoln,[723] early in the anti-slavery struggle, Schmucker supported the African colonization movement. Later he aggressively promoted the organization of emancipation societies,[724] and his home in Gettysburg became a station in the Underground Railroad.[725] In 1835, due to Schmucker's influence, Daniel A. Payne was admitted to the Gettysburg Seminary.[726] Payne was the first African-American to receive his theological education in a Lutheran seminary. Payne later became a bishop in the African Methodist Episcopal Church and the first president of Wilberforce University.[727]

Despite "violent opposition amongst the German community (they regarded prohibition as an attempt to infringe upon their civil rights) that some even menaced personal violence,"[728] he was an early and effective champion of the prohibitionist cause.

---

[720] Schmucker, Frederick K. Wentz, ed., Introduction, *Fraternal Appeal,* p.5

[721] Lueker, p.656.

[722] Schmucker, Frederick K. Wentz, ed., Introduction, *Fraternal Appeal,* p.7.

[723] Thomas J. DiLorenzo, *The Real Lincoln: A New Look at Abraham Lincoln, His Agenda, and an Unnecessary War* (Roseville, CA: Prima Publishing, 2002), p.16.

[724] Schmucker, Frederick K. Wentz, ed., *Fraternal Appeal,* p.18.

[725] Abdel Ross Wentz, *The History of Gettysburg Theological Seminary: 1826-1926* (Philadelphia: United Lutheran Publications House, 1926), p.111.

[726] Ibid.

[727] E. Clifford Nelson, p.143.

[728] John G. Morris, p.16.

Dr. Schmucker required that Gettysburg students refrain from consuming alcohol and playing cards.[729] He opposed card playing because he thought that it was a "waste of time" and that it was "calculated to sanction and encourage the gambling habits of the young and profligate."[730]

His book, *Fraternal Appeal to the American Churches on Christian Union* (1838),[731] prepared the way for one of the first attempts in modern history to create a world-wide ecumenical movement.[732] In 1846, he traveled to London, England to participate in the formation of the International Evangelical Alliance.[733] Meetings were held at London's Freemason's Hall between August 19 and 23, 1846. Frederick K. Wentz explains that the Evangelical Alliance was "the nineteenth century forerunner of the World Council of Churches."[734]

It is important to note that in the 1840s, many Protestants feared a virtual flood of Roman Catholic immigration.[735] During the 1830s, more than a half a million immigrants from Great Britain, Ireland, and Germany arrived in New York City alone.[736] During the 1840s these numbers grew even larger. Protestant nativists, such as Samuel F. B. Morse (1791-1872) of Poughkeepsie, New York,[737] feared the increasing social and political power of "hordes of Roman Catholic foreigners" coming to America. Alarmist books such as Samuel F. B. Morse's, *A Foreign Conspiracy Against the Liberties of the U.S.*, published in 1834, and Lyman Beecher's, *A Plea For the West*, published in 1835, exposed what was purported to be a Papal plot to take over the United States. Concerned evangelicals—even progressive Protestants such as S.S. Schmucker—were urged to abandon their petty sectarian differences and to unite against perceived "Romish designs."[738]

They perceived this "papist invasion" as a threat to the American System. Frederick K. Wentz explains that "anti-popery was one of the causes which Schmucker shared with other Protestants of his time and place."[739] For Dr. Schmucker, a wider Protestant

---

[729] Schmucker, Frederick K. Wentz, ed., *Fraternal Appeal,* p.18.

[730] John G. Morris, p.17.

[731] Simon Samuel Schmucker, *Fraternal Appeal to the American Churches with a Plan for Catholic Union with Apostolic Principles* (Philadelphia: Fortress Press, 1838, 1965).

[732] E. Theodore Bachman, p.49.

[733] Ibid., p.16.

[734] Schmucker, Frederick K. Wentz, ed., *Fraternal Appeal*, p.31.

[735] Samuel L. Blumenfeld, *Is Public Education Necessary?* (Boise, ID: Paradigm Company, 1981, 1985), p.160.

[736] Kenneth Silverman, *Lightening Man: The Accused Life of Samuel F. B. Morse* (Cambridge: DaCapo Press, 2003), p.139.

[737] Ibid., pp.139-142.

[738] Blumenfeld, p.160.

[739] Schmucker, Frederick K. Wentz, ed., *Fraternal Appeal*, p.17.

union—perhaps a confederation of non-Catholic denominations[740]—was not only solid theology, but it was essential for the preservation and future of the churches of the Reformation in America. In other words, for Schmucker, the pragmatic need for a unified Protestantism transcended the need for Confessional purity and separation from the Reformed. Thus, Schmucker, in the interest of Protestant unity, tended to consider confessional Lutheranism as merely "petty sectarian differences."

Dr. Schmucker was a prolific writer. He wrote more than forty books and penned countless articles.[741] His *Elements of Popular Theology* (1834) ran through nine editions. It was read by generations of American Lutheran pastors.[742] Despite his many remarkable achievements, today, Schmucker is typically remembered—and vilified in Lutheran circles—for his authorship of the anonymous and controversial *Definite Synodical Platform* (1855). This document, a proposed revision of *The Augsburg Confession,* found numerous "errors" in the original 1530 *Confession* including: approval of the mass; retention of private confession; denial of the divine obligation of the Sabbath; baptismal regeneration; and the rejection of the real presence in Holy Communion.[743] *The Definite Platform* omitted from the Apostles' Creed "the descent into hell" and excluded *The Athanasian Creed.* Other Lutheran symbols were also rejected because of their length and alleged theological errors. Thus, Dr. Schmucker taught that *The Augsburg Confession* (1530)—the basic Lutheran rallying point—was to be recognized, but he taught that in the interest of union, a distinction had to be made between "fundamental" and "non-fundamental" doctrines. [744]

Dr. Schmucker's controversial "unionist" theology was viewed by many conservatives as compromising confessional Lutheran theology.[745] Indeed, Schmucker's broad theological views scandalized European trained theologians and made later immigrant Lutherans suspicious of an American "Protestantized" Lutheranism.[746] After a long and successful teaching and scholarly career, he retired in 1864 in the mist of the "American Lutheranism controversy."[747] From 1864 until his death in 1873, at age seventy-four, he devoted himself to writing.[748]

Schmucker or Smucker?

One of Samuel Simon's sons, Samuel Mosheim Schmucker [who wrote his name "Smucker"] was a prolific author. He was born in New Market, Shenandoah County, Virginia, January 12, 1823, and he died in Philadelphia, Pennsylvania, May, 12, 1863.

---

[740] Ibid., p.28.

[741] John G. Morris, p.125.

[742] Abdel Ross Wentz, *The History of Gettysburg Theological Seminary: 1826-1926,* p.125.

[743] Ibid., p.142.

[744] Lueker, p.327.

[745] Abdel Ross Wentz, *The History of Gettysburg Theological Seminary: 1826-1926,* p.126.

[746] Particularly the General Council and members of the Lutheran Church-Missouri Synod.

[747] Schmucker, Frederick K. Wentz, ed., *Fraternal Appeal,* p.28.

[748] Ibid. p.107.

Samuel Mosheim Schmucker graduated from Washington College in Pennsylvania in 1840. After studying theology and being licensed to preach, he accepted a call from the Lutheran Church in Lewiston, Pennsylvania. In 1845 he became pastor of First Lutheran Church in Germantown, Pennsylvania. After receiving an honorable dismissal from his Synod, in October 1848, Samuel Mosheim Smucker studied law at the Philadelphia law-academy. In January 1850, he was admitted to the bar, and at once began practice. In March 1853 he removed to New York City. However, after two years, he returned to Philadelphia where he employed himself chiefly as a writer. It is interesting to note Samuel Mosheim Smucker's general literary focus on Hamiltonian-Federalist-Whig-Republican subjects and biographies.[749]

The Career of the Rev. Beale Melanchthon Schmucker

Another interesting son of Samuel Simon, the Rev. Beale Melanchthon Schmucker, was born in Gettysburg, Pennsylvania, August 26, 1827. He graduated from Pennsylvania College in 1844, and studied at Gettysburg Theological Seminary. He was licensed to preach in 1847, and in 1849, he was ordained to the Lutheran ministry by the Synod of Virginia. He received an honorary D.D. from the University of Pennsylvania in 1870. He served as pastor in Martinsburg, Virginia; Allentown, Easton, Reading, and Pottstown, Pennsylvania. He was one of the founders of the General Council in 1867.[750]

Dr. Beale Melanchthon Schmucker was "a fine liturgical scholar," who tirelessly labored to promote the liturgical and hymnological development of the Lutheran Church. Working with Charles Porterfield Krauth, A.T. Geissenhainer,[751] and Joseph Seiss, Beale M. Schmucker[752] "restored in America the liturgical tradition of the Lutheran Church in worship, hymnology, and services for ministerial acts." The result was *The Church Book of the General Council* (1868).[753]

---

[749] Samuel Mosheim Smucker's publications include: *Errors of Modern Infidelity* (1848); *Election of Judges by the People; Constitutionality of the Maine [prohibitionist] Liquor Law* (1852); *The Spanish Wife, a Play, with Memoir of Edwin Forrest* (1854); *Court and Reign of Catherine II: Empress of Russia* (1855); *Life and Reign of Nicholas I of Russia; Life of John C. Fremont, with his Explorations; Life and Times of Alexander Hamilton* (1856); *History of the Mormons, Edited and Enlarged* (1856); *Life and Times of Thomas Jefferson* and *The Yankee Slave-Driver* (1857); *Memorable Scenes in French History; Arctic Explorations and Discoveries* (1857); *Life of Dr. Elisha Kent Kane and Other American Explorers; History of Napoleon III* (1858); *History of the Four Georges; History of All Religions* (1859); *Life, Speeches, and Memorials of Daniel Webster* (1859); *Life and Times of Henry Clay; Life of Washington; Blue Laws of Connecticut*; and *History of the Modern Jews* (1860). At the time of his death he had published vol. I., of *A History of the Civil War in the United States* (1863).

[750] Lueker, p.702.

[751] A.T. Geissenhainer served as pastor of St. Paul's (Wurtemburg) 1838-1840.

[752] Luther Reed, *The Lutheran Liturgy* (Philadelphia: Mühlenberg Press, 1947), p.173.

[753] E. Clifford Nelson, p.333.

Beale M. Schmucker was also the co-editor of the *Hallesche Nachrichten* which is the primary source of information concerning the colonial history of the Lutheran Church in America.[754]

American Lutheranism

The chief aim of the American Lutheranism movement was to adapt Lutheranism to its new American environment.[755] It was also a reaction to the new surge of Lutheran Confessionalism in Germany and America. In 1830, in reaction to the Prussian Union of 1817, and inspired by the three-hundredth anniversary of the Reformation,[756] a Confessional revival was reanimating orthodox Lutheranism in Germany. This German Confessional revival, via continued waves of German immigrants, soon found its way to America. At the same time, long-assimilated Americanized Germans—this would have included the majority of mid-nineteenth century pastors and members of St, Paul's (Wurtemburg)—had a hard time comprehending the zeal of these new German speaking Confessionalists.

As we argued above, the American Lutheranist movement must be seen within the context of the wider nativist reaction to the perceived threat of Roman Catholicism. American Protestants, such as S.S. Schmucker, feared a loss of political and social control via an invasion of "papists." In American politics the infamous "Know Nothing Party" dates from this time.

The American Lutheranism movement was also an attempt to create a fusion with Lutheranism and the dominant old Puritan [Congregationalist], German Reformed and Methodist ethos found in nineteenth-century American Protestantism. An extreme example of this ethos can be seen with the Campbellite revivals,[757] which stress the principle of "the Bible is our creed." The movement had a tremendous appeal to many "untheological, anti-traditional, anti-ecclesiastical, individualistic nineteenth-century Evangelical Americans [on the western frontier]."[758] For many Americans, creeds, confessions, and clergy were emblematic of Old World religion and spiritual oppression. To this day, the "nondenominational" church movement has tremendous appeal to many American Christians.

The bottom line is that Samuel Simon Schmucker was an important and influential theological leader of "American Lutheranism" and the General Synod for more than forty years.

The General Council

The controversy that led to the creation of the General Council revolved around a complex mixture of theological issues, internal church politics, personality clashes, issues

---

[754] Lueker, p.702.

[755] Eric W. Gritsch, *Fortress Introduction to Lutheranism* (Minneapolis: Fortress Press, 1994), p.59.

[756] Ibid., p.40.

[757] A series of camp meeting revivals led by Alexander Campbell (1788-1866) and his son Thomas Campbell (1763-1854).

[758] Schmucker, Frederick K. Wentz, ed., *Fraternal Appeal,* p.9.

144

surrounding new verses old assimilated German immigrant Lutherans, and one man; i.e., Charles Porterfield Krauth (March 17, 1823–January 2, 1883).

Charles Porterfield Krauth
was the leading theologian among conservative Lutherans.
Illustration Credit: *Appleton's Cyclopedia of American Biography*,
edited by James Grant Wilson, John Fiske and Stanley L. Klos.

Charles Porterfield Krauth was the son of Gettysburg professor and theologian Charles Philip Krauth (1797–1867). He was born in Martinsburg, now in West Virginia. He was educated at Pennsylvania [Gettysburg] College and Gettysburg Lutheran Seminary. He was licensed by the Maryland Synod in 1841 and ordained in 1842. From 1842 to 1867, he served as a pastor at various Lutheran parishes.[759]

In February 1864, in the midst of "the American Lutheranism controversy," Samuel Simon Schmucker resigned as head of Gettysburg Seminary. A large number of conservative confessionalist Lutherans ["Old Lutherans"] wanted Charles Porterfield Krauth to be named as Dr. Schmucker's successor. Although he was a graduate of the Gettysburg Seminary, by 1864 Krauth had become thoroughly conservative and confessional.[760] While he advocated kindness toward its adherents, Dr. Krauth openly opposed both the theology of *The Definite Synod Platform* and of "American

---

[759] Lueker, p.451.

[760] Abdel Ross Wentz, *Lutheranism in America* (1955), p.244.

Lutheranism." At a meeting of the General Synod in York, Pennsylvania, the increasingly conservative and largely German-speaking[761] Ministerium of Pennsylvania withdrew from the General Synod.[762]

In July 1864, "after the break at York, and with no prospect of having Dr. Krauth appointed as Dr. Schmucker's successor,"[763] the Ministerium of Pennsylvania established its own seminary in Philadelphia. Here, Dr. Krauth was called as professor of systematic theology. From 1864 to 1883, Dr. Krauth faithfully served as professor at the newly formed Lutheran Theological Seminary in Philadelphia and as professor at the University of Pennsylvania. He also helped to organize and served as president (1870–1880) of, The General Council of the Evangelical Lutheran Church in North America.[764]

Charles Porterfield Krauth's most important book was *The Conservative Reformation and Its Theology* (1872). This masterful book provided a forthright rationale for maintaining strict Old World standards for Lutheran teaching, even in the confines of the New World. For Krauth, a belief in the general correctness of *The Augsburg Confession* was not enough. This document, rather, needed to be affirmed in its details, for it was "the greatest work, regarded in its historical relations, in which pure religion has been sustained by human hands... It is our shield and our sword, our ensign and our arming, the constitution of our state, the life of our body, the germ of our being."[765]

Lutheran Church-Missouri Synod leader C. F. W. Walther (1811-1887) described Krauth as, "without doubt the most eminent man in the English Lutheran Church of this country, a man of unusual learning, at home in modern as well as old theology and, what is most important, heartily devoted to the pure doctrine of the Lutheran Church."[766]

In the course of time, as passions cooled and as leading personalities on both sides retired and died, the official doctrinal basis of the General Synod gradually conformed more and more to that of the General Council's more confessional understanding of Lutheranism.

For example, in 1895, at Hagerstown, Maryland, the General Synod defined "the unaltered *Augsburg Confession* as, throughout in perfect consistence with the Word of God."[767]

In 1901, at Des Moines, Iowa, the General Synod resolved "that to make any distinction between 'fundamental' and so-called 'non-fundamental' doctrines in the

---

[761] Abdel Ross Wentz, *The Lutheran Church in American History* (1923, 1933), p.224.

[762] Ibid., p.221.

[763] Ibid. p.223.

[764] Lueker, p.451.

[765] Charles Porterfield Krauth, *The Conservative Reformation and Its Theology As Represented in the Augsburg Confession, And in the History and Literature of the Evangelical Lutheran Church* (Philadelphia, General Council Publication Board, 1872, 1913).

[766] Erwin L. Lueker, *Christian Cyclopedia.* "Charles Porterfield Krauth" (St. Louis: Concordia Publishing House, 1954), p. 451.

[767] Ibid., p.327.

146

Augsburg Confession [as S.S. Schmucker had done] is contrary to that basis as set forth in our formula of confessional subscription."[768]

And, in 1909, at Richmond, Indiana, the General Synod resolved that "the General Synod in no wise means to imply that she ignores, rejects, repudiates or antagonizes the Secondary Symbols of *The Book of Concord*, ... On the contrary, she holds those Symbols in high esteem, regards them as a most valuable body of Lutheran belief, explaining and unfolding the doctrines of *The Augsburg Confession*, ..."[769]

In 1913, at Atchison, Kansas, all confessional Symbols of the Lutheran Church were formally and officially adopted, thus paving the way for merger with the General Council. Despite this resolution, there remained a wide gap between formal adoption and actual recognition of the Confessions. Un-Lutheran doctrine and practice were generally tolerated without official censure.[770]

The General Council and the General Synod, along with other smaller Lutheran bodies, entered into a merger in 1918.[771] This merger movement had its origin in the movement for a joint celebration of the 1917 Reformation Quadricentennial.[772] Largely as a result of action by laymen, the planning committee resolved April 18, 1917, to issue a call for union of "the General Synod, the General Council and the United Synod of the South, together with all other bodies one with" them in their Lutheran faith. The merger into what became "the United Lutheran Church in America" was consummated in New York City on November 14–18, 1918.[773]

Wurtemberg's Affiliation

From the perspective of St. Paul's (Wurtemburg), "when in 1867 the question arose, should this congregation advise the Ministerium of New York to leave the General Synod, it instructed its pastor and delegate to vote against withdrawal. At a subsequent meeting, St. Paul's voted to become a charter member of the Synod of New York, which met in Red Hook, New York in October of 1867." At this same meeting, "the Rev. Dr. George Neff[774] was elected as secretary of both the Ministerium and the new Synod. He served as president of the Synod from 1878 to 1886, when he resigned before the expiration of his term of office."[775] Wolf notes that "nearly all English churches in the New York Ministerium adhered to the General Synod."[776] St. Paul's (Wurtemburg) was one of those churches.

---

[768] Ibid.

[769] Ibid.

[770] Ibid.

[771] Ibid., p.325.

[772] E. Theodore Bachmann, p.73.

[773] Lueker, p.327.

[774] Pastor of St. Paul's (Wurtemburg) 1855-1876.

[775] George Neff manuscript, *1873 Wurtemburg Church Book*.

[776] Wolf, p.369

Wurtemburg as a Two-Point Parish

Over the years, St. Paul's has been a part of several configurations of two-point parishes. Starting c.1734, "the Staatsburg Church" and then, "St. Paul's Lutheran Church of Wurtemburg," were a part of the parish led by The Evangelical Lutheran Church of St. Peter the Apostle (The Old Stone Church). In 1842, perceiving a need to establish a Lutheran church in the village of Rhinebeck, Wurtemburg pastor the Rev. Charles Adam Smith founded Third Evangelical Lutheran Church. Until he resigned in 1851, Pastor Smith served both St. Paul's (Wurtemburg) and Third Evangelical Lutheran.[777]

From 1878 to 1895, St. Paul's was yoked with Memorial Lutheran Church (Rock City).[778] The Rock City Church began as an interdenominational chapel served by "pastors of differing persuasions from neighboring villages." Lawrence writes that, "The church was dedicated on May 25, 1873, when John Schultz [a local farmer] presented the land, buildings, and furnishings to the New York and New Jersey Lutheran Ministerium. Schultz assumed the entire responsibility of the economic functioning of the church from its inception, although collections were sometimes made for special purposes, such as a bell."[779] Records indicate that the Rev. George Neff and Rev. William Nace Scholl, both from St. Paul's (Wurtemburg), officiated at the first service. The affiliation with St. Paul's (Wurtemburg) ended in 1895, when a new pastor was provided by St. Paul's Evangelical Lutheran Church in Red Hook, New York.

The two-point configuration with Memorial Rock City was renewed in 1963 and lasted until 1996. During this time, pastors lived at the 1870 Parsonage at Wurtemburg, expenses were shared, and a joint church council met several times a year to deal with issues of mutual concern.

From June 1996 to January 2000, St. Paul's (Wurtemburg) was once again part of a two-point parish with Third Evangelical Lutheran Church located in the village. For three-and-one-half years, the church that Rev. Charles Adam Smith started in 1842 in the village was once again yoked with St. Paul's (Wurtemburg). This arrangement abruptly ended on January 1, 2000, when the Rev. Mark D. Isaacs resigned from Third Evangelical Lutheran and from the clergy roster of the Evangelical Lutheran Church in America [ELCA]. In an overwhelming display of love and support, the people of St. Paul's unanimously voted to call the Rev. Mark D. Isaacs as their full-time pastor and to withdrawal from the ELCA. Many former members of Third Evangelical Lutheran Church also came over and joined St. Paul's. At this time, St. Paul's also unanimously voted to join the Evangelical Lutheran Conference and Ministerium [ELCM] a "centrist and confessional Lutheran alternative."

---

[777] Thea Lawrence, *Unity Without Uniformity: The Rhinebeck Church Community: 1718-1918* (Monroe, NY: Library Research Associates, 1992), pp.100-101.

[778] Lawrence, p.102.

[779] Ibid., p.102.

Chapter Eleven: Seminaries and the Pastors of St. Paul's (Wurtemburg)

The term "seminary" is a venerable old Pietist word taken from the Latin *seminarium*. It means "seedbed." Like the German word *Kindergarten* [i.e., literally "children's garden"], the Pietists tended to use flowery, earthy, and organic metaphors to describe the work of God and their work for God. Thus, "a seminary" is a seedbed created to grow young sprouts for the ministry. Over the past two-hundred and fifty years, five seminaries—and their graduates—have had a major influence on the spiritual life of the people of St. Paul's Lutheran Church of Wurtemburg.

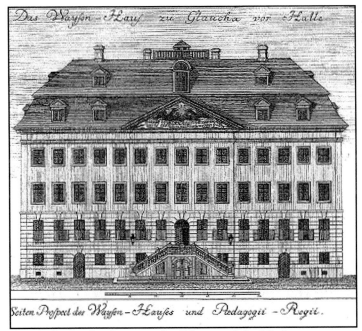

The Halle Institution was the Mecca of the Pietist movement..

The first is **Halle University**.[780] Halle provided two—possibly as many as five—of the early pastors that served St. Paul's. The Halle Institution was founded by one of Philip Jacob Spener's (1635-1705) greatest disciples. This was the energetic organizer, August Herman Francke (1663-1727).[781]

At the University of Leipzig, August Herman Francke, and two others, formed the *collegium philobiblicum* for the exegetical study of *The Holy Bible*.[782] Soon, because of

---

[780] In December of 2004, I briefly visited Halle University. From 1945-1989, Halle was located in the old East Germany (1945-1989), so the buildings are in need of repair and restoration. Despite years of war, and official communist neglect, the institution still stands.

[781] W.R. Ward, *Christianity Under the Ancien Regime: 1648-1789* (New York: Cambridge University Press, 1999), p.79.

[782] Tappert, p.21.

his Pietist views, Francke was forced out of the university.[783] In 1694, the Elector of Brandenburg, Frederick III, opened the university in Halle. Philip Jacob Spener helped Francke secure an academic appointment at Halle University.[784]

August Hermann Francke statue in Halle, Germany

In addition to appointing August Hermann Francke, Elector Frederick III also appointed the famous legal scholar, Christian Thomasius (1655-1728). In 1687, while at the University of Leipzig, Thomasius made the daring innovation of lecturing in German instead of Latin. The following year, in a provocative monthly periodical, he ridiculed the failed and stiff teaching methods of the conservative and orthodox German academics. Thomasius also openly sided with the Pietists in their controversy with Orthodox Lutherans. He even defended so-called "mixed marriages" between Lutheran and Calvinist Protestants.

Halle University

> Rev. Johannes Christopher Hartwick, 1746-1758
> Rev. Frederick Henry Quitman, D.D., 1798-1825
> (?) Rev. Johannes Fredrick Ries, 1760-1783
> (?) Rev. George Heinrich Pfeiffer, 1784-1794

---

[783] Peter C. Erb, ed., *Pietists: Selected Writings* (New York: Paulist Press, 1983), p.9.

[784] W.R. Ward, p.80.

Through Francke's organizational genius, energy, and influence, Halle University and a network of related institutions, including bible societies, orphanages, trade schools, etc., became the literal Pietist "New Jerusalem," i.e., the world epicenter of the Pietist movement.[785] Thus, under Francke's leadership Halle became a seedbed for the new piety and the academic citadel of the Pietist movement.[786]

August Herman Francke

In 1695, August Herman Francke established a school for the poor. Three years later, he founded the Halle Orphanage. This orphanage, devoted exclusively to the care and education of orphans, was the first such institution in Germany. Additional schools, ministering to the needs of children, both boys and girls of all socio-economic classes, were added. Poor students were provided with free food from royal patrons. In December of 1698, Francke listed twenty-three different schools at Halle that served more than five-hundred children.[787]

In addition, Halle included enterprises such, as a poorhouse, a hospital, an apothecary shop,[788] and a print shop devoted to the mass production of religious literature and the publication of Bibles for distribution in Germany and abroad.[789] In addition to

---

[785] Gritsch, *Lutheranism*, p.33.

[786] Ibid., p.23.

[787] Peter C. Erb, *Pietism*, pp.163-166.

[788] Pietists were interesting in herbs and the science of healing.

[789] W.R. Ward, p.81.

"internal missions," Francke and the Halle Institution also supported a worldwide network of foreign missions.[790] From Halle, missionaries were sent to India, Africa, and America.[791] Many of the pastors who ministered to Lutherans in colonial America, including the Rev. Johannes Christopher Hartwick (1714-1796),[792] and the Rev. Dr. Fredrick Henry Quitman (1760-1832), in Rhinebeck, New York, were commissioned and sent out from Halle. In addition, Justus Falckner (1672-1723), the first Lutheran pastor ordained in America, was a Halle graduate.[793]

Francke's Halle Institution was neither a church nor a state, yet through hard work and innovative management he was able to market Halle products in faraway places such as America, Lapland, Russia, and India. The entrepreneurial Francke was able to generate an income sufficient to support this mammoth enterprise.[794] August Herman Francke was "gifted with limitless energy, boundless enthusiasm, great organizational ability, and a flair for what later ages would call public relations."[795]

Thus, of August Herman Francke, Max Weber writes,"work in a calling was also for Francke the ascetic means *par excellence*."[796] He adds, "He was firmly convinced (as were the Puritans…) that God himself, through the success of the believer's work, was blessing His chosen."[797]

Francke's son, Gotthilf August Francke (1696-1769),[798] sent Henry Melchior Mühlenberg (1711-1787) to America to become the organizer of the colonial Lutheran Church. Mühlenberg, though not the first Lutheran pastor on the scene, has been called "the patriarch of American Lutheranism."[799] Mühlenberg planted many Lutheran churches and organized scattered German settlers into congregations.[800] His theology was clearly shaped by Hallensian Pietism, as was the case of most of his colleagues. Mühlenberg's reports; i.e., *Hallische Nachrichten [Halle Reports]*,[801] represent the most complete record of early Lutheran Church life in America.

---

[790] Holborn, p.138.

[791] Ibid., pp.56-57.

[792] Ronald H. Bailey, *Hartwick College: A Bicentennial History: 1797-1997* (Oneonta, NY: Hartwick College), p.19.

[793] Abdel Ross Wentz, *The History of Gettysburg Theological Seminary: 1826-1926* (Philadelphia: United Lutheran Publications House, 1926), p.18.

[794] W.R. Ward, p.81.

[795] Robert G. Clouse, *The Church in the Age of Orthodoxy and the Enlightenment: Consolidation and Challenge from 1600 to 1800* (St. Louis: Concordia Press, 1980), p.78.

[796] Max Weber, translated by Stephen Kalberg, *The Protestant Ethic and the Spirit of Capitalism* (Los Angeles: Roxbury Publishing Company, 1904-1905), 2002), p.84.

[797] Ibid.

[798] Edmund Jacob Wolf, *The Lutherans in America* (New York: J.A. Hill & Co., 1889), p.236.

[799] Bergendorf, pp.191-193.

[800] Gritsch, *Lutheranism*, pp.57-58.

[801] Wolf, *The Lutherans in America*, p.240.

During the summer of 1750 Mühlenberg made a trip to upstate New York to intercede for the Rev. Johannes Christopher Hartwick in a dispute—eighteenth century "conflict resolution"—when Hartwick was serving as the pastor of the Evangelical Lutheran Church of St. Peter the Apostle (the Old Stone Church) in Rhinebeck, New York.[802] Mühlenberg's 1750 visit included a visit to "the Staatsburg Church."

Abdel Ross Wentz notes that, sometime after 1770, "Halle could no longer be relied on as a source of ministerial supply." He adds that by this time, "the home of Pietist learning was changing. The Halle of Mühlenberg's acquaintance had passed, and the new teachers were not so firmly Lutheran and evangelical nor did they inculcate the same religious fervor and warm Christian piety as the Francke's had done."[803] This was the new age of the Enlightenment and Rationalism.

The rise of Rationalism at Halle, coupled with the outbreak of the American Revolution, created a clergy crisis in America. To supply the demand for Lutheran clergymen, an informal system of private tutoring in theology was established. The Rev. Dr. Fredrick Henry Quitman tutored many theological students here in Rhinebeck, New York. Pastors George Heinrich Pfeiffer, William J. Eyer, and Johann Friedrich Ernst may have been trained in this way.

Augustus Theodosius Geissenhainer was tutored by his well-known uncle the Rev. Fredrick William Geissenhainer, Sr. Prior to coming to America, the Rev. Fredrick William Geissenhainer "had taught at the University of Gottingen.[804] According to Beale M. Schmucker, in the fall of 1823, Augustus Theodosius Geissenhainer was sent to New York City to study for the ministry with his uncle.[805]

Interestingly, when Samuel Simon Schmucker learned that the Halle Institution had been severely damaged and neglected, both during and following the Napoleonic Wars, he, and other American Lutherans, helped to raise funds to reestablish the Institution. Thus, years later, the fruit and seeds of Halle University returned to reinvigorate the world center and fountainhead of Pietistic Lutheranism.

Hartwick Seminary

Hartwick Seminary was founded in 1797 to meet the need for educated Lutheran pastors in America. This wonderful New York institution provided seven pastors who faithfully served the people of St. Paul's (Wurtemburg).

Sometime prior to 1760, the eccentric Johannes Christopher Hartwick acquired more that 20,000 acres from the Mohawks, in the wilderness of what is now Otsego County, New York. Apparently, his desire was to create a utopian Christian society in the virgin wilderness. He died in 1796, without having fulfilled his dream for a "New Jerusalem," but left detailed instructions in his will for the foundation of a seminary. However, the executors of his will, Jeremiah Van Rensselaer and Frederick A. Mühlenberg had

---

[802] Bailey, p.22.

[803] Abdel Ross Wentz, *The History of Gettysburg Theological Seminary: 1826-1926,* p.39.

[804] Henry Hardy Heins, *Throughout All The Years: The Bicentennial Story of Hartwick in America, 1746-1946* (Oneonta, NY: Trustees of Hartwick College, 1946), p.22.

[805] Beale M. Schmucker, *Memorial of Augustus Theodosius Geissenhainer* (Philadelphia: The Ministerium of Pennsylvania, 1883), p.5.

difficulty enacting Hartwick's wishes because "he had designated Jesus Christ as his heir."[806]

Hartwick Seminary was founded in 1797.
Photo from Henry Hardy Heins, *Throughout All the Years: Hartwick*, 1746-1946.

Eventually, the executors of Hartwick's will did manage to get through the numerous legal problems and founded Hartwick Seminary. On September 15, 1797, the first Lutheran Seminary in America was officially established.[807] However, a decision on the final location of the school was postponed.[808]

Dr. John Christopher Kunze (1744-1807), the son-in-law of Henry Melchior Mühlenberg, was named Director, and taught theology at his home in New York City.[809] The Rev. Anthony Theodore Braun taught sciences and languages at Albany, New York[810] and Rev. John Frederick Ernst—who had served as pastor in Rhinebeck from 1794-1798—taught elementary school on the Hartwick Patent near Cooperstown. Henry Hardy Heins states that, "Ernst had been sent to the Hartwick Patent in the wilds of Otsego County as a feeler move to see if the location might be suitable for possible future

---

[806] Heins, pp.14-17.

[807] Ibid., p.16.

[808] Ibid., p.17.

[809] Ibid.

[810] Ibid.

154

establishment of the whole institution."[811] Heins adds, by 1803, Ernst "was back in Pennsylvania from whence he had come."[812]

Hartwick Seminary,
Name, Tenure at St. Paul's, *(Graduation Date)*
Rev. Charles Adam Smith, D.D., 1840-1850, *(1830))*
Rev. John L. Kling, 1881-1887, recalled 1908-1913, *(1865)*
Rev. Chauncey W. Diefendorf 1895-1898, *(c.1862)*
Rev. Roscoe C. Wright, D.D., 1899-1907, *(c.1899)*
Rev. William Gibson Boomhower, D.D., 1914-1916, *(1914)*
Rev. Oscar B. Noran, 1917-1919, *(unknown)*
Rev. E. L. Davison, 1919-1924, *(1913)*

After several years of debate and deliberation concerning the permanent location of the seminary, and due to the persistence of the residents of the Hartwick Patent, the first seminary building was established at the Otsego County location, in 1815.[813]

At this time, the Rev. Ernest Lewis Hazelius (1777-1853) became the first principal. Dr. Hazelius held this position for fifteen years, until 1830, when he accepted a position at the Gettysburg Lutheran Seminary.[814] He later became a professor at the Classical and Theological Institute of the Synod of South Carolina.

Hartwick Seminary offered an academy and a theological department. In 1816, it was incorporated with twelve appointed trustees, the majority of whom were to be Lutheran clergymen. During the first twenty years the school averaged between sixty and seventy students. In the late 1830's and 1840's, enrollment dropped nearly in half. Women were admitted for the first time in 1851, bringing the enrollment to eighty-nine and in the 1880's, it was over one hundred.

Throughout its existence, Hartwick Seminary struggled to attract new students and financial support. Abdel Ross Wentz states that Hartwick struggled because, "the institution was not under [direct] synodical jurisdiction... and its remote location seriously hindered its work."[815]

In an interesting statement in the *Hartwick Seminary Catalog of 1919,* the school attempted to overcome this objection when they argued, "a simple glance at any railroad map will show the ideal location of the school with regard to accessibility. However many larger New York schools may feel about it, geographically Hartwick Seminary is the hub of the state."[816]

---

[811] Ibid., p.18.

[812] Ibid., p.19.

[813] Ibid., pp.25-26.

[814] Ibid., pp.29-31.

[815] Abdel Ross Wentz, *A Basic History of Lutheranism in America* (Philadelphia: Mühlenberg Press, 1955), p.82.

[816] *Hartwick Seminary Catalog,* 1919, p.7.

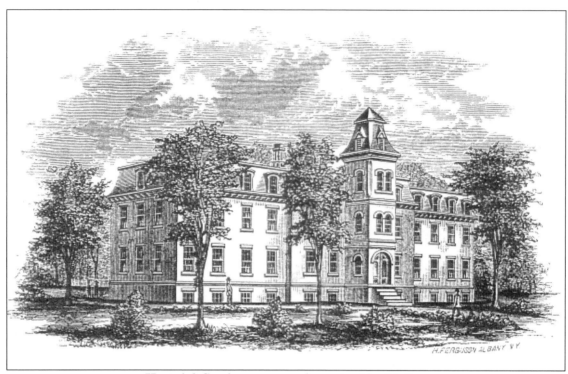

Hartwick Seminary was an important institution
for nineteenth century Lutheranism in Upstate New York.
Illustration Credit: Edmund Jacob Wolf, *Lutherans in America*, J.A. Hill & Co., 1889.

In the early years of the school, before being inaugurated, full-time professors at Hartwick were required to publicly affirm and sign this statement:

> I solemnly declare in the presence of God and the Trustees of this Seminary, that I do *ex animo* believe the Scriptures of the Old and New Testament to be the inspired word of God and the only perfect rule of faith and practice. I believe *The Augsburg Confession* (1530) to be a summary and just exhibition of the fundamental doctrines of the word of God. I declare that I approve of the general principles of church government adopted by the Lutheran Church in this Country and believe them to be consistent with the Word of God. And I do solemnly promise not to teach anything, either directly or by insinuation, which shall appear to me to contradict or to be in any degree more or less remote, inconsistent with the doctrines or principles avowed in this declaration. On the contrary, I promise, by the aid of God, to vindicate and inculcate these doctrines and principles in opposition to the views of Atheists, Deists, Jews, Socinians, Unitarians, Calvinists, Arians, Universalists, Pelagians, Antinomians, and all other errorists, while I remain a professor in this Seminary.[817]

---

[817] Heins, p.37.

In 1888, the Classical Department introduced the freshman year of a Collegiate Course, and in 1927, it expanded to a four-year college and was moved to Oneonta, New York. It continues to the present day as "Hartwick College." The Theological Department took the name Hartwick Seminary when it moved to Brooklyn, New York, in 1930. After years of financial struggle, the Seminary officially closed in the spring of 1940.[818] The Academy remained at the original location until 1934, when classes ceased.[819]

Hartwick Seminary, although it officially closed in 1940, had a profound influence on the piety of St. Paul's. In addition to supplying eight pastors, three sons of St. Paul's, who became clergymen, also attended Hartwick Seminary; i.e., the Rev. William Edwin Traver (1847-1930), the Rev. Chester Henry Traver (1848-1929), and the Rev. John Gideon Traver (1863-1941).[820] In addition, another son of St. Paul's, the Rev. Roy Steward, current president of the Evangelical Lutheran Conference and Ministerium, graduated from Hartwick College. Hartwick Seminary is fondly remembered in the records and archives of St. Paul's (Wurtemburg).

The Lutheran Theological Seminary at Gettysburg was founded in 1826. Nine of the thirty pastors who have served at St. Paul's (Wurtemburg) were educated at the Gettysburg Seminary. It is interesting to note that Gettysburg was selected for the location of the General Synod's new seminary for the same reason that generals on both sides during the American Civil War chose this location for the decisive battle, July 1, 2, and 3, 1863; i.e., that Gettysburg—even in 1826!—was located on an excellent turnpike supported by a hub of roads.[821]

Lutheran Theological Seminary-Gettysburg
Name, Tenure at St. Paul's, *(Graduation Date)*
Rev. William Nace Scholl, D.D., 1850-1855, *(1833)*
Rev. George Neff, D.D., 1855-1876, *(1842)*
Rev. Joseph G. Griffith, D.D., 1876 -1881, *(1867)*
Rev. George William Fortney, 1888-1895; *(1873)*
Rev. Herbert Finch, 1949-1954, *(1902)*
Rev. Rolf W. Eschke, 1959-1962, *(unknown)*
Rev. William Howard Beck, D.Min., 1968-1970, *(1966)*
Rev. Daniel M. Strobel, 1978-1984, *(1978)*
Rev. Mark D. Isaacs, S.T.M., D.Min., Ph.D., 1996-present *(1992)*

The School of Theology at Susquehanna University supplied one pastor, Elder Jay Himes. Susquehanna University was founded in 1858, in Selinsgrove, Pennsylvania, as "the Missionary Institute." Abdel Ross Wentz states that the Missionary Institute was

---

[818] Ibid., p.107.

[819] http://info.hartwick.edu/library/archives/seminary/moreinfo.html#backlist <June 3, 2006>

[820] Heins, p.134.

[821] Abdel Ross Wentz, *The History of Gettysburg Theological Seminary: 1826-1926* (Philadelphia: United Lutheran Publication House, 1926), p.99.

founded due to a "difference of opinion within the General Synod."[822] Wolf explains that the original intent of the Missionary Institute "was to prepare for the Lutheran ministry such candidates as were either too far advanced in years, or prevented by other circumstances, from pursuing a collegiate course and full theological curriculum."[823]

Theological School at Susquehanna University
Name**,** Tenure at St. Paul's, *(Graduation Date)*
Rev. Elder Jay Himes, 1924-1946 *(c.1924)*

The Lutheran Theological Seminary at Philadelphia was founded in 1864. The roots of the Philadelphia Lutheran Seminary go back to 1747, and the founding of the first Lutheran Synod in North America; i.e., the Ministerium of Pennsylvania, by Halle missionary and church planter Henry Melchior Mühlenberg. The Lutheran Theological Seminary at Philadelphia was founded in 1864, as a conservative reaction to the "American Lutheranism" controversy and the resultant General Synod-General Conference schism. This separation was partly in response to the theology of the Lutheran Theological Seminary at Gettysburg, which was perceived by many more conservative Lutherans as being too committed to American cultural accommodation rather than confessional Lutheran orthodoxy.

Lutheran Theological Seminary-Philadelphia
Name**,** Tenure at St. Paul's, *(Graduation Date)*
Rev. Frederick Charles Dunn, 1963-1967, *(1963)*
Rev. Sylvester Bader, 1970-1977, *(1938)*
Rev. Richard Mowry, 1984-1996, *(1968)*

It is interesting to note that *The Book of Concord* (1580) has been officially translated and edited three times by members of the Philadelphia Lutheran Seminary faculty; i.e., Henry Eyster Jacobs (1911), Theodore G. Tappert (1959) and Timothy J. Wengert (2000).

Reflecting the influence of the New York Synod, after 1963 Philadelphia Seminary supplied three pastors; i.e., Dunn, Bader, and Mowry. For two-hundred and three years, until Philadelphia graduate Pastor Fred Dunn arrived in 1963, the pastors who have served the people of St. Paul's (Wurtemburg) were educated at Halle University, Hartwick Seminary, and Gettysburg Seminary.

---

[822] Abdel Ross Wentz, *A Basic History of Lutheranism in America*, p.112.

[823] Edmund Jacob Wolf, *The Lutherans in America: A Story of Struggle, Progress, Influence and Marvelous Growth* (New York: J.A. Hill & Co., 1889), p.344.

Seminary Affiliation Unknown
    Rev. Johann Friedrich Ernst, 1794-1798
    Rev. William J. Eyer, 1825-1837
    Rev. Augustus Theodosius Geissenhainer, 1838-1840[824]
    Rev. Carl E. Rosomer, 1947-1949
    Rev. John L. de Papp, 1955-1958

---

[824] Privately tutored by his well known uncle the Rev. Fredrick William Geissenhainer, Sr.

Chapter Twelve: Clergy Who Have Served St. Paul's (Wurtemburg)

Historically, trying to procure a pastor for St. Paul's was not an easy proposition. For example, the Church Council Minutes of September 4, 1916 state that "the candidacy of Rev. T. W. Keller as Pastor of our Church was considered... and the election of Rev. Keller was declared unanimous." However, a notation in the Minutes from September 11, 1916 state, " Rev. Keller by letter to the Secretary declined the Call to come to Wurtemburg... His wife refusing to come out in the open country."[825]

During the past two-hundred and fifty years, the people of St. Paul's have been served by at least thirty pastors. For some of these pastors, all that we know is that they were here. Others preached in Wurtemburg, and went on to write books, to serve the Synod or Ministerium in leadership positions, or to teach at Hartwick Seminary. Some left the ministry. A few changed denominations. All of them contributed to the unique character and history of St. Paul's.

John Christopher Hartwick, or Johannes Christophorus Hartwig[826] (January 6, 1714-July 17, 1796), was an eccentric, misogynistic, idealistic Pietist Lutheran pastor who served Palatine congregations in the Hudson River Valley—including the Staatsburg Church—from 1746 until 1758. His name is associated with both Hartwick Seminary (1779 to 1940) and Hartwick College (1927 to the present).

He was born in Molschleben, in the Duchy of Saxe-Gotha, in the province of Thuringia, and educated at Halle University. His father was Andreas Hartwig, and we know that Johannes had an older sister named Ana Barbara Brigitta, and two younger twin brothers named Sebastian and Conrad.[827] Henry Hardy Heins states that, other than these few names, "the early life of Hartwick is almost completely lost in obscurity."[828]

However, one source lists Hartwick as a theology student from Molschleben "connected for a short time with Dr. J. H. Callenberg's *Institutum Judaicum*; i.e., a school in Halle that existed from 1728 to 1791, to "train missionaries for work among the Jews and Mohammedans."[829]

---

[825] *Church Record: Wurtemburg Lutheran Church, 1895-1920* (September 4, 1916), p.78. NOTE: See Wurtemburg Archives # 139.

[826] Heins notes that "the name has suffered a large variety of spellings, including Hartwyk, Hartwich, Hardwig, Hardwick, and Hardwicke. J.C.H. was never consistent himself, but he usually signed his name 'Hardwick.'" Heins, p.1.

[827] Ibid.

[828] Ibid.

[829] Ibid., p.2.

For eschatological reasons, the conversion of the Jews was a particular Pietist concern.[830] For example, in *Pia Desideria* (1675), Philip Jacob Spener writes, "in order for the Jews to be converted the True Church must be in a holier state than now if it's holy life is to be a means of conversion, or at least the implements to such conversion."[831]

While at Halle University, Hartwick met and studied with the great future patriarch of the Lutheran church in America, Henry Melchior Mühlenberg (1711-1787).[832] This Halle-forged association would later have implications for the future of Lutheranism in Upstate New York.

Following the completion of his studies at Halle, Dr. Philipp David Kräuter of London,[833] and Dr. Wagner of Hamburg negotiated a call for Hartwick in the central Hudson Valley parish of East Camp and Rhinebeck.[834] This would have included the people meeting for worship at "the Staatsburg Church." At the time, ""the Staatsburg Church" was a preaching outpost on the Stephen Fraleigh patent.[835]

Although Hartwick had been studying at the Pietist Halle University, his call came from the orthodox Hamburg Consistory.[836] After receiving this call, on November 24, 1745, Hartwick was ordained by Dr. Philipp David Kräuter in London's German Trinity Lutheran Church.[837]

In 1746, Hartwick arrived in the Hudson River Valley. Records indicate that he spent twelve years as a pastor in the area (1746 to 1758), riding a circuit that included Rhinebeck (the Evangelical Lutheran Church of St. Peter the Apostle), Staatsburg (later St. Paul's Wurtemburg), East Camp (Germantown), Ancram, and Tarbush (Manorton).[838]

Falckner and Berkenmeyer: Lutheran Clergy Pioneers

Justus Falckner, who had also been educated at the Halle University, arrived in America in 1703. On November 24, 1703, he became the first Lutheran pastor ordained in America. For the next twenty years, Falckner devoted himself to establishing and

---

[830] See Mark D. Isaacs, *THE END? Textual Criticism and Apocalyptic Speculation in Johann Albrecht Bengel: Lessons to be learned from the Godly scholar who calculated the Second Coming of Jesus Christ as June 18, 1836* (Boca Raton, FL: Universal Publishers, 2008).

[831] Spener, p.77.

[832] Decker, p.23.

[833] Dr. Philipp David Kräuter served as pastor of the Hamburg Trinity Lutheran Church in London from 1742 to 1767. *The Albany Protocol*, p.525.

[834] Heins, p.2.

[835] Edward M. Smith, *Documentary History of Rhinebeck, in Dutchess County, New York* (Rhinebeck, 1881, 1974 reprint edition), p.107.

[836] Shelley Burtner Wallace, "John Christopher Hartwick: Orthodox and Pietism," Hartwick College's alumni magazine *THE WICK* , Summer, 1996.

[837] Heins, p.2.

[838] Ibid., p.2.

maintaining congregations in New Jersey and New York, including small-scattered congregations in the Hudson River Valley. He died in 1723.[839]

Two years after Falckner's death, the Rev. Wilhelm Christoph Berkenmeyer (1687-1751), an authoritarian old-line orthodox Lutheran pastor from Hamburg, Germany arrived in New York City.[840] He had studied theology at the orthodox University of Altdorf. Berkenmeyer "would have nothing to do with Pietism in any form... theologically he would be classified as an ultraconservative."[841]

Berkenmeyer assumed the authority of superintendent of all Lutheran parishes in New York and New Jersey. By 1735, he had revised "the Amsterdam Church Constitution," making it "more suitable for the colonies." "More suitable" meant that Dutch and German Lutheran churches in the New York and New Jersey area were to be bound together under his charge "in a synod of sort."[842] Establishing a headquarters in the Upper Hudson Parish of Loonenburg (now Athens, New York), the "arbitrary and autocratic"[843] Berkenmeyer required that his forty-eight-page orthodox constitution be signed by all area church councils and pastors. He also required that congregations accept only "orthodox Lutheran clergy from academies in Hamburg, London, or Amsterdam."[844] Not surprisingly, Berkenmeyer's strict supervision and authoritarian manner were not always welcomed by the area parishes and clergy.

One such conflict involved the Rev. Johannes Spahler, who had refused to sign Berkenmeyer's Amsterdam Constitution. Instead, Spahler used the Nassau-Itzstein and Rhenish Constitution. Starting in 1732, Pastor Spahler served as pastor of the Lutheran churches in Rhinebeck (St. Peter's) and Germantown.

When he arrived in the area, Spahler conducted house-to-house visits with parish members. During these visits he was shocked that young and old alike "knew nothing at all, and some who could hardly recite the Lord's Prayer or the Creed."[845] Some had not received Holy Communion for many years, and others had never received the Sacrament. Some children were so uneducated that they did not know what a pastor was. Others, "ran away into the woods or hid when the pastor came."[846]

In 1736, Berkenmeyer grew frustrated with Spahler because he refused both to sign the Amsterdam Constitution and to recognize him as "Superintendent." In an effort to undermine Spahler, Berkenmeyer invited parishioners from Germantown and Rhinebeck to meet with him to express their dissatisfaction.[847]

---

[839] Justus Falckner, translated and edited by Martin Kessler, *Fundamental Instruction: Justus Faulkner's Catechism* (Delhi, NY: American Lutheran Publicity Bureau, 2003), p.16.

[840] Nelson, p.15.

[841] Ruth Decker, p.19.

[842] Ibid., p.19.

[843] Ibid.

[844] Wallace, *THE WICK.*

[845] Decker, p.21.

[846] Ibid., p.21.

[847] Ibid., p. 22.

Spahler, apparently a man with "an independent disposition," hardened his position. One Sunday morning Berkenmeyer arrived from across the Hudson River at one of Spahler's churches to confront him. A long and heated public argument ensued. In the end, Spahler refused to sign the Amsterdam Constitution or submit to Berkenmeyer's authority. Disgusted with the entire episode, Spahler soon resigned and left the area. Berkenmeyer then filled the vacant position, leading the congregations at Rhinebeck, East Camp, Tar Bush, Ancram, and Staatsburg for the next ten years.[848] Because Berkenmeyer was based on the west side of the Hudson River in Loonenburg, and because the congregations on the east side of the Hudson River were scattered, it is doubtful that his pastoral care was very effective.

In 1746, after several calls for relief, Berkenmeyer's replacement for the parishes on the east side of the Hudson River was dispatched from London. Thus, Johannes Christopher Hartwick arrived to take over these scattered parishes. Upon his arrival, apparently in an effort to avoid another Spahler-like conflict with the heavy-handed Berkenmeyer, Hartwick signed the Amsterdam Constitution.

However, for Berkenmeyer, adherence to the Amsterdam Constitution was not enough. He soon charged that Hartwick was a "crypto-Herrnhuter [i.e., a radical Pietist]." Just as he had done a few years before with Spahler, working with a few disgruntled members of the Rhinebeck congregations, Berkenmeyer sought to undermine and depose Hartwick.

Thus, thanks to Berkenmeyer's incitements and intrigues [and undoubtedly Hartwick's eccentric behavior!], a full-blown church conflict erupted. Hartwick later wrote that, during the conflict, "I fought with the wild animals in Rhinebeck, after the fashion of men, since Berkenmeyer's 'epicurean' followers attacked me in church, not only with words, but also with fists, tore off my wig, hit me in the face and wanted forcefully to drag me out of the church."[849]

During the summer of 1750, Henry Melchior Mühlenberg, the father of American Lutheranism, traveled from Pennsylvania in an attempt to settle the dispute between Hartwick, Berkenmeyer, and the Rhinebeck area congregations.[850] Mühlenberg was apparently able to negotiate an uneasy truce between all factions. The wounded Hartwick remained in the area until 1758, when he resigned.[851]

While Pastor Berkenmeyer was certainly an autocratic manipulator, Hartwick did not help his own situation. Hartwick was a true eccentric, who has been described as "restless, desultory, and uncouth." He was arrogant, blunt, and unkept. He often preached in his blanket coat and he changed his linen infrequently. Like Berkenmeyer, Hartwick had a rigid personality. He had little tolerance for his parishioners' flaws and vices. He reportedly forced his parishioners to sign a covenant that "they would forswear

---

[848] Ibid., p.22.

[849] Ronald H. Bailey, *Hartwick College: A Bicentennial History (1797-1997)* (Hartwick College, Oneonta, New York, 1997), p.21.

[850] *The Journals of Henry Melchior Mühlenberg,* translated by Theodore G. Tappert and John W. Doberstein (Philadelphia: The Evangelical Lutheran Ministerium of Pennsylvania and Adjacent States and The Mühlenberg Press, 1942, 1945, 1958), vol. I, p.252.

[851] Bailey, p.22-24.

shooting, horse racing, boozing, and dancing."[852] Hartwick was known for his epic two-hour sermons and for his long rambling prayers. It was said that servants dreaded visits from Pastor Hartwick because of his long prayers before eating meals.

In addition, the peculiar Hartwick was a determined woman hater. He was such a fanatical misogynist that if he saw that he was about to meet a woman on the road he would cross over, or even to leap over a fence in order to avoid her. He regarded women as "a bosom serpent, a domestic evil, a night invasion, and a mid-day devil."[853]

Once, when one of Hartwick's epic sermons happened to be interrupted by the barking of a dog, with great indignation he exclaimed that people "had better keep their dogs and children at home, and it would not matter if they kept their women there too."[854]

With his undiplomatic outbursts and odd behavior, he frequently alienated his congregations and the area clergy.

At the same time, in many ways, the idealistic and visionary John Christopher Hartwick was a man ahead of his time. In the spring of 1764, while living in Philadelphia, Hartwick wrote a newspaper article vehemently protesting the death penalty for theft on the grounds that such a punishment was contrary to divine law. Reportedly, city officials were so incensed that they suppressed the article and almost threw the hapless Hartwick into prison.[855]

In opposition to the exclusiveness of private schools, Hartwick also envisioned State-run educational institutions. In his will, Hartwick expressed the desire that his estate be used to establish a public school and not a private school.[856]

After his service in Rhinebeck, for the remainder of his life, Hartwick apparently traveled from place to place living off of the goodwill and hospitality of friends and acquaintances. Perhaps it was his odd personality, or perhaps it was his inability to find a congregation willing to submit to his strict moral dictates that confirmed Hartwick's belief that American society needed to be reformed by regulating settlement patterns and enforcing a disciplined code for each community. Traces of his "missionary service" have been found in more than twenty Lutheran congregations from Waldoboro, Maine to Frederick, Maryland.[857]

In 1796, Hartwick died suddenly of asthma at Clermont Manor,[858] the home of Robert R. Livingston (1746-1813). He was first buried in the old Lutheran churchyard in Germantown, New York.[859] In February 1798, his remains were relocated to Ebenezer (now First) Lutheran Church in Albany, and interred in the chancel floor under a white

---

[852] Wallace, *THE WICK.*

[853] Heins, pp.4-5.

[854] Ibid.

[855] Ibid., p.6.

[856] Ibid., p.7.

[857] Ibid., p.6.

[858] Ibid,. p.10.

[859] Decker, p.25.

marble "sepulcher stone."[860] In 1816, Ebenezer Church was rebuilt, and Hartwick's remains were disinterred and removed to a city cemetery in Albany. Then, in 1868, this old cemetery became part of Albany's new Washington Park. Bodies were removed to the Albany Rural Cemetery. However, in a letter dated October 4, 1945, the superintendent of the Albany Cemetery Association stated that "the remains of John Christopher Hartwick were not among those so moved."[861] Thus, his mortal remains are somewhere in Albany's Washington Square Park.[862]

John Christopher Hartwick died in 1794 at Clermont, the home of "Chancellor" Robert R. Livingston (1746-1813). Among other accomplishments, Livingston was a member of "the Committee of Five" that drafted the Declaration of Independence (1776).
In 1803, while serving as U.S. Minister to France under President Thomas Jefferson, he negotiated the Louisiana Purchase.
Livingston was also a active Freemason.
In 1784, he was appointed the first Grand Master of the Grand Lodge of New York.

Ordinarily, the death of an eccentric parishless Lutheran clergyman would have gone largely unnoticed by a majority of people. However, this was not the case with John Christopher Hartwick. Starting in 1754, Hartwick made a series of land purchases, obtaining the majority of a 24,000 acre patent from the Mohawk Indians in Otesgo County, New York.[863] Hartwick's vision was to lease his wilderness land to suitable Christian settlers for the establishment of a utopian "New Jerusalem." Hartwick believed that by regulating settlement patterns, and by enforcing a strict moral code, American

---

[860] Heins, p.13.

[861] Ibid., p.14.

[862] Ibid.

[863] Ibid, p.5.

society could be reformed. He envisioned a utopian community dedicated to the principles of pious living.[864]

To accomplish this vision, Hartwick commissioned his neighboring landowner, Judge William Cooper to help build his "New Jerusalem." The practical Cooper essentially ignored Hartwick's criteria of attracting Christian tenants and leased the valuable property indiscriminately to all those willing to pay. In the end, most—if not all—of Cooper's tenants had little interest in Hartwick's utopian Christian scheme.[865]

Hartwick died in 1796 without having fulfilled his dream for a "New Jerusalem," but left complete instructions in his will for the organization of a seminary. Hartwick left his largely undeveloped land to endow "an institution for training up young men to become missionaries among the Indians according to *The Augsburg Confession* (1530) and the tenets of the Evangelical Lutheran Church."[866]

The executors of his will, Jeremiah Van Rensselaer and Frederick A. Mühlenberg [son of Henry Melchior Mühlenberg] had difficulty enacting Hartwick's wishes because he complicated matters by designating Jesus Christ as his heir. Despite this, the executors did manage to get through that and other complex legal challenges. Thus, in September 1797, they founded Hartwick Seminary, the first Lutheran Seminary in America. However, the decision on the final location of the school was postponed. Dr. John Christopher Kunze, son-in-law of Henry Melchior Mühlenberg, was named director, and taught theology at his home in New York City;[867] the Rev. Anthony Theodore Braun taught sciences and languages at Albany,[868] and the Rev. John Frederick Ernst taught elementary school on the Hartwick Patent.[869]

There continued to be a debate about the permanent location of the Seminary but, due to the persistence of the residents of the Hartwick Patent, the first seminary building was established there in 1815, and Rev. Ernest Lewis Hazelius became the first principal.

During the debate on where to locate Hartwick's seminary, Rhinebeck was also considered as a location, with the Rev. Dr. Frederick Henry Quitman being named as professor of theology.[870] In 1799, Dr. Quitman's congregation [the Evangelical Lutheran Church of St. Peter the Apostle, and perhaps the Staatsburg Church] made a generous offer of land and money in an effort to have the seminary located in Rhinebeck. Heins states that it was likely that, if the offer had been accepted, Dr. Quitman would have been the permanent theological professor [at the time, Quitman was one of the best-educated and most experienced Lutheran pastors in America]. However, "since he was an outspoken Rationalist this would have probably not have helped the school's influence any."[871]

---

[864] Ibid., p.7.

[865] Ibid., p.8.

[866] Ibid., p.7.

[867] Ibid., p.17.

[868] Ibid.

[869] Ibid., p.8.

[870] Ibid., p.23.

[871] Ibid., p.23.

After years of financial struggle, Hartwick Seminary was officially closed in 1940. In 1927, the Seminary relocated to Oneonta, New York and became Hartwick College, a four year liberal arts college.[872] The archives of Hartwick Seminary, including many rare theology books brought from Germany, are housed in the campus library at Hartwick College.

Rev. Johann Friederich Ries (1722-1791), who succeeded John Christopher Hartwick on January 7, 1759,[873] served in Rhinebeck for more than twenty-four years (March 7, 1760 to January 5, 1783), including during the American Revolution.[874] The Rev. George Neff states that, "the first minister who preached to this people was Pastor Ries, who commenced his labor in 1760 and continued faithfully among them a number of years."[875] Lawrence states that "Johannes Ries, who pastored at the Evangelical Lutheran Church of St. Peter the Apostle, was also at Wurtemburg [i.e., "the Staatsburg Church"] in 1760 and performed the first baptism in the congregation."[876]

Ries [pronounced "Reece"] was a native of Rothenburg-on-the-Tauber.[877] He was the son of a Lutheran pastor, and he was "regularly ordained by the Consistory of Rothenburg."[878] In Germany, he studied both medicine and theology.[879] Although there is no proof, Ries may have been trained at the Halle Institution. He came to the Central Hudson Parish sometime prior to 1760.[880]

The Rev. J. A. Earnest, D.D., states that "Ries seems to have lived in New York City in 1750." After the 1750 "conflict resolution" conference in Rhinebeck, Henry Melchior Mühlenberg and John Christopher Hartwick, apparently, stopped to visit Ries in September on there way back to Pennsylvania.[881] Perhaps it was this visit that planted the seed in Pastor Ries' mind that led to his later ministry among the scattered congregations of the Hudson River Valley.

---

[872] Ronald H. Bailey, *Hartwick College: A Bicentennial History: 1797-1997* (Oneonta, NY: Hartwick College).

[873] The Rev. J. A. Earnest, "Centennial Address given at the Evangelical Lutheran Church of St. Peter the Apostle in Rhinebeck, New York, September 2, 1886," p. 10. Archives of St. Paul's (Wurtemburg).

[874] Ibid.

[875] George Neff, *1873 Wurtemburg Church Record Book*.

[876] Lawrence, p.99.

[877] A group from St. Paul's (Wurtemburg) had the privilege of spending several days in Rothenburg-on-Tauber in December 2004. It is a quant and remarkable "walled" medieval German city.

[878] Simon Hart and Harry J. Kreider, p.369.

[879] Decker, p.28.

[880] Walter V. Miller, *Christ's Lutheran Church, Germantown, New York; 250th Anniversary: 1710-1960* (Germantown, N.Y.: Christ Lutheran Church, 1960), p.30.

[881] Ibid.

During his career, Pastor Ries served many parishes, including German congregations in New York City, and then in Stone Arabia.[882] In this area, Pastor Ries served the Evangelical Lutheran Church of St. Peter the Apostle, the Staatsburg Church, Christ's Lutheran (East Camp-Germantown),[883] and St. Thomas Lutheran Church[884] in Churchtown, New York.

In December 2006, Pastor Mark D. Isaacs led a tour group from St. Paul's (Wurtemburg) to "Lutherland," Germany. Among the sites we visited was Rothenburg-on-Tauber, the home of our first pastor Johannes Ries.
Photo: Linda A. Isaacs.

While in Pennsylvania, prior to coming to New York, Mühlenberg "advised Ries to avoid New York church politics;"[885] i.e., the self-appointed orthodox Lutheran overseer the Rev. Wilhelm Christoph Berkenmeyer of Loonenburg.[886] Thus, Pastor Ries aligned himself with the Hallean Pietist Mühlenberg against the controlling heavy handed Orthodoxy of Berkenmeyer.[887]

---

[882] Simon Hart and Harry J. Kreider, p.370.

[883] Founded in 1710.

[884] Founded in 1730.

[885] Lawrence, p.15.

[886] Ibid., p.7.

[887] Decker, p.29.

Upon his death in 1791, "Ries was buried under the altar of St. Thomas Lutheran Church in Churchtown, New York."[888] Apparently this church building stood where the present cemetery is located.[889] Pastor Ries' headstone can still be found in the St. Thomas Cemetery.

According to Dr. George Neff, "Rev. John F. Ries"
was "the first minister who preached to this people."
His headstone, [when this picture was taken]
was located perpendicular to two other headstones.
It has obviously been relocated from his original grave.
Photo: The Rev. Dr. Mark D. Isaacs.

Rev. George Heinrich Pfeiffer was born in Germany c.1747. He died in Rhinebeck on October 26, 1827. Pastor Pfeiffer served St. Paul's (Wurtemburg) for more than twelve years—from May 17, 1784 until 1794.

According to J.A. Earnest, in his old age, "Mr. Pfeiffer was much afflicted by impairment of the reason" and he "continued to reside among his people until his death." During this time, he "was the recipient of many kindnesses from his distinguished successor [Dr. Quitman] and the regular beneficiary of the New York Ministerium." For many years the New York Ministerium solicited voluntary contributions to financially support this faithful old minister.[890]

---

[888] Ibid., p.29.

[889] Ibid.

[890] The Rev. J. A. Earnest, "Centennial Address," p.10.

Pastor Pfeiffer is buried in the churchyard of the Evangelical Lutheran Church of St. Peter the Apostle ["the Old Stone Church"] in Rhinebeck, and the stone bears the inscription; *"Sacred to the memory of Rev. George Heinrich Pfeiffer, a native of Germany, pastor of the Lutheran congregation in Rhinebeck, who died October 26, 1827, aged about 80 years."*[891]

Pastor George Pfeiffer's grave and headstone
can still be found in the churchyard of the Old Stone Church.
The inscription has been badly eroded by acid rain.
Photo: The Rev. Dr. Mark D. Isaacs.

Rev. Johann Friedrich Ernst (1748-1805) served St. Paul's (Wurtemburg)—and area parishes—from 1794 until 1798. Walter V. Miller writes that "it is said that this man was not German-born, but that he hailed from Pennsylvania. His family consisted of seven children; four daughters and three sons. For some reason the new pastor was unable to conduct the affairs of his pastorate in a harmonious manner."[892] Ruth Decker states that "his pastorate was marked with conflict and dissent."[893] Thus, after four years Ernst resigned his charge and returned to Pennsylvania.

Later in 1798, the Rev. John Frederick Ernst apparently relocated to what is now the Cooperstown, New York area. From 1797 to 1802, he was listed as "Pastor of the Hartwick Patent."[894] According to Heins, "Ernst was appointed [by the executors of

---

[891] James H. Smith provides the text inscribed on Pastor Pfeiffer's tombstone, p.274.

[892] Miller, p.32.

[893] Decker, p.29.

[894] Heins, p.61.

Hartwick's will] to settle as pastor in the Hartwick tract in Otsego County on condition that the residents thereof extend to him a call to preach and to instruct the inhabitants in the lower school branches."[895] Evidently, Pastor Ernst was sent to this area, "mainly as a feeler move to see if the location might be suitable for the possible future establishment of the whole institution [i.e., The Hartwick Seminary].[896] At the time, Pastor Ernst was the second regularly employed clergyman in the village of Cooperstown. When Hartwick Seminary was opened "Ernst became a member of the faculty."[897]

The Rev. Frederick Henry Quitman, D.D.,[898] served as pastor of St. Paul's Lutheran Church of Wurtemburg from February 18, 1798 to August 23, 1825. In addition to Wurtemburg, he also served Lutheran churches in Rhinebeck, Germantown, and Livingston.[899] He was the son of Stephen Henry and Anna Quitman. He was born August 7, 1760, in the Duchy of Cleves in Westphalia on an island in the lower Rhine. His father, Stephen Henry Quitman, held an important office in the Prussian Government.

Frederick Henry Quitman, manifesting at an early age a great love for books, more than common intelligence, and superior talents and application to study, was placed by his father into the celebrated school of Halle.[900] After receiving the advantage of a liberal education, Frederick then transferred to Halle University to become a Lutheran clergyman. Aware of his considerable talents and abilities, his immediate family and friends were not in favor of his entering the ministry. But his predilection for that profession was too strong to be yielded.

Quitman studied at Halle University during the period of "Illumination," under such lights as George Christian Knapp (1753-1825), August Herman Niemeyer (1754-1828), Johann Salomo Semler (1725-1791), and other eminent professors of the Rationalist School. At the time, Halle University, which had been the seat of the Pietist movement, had shifted to the new *Aufklarung* Rationalism.[901] At the same time, Hines explains that while "Dr. Quitman was a staunch supporter of the unpopular Rationalistic school of theology… he did not force anyone to share his [liberal] views."[902]

---

[895] Ibid.

[896] Ibid., p.18.

[897] Miller, p.32 and Heins, p.22.

[898] Taken from *The Minutes of the 27th Synod of the Evangelical Lutheran Ministerium of New York and Adjacent Parts* held in Albany, New York, October 15, 1832 (Hudson, NY: Ashbol Stoddard, 1832), p.15. Light edits and clarifications have been included to deepen the understanding of the modern reader.

[899] William Hull, *History of the Lutheran Church in Dutchess County* (New York, J.E. Wible Printer: Gettysburg, PA, 1881), p.7.

[900] At this time the Halle Institution in Halle, Germany was the Mecca of the world-wide Lutheran Pietist movement.

[901] Dr. Quitman's "German Rationalist" approach to philosophy and theology made him a favorite scapegoat for orthodox Lutheran Confessionalists later in the nineteenth century.

[902] Heins, p.16.

After completing his academic course with honors, and spending two years as a *private docent* [a tutor] to the family of the Prince of Waldeck Frederick, he became connected with the Lutheran Consistory of the United [Dutch] Provinces. In 1783, he was ordained by that body, and sent to be pastor of the Lutheran congregation in the Island of Curacao. Rev. Quitman remained in this situation, useful, respected, and happy, for the space of fourteen years. During the summer of 1795, he was induced, when political convulsions [a slave rebellion in Curacao!] forced him, to convey his wife and children to Philadelphia. He had the intention of returning to Holland after a short time.[903]

The Rev. Frederick Henry Quitman, D.D.
Art Credit: Rhinebeck Historical Society.

At this point "Providence frustrated this design." There was a profound shortage of German-speaking Lutheran pastors willing to serve in the rustic wilds of Upstate New York. Learning of this need, Quitman saw a far more extensive field of action than in his native land. Thus, "he was determined to spend the residue of his life on this side of the Atlantic."[904]

For more than thirty years, Dr. Quitman divided his time among a number of small and scattered Lutheran churches in the Hudson River Valley. These congregations were dispersed groupings of German-speaking farmers and craftsmen. During his ministry, Dr. Quitman often preached seven or eight times a week, in either German, Low Dutch,

---

[903] Earnest, p.11.

[904] J.C. Jennson, *American Lutheran Biographies* (Milwaukee, 1890), p.76.

or English.[905] In addition to Greek, Latin, and Hebrew, Dr. Quitman could also speak French and Swedish.[906]

During his lifetime, he "had the reputation for being one of the most learned and eloquent men in the Lutheran Church in this country."[907] "In his preaching he was brief, biblical, practical and impressive inculcating with great energy the Christian gospel... [and] He never used a manuscript in the pulpit."[908]

A Rare Painting of Dr. Quitman
Source: Wilson Library at the University of North Carolina.

Quitman first served the associated churches of Schoharie and Kobles Kill [until 1798[909]]; and afterwards he served congregations in Rhinebeck, Wurtemburg, Germantown, and Livingston.

The Old Stone Church Parsonage [i.e., "The Quitman House"] was built for Rev. Quitman in 1798, and was enlarged during the ministry of the Rev. Fredrick M. Bird.[910] Dr. Quitman's call required him to preach eighteen Sundays and three festival days at the Evangelical Lutheran Church of St. Peter the Apostle in Rhinebeck; eighteen Sundays and three festival days at Germantown; nine Sundays and one festival day at Wurtemburg; and seven Sundays and one festival day at Livingston.

---

[905] Edmund Jacob Wolf, *The Lutherans in America* (New York: J.A. Hill & Co., 1889), p.306.

[906] Earnest, p.11.

[907] Ibid.

[908] Wackerhagen, pp.57-58.

[909] Ibid.

[910] Hull, p.9.

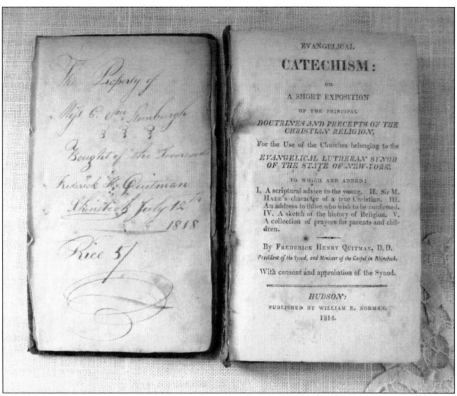

Dr. Quitman's "Evangelical Catechism (1814)" proved to be
very controversial among more conservative Lutherans.
Source: The archives of the Quitman House.

His salary from the Evangelical Lutheran Church of St. Peter the Apostle was thirty pounds New York currency—which was $750—ten bushels of wheat, and the use of the parsonage and church lands. From the Germantown congregation, he was paid thirty-five pounds and eight bushels of wheat, firewood, and use of parsonage and church lands, or twenty-five pounds additional if he did not choose to use them. From Wurtemburg he received thirty pounds and eight bushels of wheat. From Livingston, he received twenty-five pounds and eight bushels of wheat. It is interesting to note early American clergymen, because there was a shortage of coinage and specie, were often paid in kind in a barter arrangement by their farmer members.

His call from St. Paul's Lutheran Church of Wurtemburg came with a resolution, that he should notice the names attached to the call, and that he should be free from all pastoral duties to those who contributed nothing to the support of the Church.[911]

After the decease of the venerable Dr. John Christopher Kunze (August 5, 1744-July 24, 1807),[912] Dr. Quitman was elected President of the Evangelical Lutheran Ministerium of the State of New York and Adjacent Parts; to which from one term to another, he was unanimously reelected, until 1825, when he declined reappointment due to his inability to

---

[911] Several copies of his various calls [contracts] are in Wurtemburg archives.

[912] Dr. John Christopher Kunze, born in Leipzig, Germany, was an outstanding educator and Lutheran pastor. He was a coadjutor to Henry Mühlenberg—the patriarch of American Lutheranism—and professor of Oriental Languages at Columbia University (1784-1787) and professor at Hartwick Seminary until his death in 1807 (Heins, p.17).

travel. And so, for eighteen years, from 1807-1825, Dr. Quitman was "the forceful president of the New York Ministerium."[913]

In 1811, he received the honorary degree of Doctor of Divinity from Harvard University. To date, Dr. Quitman is the only Lutheran clergyman to receive this honor. And, so long as the condition of his health permitted him to attend their meetings he continued at the head of the Board of Trustees of Hartwick Seminary, through the partiality of his colleagues.

Dr. Quitman's "personal appearance was very imposing," he possessed a frame of uncommon vigor."[914] His "well-proportioned and ever erect frame stood full six feet high and was of great bulk, weighing generally about, and sometimes above three hundred pounds."[915] He had a mind of extraordinary power. Gifted with an astonishing memory, an acute judgment, and untiring industry, Dr. Quitman gathered for himself and others large stores of general knowledge, especially of theological science. He had "a fine personal appearance, and a cheerful disposition."[916] As a preacher, "he was universally confessed to be mighty in the Scriptures, convincing, eloquent, pathetic; and as a catechist, few in our country have equaled him."[917]

During this time, in addition to the toilsome functions of a parish pastor, Dr. Quitman also served as a private tutor of theological candidates. Dr. Quitman taught candidates both sacred and classical literature. Lutheran historian Abdel Ross Wentz notes that, "Dr, Quitman… instructed many young men in those parts in their theological branches."[918] He was rarely without students in one or other of these departments.[919]

Long before missionary efforts were employed by our communion in the State of' New York, and while the number of its clergymen was very small, Dr. Quitman was accustomed to pay an annual visit to outlaying destitute settlements and new societies riding a circuit of from one- hundred to two-hundred miles. On these visits Dr. Quitman would daily dispense the word of salvation, and administer the ordinances of the Gospel. On these trips, "his dwelling was the abode of hospitality; and his conversation, independent of the information it yielded, was marked by pleasantly good humor, and very unusual variety of topics and illustrations. One of the most striking traits of his character was frankness that abhorred all concealment and artifice."[920]

---

[913] Abdel Ross Wentz, *The Lutheran Church in American History* (Philadelphia: United Lutheran Publishing House, 1933), p.60

[914] April 23, 1851 letter from Rev. Augustus Wackerhagen, D.D. (1774-1865), his son-in-law, John G. Morris, *Fifty Years in the Lutheran Ministry* (Baltimore: James Young, 1878), p.57

[915] Ibid.

[916] John G. Morris, p.61.

[917] Ibid.

[918] Abdel Ross Wentz, *The Lutheran Church in American History*, p.60.

[919] In the days prior to the founding of theological seminaries such as Hartwick (1797) and Gettysburg (1826), potential Lutheran pastors would often study privately with a well educated pastor prior to ordination.

[920] From *The Minutes of the 27th Synod of the Evangelical Lutheran Ministerium of New York and Adjacent Parts* held in Albany, New York, October 15, 1832, p.15.

For example, once an aged female member of his congregation examined Dr. Quitman's face and asked, "Dominie, have you had the small pox?" "No, mother," he replied, "it has had me!"[921]

Another time, a cynical and skeptical old man, who was displeased with Dr. Quitman's exercise of pastoral authority, stated with a taunting air, "And what are ministers then?" The Doctor stated, "we are grindstones to grind rough people smooth."[922]

Although constitutionally ardent, and occasionally betrayed into vehemence by collision with those of similar ardor, Dr. Quitman cherished no feelings of ill will toward anyone, and gladly acknowledged merit wherever he discerned it.

The Rev. G.A. Linter, D.D., relates a story that illustrates the broad and liberal views of Dr. Quitman. Once, the Doctor was invited to preach at a gathering of Free and Accepted Masons. A member of the Evangelical Lutheran Church of St. Peter the Apostle [the Old Stone Church] heard about it. The concerned member came to the Parsonage to express his opposition to the matter. The member said to Dr. Quitman "My dear Pastor, I have understood that you are to preach before that Society which is in league with the Devil; and I could not rest till I had come and told you my feelings on the subject."[923]

"I am sorry," said the Doctor, "that you feel so, and to satisfy you that I intend to do no evil, I will read you the sermon which I have written for the occasion." So he produced the sermon; and, as he read the text, the simple-hearted man exclaimed, "My dear Sir, are you going to preach to these Freemasons from *The Holy Bible*? Then, I have no objection. If it is all right, I'll come and hear you." So he did, and was much pleased and edified by the sermon.[924]

The fear of man, or the fear of consequences, never drove Dr. Quitman from a purpose formed under the conviction of duty. And, while liberal [i.e., an enlightened Pietist Lutheran] in his principles, and most heartily opposed to schemes that seem to favor the imposition of a yoke upon the brethren, Dr. Quitman was nevertheless equally averse from controversy, and from all tendencies to lawlessness [i.e., antinomianalism] and confusion [i.e., lack of good order]. Dr. Quitman's grand aim in the sacred desk [the pulpit], was the inculcation of the plain, but with practical and mighty truths and lessons of the religion of the crucified and exalted Redeemer.[925]

In 1815, Dr. Quitman relinquished the charge at Germantown and Livingston, having prevailed upon them to call a minister for themselves. And, in 1824, in consequence of increasing infirmities, he was forced to relinquish his call at St. Paul's (Wurtemburg).

---

[921] John G. Morris, p.58.

[922] Ibid., p.59.

[923] Ibid.

[924] Ibid., p.61.

[925] From *The Minutes of the 27th Synod of the Evangelical Lutheran Ministerium of New York and Adjacent Parts* held in Albany, New York, October 15, 1832, p.15.

Dr. George Neff wrote, "In the year 1825, his health failing, and becoming feeble with age, he had to be carried into the pulpit where he preached sitting down and where he engaged in the regular Service of the sanctuary."[926]

In 1828, he was compelled by failing health, "to the deep regret of his parishioners at the Old Stone Church, to retire from all public labors." The *1832 Synod Minutes* state that "Growing weakness had confined him to his dwelling and chamber until Tuesday, June 26, [1832], when it pleased the parent of mercies to release him by the hand of' death from the sorrows and troubles of' this changeful world."[927]

The *1832 Synod Minutes* add:

> What amount of good resulted from the services of our departed friend cannot now be fully known, and will be disclosed in the final issue of human affairs. Dr. Quitman's example of indefatigable diligence, whilst enabled to work in the vineyard of the Lord, is well adapted to stimulate the zeal of those who have succeeded him in the same momentous vocation. And the last years of Dr. Quitman's life, though cheered by domestic affection and Christian hope, present an instance, calculated to inspire habitual humility and prayerful dependence on God, of the feebleness and imbecility, to which, in God's unsearchable wisdom, many of the most richly endowed among his children are suffered to be cast down.[928]

Rev. Chester H. Traver, D.D. wrote, "He was a man of commanding presence, highly respected by all just persons, but fearless anywhere. A large congregation assembled in 1832 at the Evangelical Lutheran Church of St. Peter the Apostle [the Old Stone Church] to pay tribute to his worth as a man, a citizen, and as a pastor and preacher."[929]

Dr. Quitman was buried in the churchyard in a grave that is located roughly half way between the Parsonage [the Quitman House] and the Evangelical Lutheran Church of St. Peter the Apostle, one of the congregations that he faithfully served for years. He was twice married. His first wife died in Curacao prior to his relocation to Rhinebeck. He left behind three daughters and four sons. One son, John Anthony Quitman, was a Brigadier General in the Mexican-American War, and he went on to serve as a Governor and Congressman from the State of Mississippi.

Lutheran historian Dr. Abdel Ross Wentz notes that "The Quitman Catechism... [was controversial] because it denied the inspiration and authority of *The Holy Bible* and

---

[926] George Neff, "Historical Sketch," *1873 Wurtemburg Church Record Book*.

[927] From *The Minutes of the 27th Synod of the Evangelical Lutheran Ministerium of New York and Adjacent Parts* held in Albany, New York, October 15, 1832, p.15.

[928] Ibid.

[929] Chester Henry Traver, "Rev. Chester Traver's History of Wurttemburgh Church: Former Rhinebecker Writes Interesting Sketch St. Paul's Lutheran Church" *The Rhinebeck Gazette*, September 18, 1915.

set at nought many of the main doctrines of the Lutheran Confessions and the Apostle's Creed... did not sell.*930*

Dr. Quitman's grave is located in the Churchyard of the Old Stone Church
Photo: The Rev. Dr. Mark D. Isaacs.

Dr. Quitman's publications are: *A Treatise on Magic, or the Intercourse between Spirits and Men* (1810); *An Evangelical Catechism, or a Short Exposition of the Principle Doctrines and Precepts of the Christian Religion* (1814); *Three Sermons, Preached Before the Evangelical Lutheran Synod in the town of Claverack, New York, September 1817* [the 300th anniversary of the posting of *The Ninety-Five Thesis* by Martin Luther in Wittenberg, Germany] (Hudson: William E. Norman, 1817);[931] and a hymnbook (1814).[932]

---

[930] Abdel Ross Wentz, *The Lutheran Church in American History*, p.117. A copy of Dr. Quitman's Catechism is on display at the Quitman House in Rhinebeck, New York, two copies are also available in the rare book room at the Lutheran Theological Seminary in Gettysburg, Pennsylvania.

[931] A copy is in the rare book archives of the Lutheran Theological Seminary in Philadelphia, Pennsylvania.

[932] Dr. Quitman's hymnbook proved to be quite controversial. Luther Reed condemns Quitman's hymnal as "Rationalistic... long-winded, didactic, [and] anemic form of the 'liturgy' issued... in

Dr. Quitman lived with his family in the parsonage at the Evangelical Lutheran Church of St. Peter the Apostle (The Old Stone Church). The Quitman House has been restored and preserved by volunteers belonging to the Quitman Resource Center for Preservation, Inc.

John Anthony Quitman (1799-1858), born in Rhinebeck, New York, on September 1, 1799, was the remarkable son of Dr. Frederick Henry and Anna Elizabeth (Huecke) Quitman.

General, Governor, and Congressman
John Anthony Quitman
Photo: Quitman House, Rhinebeck, New York.

John Anthony Quitman grew up in the parsonage of the Evangelical Lutheran Church of St. Peter the Apostle in Rhinebeck. John's father, the Rev. Dr. Frederick Quitman, intended for John to enter the ministry. He was sent to study at the Hartwick Seminary. After graduating in 1816, instead of going into the ministry, he became a tutor in its classical department. Heins notes that John A. Quitman was "the first in Hartwick's succession of distinguished alumni [to achieve success and fame] outside [of the ranks of] the clergy."[933]

1814 under the authority of the New York Ministerium... [it was] ...thoroughly unevangelical and antiliturgical." Reed, *Worship*, p.372.

[933] Heins, p.38.

In 1818, he taught at Mount Airy College in Germantown, Pennsylvania. Quitman moved to Ohio to study law in 1819. In 1820, he was admitted to the bar, and moved to Chillicothe, Ohio, and then, in 1821 he removed to Natchez, Mississippi.[934] At the time Mississippi was on the American frontier, and it provided many opportunities for ambitious young men.

In Mississippi, as a transplanted northerner, John Anthony Quitman became a wealthy and influential plantation owner, lawyer, military officer, and politician. He owned four plantations, and more than 400 slaves. As a politician, Quitman identified himself with those opposed to dueling, gambling, and other vices. He was a Jeffersonian-Jacksonian Democrat who held strong secessionist views. Ironically, John Anthony Quitman, born in Rhinebeck, New York, became more southern than most Southerners.

Elected to the Mississippi legislature in 1827, Quitman served as Chancellor of the Superior Court (1828-1834), a member of the Constitutional Committee (1832), and in 1835 he served as President of the Senate, and for a short time, acting Governor of Mississippi. He fought for the Independence of Texas in 1836, and in 1839, he was elected judge of the court of errors and appeals.

John Anthony Quitman helped found the Natchez Fencibles Volunteer Militia Company, and he served as brigade inspector and major general in the Mississippi militia. On July 1, 1846, at the outbreak of the Mexican-American War (1846-1848), he was commissioned a Brigadier-General of volunteers by President James K. Polk. He rendered gallant and noble service during the Mexican War under Generals Zachary Taylor and Winfield Scott. During the war, Quitman fought in the Battle of Monterrey, and he marched from Vera Cruz to Mexico City. On April 14, 1847, for his role at the Battle of Monterey, he was commissioned as a major general in the Regular Army.

On September 13, 1847, in the stuff of legend, during the Battle of Chapultepec, General Quitman—wearing only one boot [he abandoned his other boot stuck in the battlefield mud]—led a battalion of U.S. Marines into "the halls of Montezuma."[935] Through sheer will and determination, his division fearlessly assaulted the nearly impregnable castle at Chapultepec. In the face of deadly enemy fire, dashing across the open plain, carrying the artillery they found on their route, Quitman's troops forced their way up the side of the steep hill on which the ancient fortress was built. Having gained the summit, they assaulted the Chapultepec Castle, thereby securing the key to Mexico City. In the afternoon of that day, after receiving the formal surrender of the citadel, Quitman led his division in an attack on the Belen Gate. At bayonet point, his troops were the first within the walls of Mexico City.

For his battlefield heroics, General Winfield Scott appointed John Anthony Quitman civil and military governor of Mexico City.[936] He was awarded a congressional sword [this was the early 19th century equivalent of the modern Congressional Medal of Honor!]. Gen. Quitman also served as the first President of the Aztec Club of 1847 [the

---

[934] Ibid.

[935] Clarence B. Carson, *A Basic History of the United States: The Sections and the Civil War, 1826-1877* (Phenix, AL: American Textbook Committee, 1985, 2001), vol.3, p.117.

[936] Ibid.

military society of the Mexican-American War]. He was honorably discharged on July 20, 1848.

"For the Hall of Montezuma…"
Gen. Quitman and Battalion of U.S. Marines Entering Mexico Cit.
Notice, the General is missing his left boot!
Source: Tom Lovell, *For the U. S. Marine Corps.*

After the War, Quitman was elected as the fifteenth governor of Mississippi (1850-1851), and also served as a U.S. representative in Congress (1855-1858). He was a champion of slavery and states' rights. He used his political clout and influence in an attempt to persuade Mississippi to secede from the Union during the 1850s. Asserting the right of secession and the desirability of forming a confederacy of the slave-holding states, Quitman anticipated by nearly ten years the action which led to the American Civil War.

Also during the 1850s, John Anthony Quitman was also involved with the Filibuster of Cuba; i.e., an effort by Southern politicians and business leaders to take over Cuba in an attempt to bring an additional slave state into the Union.[937] The Filibuster effort failed, and Quitman barely escaped being sent to prison for his involvement in the affair.

Quitman died at his plantation, "Monmouth," near Natchez, Mississippi, on July 17, 1858. Presumably, he died from the effects of National Hotel disease contracted in Washington, D.C., during the inauguration of fellow Democrat President James Buchanan.

Most historians agree that had Quitman not suddenly died, because of his military experience and his political influence, he would have been offered command of the Confederate forces at the outbreak of the Civil War (1861-1865).

---

[937] Paul Johnson, *A History of the American People* (New York: HarperCollins, 1997), p.427.

Quitman is remembered today with a New York State commemorative historical plaque at the Quitman House in Rhinebeck, New York. In his honor, three towns bear his name; i.e., Quitman Texas; Quitman, Mississippi; and Quitman, Georgia. In addition, his Mississippi home, Monmouth Plantation, has been restored and preserved, and is now a popular bed and breakfast inn.

John A. Quitman, born in Rhinebeck, New York
became more southern than most Southerners.
Photo by the Rev. Mark D. Isaacs.

The Rev. William J. Eyer served as pastor of St. Paul's (Wurtemburg) from September 1825 to September 1837.[938] Alvah G. Frost reports that, "At the close of Dr. Quitman's labors (1824), the English language was making rapid progress among the children of the early settlers, and the agitation of English preaching fairly commenced, so that shortly after Rev. Eyer came, the English language occupied the entire service. He also became the exclusive pastor of the church."[939]

The Rev. Augustus Theodosius Geissenhainer accepted a call to St. Paul's (Wurtemburg) on June 8, 1838. Augustus Theodosius Geissenhainer was the son of the Rev. Henry Anastasias Geissenhainer and Anna Maria Schaerer Geissenhainer of Whitpain Township, Montgomery County, Pennsylvania. He was born in Whitpain Township on July 11, 1814.

In the fall of 1823, Augustus Theodosius Geissenhainer was sent to New York City to study for the ministry with his well-known uncle, the Rev. Fredrick William Geissenhainer, Sr.[940] The Rev. Beale M. Schmucker wrote that, "from his uncle, in the

---

[938] *1873 Church Book.*

[939] Alvah G. Frost, p.11.

[940] Beale M. Schmucker, *Memorial of Augustus Theodosius Geissenhainer* (Philadelphia: The Ministerium of Pennsylvania, 1883), p.5.

years of his preparation and early ministry, he had received a profound reverence for the true faith of our Church, as set forth in her Symbols [e.g., *The Book of Concord* (1580)], and [during his long ministry] his conviction of its accordance with Scripture grew ever stronger. He had an abhorrence of all compromises and concealments. No more loyal Lutheran lived than he."[941]

The Rev. Augustus Theodosius Geissenhainer
Photo: St. Peter's Evangelical Lutheran Church, Bethlehem, Pennsylvania.

Augustus Theodosius Geissenhainer was licensed on September 15, 1835, at the age of twenty-one, at a meeting of the New York Ministerium held at Palatine, Montgomery County, New York. Until being called to St. Paul's (Wurtemburg), he acted as an assistant to his uncle, the Rev. Fredrick William Geissenhainer, Sr., whose health was feeble. His uncle died on May 27, 1838.

At his installation as pastor at Wurtemburg, in September, 1838, his brother, Rev. Dr. Frederick William Geissenhainer, Jr. (1797-1879) was assisted by the Rev. Augustus Wackerhagen, D.D. (1774-1865).[942] The Rev. A. T. Geissenhainer remained at St. Paul's (Wurtemburg) for only two years; i.e., until August 1840, when he took a call to St. John's, a union church located in Orwingsburg, Schuykill County, Pennsylvania.[943]

---

[941] Ibid., p.10.

[942] Chester Henry Traver, *The Rhinebeck Gazette*, (1915).

[943] Beale M. Schmucker, p. 6-7.

Here, in 1844, Pastor Geissenhainer was instrumental in the formation of a new Lutheran congregation named, "St. Paul's Lutheran Church."[944]

During his career, the Rev. A.T. Geissenhainer was an effective organizer and church planter. In his efforts to propagate the Gospel he served many new congregations, primarily in Pennsylvania and New Jersey. The Rev. Beale M. Schmucker explained that, "a large part of the ministerial labor of Mr. Geissenhainer was devoted to the formation of missionary congregations, and to feeble pastorates which were able to furnish but a small part of income necessary to the support of his family."[945]

After the death of his first wife, the Rev. A. T. Geissenhainer married Eleonora Schmucker,[946] the daughter of the Rev. Samuel Simon Schmucker, the founder of Gettysburg College and of the Gettysburg Lutheran Seminary.[947] Interestingly, during the "American Lutheranism" controversy, which led to the formation of the General Council, many of Samuel Simon Schmucker's own students—and members of his own family, including his son, Beale M. Schmucker, and two of his sons-in-law, Benjamin Sadtler and Augustus Theodosius Geissenhainer—sided with Charles Porterfield Krauth and became leaders of the more conservative party.[948]

During this General Synod-General Council controversy, Pastor Geissenhainer sided with the General Council and was elected treasurer of the Ministerium of Pennsylvania. He served in this position from 1864 to 1877.

At the first meeting in which he served as treasurer, it was decided to start a new seminary in Philadelphia [i.e., the present Lutheran Theological Seminary at Philadelphia]. The Rev. Beale M. Schmucker writes that, despite the fact that the new seminary was expected to carry its own expenses, "with the inception of that work began the serious responsibility and burden of the treasurer's office."

Pastor Geissenhainer was charged with the responsibility of collecting, investing, and managing an often inadequate income stream. As a result, this position brought Pastor Geissenhainer many additional cares and anxieties. Beale M. Schmucker reported that during times of financial crisis, "he frequently advanced of his own moneys, at times even to the extent of several thousand dollars, in order to tide over times of embarrassment."[949]

In addition to being a pastor, and a leader with in the General Council, the Rev. A. T. Geissenhainer also became known as "a diligent liturgical scholar."[950] In his classic book, *The Lutheran Liturgy* (1947), the Rev. Dr. Luther Reed (1873-1972) mentions Pastor Geissenhainer's scholarly contributions.

---

[944] Ibid.

[945] Ibid., p.9.

[946] Ibid. p.8. Eleonora Schmucker Geissenhainer (1831-1881) is buried in the Evergreen Cemetery in Gettysburg, Pennsylvania. This is the cemetery that gave the name to the famous "Cemetery Ridge" during the Battle of Gettysburg (July 1-3, 1863).

[947] Luther Reed, p.173.

[948] Wentz, p.61.

[949] Beale M. Schmucker, p.9.

[950] Wentz, p.61.

The Ministerium of Pennsylvania took steps at once to translate this German Liturgy of 1855 into English. A committee consisting of Drs. C. F. Schaeffer, C. W. Schaeffer, C. F. Welden, G. F. Krotel, and B. M. Schmucker was appointed. Since these men possessed high literary culture and were students of the liturgy, their work soon became much more than mere translation. The influence of recent liturgical reform in Germany and England was definitely felt. The Rev. A. T. Geissenhainer, F. W. Conrad, and J. Kohler were subsequently added to the committee. Various features of the German Liturgy of 1855 were omitted; other features were introduced, all-as the preface states 'for the purpose of securing a stricter conformity to the general usage of the ancient and purest liturgies of the Lutheran Church.' A selection of introits, chiefly from the Bavarian agenda, was included; the Nicene Creed was introduced 'for occasional use;' and the General Prayer was placed after the Sermon. A condensation of Loehe's preface to his liturgy of 1844 was included. Dr. Beale Melanchthon Schmucker and A.T. Geissenhainer were largely responsible for the final form. The book was published by Lindsay and Blakiston of Philadelphia in 1860 under the title: *A Liturgy for the Use of the Evangelical Lutheran Church.*[951]

Rev. Augustus Theodosius Geissenhainer died suddenly on March 2, 1882.[952]

The Rev. Charles Adam Smith, D.D. (June 25, 1809–February 15, 1879), came to Wurtemburg in 1840, from the Lutheran Church in Stone Arabia, Montgomery County, New York. After a prolonged vacancy, acting under the advice of New York Ministerium President, the Rev. Dr. Henry Newman Pohlman (March 8, 1800-January 20, 1874), a committee of one was sent to Stone Arabia from St. Paul's Lutheran Church of Wurtemburg to interview the Rev. Charles Adam Smith. As a result of this visit, Pastor Smith was persuaded to accept a call to St. Paul's. His first baptism was June 19, 1842, and the last December 25, 1849, in all, forty-nine people.[953]

The Rev. Charles Adam Smith was born in New York City. As a young boy, he was left an orphan. By extraordinary studiousness, industry, and energy, he prepared himself for Hartwick Seminary. At Hartwick, Charles Adam Smith overcame the odds, and completed a classical and theological course under the Rev. Ernest Lewis Hazellius, D.D. (1777-1853).[954] He graduated from Hartwick Seminary in 1830, and he was ordained into the Lutheran ministry at the early age of twenty-one.[955]

---

[951] Reed, p.173.

[952] Beale M. Schmucker, p.6.

[953] Chester Henry Traver, *The Rhinebeck Gazette*, (1915).

[954] Dr. Hazellius was an important Lutheran theologian, professor, and author who taught at Hartwick Seminary from 1815-1830; Gettysburg Seminary from 1830-1833; and the Classical and Theological Institute of the Synod of South Carolina from 1834-1853. Among his works are a translation of the odd and interesting oculist, novelist, economist, and Pietist mystic named Johann Heinrich Jung-Stilling; i.e., *The Life of John Henry Stilling, Doctor of Medicine and Philosophy, Court Counselor and Professor of Political Economy in the University of Marburg in Germany and Author of Many Religious Works* (Gettysburg: Press of the Theological Seminary, N.G. Neinstedt Printer, 1831). For a lengthy discussion of the life and career of Johann Heinrich Jung-Stilling see Mark D. Isaacs, *THE END? Textual Criticism and Apocalyptic Speculation in Johann Albrecht Bengel (1687-1752): Lessons to be learned from the Godly scholar who*

Before serving the Lutheran Church in Stone Arabia, New York, Charles Adam Smith was ordained into the ministry of the Lutheran Church, in 1830, and was pastor successively, in Palatine Bridge, New York, and in Baltimore, Maryland, where he was also an editor of *The Lutheran Observer*. His first pastorate was at Palatine Bridge, New York, in which he served for about seven years. His next call was to Baltimore, Maryland to take charge of a new church enterprise in that city. While in Baltimore, he was associated with Dr. Benjamin Kurtz (1795-1865)[956] as a writer for *The Lutheran Observer*. Abdel Ross Wentz states that, Kurtz "was a stormy petrel of the 'American Lutheran' movement, a keen debater, and a vigorous writer."[957]

During this time, Pastor Smith also prepared and published in connection with Dr. John Gottlieb Morris (1803-1895),[958] a *Popular Exposition of the Gospels: Designed for the Use of Families, Bible Classes, and Sunday Schools* (1840), in four volumes, on the plan of *Albert Barnes' Notes on the Old and New Testament*. Dr. John Gottlieb Morris was also an influential theological and political ally of Dr. Benjamin Kurtz.[959]

In 1872, Dr. George Neff stated that, during his time at St. Paul's (Wurtemburg), 1840-1850, Pastor Smith "labored zealously and faithfully."[960] How *zealously* and how *faithfully*? In 1915, the Rev. Chester H. Traver recalled that Pastor Smith, "was among 'the New Measures' men of that day, believing in revivals and temperance."[961]

---

calculated the Second Coming of Jesus Christ as June 18, 1836 (Phoenix, AZ: Robert Welsh University Classical Press, 2010.

[955] *The Lutheran Observer*, "Death of Rev. Charles A. Smith, D.D.," vol.47, p.1, February 21, 1879.

[956] Dr. Benjamin Kurtz was regarded as one of the most eloquent men of his time. He was a zealous advocate of revivals [New Measures], and had very little sympathy with the confessional writings of the Lutheran Church. He was one of the founders of the General Synod, and of the Gettysburg Seminary. For more than thirty years he served as a trustee of Pennsylvania [later Gettysburg] College, and on the board of directors of the Gettysburg Seminary. He was also the founder of Missionary Institute at Selinsgrove, Pennsylvania. During his two European tours, in 1825 and 1846, he contributed interesting incidents and reminiscences to the *Lutheran Intelligencer* and to the *Lutheran Observer*, of which he was editor at the time.

[957] Abdel Ross Wentz, *A Basic History of Lutheranism in American* (Philadelphia: Mühlenberg Press, 1955), p.139.

[958] Dr. John Gottlieb Morris, a nationally prominent Lutheran pastor and author, was the first librarian of the Peabody Institute in Baltimore, founder of Lutherville, Maryland, and of the Lutherville Female Academy. Morris argued that there was a direct relationship between geology and biblical revelation. He was also an early geological and botanical scientist whose collection of specimens were fundamental to the development of the early Smithsonian Institution. Throughout his career, he tirelessly fought for the advancement of knowledge, culture, and morality. See, Michael J. Kurtz, *John Gottlieb Morris: Man of God, Man of Science* (The Maryland Historical Society, 1997).

[959] See John G. Morris, *Fifty Years in the Lutheran Ministry* (Baltimore: James Young, 1878), pp.137-140.

[960] Neff, *1873 Wurtemburg Church Record Book*.

[961] Chester H. Traver, *The Rhinebeck Gazette*, (1915).

The term "New Measures" was the name given to a series of revivals and related practices that followed after Rationalism had spent itself early in the nineteenth century. In some areas, primarily in Western New York State, this movement was prevalent from c. 1830. A "New Measures man" was a practitioner of the revivalistic preaching methods of Charles Grandison Finney (1792-1875). Finney, from "the burnt-over district" in Upstate New York, became president of Oberlin College in Ohio. From Oberlin, Finney hoped to prepare, "a new race of revival preachers" to awaken "backslidden Christians" to the attainable duty of practicing Christian perfectionism as commanded in Matthew 5:48.[962]

Within the Lutheran Church, "New Measures" were advocated by influential writers such as the Rev. Dr. Benjamin Kurtz. Opponents regarded it as incompatible with traditional Lutheranism. At this time, the agitations and controversies between old and new school Lutherans, or evangelical religion and heterodoxy and formalism, began to sweep over the region. They usually took the form of a contest between the advocates of prayer meetings and revivals, and those who opposed them. There was often great excitement and much bitterness, and even violence, manifested by the opponents of "New Measures."

An 1879 article, which appeared in *The Lutheran Observer,* stated that Dr. Smith, "as a New Measures man, took a decided stand in favor of revivals, and after some years of earnest labor, opposition and strife, the opponents of evangelical measures withdrew from the church having friends of revivals in full position."[963]

Evidently, Pastor Smith's "New Measures" awakened such bitter hostility that a "dissatisfied portion" of the members of St. Paul's withdrew their membership from the Church. In September 1848, the dissatisfied portion from Wurtemburg appealed to the New York Ministerium that held its fifty-third session at St. Paul's Evangelical Lutheran in Red Hook, New York. After hearing the case, the New York Ministerium adopted a resolution that states:

> Resolved that the control of the church property being placed by law under the trustees in office, it is out of our power to interfere in the affairs of the Wurtemburg Church; therefore the declaration from former members of that congregation cannot be sustained by this Synod.[964]

The Ministerium decree added:

> Resolved, that this Synod cherished undiminished confidence in the ministerial character and deportment of Rev. Charles Adam Smith and in the present congregational organization of the Wurtemburg Church; and we believe

---

[962] Erwin L. Lueker, *Christian Cyclopedia.* "New Measures," (St. Louis: Concordia Publishing House, 2000.)

[963] *The Lutheran Observer*, February 21, 1879.

[964] Chester H. Traver, *The Rhinebeck Gazette*, (1915).

that in the course which he has pursued as pastor of said Church he had been actuated by a solemn sense of duty to God and the interests of vital religion.[965]

The Rev. Chester Henry Traver adds that, during the bitter struggle, "as Rev. Smith came to church one Sabbath, he saw many intently looking up into the basswood tree standing along the west fence. His enemies had placed his effigy there."[966]

The Rev. Charles Adam Smith is buried in Schoharie, New York[967]
Photo by the Rev. Mark D. Isaacs.

At this same time, the secretary of St. Paul's (Wurtemburg) was warned not to pass a certain barn where the seceders held their meetings. In support of Pastor Smith, he replied, "I cannot die in a better cause."[968]

Also, during the ministry of the Rev. Dr. Charles Adam Smith, a new Lutheran church—The Third Evangelical Lutheran Church[969]—was organized in the village of Rhinebeck. When Dr. Smith served as pastor of the Wurtemburg Church (1840-1850), there was no parsonage. As a result, as his predecessors had done, Pastor Smith lived in

---

[965] Ibid.

[966] Ibid.

[967] It took the author eleven years to find the location of Dr. Smith's grave. The breakthrough came via the excellent archives at the Lutheran Theological Seminary at Philadelphia.

[968] Ibid.

[969] Founded in 1842.

the village of Rhinebeck. Seeing a need for a Lutheran Church in the growing village of Rhinebeck, Pastor Smith began holding Sunday evening services at the First Baptist Church (founded in 1821). For several years, Pastor Smith preached in the forenoon on alternate Sundays in the two churches. Soon after, a portion of the Wurtemburg congregation united with others in the village of Rhinebeck, and organized a new congregation and erected there a handsome new church on Livingston Street.[970] Hence, Pastor Smith is remembered as being the founding pastor of Third Evangelical Lutheran Church. In 1849, when both churches desired a morning service, Pastor Smith relinquished his call at Wurtemburg, and became pastor exclusively at the village church in Rhinebeck.

In addition to his pastoral duties, from 1846 until 1856, Charles Adam Smith also served on the Board of Trustees of Hartwick Seminary.[971]

Pastor Smith served Third Evangelical Lutheran Church in the village exclusively until 1852, when he accepted "an urgent call" from Christ Lutheran Church in Easton, Pennsylvania.[972] He served in Easton for three years when he was called to become pastor of St. Mark's Lutheran Church, on the corner of Thirteenth and Spring Garden Streets, in Philadelphia. Here, he ministered for a short time.

After removing to Philadelphia, under the auspices of the Lutheran Publications Board, Charles Adam Smith originated and published a monthly home journal entitled *The Evangelical Magazine*, which, after adopting several names, became *The Lutheran and Missionary*. He continued to serve as editor until it was merged with *The Lutheran Home Journal*.

He then opened a select school for young ladies, and served as a supply pastor for the Western Presbyterian Church in Philadelphia, from which he subsequently accepted a pastoral call, and thus became united with the Presbyterian Church. After a pastorate of about seven years, he accepted a call from the Presbyterian Church at East Orange, New Jersey. After serving for five years, he resigned for health reasons, returned to Philadelphia, and devoted himself exclusively to literary pursuits.

At this point, Dr. Smith, accompanied by his wife, visited Europe. The couple spent nearly a year abroad, mostly in Germany among the historical sites of the Lutheran Reformation. During this time, Smith wrote a series of interesting articles concerning his European travels. These articles were published in *The Lutheran Observer*.

After returning from Europe, he resided in Philadelphia and was actively engaged in writing and preaching, more or less as a supply for pastors during their absence on vacations and other times.

Dr. Smith was an able and accomplished writer, and during an active ministry of forty years published quite a number of interesting and valuable works. He translated many works from German, including *Krummacher's Parables* (New York, 1833); and, is the author of *The Catechumen's Guide* (Albany, 1837); *Popular Exposition of the Gospels*, with Reverend John Gottlieb Morris (Baltimore, 1840); *Illustrations of Faith* (Albany, 1850); *Men of the Olden Time* (Philadelphia, 1858); *Before the Flood and After*

---

[970] Hull, p. 13.

[971] Heins, p.182.

[972] "The [Third] Lutheran Church Burns," *The Rhinebeck Gazette*, July 10, 1909.

(1868); *Among the Lilies* (1872); *Inlets and Outlets* (1872); and *Stoneridge, a Series of Pastoral Sketches* (1877)."[973] *Stonebridge* was "a collection of pastoral sketches from his early ministry, some of which have appeared in the columns of *The Lutheran Observer* which have been often enriched by the products of his graceful pen."[974]

Following his death in 1879, *The Lutheran Observer* stated:

> Our personal relations with him were most cordial and intimate for years, and our deep sense of loss at this unexpected departure from earth, we cannot here fully express. Earnest and positive, he was yet genial, frank, manly, and sincere in his relationships and intercourse—a man of true honor and without guile.[975]

The Lutheran Observer also reported:

> …he was conscious of his approaching end, and his family was summoned to his bedside to receive his parting benediction. One of his sons offered a prayer, and then in faint accents he expressed his unshaken trust in Christ whose salvation he had so long proclaimed to perishing men. A few moments after, his spirit gently passed away. His death occurred at his residence in Philadelphia on Saturday afternoon February 15, 1879 after an illness of one week from a violent attack of pleuro pneumonia.[976]

Charles Adam Smith left a wife, four sons, and one daughter. His funeral services took place Tuesday, February 18, 1879, at noon at St. Mathew's Lutheran Church. The Rev. William Miller Baum, D.D. presided.[977] His remains were removed to Schoharie, New York where several other members of the family are entombed.[978]

The Rev. William Nace Scholl, D.D., (September 9, 1805-June 12, 1889), became the pastor of St. Paul's in 1851. His first baptism was dated April 13, 1851, and the last, February 18, 1855.

In 1851, in his report to the Synod, Pastor Scholl stated:

> I took charge of St. Paul's Church, Wurtemburg, on the first of April last [i.e., 1850]; and have preached regularly, and with an increasing number of attentive hearers, and the prospect of doing good under the Great Head of the Church is encouraging. The church building has been lately repaired and refitted

---

[973] James Grant Wilson and John Fiske, ed., *Appleton's Cyclopedia of American Biography* (New York: D. Appleton and Company, 1887-1889).

[974] *The Lutheran Observer*, "Death of Rev. Charles A. Smith, D.D.," vol.47, February 21, 1879.

[975] Ibid.

[976] Ibid.

[977] The Rev. William Miller Baum, D.D., (1825-1902) graduated from the Gettysburg Lutheran Seminary in 1846. He served as pastor of St. Matthew's Lutheran Church in Philadelphia from 1874-1902.

[978] *The Lutheran Observer*, February 21, 1879.

at the expense of nearly $400, and now compares favorably with any of our country churches. The people appear to be much encouraged, and anticipate a brighter day. We trust that a considerable amount will be raised the coming year, for the cause of domestic and foreign missions, and of benevolence.

The Rev. Chester H. Traver wrote, "The parsonage was then in the village [of Rhinebeck]. Dr. Scholl did not keep any horse, but was always very prompt [a walk of more than four miles!]. He also preached at Clinton Hollow or Schultzville in the afternoon, walking to and fro [more than six miles from Wurtemburg!]. His Christian spirit won nearly all. His style was peculiar, but he was thoroughly scriptural in his preaching and conscientiously faithful in his pastoral work."[979] Traver adds that during his pastorate, the church was repaired and refitted at a cost of $400.[980]

Also, during his pastorate, "a new cemetery was established"[981] at Wurtemburg.

Later in his career, 1865 to 1889, the Rev. Dr. William Nace Scholl served as Principal and then President of the Hartwick Seminary. Dr. Scholl also served as acting Professor of Theology at Hartwick Seminary from 1869-1870.[982]

In February 1865, while serving Zion Lutheran Church in Athens, New York, Pastor Scholl was elected Principal of Hartwick Seminary. In his role as Principal, Dr. Scholl "spent most of his principalship in the field" attempting to raise money for the perennially cash starved Seminary.[983] His fund raising efforts—difficult in normal times—were further frustrated following the General Synod-General Council schism of 1866. Due to failing eyesight, in June 1870, Dr. Scholl was forced to resign. He had served a total of nine years as President of the Board at Hartwick. And, he served for a total of thirty-five years as a trustee.[984]

The Rev. George Neff, D.D., (December 23, 1813-August 6, 1900), served as pastor of St. Paul's for twenty-one years; i.e., from July 1855 to July 1876. Dr. Neff was widely known in northern Dutchess County, where he was highly esteemed as an earnest and faithful pastor.

George Neff was born on December 23, 1813, in Philadelphia. The Neff family tree has its roots in Switzerland, where the chief ancestor, in the struggle of Protestantism in Southern Europe, rescued the standard of Zurich from desecration and received marked distinction.[985]

His father, Rudolph Neff, was for many years, a successful Philadelphia merchant. Rudolph Neff was born August 29, 1776, in Philadelphia County, Oxford Township, Germantown, Pennsylvania. Rudolph died June 11, 1857. He married Margaret (Rudi)

---

[979] Chester H. Traver, *The Rhinebeck Gazette*, (1915).

[980] Ibid.

[981] Lawrence, p.100.

[982] Heins, p.159.

[983] Ibid., p.55.

[984] Ibid., p.61.

[985] *The Poughkeepsie [Sunday] Courier*, "Rev. George Neff," August 12, 1900, p.1.

Rugan on December 4, 1802, in Philadelphia County, Pennsylvania, at the First Reformed Church. She was born May 24, 1780. Margaret died January 23, 1861. They had eleven children.[986]

The Rev. George Neff, D.D.
Photo: Archives of St. Paul's Lutheran Church of Wurtemburg.

George Neff entered the University of Pennsylvania, and after graduating [B.A. degree], he went to the Theological Seminary at Gettysburg to pursue his studies for the ministry. He graduated in 1842.[987] While there he was elected to the Professorship of Latin and Mathematics at Hartwick Seminary.

On September 13, 1842, Pastor Neff was licensed to preach the gospel by the New York Ministerium, and in 1844, he received his first call from Trinity Lutheran Church [served 1842-1847], a new congregation in Philadelphia. There, he labored under many discouragements, but he was successful in placing it on a solid basis, and by 1900, Trinity Lutheran Church was one of the largest, most active and liberal churches in the city. He also served Lutheran churches in Saddle River, New Jersey, from 1847 to 1850, and in Passyunk, Pennsylvania, from 1850 to 1855.[988]

---

[986] Ibid.

[987] Abdel Ross Wentz, *History of Gettysburg Theological Seminary*, p.384.

[988] *The Poughkeepsie [Sunday] Courier*, "Rev. George Neff," August 12, 1900, p.1.

The Rev. George Neff was installed as pastor of St. Paul's (Wurtemburg) on October 11, 1855, by Revs. Drs. H. N. Pohlman, William D. Strobel and M. Sheeleigh. During his ministry at Wurtemburg, he performed eighty-seven infant baptisms.

According to his obituary, "[while in Passyunk, Pennsylvania] his health failing and anxious to make a change, he accepted a call to St. Paul's Lutheran Church of Wurtemburg in Rhinebeck, New York."[989]

When Pastor Neff was called to the Wurtemburg Church "it was a large field for usefulness but unfortunate divisions had taken place [within the congregation] which rendered the work one of considerable responsibility. But an earnest, judicious labor of twenty-one years healed the difficulties, restored them again to unity, and prosperity followed. Extensive improvements were made to the church building and surroundings, and in the twenty-one years scarcely a note of discord disturbed the harmony between the pastor and his people."[990]

"Shortly after" Pastor Neff's "settlement, he preached altogether in the English language and ministered exclusively to the Wurtemburg Church."[991] The Rev. Chester H. Traver wrote, "He fostered the advanced ideas of his predecessors. By his genial spirit he won the respect of the people."[992]

In addition to these pastoral duties at St. Paul's, he served for fifteen years as the secretary of the New York and New Jersey Synod and for eight years as the president (1878-1886). During this time, he acquired a large experience of ecclesiastical and congregational working and development. Through his wise leadership, Pastor Neff was able to secure the co-operation of both the synod and the churches.

The Rev. Chester H. Traver wrote, "a Wurtemburg parishioner never informed his pastor when sick." After his recovery, the man bitterly complained in the community, and within the congregation, that the pastor had not visited him during his illness. Upon learning of this, Pastor Neff went to the man's home and appeared, "very much aggrieved and vexed" saying, "I don't know why you treat me so rudely. You have sent for the doctor, but you have neglected me." The man was surprised, and humbly apologized to Dr. Neff.[993]

The Rev. Chester H. Traver stated that Dr. Neff "was apt in his answers to fault-finders among his parishioners." Once a woman repeatedly asked, "Why don't you come to visit me? Come any time." Pastor Neff did so, and said that he would come again. "A third visit," wrote Traver, "conquered her desire for frequent visits."[994]

---

[989] Ibid.

[990] Ibid.

[991] Howard H. Morse, *Historic Old Rhinebeck* (Rhinebeck, New York, 1908), p.151

[992] Chester H. Traver, *The Rhinebeck Gazette*, (1915).

[993] Chester H. Traver, "Death of Rev. George Neff, D.D." See obituary clip in *Mrs. Samuel S. Frost's (1819-1912) Scrapbook,* (St. Paul's Archives), p.23.

[994] Ibid.

In 1876, Dr. Neff moved to Poughkeepsie "to take a little needful rest."[995] It was not long before he was invited to take charge of the Cherry Street Chapel in Poughkeepsie, where he conducted a Bible class and preached Sunday and Wednesday evenings.

Just at this time, the Presbyterian Church of Freedom Plains, seven miles east of the city of Poughkeepsie, became greatly disturbed by serious difficulties, which threatened their peace and prosperity. Dr. Neff was invited to supply their pulpit for one Sunday morning, which resulted in a continued supply for nearly two years. Harmony was again restored. The members became more deeply interested in church work. Several hundred dollars were raised for improvements and beautifying their church. As a result, it became one of the most beautiful churches in that section of the county.

Dr. George Neff, and his wife Elisabeth,
are buried in the Poughkeepsie Rural Cemetery.
Photo" Rev. Mark D. Isaacs

After his supply work with the Presbyterian Church, he relocated to Philadelphia and remained there until his health became impaired. He then relocated to his daughter's home in Poughkeepsie, New York.

In 1886, the degree of Doctor of Divinity was conferred upon him by the Wittenberg College of Springfield, Ohio, and the synod of, which he was a member, placed his name on the roll of honor, "*Senior Ministerii.*"

Pastor Neff's wife, Elisabeth Rugan Neff, died in July 1883. The couple had two children John Rugan Neff and Susanna R. Neff Ackert.[996] Susanna's husband, Philip

---

[995] Chester H. Traver, *The Rhinebeck Gazette*, (1915).

Edgar Ackert was the City Attorney in Poughkeepsie. John Rugan Neff, after attending Hartwick Seminary for two years, moved to Pennsylvania and became a successful merchant near Philadelphia.[997]

On Monday, August 6, 1900, at the age of 88, Dr. Neff died at the home of his daughter, Mrs. Philip Edgar Ackert [Susanna R. Neff Ackert (d.1928)] on South Clinton Street in Poughkeepsie, New York. The funeral was held from his late home on Wednesday August 8, 1900 at 2:00 PM. The Rev. George and Elisabeth R. Neff are buried in the Poughkeepsie Rural Cemetery.[998]

Civil War Veteran, the Rev. Joseph G. Griffith.
Photo: W.H. Walker, Photographer, Chatham Village, New York.
Archives of St. Paul's Lutheran Church of Wurtemburg.

The Rev. Joseph G. Griffith, D.D. was born in Bucks County, Pennsylvania, on February 11, 1839. He attended Pennsylvania [Gettysburg] College, 1863-1865, and he graduated from Gettysburg Lutheran Seminary in 1867.[999] He was licensed by the Eastern Pennsylvania Synod in 1867, and ordained at Sunbury, Pennsylvania, by the Susquehanna Synod in 1868.

---

[996] *The Poughkeepsie [Sunday] Courier*, p.1.

[997] Chester H. Traver, "The Death of Rev. George Neff, D.D." See obituary clipping in *Mrs. Samuel S. Frost's (1819-1912) Scrapbook,* (St. Paul's Archives), p.23.

[998] *The Poughkeepsie [Sunday] Courier*, "Rev. George Neff," p.1, August 12, 1900.

[999] Wentz, p.436.

During the Civil War, Joseph G. Griffith enlisted in the Pennsylvania Militia, 31st Regiment, Co. D. The 31st Regiment of the Pennsylvania Militia fought in some of the most significant battles of the American Civil War, including: Manassas [First Bull Run]; Fredericksburg; the Seven Days; Gaines Mill; Malvern Hill; Second Bull Run; the Battles of South Mountain and Antietam; the Battle of Gettysburg; the Battles of the Wilderness; Spotsylvania and Spotsylvania Court House. The 31st Regiment was mustered out of service on June 16, 1864.[1000]

Rev. Joseph G. Griffith.
Photo by John Coumbe, Rhinebeck, New York.
Photo: Archives of St. Paul's Lutheran Church of Wurtemburg.

In addition to St. Paul's (Wurtemburg), which he served from 1876 to 1881, Pastor Griffith served churches in Clermont, New York, 1873 to 1875; Chatham, New York, 1875 to 1876; Oriole, Pennsylvania, 1882 to 1884; Ramsey, New Jersey, 1884 to 1886; Auburn, Nebraska., 1886 to 1890; St. Mark's in Omaha, Nebraska., 1890 to 1892; Lawrence, Kansas 1893 to 1897; and Montoursville, Pennsylvania, 1897 to 1899. Dr. Griffith served as pastor in Williamsport, Pennsylvania 1867 to 1873, and again from 1899 to 1903. On February 1, 1872, Pastor Griffith married Clara M. Lewars. The couple had no children.

[1000] Frederick H. Dyer, *A Compendium of the War of the Rebellion Compiled and Arranged from Official Records of the Federal and Confederate Armies, Reports of the Adjutant Generals of the Several States, the Army Registers, and Other Reliable Documents and Sources* (Des Moines, Iowa: The Dyer Publishing Company, 1908).

While in Kansas, from 1887 to 1897, Dr. Griffith also served as a trustee of Midland College in Atchison. Midland College was founded in 1883, in Atchison, Kansas by German Lutheran immigrants. The college moved to Fremont, Nebraska, in 1919. In 1962, Luther College in Wahoo, Nebraska merged with Midland Lutheran College.

The Rev. Dr. John Gideon Traver writes that, "He answered 'here' to Heaven's roll call from Montoursville [five miles east of Williamsport], Lycoming County, Pennsylvania, December 11, 1907."[1001]

On July 17, 1996 Montoursville became tragically famous when TWA Flight 800 exploded off East Moriches, New York, with the loss of two-hundred-and-thirty lives. On board were sixteen students from Montoursville High School and their five adult chaperones, who were on a class trip to France as part of a student exchange program.

Rev. John Kling as he appeared during his first tenure.
Photo: Archives of St. Paul's Lutheran Church of Wurtemburg.

The Rev. John L. Kling was installed as pastor on November 17, 1881, by the Rev. George Neff, D.D., the Rev. John A. Earnest, D.D.,[1002] and the Rev. Samuel A. Weikert.[1003] Pastor Kling served at St. Paul's until the spring of 1887.

[1001] Chester H. Traver, *The Rhinebeck Gazette*, (1915).

[1002] At the time the Rev. John A. Earnest was the pastor of The Lutheran Church of St. Peter the Apostle (the Old Stone Church) in Rhinebeck.

[1003] At the time, the Rev. Samuel A. Weikert was the pastor of St. Paul's Evangelical Lutheran Church in Red Hook, New York.

One of many significant events of his pastorate was the organizing here of the Woman's Home and Foreign Missionary Convention of the New York and New Jersey Synod, with Mrs. J. G. Griffith as president, Mrs. Frank Lown, recording secretary, and Mrs. A. Allendorf, treasurer.

The Rev. George William Fortney (December 27, 1845-August 30, 1909) served St. Paul's (Wurtemburg) for seven-and-one-half years—from December 22, 1887, to May 26, 1895—until he accepted a call to Turbotsville, Pennsylvania He was ordained into the Lutheran ministry in 1880. He was installed by the Rev. Chester H. Traver[1004] and the Rev. Samuel A. Weikert.[1005] In August, 1890, a Ladies' Aid Society was formed which over the next twenty-five years collected more than $2000 toward the incidental expenses of the church property.

Rev. George W. Fortney
Photo: Schaffer Photographers, Poughkeepsie, New York.
Archives of St. Paul's Lutheran Church of Wurtemburg.

In the summer of 1892, as preparatory to the entertainment of both the Synod and the Woman's Convention, the interior of St. Paul's was repapered and painted, the pulpit

---

[1004] At the time the Rev. Chester H. Traver was the pastor of The Lutheran Church of St. Peter the Apostle (the Old Stone Church) in Rhinebeck.

[1005] Following the death of the Venerable Rev. Dr. Henry Lafayette Ziegenfuss (February 8, 1894) the Rev. Samuel A. Weikert became and Episcopalian priest and the Rector of Christ Church in Poughkeepsie.

platform was lowered and a new pulpit placed upon it. The organ and choir were removed from the gallery to the right side of the pulpit. The officers presented a new pulpit Bible. At the re-opening, August 22, 1892, Rev. Dr. Henry Ziegler, father-in-law of the pastor, preached the sermon.[1006]

The Rev. Dr. Henry Ziegler (1816-1898) preached at the Grand Reopening of St. Paul's (Wurtemburg) held on August 22, 1892.

The Rev. Dr. Henry Ziegler was a well-known Pietist Lutheran pastor, church planter, evangelist, and theologian. He was born near Old Fort, Centre County, Pennsylvania, August 19, 1816. He graduated from Pennsylvania [Gettysburg] College, Gettysburg, in 1841, and at Gettysburg Lutheran Theological Seminary in 1843, and in the latter year was licensed to preach. He was pastor at Selinsgrove, Pennsylvania, in 1843 to 1845, traveling missionary and missionary president of Pittsburg synod in 1845 to 1850, pastor at Williamsport, Pennsylvania, in 1850 to 1853, agent for the Parent education society, residing at Selinsgrove, Pennsylvania, in 1853 to 1855, pastor at Salona, Pennsylvania, in 1855 to 1858, and professor of theology at the Missionary Institute [now Susquehanna University], Selinsgrove, Pennsylvania, in 1858 to 1881. Failing health then compelled him to retire from active duties.

Dr. Ziegler received the honorary degree of D.D. in 1860 from Wittenberg College, Springfield, Ohio. He had a wide reputation as an author, and as a teacher of theology he has been eminently successful. Before his health failed he was a frequent contributor to church periodicals, especially *The Evangelical Review and Lutheran Quarterly* and *The Lutheran Observer* [the leading periodical of the General Synod]. Besides numerous baccalaureate and other addresses, he published *Treatise on Natural Theology* (1860); *Treatise on Apologetic Theology* (1861); *Catechetics—Historical, Theoretical, and Practical* (Philadelphia, 1873); *The Pastor, his Relation to Christ and the Church* (1876);

[1006] *The Rhinebeck Gazette*, August 26, 1892. Anna Lorena Gunn Ziegler was born on August 17, 1850 in Williamsport, Pennsylvania.

"The Preacher, his Relation to the Study and the Pulpit" (1876); *Dogmatic Theology* (Selinsgrove, Pennsylvania, 1878); and *The Value to the Lutheran Church of her Confessions: An Essay* (Philadelphia, 1878).[1007] Pastor Ziegler died November 26, 1898, in Selinsgrove, Pennsylvania.[1008]

From Tuesday, October 4, until Sunday October 9, 1892, the New York and New Jersey Synod met at the newly renovated St. Paul's (Wurtemburg).[1009] An article in *The Lutheran Observer* reports:

> Bountiful provision had been made for the care and comfort of the Synod by this kind people and their thoughtful pastor. The Synod was well entertained, and that is the rule among our churches; but the interest manifested in the business of synod, as attested by large numbers who were present at all its meetings was above average.[1010]

The Lutheran Observer continued, "Good strong addresses were delivered on education, missions, etc. by the speakers appointed by Synod and by the secretaries of the Boards."

They added, "resolutions were passed with strong majorities recommending to pastors and people the peaceable introduction and use of the Common Service [hymnbook]; recommending also the use of this Service at synodical communions; and instructing the delegation to the General Synod to vote against a re-opening of the subject in that body."[1011]

"The committee on the new Catechism of the General Synod suggested several improvements, and recommended its adoption, not as perfect, but as a useful book for pastors in the work of catechization."[1012]

At the Synod meeting:

> The trustees of the Hartwick Seminary reported that this institution is in the most prosperous condition, that the buildings have been repaired so that they are now in better condition than they have been for years, and asked that the churches take a special collection on the Day of Prayer for colleges to pay for repairs, improvements, etc.[1013]

[1007] *Appleton's Cyclopedia of American Biography*, edited by James Grant Wilson, John Fiske and Stanley L. Klos. Six volumes, New York: D. Appleton and Company, 1887-1889 and 1999. http://famousamericans.net/henryziegler/

[1008] Abdel Ross Wentz, *History of the Gettysburg Theological Seminary: 1826-1926* (Philadelphia: United Lutheran Publications House, 1926), p.387.

[1009] *The Lutheran Observer*, J.L. Kistler, October 1892, [clipping #107 in the St. Paul's Archives.]

[1010] Ibid.

[1011] Ibid.

[1012] Ibid.

[1013] Ibid.

Again, it is important to note this long-run historic link to Hartwick Seminary. A majority of the pastors who served St. Paul's (Wurtemburg) were trained at Hartwick Seminary.

Also, at the Synod meeting was "the celebration of the semi-centennial of the ministry of Rev. George Neff... Dr. Neff as licensed in the same church in which synod was assembled, September 13, 1842 [i.e., the Synod met at St. Paul's (Wurtemburg) in 1842], and served this same charge as pastor many years [Dr. Neff served St. Paul's from July 1855-July 1876]."

In 1892 the Rev. Archibald Edwin Deitz, D.D. (1869-1965)
was ordained at St. Paul's (Wurtemburg).
He went on to serve as a Lutheran Pastor for seventy-three years!
Photo Source: Henry Hardy Heins, *Throughout All the Years, Hartwick, 1746-1946.*

Also of interest, at this Synod meeting, the Rev. Archibald Edwin Deitz, D.D., (1869-1965) was ordained. At the time, Pastor Dietz had been called to serve Third Evangelical Lutheran Church in the village of Rhinebeck. He served as pastor of Third from 1892 to 1898.[1014]   During this time, on October 18, 1893, he married a Rhinebeck girl "[Caroline W. Secor the daughter of H. L. Secor."[1015]   Caroline died in Riverside, California on December 18, 1907. Archibald married Marie B. Lederle on August 3, 1919, at All Soul's Lutheran Church in Jersey City, New Jersey. The marriage ceremony was performed by Archibald's brother, Rev. Raymond Charles Deitz.

[1014] Rev. Mark D. Isaacs, *The 150th Anniversary of Third Evangelical Lutheran Church* (Rhinebeck, New York: 1842-1992), p.19.

[1015] Howard H. Morse, *Historic Old Rhinebeck* (Rhinebeck, New York, 1908), p.186.

Dr. Deitz attended Hartwick Seminary, and was a Gettysburg Seminary graduate (1892). He went on to serve as Professor of Theology, Dean, and then President of Hartwick Seminary (c.1920). Dr. Deitz was the author of several books on theology and Greek translations. He remained active until his death in 1965 spending an incredible seventy-three years in the Lutheran ministry![1016] Rev. Dr. Archibald E. Deitz died on November 14, 1965, at the Jersey City Medical Center in Jersey City, New Jersey, at the age of 96 years old.

For the one hundred and fiftieth anniversary of St. Paul's (Wurtemburg) [i.e., 1910] the Rev. George W. Fortney wrote a letter to the Rev. Chester H. Traver. In this letter, he recalled his tenure at St. Paul's (Wurtemburg). Pastor Fortney wrote, "I had a reasonably prosperous pastorate during my stay and a very pleasant experience among the people. I shall ever recall my work there with pleasure."[1017]

The Rev. George W. Fortney died in Suffern, New York, on August 30, 1909. The Rev. Chester H. Traver wrote, "He possessed a vigorous mind, well disciplined by study and teaching, was a good sermonizer, an acceptable preacher and an ardent advocate of temperance. He was well skilled in music and could lead and drill his church choir."[1018]

The Rev. Chauncey Diefendorf
Photo: Archives of St. Paul's Lutheran Church of Wurtemburg.

[1016] Ibid.

[1017] Chester H. Traver, *The Lutheran Quarterly* (1916), p.395.

[1018] Ibid.

The Rev. Chauncey Diefendorf served as pastor from September 1, 1895, to November 27, 1898, when he removed to Lawyersville near Cobleskill, New York. He was installed as Pastor of St. Paul's by Rev. Dr. William H. Luckenbach, president of the Synod. The Rev. Chester H. Traver, D.D., addressed the congregation and Rev. Archibald E. Dietz, D.D. delivered the charge.

Pastor Diefendorf was born on February 1838. He attended the Hartwick Seminary and Selinsgrove University in Pennsylvania in preparation for the ministry. Rev. Chauncey Diefendorf of Leesville, New York and Melissa Weatherwax of East Greenbush, New York were married at the Evangelical Lutheran Church of West Sand Lake, Sand Lake, Rensselaer County, New York on June 8, 1871. At the time, Pastor Diefendorf was serving as pastor of that church.

He died in his home in Fort Plain, New York, November 19, 1909. He was buried at the Fort Plain Cemetery. The Rev. Dr. George U. Wenner, president of Synod, preached the funeral sermon. In his obituary Pastor Diefendorf stated that, "he was kind and faithful in his church, and he had a large circle of friends."[1019] In 1916, the Rev. Chester H. Traver wrote, "the Rev. Chauncey Diefendorf was a devoted and faithful laborer, and won many stars for his crown."[1020]

The Rev. Chauncey Diefendorf (1838-1909)
is buried at the Fort Plain Cemetery
next to his wife Melissa and their two infant children.
Photo: Linda A. Isaacs

The Rev. Roscoe C. Wright, D.D., served as pastor from April 2, 1899, to September 1907. He was installed May 28, 1899, by the Revs. W. W. Gulick, Laurent

---

[1019] "The Rev. C. Diefendorf Passes Away: Esteemed Lutheran Clergyman Died Last Night," Fort Plain newspaper, February 20, 1909. See obituary clipping in *Mrs. Samuel S. Frost's (1819-1912) Scrapbook,* (St. Paul's Archives), p.46.

[1020] Ibid.

Dryer Wells, D.D.,[1021] and Archibald E. Deitz.   Pastor Wright attended Gettysburg College and Hartwick Seminary.

The Rev. Roscoe C. Wright
Photo: Archives of St. Paul's Lutheran Church of Wurtemburg.

During his pastorate at Wurtemburg, the church was reroofed, repainted, and repapered.   A new lectern was added, and a new organ and a new furnace were purchased. Also at this time, the Social Hall kitchen was enlarged.[1022] During his second year, the Seventeenth Annual Convention of the Woman's Home and Foreign Missionary Society was held at Wurtemburg from October 3 to 5, 1901. In 1907, Pastor Wright resigned to accept a call in Amsterdam, New York.

[1021] The Rev. Laurent Dryer Wells, D.D was a faithful Lutheran pastor who served the Church from more than forty-nine years. He graduated from Hartwick Theological Seminary in 1867. He served congregations in Saddle River, New Jersey; Canajoharie, New York; Valatie, New York; Shamokin Pennsylvania; Fayette, New York; Third Evangelical Lutheran Church, Rhinebeck, New York (1899-1909); and Ramapo, New York. Dr. Wells was serving as pastor of Third Evangelical Lutheran Church in Rhinebeck, New York when, on July 10, 1909, a fire destroyed the building. He resigned this call on July 22, 1909. His wife Mary (Minnie) Samantha Benton (married May 20, 1868) died in Rhinebeck, New York May 26, 1902 [age 59 years, 8 months, and 5 days]. Dr. Wells is buried next to his wife in the Wells Family Plot in Midddleburgh, New York. Source: Obituary, *The Rhinebeck Gazette*, June 24, 1916.

[1022] Chester H. Traver, *The Rhinebeck Gazette*, (1915).

Toward the end of his career, Pastor Wright became a well-respected Reformed clergyman. He served the Dutch Reformed Church in Chatham, New York, for fifteen years prior to his death.[1023] During his career, he served churches in Rhinebeck, Amsterdam, Highland, Millerton, and Chatham.

The Rev. John L. Kling.
Photo: Archives of St. Paul's Lutheran Church of Wurtemburg.

The Rev. John L. Kling, (July 1, 1838-February 2, 1923). The Rev. Kling, "the Grover Cleveland of St. Paul's,"[1024] served two non-consecutive terms as pastor. The first tenure was from September 1, 1881 until June 1, 1887, and the second tenure was from February 1908 until December 1913, when he resigned due to age and health reasons. His recall after an absence of twenty years was proof of the high esteem that the members of St. Paul's held Pastor Kling. He was installed April 12, 1908, by Rev. Laurent Dryer Wells, D.D., pastor of Third Evangelical Lutheran Church acting for the Synod President. Rev. D. W. Lawrence addressed the people.

On Saturday, July 10, 1909, while Pastor Kling served as pastor in Wurtemburg, a disastrous fire occurred at about midday at Third Evangelical Lutheran Church in the village of Rhinebeck. "The flames were first seen by Dr. Laurent Dryer Wells the pastor, who resided in the parsonage just east of the church. He at once rushed to the nearest

---

[1023] See obituary, "Pastor's Death Occurred Today," in *Mrs. Samuel S. Frost's (1819-1912) Scrapbook,* (St. Paul's Archives), p.45.

[1024] The Rev. John L. Kling is the only pastor to have served two nonconsecutive terms as pastor of St Paul's.

alarm box at the corner of East Market and Center Street… the alarm was turned in at 11:40 AM."[1025]

Church Organist Alice Traver Coon recalled, "just as I had reached home [from practicing the organ at church] on July 10, 1909 the firebell sounded. Our dear church was in flames."[1026]

According to *The Rhinebeck Gazette* the building caught fire:

> …from a burning pile of rubbish near the northeast corner of the building. Two sections of boardwalk used in the winter, projecting from the pile, were leaning against the rear wall of the church, and were in flames as well as the building above them. The fire spread rapidly to the roof, burning through the cornice. The fire raged for nearly half an hour before a portion of the roof fell, carrying the ceiling with it into the nave of the church. The bell in the tower rang intermittently until it fell in red hot pieces upon the stone porch below. When the fire was finally extinguished at about 2:00 PM, only the walls and floor were left in place, but all beyond repair. The building had been constructed of wood. The loss was estimated at $10,000.[1027]

Colonel John Jacob Astor IV (1864–1912)[1028] and his young son William Vincent Astor (1891-1959)[1029] "witnessed the fire from the latter's new automobile."[1030] John Jacob Astor, who was made a colonel during the Spanish-American War, lived at the near by Ferncliff Estate.

In 1909, Astor divorced his wife Ava Lowle Willing—a famously beautiful and famously spoiled heiress from Philadelphia—and on September 9, 1911, married eighteen year old Madeleine Talmadge Force in his mother's ballroom at Beechwood, the family's Newport, Rhode Island, home. The divorce and remarriage to Madeleine, who was a year younger than John Jacob Astor's son Vincent Astor, caused a scandal in Gilded Age high society. To avoid the spotlight, John Jacob Astor IV and Madeleine took an extended honeymoon to Europe and Egypt to wait for the gossip to calm down.

[1025] *The Rhinebeck Gazette,* "The Lutheran Church Burns: Completely Destroyed by Fire Saturday." July 16, 1909, p.1.

[1026] Ibid.

[1027] Ibid.

[1028] Among Astor's accomplishments was an 1894 science fiction novel entitled *A Journey in Other Worlds,* about a life in the year 2000, on the planets Saturn and Jupiter. He also patented several inventions, including a bicycle brake in 1898, a "vibratory disintegrator" used to produce gas from peat moss, a pneumatic road-improver, and helped develop a turbine engine. Astor made millions in real estate and in 1897, Astor built the Astoria Hotel which adjoined Astor's cousin, William Waldorf Astor's, Waldorf Hotel in New York City, the complex became known as the Waldorf-Astoria Hotel.

[1029] While a student at Harvard University in 1912, Vincent Astor inherited an estimated $200 million when his father went down with the *Titanic.*

[1030] Ibid.

While traveling, Madeleine became pregnant, and wanting the child born in the United States, the Astors booked first-class passage on the maiden voyage of the *Titanic*. They boarded the *Titanic* at Cherbourg, France. Astor was the richest person on the ship and, along with his wife, his party included his manservant, his wife's maid and nurse, and his pet Airedale, Kitty.

Colonel John Jacob Astor IV (1864–1912)

At 11:40 PM on April 14, 1912 the *Titanic* hit an iceberg and began sinking. At first, Astor did not believe the ship was in any serious danger, but later helped his wife into a lifeboat. He asked if he could join his wife, mentioning her "delicate condition," but the officer in charge said no men until all the women and children were safely away. Astor reportedly stood back, asked for the lifeboat number, lit a cigarette, and tossed his gloves to Madeleine. Madeleine survived, and he perished.

John Jacob Astor's body was one of the few that were recovered. His body was recovered by the *MacKay-Bennett* on April 22. Because his body was badly crushed and covered in soot, Astor is believed to have been smashed by the first smokestack as it fell from the Titanic. His body was identified by the initials sewn on the lapel of his jacket. Among the items found on him were £225, $2440, and a gold watch which his son, Vincent wore the rest of his life. His funeral was held at the Church of the Messiah in Rhinebeck.

The Gazette reported that, "Mrs. Wells, the pastor's wife, was prostrated when she learned of the fire. She shortly recovered."[1031]

[1031] Ibid.

The fire virtually destroyed the church building. In addition to the building, writes Mrs. Alice Traver Coon, "one of our losses was the Estey organ."

After the fire, for two years, the congregation was without a pastor. During this time Third Lutheran was served by supply pastors, most often by the Rev. John L. Kling of St. Paul's Wurtemburg. Through the hard work and loyal efforts of the members, a new church was erected, incorporating the front wall of the original church. Mrs. Alice Traver Coon reported that while the new building was being constructed, "services were held either in our parsonage or in the Baptist or Reformed chapels, loaned for our use."[1032]

The Rev. Walter D. Miller, D.D., preached for the first time in the new building on Palm Sunday, April 9, 1911. On July 9, 1912, the new building was dedicated. The second church cost $8,000.

This photograph was taken on August 13, 1913
at the 1870 Lutheran Parsonage in Wurtemburg on the occasion of the Golden Wedding
Anniversary of the Rev. and Mrs. John L. Kling.
Pastor and Mrs. Kling are seated in the front center of the photograph.
Photo: Archives of St. Paul's Lutheran Church of Wurtemburg.

Fiftieth Wedding Anniversary Celebration at the 1870 Parsonage

The Rev. John L. Kling married Almira Lehman on August 18, 1863, in Sharon, Schoharie County, New York. On August 13, 1913, at the 1870 Lutheran Parsonage, a

---

[1032] *The Rhinebeck Gazette,* July 16, 1909, p.1.

gala celebration of their Fiftieth Wedding Anniversary was held. More than two-hundred and-fifty guests celebrated with the happy couple.[1033]

Mrs. Kling died on February 22, 1914, in Chicago at the home of their daughter where they had gone to spend the winter. Her obituary states that, "Mrs. Kling was dearly loved by all who knew her and her memory will be enduring."[1034]

The couple had two sons Marcus Kling of Washington, and Irving Kling of Chicago, and two daughters, Mrs. George Crusius of Wurtemburg, and Mrs. William T. Snively of Chicago. They also had several grandchildren.

Pastor Kling's father and mother died in 1894, within two days of each other, both at the age of seventy-nine. His grandfather, Jacob Kling, had twelve children, nine sons and three daughters. Jacob Kling, "was accidentally killed at the age of ninety-nine."[1035]

Pastor Kling's resignation from St. Paul's took effect on December 1, 1913. He went on to serve a Lutheran congregation in East Schodack, New York. Interestingly, Pastor Kling had previously served this congregation forty-two years earlier! While in East Schodack, New York Pastor Kling married Mrs. Phoebe Miller.

Almira Lehman Kling (1841-1914)
Photo: Archives of St. Paul's

Pastor John Kling died in East Schodack, on February 2, 1923. The Rev. John Kling was buried next to his wife Almira in the Slate Hill Cemetery in Sharon, New York.[1036]

[1033] Ibid.

[1034] "Recent Deaths: Mrs. John Kling," *The Rhinebeck Gazette*, February 28, 1914, p.1.

[1035] "Rev. and Mrs. John Kling Have Golden Wedding," *The Rhinebeck Gazette*, August 16, 1913, p.1.

[1036] See obituary, "Rev. John Kling Dies At East Schodack," in *Mrs. Samuel S. Frost's (1819-1912) Scrapbook,* (St. Paul's Archives), p.16.

The Rev. John Kling (1838-1923)
Photo: Linda A. Isaacs

The Rev. William Gibson Boomhower, D.D., was born in East Berne, New York on January 15, 1891. He was a graduate of both the classical and theological departments of Hartwick Seminary.

*Pastor Boomhower was called to St. Paul's
directly from Hartwick Seminary.*
Photo: Archives of St. Paul's (Wurtemburg).

During his last year at Hartwick Seminary he occasionally supplied the Wurtemburg pulpit. When he graduated in 1914, St. Paul's extended a call which began in July 1914.

William Gibson Boomhower was examined and ordained by the Lutheran Synod of New York at Paterson, New Jersey, October 1, 1914, and installed at St. Paul's the same month.

In 1916, Pastor Boomhower accepted a call to Gilead Lutheran Church in Center Brunswick, New York. He served here until 1919, when he became General Secretary of the New Jersey Sunday School Association.

The Rev. William G. Boomhower
Photo: Alice Boomhower of Rhinebeck.

He married Mildred Elze (1899-1970) on June 26, 1920. During his long ministry, his wife Mildred served as a faithful co-worker. The shared tombstone bares their inscription, "Together they lived to serve their Lord in His Church." In 1921, he accepted a call to Redeemer Lutheran Church in Troy, New York.

From 1922 to 1929, William G. Boomhower served as pastor of Zion Lutheran Church in Cobleskill, New York. In 1928, he was awarded an honorary Degree of Doctor of Divinity from Hartwick College.

From 1929 to 1935, he served as pastor of the Lutheran Church of Our Savior in Jersey City, New Jersey. From 1935 to 1941, he served Temple Lutheran Church in Philadelphia. From 1941 to 1944, he served at Atonement Lutheran Church in Oneonta, New York, where he also served as part-time instructor at Hartwick College. From 1944 to 1951, he served as pastor of St. Paul's Lutheran Church in Brooklyn. From 1951 to 1957, he was recalled to Gilead Lutheran Church in Center Brunswick, New York.[1037]

As a young man, while attending Hartwick College, the Rev. Roy Steward recalls many joyful meetings and dinners with Dr. Boomhower, who shared his many experiences in the ministry, as well as his time at St. Paul's (Wurtemburg). Pastor Boomhower died in 1974, and he is buried in Cobleskill, New York.

The Rev. Oscar B. Noran served St. Paul's from July 1, 1917, until March 30, 1919. Prior to coming to Wurtemburg Pastor Noran served as Assistant Teacher (1914 to 1916) at Hartwick Seminary.[1038] Pastor Noren's Letter of Call, signed April 8, 1917, is on file in the archives of St. Paul's.[1039] According to the Call, Pastor Noran was to be paid $800.00 per year in twelve monthly payments. Adjusting for inflation, by applying the CPI price adjuster, this works out to $13,267.43 (2009) per year.

The Rev. E.L. Davison served St. Paul's from July 20, 1919, until November 30, 1924. During his tenure, significant changes were made to the chancel area of the church. *The Minutes of the Lutheran Brotherhood* men's group for December 20, 1920, state that the Rev. E. L. Davison instructed the men of the church on the "reasons for his desire to change the arrangement of the Altar."[1040]

During the tenure of Pastor Davison, in February of 1921, the "Jesus the Good Shepherd" stained glass window was installed.[1041] This window has brought inspiration, comfort and joy to generations of Wurtemburg worshippers.

The Rev. Elder Jay Himes served as pastor of St. Paul's from May 10, 1924 to September 15, 1946. Pastor Himes graduated from the Theology School of Susquehanna University. Pastor Himes was born in Brookville, Pennsylvania, and died of a sudden heart attack at age sixty-three in Hazelton, Pennsylvania. He died on December 29, 1950; and his tombstone death date incorrectly states, "1951."

During his tenure as pastor of St. Paul's he worked as a rural mail carrier. He was also a woodworker, raised chickens, and sold eggs. The late Mary Traver Baas owned a beautiful little end table with inlayed wood that Pastor Himes made in his shop behind the 1870 Parsonage. He was also a Freemason and member of the Grange.

[1037] Information for this profile was taken from a program for "A Community Testimonial Honoring Dr. William G. Boomhower," held at the State University Dining Hall, Cobleskill, New York, May 25, 1964. A copy of this program is in the archives of St. Paul's Lutheran Church of Wurtemburg.

[1038] Heins, p.167.

[1039] Archives of St. Paul's, file folder #103.

[1040] *Minutes of the Lutheran Brotherhood* (1915-1927), p.123. St. Paul's Archives.

[1041] John 10: 11 "I am the good shepherd: the good shepherd gives his life for the sheep."

The Rev. Elder Jay Himes
Photo: Archives of St. Paul's Lutheran Church of Wurtemburg.

Pastor Himes was married to May K. Cotting (1892-1968). They are buried together in the Cotting Family plot in the Cemetery of the Evangelical Lutheran Church of St. Peter the Apostle (The Old Stone Church) in Rhinebeck, New York.

Pastor Himes is buried at the Old Stone Church Cemetery
Photo by the Rev. Mark D. Isaacs.

The Rev. Carl A. Romoser was duly installed as Pastor of St. Paul's on November 16, 1947. Evidently all did not go well for Pastor Romoser. In the Spring of 1949 a petition was circulated among the members of St. Paul's. It read:

214

"The undersigned members of our Church believe that because of misunderstanding, lack of good fellowship, and cooperation, and untactful remarks and acts by our pastor, that a condition now exists which makes a further friendly relationship between our pastor and congregation impossible. And, we believe that the present relationship is a deterrent to the future welfare and growth of our Church. We therefore regretfully petition the Council to ask for the resignation of our Pastor."[1042]

This petition was signed by twenty-five leading members of the Church.[1043] The petition sparked a special congregation meeting which was held On June 5, 1949. This meeting was presided over by United Lutheran Synod President the Rev. Frederick R. Knubel, D.D. After reading the Constitution of the United Lutheran Synod on "the qualifications necessary to vote upon the question before the meeting," a motion was made, and seconded, that "the contractual relationship between Pastor Romoser and the congregation be terminated."[1044]

Ballots were then distributed and it was announce that twenty-seven votes [unanimous] were cast in favor of terminating the pastor's contract.[1045]

There are rumors that he had a severe drinking problem. In a recent interview, one of our long-time members recalled that "Pastor Rosomer spent more time in the saloon in Upper Red Hook than he did doing his job." She added that in a "painful action," he had to be removed from his Church leadership position. After 1949, there are no records of what happened to him.

The Rev. Herbert Finch was born in Ramsey, New Jersey, on February 18, 1877. He was the son of Simon and Mary (Rupp) Finch. In 1894, at the age of seventeen, he entered Gettysburg College. Following his graduation in 1898, he taught school for a year. In 1899, he entered the Gettysburg Lutheran Theological Seminary and graduated in 1902.[1046] From 1906 to 1907, he studied at the University of Pennsylvania. From 1908 to 1910 Pastor Finch was a student at the University of Berlin. During this time he traveled extensively in Europe.[1047]

Pastor Finch was ordained in 1902 by the Western Pennsylvania Synod. From 1902 to 1908, he served as pastor of Gethsemane Lutheran Church in Philadelphia. From 1909 to 1923, he served as pastor of St. Paul's Lutheran Church in Johnstown, New York.

[1042] A copy of this document, with original signatures can found inserted between page 252 and page 253 of the *Church Record: Wurtemburg Lutheran Church, 1920-1951.* NOTE: See Wurtemburg Archives # 139.

[1043] *Church Record: Wurtemburg Lutheran Church, 1920-1951* (Letter dated June 5 1949), p.253. NOTE: See Wurtemburg Archives # 139.

[1044] Ibid.

[1045] Ibid.

[1046] Adel Ross Wentz, *History of the Gettysburg Theological Seminary*, 1926, p.533.

[1047] St. Paul's Archives, September 17, 1952 letter from the Rev. Herbert Finch. Document #52.

In 1924, Pastor Finch was called to the Trinity Evangelical Lutheran Church in Charleston, West Virginia which was organized on October 16, 1924. While serving as the first pastor of Trinity, "the fledgling congregation worshiped in the local YWCA for four years."[1048] In 1928, the congregation moved into their first sanctuary on Lee and Elizabeth Streets in Charleston. Pastor Finch resigned on October 31, 1928.

The Rev. Herbert Finch
Photo: Trinity Evangelical Lutheran Church
in Charleston, West Virginia.

By appointment from the Board of Social Missions of the United Lutheran Church, Pastor Finch then served as Chaplain at the Wassaic State School in Wassaic, New York. While serving as Chaplain in Wassaic he was called to St. Paul's (Wurtemburg) as stated supply on October 3, 1949. He served in this capacity until 1954.

In 1952, at the age of seventy-five, and in the fiftieth year of his ordination, Pastor Finch wrote, "I have been, outside of parish relations, President of the Hartwick Conference of the Synod of New York; Secretary of the Synod of New York (General Synod); and President of the West Virginia Conference of the Synod of West Virginia."[1049]

At St. Paul's (Wurtemburg) the Rev. Herbert Finch is remembered as "the wonderful older gentleman who came from Wassaic." The congregation also has fond memories of his wife Virginia Washburn Finch. After their service here at St. Paul's the couple retired to Penny Farms near Jacksonville, Florida. Penny Farms is a non-denominational Christian retirement community founded by J.C. Penny in 1926. Pastor Finch and his wife Virginia are buried in the Mahwah Cemetery in Bergen County, New Jersey.

[1048] http://www.trinitywv.org/history.shtml <November 4, 2006>

[1049] Ibid.

The Rev. John L. de Papp served at St. Paul's from 1955 to 1958. Prior to coming to St. Paul's, he served as pastor of St. Peter's Lutheran Church in Greenport, Long Island. During his tenure at St. Paul's, he was deeply involved in efforts to aid and resettle refugees from the courageous but failed 1956 Hungarian Uprising against the Soviet Union. On November 30, 1958, Pastor De Papp resigned and accepted a call to St. Luke's Lutheran Church in Valatie, New York.

The Rev. Rolf W. Eschke graduated from Gettysburg Lutheran Theological Seminary in 1959. Pastor Eschke served at St. Paul's (Wurtemburg) from September 1, 1959, until August 31, 1962.

The Rev. Roy Steward, who was a young man at this time, has many fond memories of Pastor Eschke's pastorate. Pastor Roy recalls that Pastor Eschke, who came from a more conservative-evangelical perspective, was an excellent preacher and Bible teacher.

The Rev. Rolf W. Eschke
Photo: St. Paul's Archives.

After leaving St. Paul's, Pastor Eschke accepted a call to Trinity Evangelical Lutheran Church in West Sand Lake, New York. He eventually left the Lutheran Church in America and took a call at the Newark Valley First Congregational Church, located in Newark Valley, New York. He served as a pastor in the United Church of Christ until his retirement.

Pastor Eschke visited St. Paul's for the gala celebration of our 250th Anniversary held on September 19, 2010. He delighted members and friends with recollections of his time spent at St. Paul's. He also recounted the festivities for the 200th Anniversary held in 1960. At this celebration Eleanor Roosevelt visited Wurtemburg.

The Rev. Frederick Charles Dunn was born in 1924. After serving in the U.S. Navy Submarine Corps during the Second World War, Pastor Dunn graduated from Wagner College, in 1959, and the Lutheran Theological Seminary at Philadelphia, in 1963. He was installed as pastor of St. Paul's on October 1, 1963.

After serving at St. Paul's until December 31, 1967, Pastor Dunn accepted a call to Trinity Lutheran Church in Kingston, New York. After a challenging tenure at Trinity, he left the ministry and worked at IBM until his retirement. He died in 1984, and is buried in the Wurtemburg Cemetery.

The Rev. Roy Steward, who was in high school during Pastor Dunn's ministry at St. Paul's, has many fond memories of Pastor Dunn. In fact, according to Pastor Steward, "it was Pastor Dunn who repeatedly raised the possibility with me of pursuing seminary studies."[1050]

The Rev. Frederick Charles Dunn
Photo: Archives of St. Paul's Lutheran Church of Wurtemburg.

Pastor Roy recalls that, "my response was to state that I wanted to be a dairy farmer and that the Church needed lay leaders as much as clergy." In the end, after graduating from Hartwick College, Roy Steward attended Gettysburg Seminary and became a Lutheran pastor.

The Rev. William H. Beck, D.Min. was born on December 30, 1940. He is the son of Lester and Eva Beck of Altoona, Pennsylvania. He graduated from East Stroudsburg University where he met his wife Greta Ewe. They were married at St. Paul's Lutheran Church in Tannersville, Pennsylvania.

After completing his M.Div. degree at the Gettysburg Theological Seminary (1966), he was ordained by the Lutheran Church in America (LCA). His first call was to a three point parish in Brodheadsville, Pennsylvania. While serving this parish he worked on his master's degree from Princeton Theological Seminary. He received his M.Th. degree in 1968.

So that he could do work on his doctorate from the Hartford Seminary Foundation, Pastor Beck accepted a call to St. Paul's (Wurtemburg) and Memorial (Rock City) in Rhinebeck, New York. He served as pastor of St. Paul's from September 1, 1968 until March 14, 1970, when he accepted a call to Jefferson Lutheran Parish in Codorus, Pennsylvania. Pastor Beck had previously done his internship at this parish in York County, Pennsylvania. While serving this congregation, Pastor Beck completed his

---

[1050] September 1, 2006 E-mail to the Rev. Mark D. Isaacs. Document preserved in Archive Folder #52.

doctoral work and received his D.Min. degree from Lancaster Theological Seminary in 1975.

Dr. Beck and his wife visited St. Paul's during the Summer of 2009.
Photo: Linda A. Isaacs

While in Seminary, Pastor Beck served as a reservist in the Marine Corps. Later, he joined the Army Reserve and served as a chaplain. During the Gulf War, at the age of 50, he was called into active duty. He served in Saudi Arabia during Operation Desert Storm. Pastor Beck retired at the rank of Lieutenant Colonel.

After serving many parishes in York County—including Mt. Carmel Lutheran Church (twenty-one years) and St. Paul's (Dubs) Lutheran Church (seven years)—Pastor Beck retired from active parish ministry on June 30, 2008.

Rev. Sylvester Bader served St. Paul's from 1970 to 1977. He graduated from the Lutheran Theological Seminary-Philadelphia in 1938. Prior to coming to St. Paul's he served Covenant Lutheran Church in Ridgewood, New York from 1938-1970. Pastor Bader served St. Paul's at the very end of his long career as a Lutheran pastor. Pastor died in Bayonne, New Jersey.

A few years ago, Pastor Bader's daughter stopped by the 1870 Parsonage. She had grown up in the old house and was interested in seeing how the place had been changed and renovated. She fondly recalled playing in the cemetery and in the old barn that once stood behind the Parsonage.

The Rev. Sylvester Bader
Photo: Archives of St. Paul's Lutheran Church of Wurtemburg.

The Rev. Daniel M. Strobel came to St. Paul's directly from the Lutheran Theological Seminary-Gettysburg after receiving his M.Div. degree. He served St. Paul's from 1978 to 1984, when he accepted a call to St. Andrews's Lutheran Church in Speedway-Indianapolis, Indiana. Older members speak fondly of his enthusiasm and of his faithfulness.

The Rev. Daniel and Nancy Strobel

After attending the Lutheran Theological Seminary in Chicago, Pastor Dan and Nancy Strobel's son Ronald was ordained into the Lutheran ministry on January 30, 2010. Pastor Ron currently serves Holy Trinity Lutheran Church in Chassell, Michigan.

220

The Rev. Richard Mowry served at St. Paul's (Wurtemburg) and Memorial (Rock City) from 1984 to June of 1996. Pastor Mowry graduated from the Lutheran Theological Seminary at Philadelphia in 1968. In addition to serving as pastor, he was active in the community. He served as a volunteer Fire Policeman for the Rhinebeck Volunteer Fire Department. When the beeper would sound, Pastor Mowry would go racing to the scene.

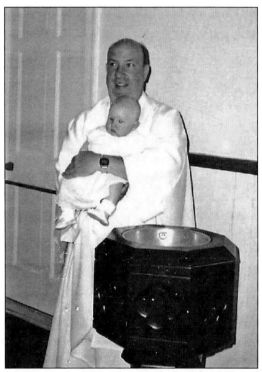

Pastor Mowery holding the newly baptized Jared King.
Photo: Barbara King family archives.

The Rev. Mark D. Isaacs, M.Div., S.T.M., D.Min., Th.D., Ph.D. has served St. Paul's from June 29, 1996, to the present. Pastor Mark—born in Minneapolis, Minnesota (September 16, 1955) and baptized in Hazel Run, Minnesota—has lived most of his life on the East Coast, in Maryland, New Jersey, Massachusetts, Pennsylvania, and Upstate New York. He earned a B.A. in Economics from Westfield State College (1980); a Master of Divinity degree (1992); and a Master of Sacred Theology degree (2005) from the Lutheran Theological Seminary at Gettysburg. He earned his Ph.D., *Summa Cum Laude*, from Trinity Theological Seminary in Newburgh, Indiana (2005).[1051] Pastor Mark also received a Doctor of Ministry degree from the Lutheran Theological Seminary at Philadelphia in May 2007, and a Doctor of Theology degree from the Newburgh Theological Seminary in Newburgh, Indiana (2008). He has done post-doctoral work at the International Academy of Apologetics, Evangelism, and Human Rights in Strasbourg,

---

[1051] See Mark D. Isaacs, *Centennial Rumination on Max Weber's The Protestant Ethic and the Sprit of Capitalism* (Boca Raton, FL: Dissertation.com, 2005).

France (summer 2007 and 2009). The Academy is held at the *Aumonerie Universitaire Protestante* (AUP) at the University of Strasbourg.

The young Rev. Mark D. Isaacs (c.1995)
Photo: Archives of St. Paul's (Wurtemburg)

Before attending Seminary, Pastor Mark worked as a research economist, business editor, and economics writer. Since July 1, 1996, he has served as pastor of St. Paul's Lutheran Church of Wurtemburg. Since December 1999, Pastor Mark has also served as an adjunct professor in several area colleges, including, Marist College, Mount Saint Mary College, and the State University of New York-Ulster. As an adjunct professor, he teaches courses such as economics, Christian worldviews and values, marketing, comparative religions, western civilization, geography, and American history.

Recalling how he first came to Rhinebeck, Pastor Mark states,

> In the spring of 1992, while I was a senior at Gettysburg Seminary, as a part of the call process from the Evangelical Lutheran Church in America [ELCA], I was interviewed by three bishops at a Region Eight meeting in Philadelphia. I interviewed with the bishop from the Upstate New York Synod, the bishop from the Northeast Pennsylvania Synod, and the bishop from the Metro New York Synod. At the time, William H. Lazareth [an outspoken incense, cope, miter, and crosier liturgical reformer *and* dogmatic theological liberal!] was serving as Metro New York Bishop. During the interview, we developed an immediate and mutual antipathy toward each other. We did not connect, and we did not relate on any level. At the conclusion of the interview, I shrugged off the entire experience and "wrote off" the Metro New York Synod.

Pastor Mark added that, "at the end of the day, when the bishops announced their selections, I was astonished that I had been selected for the Metro New York Synod. I was then told that I was going to be sent to Third Evangelical Lutheran Church in the village of Rhinebeck, New York. Never having heard of Rhinebeck before—coming from the New England Synod—and after four years of Seminary poverty, I was eager to begin my full-time ministry. I welcomed the challenge."

Pastor Mark recalled that, "as a part of the call process, I was invited to Rhinebeck to meet the call committee." Thus, in April 1996, he drove up to Rhinebeck, New York from Gettysburg, Pennsylvania.

He stated "It was a dark and stormy night when I drove into Rhinebeck for the first time. Ironically, my first night in Rhinebeck was spent in the 1870 Parsonage at St. Paul's (Wurtemburg). The Rev. Richard Mowry was pastor of St. Paul's at the time, and interim pastor of Third Lutheran Church. Seeking to save money on the cost of a motel, it was decided that I should spend the night at the Wurtemburg Parsonage. Pastor Mowry was a bachelor who illuminated his home with multiple dozens of candles. In the dark, and with the rain, and with the candles, the old house—in the middle of two cemeteries—looked like something out of a Gothic horror novel. I spent a sleepless night on an old lumpy mattress in the guest room. As the thunder and lightening crashed and rumbled, I was sure that I saw the eyes move on a portrait hanging on the wall! Little did I know that, in January 2000—after several coats of paint—this same room was to become my bedroom!"

After meeting with the call committee, I was called to Third Evangelical Lutheran Church and ordained by ELCA Bishop William H. Lazareth on June 21, 1992.

Pastor Mark stated that, "a few weeks after arriving in Rhinebeck, I learned that Bishop William H. Lazareth, and the Call Committee from Third, had been less than honest about my predecessor's situation, and about the dismal condition of the congregation. Even by first-call challenge situations, it was pretty much of a worst-case scenario. Despite this, I resolved to make the best of a difficult situation."

From mid-1992 until mid-1999, Third Lutheran experienced solid growth in both new members and income. During this time, average attendance increased from twenty to around eighty-five.

On July 1, 1996, after Pastor Mowry's resignation, Pastor Isaacs was appointed Interim Pastor of St. Paul's (Wurtemburg). At the time, St. Paul's was a small, struggling, rural congregation. Attendance averaged around twenty, and both the 1870 Parsonage and the church building was in disrepair.

From the perspective of Lutheranism, Rhinebeck and Red Hook, New York, are peculiar. History had endowed this region with four struggling Lutheran congregations, served by three ELCA pastors who were all paid below Synod minimum. Over the years, through maladministration and benign neglect from the ULC, LCA, and the current ELCA Metro Synod, all four churches were in a state of chaos and dysfunction, locked in negative growth trends.

From 1963 until 1996, Memorial (Rock City) Lutheran Church and St. Paul's (Wurtemburg) were configured as a two-point parish. After thirty-three years it was clear that this two point parish arrangement had not benefited either congregation. The logical thing to do was to set up a pair of two-point parishes; i.e., Third and St. Paul's (Wurtemburg), and St. Paul's (Red Hook) and Memorial (Rock City).

From Pastor Mark's perspective, this new arrangement worked from July 1, 1996 until November 1, 1999. During this time, services were held at 9:00 AM at Wurtemburg and at 11:00 AM in the village at Third. Ziegenfuss University [our weekly adult Bible study and current issues class] and confirmation classes were combined, church councils from both churches met separately and jointly [as needed]. Combined Lenten and special services were held as well as social functions. Periodically, there were minor open—and behind the scenes—disagreements over budget issues and summer worship times. Despite this, stated Pastor Mark, "I felt that things were going very well. I continued to push hard for a formal two-point parish arrangement."

An older, and possibly wiser, Rev. Dr. Mark D. Isaacs
Photo: Linda A. Isaacs

However, despite sincere efforts to form a two-point parish, a conflict at Third Lutheran erupted and escalated to the point where the only resolution was for Pastor Mark to resign.[1052] Seeking advice from the Hudson Conference Dean, Pastor Mark was told that "if he resigned from one church he had to resign from both churches." Hence, on Sunday October 17, 1999, he resigned from both churches. However, the people of St. Paul's (Wurtemburg), in a dramatic and spontaneous gesture of love and support, refused to accept Pastor Mark's resignation. In response to their love and support, Pastor Mark decided to continue to serve at St. Paul's. The Metro Synod objected, and on January 1, 2000, Pastor Mark resigned from the ELCA clergy roster.

Since it was a violation of the ELCA constitution to have a non-rostered ELCA clergyperson serving an ELCA congregation, St. Paul's began to search for an alternative

---

[1052] See G. Lloyd Rediger, *The Clergy Killers: Guidance for Pastors and Congregations Under Attack* (Louisville: Westminster John Knox Press, 1997).

to the ELCA. A committee was formed to investigate the theological positions and constitutions of a host of national Lutheran organizations and synods. After an exhaustive search, the congregation selected the Evangelical Lutheran Conference and Ministerium [ELCM]. The ELCM is a centrist Lutheran denomination founded by the Rev. Roy Stewart of Altoona, Pennsylvania, a son of St. Paul's (Wurtemburg). Pastor Mark had met Pastor Roy Stewart several years earlier and had always respected and admired his theological perspective and his down to earth attitude.

The Rev. Dr. Mark D. Isaacs and Linda A. Isaacs
Photo: Barbara King

On January 9, 2000, the Rev. Mark D. Isaacs was officially received onto the clergy roster of the Evangelical Lutheran Conference and Ministerium.[1053]

After St. Paul's decided to defy the ELCA and issue a call to Pastor Mark, attorneys got involved, and threats—such as seizing the church property—were made by the Metro New York Synod. Rather than buckle to these threats, the people of St. Paul's rallied behind their Church and behind Pastor Mark. Per the constitution, two back-to-back congregational votes were taken to leave the ELCA, and to join another Lutheran body. These dramatic votes were both unanimous. Hence, since May 2000, St. Paul's (Wurtemburg) has officially been a member of the Evangelical Lutheran Conference and Ministerium.

Looking back on the challenging crisis of October 1999 to January 2000, Pastor Mark, and the people of St. Paul's, are grateful for the experience. Almost from the time of his ordination in 1992, Pastor Mark, as a moderate to conservative Lutheran with

---

[1053] January 12, 2000 Letter to Metro New York Synod Bishop Stephen P. Bouman from the Rev. Mark D. Isaacs. Archive of St. Paul's Lutheran Church of Wurtemburg.

Pietist leanings, had generally felt excluded and alienated from the extremely theologically liberal ELCA.[1054]

According to Pastor Mark, "this crisis offered a rare moment of clarity. In the end, without this bitter experience, I probably would have spent the remainder of my career merely muddling along and being frustrated with denominational politics and endless petty synod intrigues. As an ELCM pastor, I have been granted a new freedom. The entire experience has reinvigorated my commitment to serving Christ in this special place and during this critical time."

In addition, since January 2000, the people of St. Paul's have responded with their hands, hearts, and wallets. The 1802 Church building has undergone extensive repairs and improvements. The 1870 Parsonage has also been totally refurbished. For example, during the winter of 2006, a major $30,000 kitchen renovation was accomplished. The demolition of the old kitchen and much of the reconstruction were done by congregational volunteers.

Today, as a member of the Evangelical Lutheran Conference and Ministerium, St. Paul's (Wurtemburg) is an active and growing congregation. Since January 2001, St. Paul's has grown from an average attendance of twenty to twenty-five, to about one-hundred. Thanks to a committed cadre of leaders, teachers and parents the Sunday School is thriving, and many new non-Lutheran families have joined our congregation.

The painful events of the fall of 1999 closed one door, and opened a series of exciting new options and opportunities for both St. Paul's and for the ministry of Pastor Mark. Pastor Mark recently stated that, "I am grateful for the opportunity to serve historic St. Paul's Lutheran Church of Wurtemburg, and I look forward to a continued time of growth and expansion."

An Active Freemason

In his free time, the Rev. Mark D. Isaacs is an active and enthusiastic Freemason. He was made a Mason on June 13, 1983 at Elm-Belcher Lodge, A.F. & A.M. in Agawam, Massachusetts. Currently he is a member of Hendrick Hudson Lodge No. 875, F.& A.M., Red Hook, N.Y.; Warren Lodge, No.32, Shultzville, N.Y.; Poughkeepsie Chapter, No. 172; King Solomon Council; Poughkeepsie Commandery, No. 43; The Ancient and Accepted Scottish Rite, The Valley of the Hudson [Lodge of Perfection and Council of the Princes of Jerusalem]; Valley of Schenectady [Chapter and Consistory]; Cyprus Temple, A.A.O.N.M.S. of Albany; The Royal Order of Scotland; The Allied Masonic Degrees; The Grand College of Rites of the United States of America; The American Lodge of Research; The Thomas Smith Webb Chapter of Research; The Southern California Research Lodge; The Philalethes Society; and The Scottish Rite Research Society.

Dr. Isaacs also serves as the Grand Chaplain of the Grand Lodge of Free and Accepted Masons of the State of New York [Appointed 2010]; the Grand Chaplain of the Grand Chapter of Royal Arch Masons of the State of New York [Appointed 2009]; the Grand Chaplain of the Grand Council of Cryptic Masons of the State of New York [Appointed 2010]; and the Associate Grand Prelate of the Grand Commandery of Knights

---

[1054] See Thomas C. Reeves, *The Empty Church: The Suicide of Liberal Christianity* (New York: The Free Press, 1996).

Templar of the State of New York [Appointed 2009]. In 2011 he had the high honor of being appointed General Grand Chaplain of the General Grand Chapter of Royal Arch Masons International.

Holy Land Pilgrimage

In March 2010, Pastor Mark was selected by the Grand Commandery of Knights Templar of the State of New York to participate in the 28th Annual Holy Land Pilgrimage. Each Spring, the Knights Templar send two clergypersons per state on a twelve day all expense paid Holy Land Pilgrimage. Clergypersons do not need to be Masons in order to participate in this program. The purpose of this program—this ministry—is to send worthy clergypersons to Israel to see the holy sites. Standing by the shore of the Sea of Galilee, seeing Bethlehem, the Temple Mount in Jerusalem, the Shrine of the Book [where the Dead Sea Scrolls are housed] and the Church of the Holy Sepulture adds a new dimension to reading, teaching, and preaching. *The Holy Bible* really comes alive when you are able to walk the land and see the locations of key events.

Pastor Mark stated that:

> During the eleven days that we were in Israel, we saw many remarkable things. However, at the top of the list, was a visit to a place, that despite years of Bible reading, and formal Seminary training, I was not particularly aware of. Today, the place is known as *Tel Bet She'an.*

A "tel" is an artificial mound containing multiple layers of debris from repeated destructions and rebuildings that accumulates over the centuries. Archaeologists cut through the layers of a tel, like the layers of a birthday cake, to recover and reconstruct the culture and the events of previous inhabitants.

In *The Holy Bible,* this place was known as "Beth Shean." In the New Testament, it was known as one of "the ten cities of the Decapolis." During the Roman Period, time of Jesus of Nazareth (c.7 B.C.-33 A.D.),[1055] the city was called "Scythopolis, or Nysa-Scythopolis [since at some point it had apparently been repopulated by a group of fierce Indo-European Scythian mercenaries]."

Bet She'an / Beth Shean / Scythopolis is remarkable because it has been inhabited by human beings since at least the Late Neolithic Period, i.e., nearly 7,000 years ago. Archaeologists have also recovered and dated artifacts back to the Chalcolithic Period (c.4500-3300 B.C.). The site is located just south of the Harod River in the Galilee on a major junction of the Jordan and Jezreel valleys.[1056]

During the Late Canaanite Period (16th to 12th century B.C.) the city was conquered and held by the Egyptians for more than two-hundred years. Apparently, during the days of Joshua and the Judges, the Israelite tribes were unable to conquer the Canaanites who lived in the area. Later, after a vicious battle waged on nearby Mount Gilboa, the

---

[1055] Interestingly, according the Gospels, Jesus of Nazareth never visited the major Hellenized Galilean cities of Tiberius, Sepphoris, or Scythopolis!

[1056] Miriam Feinberg Vamosh, *National Parks of Israel: Beit She'an: Capital of the Decapolis* (Israel: Eretz Ha-Tzvi, Inc, 1996).

Philistines slew King Saul (1051-1011 B.C.) and his son's (I Samuel 31:8-10). The Philistines then displayed the decapitated and mutilated bodies on the city's walls. During the reign of King Solomon (971-931 B.C.), the city finally fell under Israelite control (I Kings 4:12).

Pastor Mark at Qumran with Cave Four in the background.
Here the Dead Seas Scrolls were written, studied,
and hidden until they were recovered in 1947.

In 732 B.C., the Assyrian armies destroyed and captured the city. Apparently, Beth Shean was abandon until the arrival of Alexander the Great (356-323 B.C.) and the Greeks. Following the death of Alexander in Babylon at the age of 33, the rebuilt city changed hands between the Egyptian Ptolemies and the Syrian Seleucids. At this time, the city became thoroughly Hellenized complete with an elegant theater, a basilica, a nyphaeum [a monumental public fountain], a bustling marketplace, a hippodrome, a elaborate bathhouse, and a temple dedicated to the Greek god Dionysus [the god of wine and unbridled emotions].

After the Maccabean revolt (167-134 B.C.), the Hasmoneans (c.104 B.C.) took control of the city. The city then fell to Roman domination when Pompey Magnus (106 B.C.-48 B.C.) subdued the region (c.63 B.C.). During the reign of Herod the Great (37 B.C.-4 B.C.) the city became the capital of a regional alliance of ten pagan Greek cities known as "the Decapolis." According to Flavius Josephus ((37 –c.100 A.D.), during *The First Jewish War* (66-70 A.D.), the Greek population of Scythopolis showed their loyalty to the Romans by massacring the entire Jewish population. The city was an important center of Greco-Roman culture until January 18, 749 A.D. when a massive earthquake [the great "Golan Earthquake"] reduced the once glorious polis to total ruins. The destruction from this catastrophe can still be seen on the site. During the Crusader Period (1099-1281 A.D.) there was a small outpost located near the site.

Archaeologists began working the tel in the 1890s, and again, during the 1920s. Today, it is still an active archaeological dig being worked by the Israeli Antiquities Authority. Although Bet She'an is not mentioned in the New Testament, this is the largest and best-preserved late Roman Period city in modern Israel. The 400 acre site is beautifully maintained as a national park.

The theater at Beth Shean-Scythopolis held more than 7,000 people.
It, along with the rest of the city,
was destroyed in the great Golan Earthquake of January 18, 749 A.D.
Photo: The Rev. Dr. Mark D. Isaacs

Today, visitors can walk among the ruins of an Egyptian temple, and a massive theater that once seated more than 7,000 spectators. There is also an impressive column lined *cardo* [i.e., a main street/business district] complete with little shops and ruined public buildings. In addition to bathhouses [featuring heated water!], there are the impressive remains of a Byzantine era public lavatory which could accommodate forty people at a time. The lavatory featured running water and marble seats!

There are several remarkable lessons to be learned from Beth Shean-Scythopolis.

First, white marble is *not* available in Israel. When you walk among the impressive ruins of a Greco-Roman city such as Scythopolis you are astonished by the amount of marble used in the construction of these once great buildings. Not only is the workmanship incredible [ancient operative masons did this work without the benefit of modern power tools!], but perhaps the most astonishing thing is that all of the marble had to be imported from quarries in either Greece or Turkey! You are left wondering how did they move massive marble blocks and marble columns hundreds and hundreds and hundreds of miles without the benefit of modern rail systems, superhighways, or trucks? Imagine the effort and the expense involved! Indeed, these were dedicated and persistent builders!

Second, in a tel, when the city is destroyed by marauding armies, a new city is built on top of the ruins of the old city. With this particular site, there is something like seventeen layers of destruction! The builders of the new city would often reuse the ashlar's that were cut by masons and used in previous structures. In other words, the buildings come and go, but the priceless stones and blocks quarried and squared by the masons were reused over and over again.

In 2010, these same stones, columns, and capitals are still visible [the Five Orders of Architecture]. These ancient stones have been carefully excavated by the archaeologist's trowel and placed on display throughout the dig site. It is astonishing when you realize that some of these stones are more than 2,000 years old, and that despite the fact that we do not know the names of the individual masons that created these objects of beauty, we can celebrate their craftsmanship all of these centuries later.

Third, it is also interesting to note that it is extremely difficult for archaeologists to attempt to reconstruct the daily lives of the people that once inhabited the various cities on this site. What were they like? What did they believe? How did they live? While these and other questions may be impossible to answer the one thing that remains for us to behold and to wonder about are the ashlar's—the beautifully hewn stones that the masons of long-ago left behind. Empires come and empires go, but the stones—silent witnesses to cunning and curious craftsmanship—remain forever! On this side of heaven, these stones are the nearest thing to eternal life.

According the Pastor Mark, "Freemasonry teaches us the eternal lessons derived from the ancient builders. As we walk among ancient ruins we are left to wonder what our long term contribution might be to the human family. How will we be remembered? Will someone be admiring our handiwork 100, 200, or a thousand years from now? Examining these ancient stones leaves us asking questions and wondering!"

Chapter Thirteen: Sons of St. Paul's (Wurtemburg) Who Became Clergymen

On June 5, 1960, with the Rev. Herbert Finch (Pastor Emeritus) and the Rev. Rolf W. Eschke (current Pastor), a special Bicentennial Service was held at St. Paul's. Participating Clergy included the Rev. Alfred L. Beck D.D., Litt.D, President of the United Lutheran Synod of New York and New England, and the Rev. Paul C. White, Ed.D., D.D., and Ph.D., Secretary of the United Lutheran Synod of New York and New England.

The bulletin for the day stated that the following sons of St. Paul's were called to the Ministry: "The Rev. William Edwin Traver; The Rev. Dr. Chester Henry Traver; The Rev. Dr. John Gideon Traver; and the Rev. Philip E. Bierbauer."

The Rev. William Edwin Traver

The first son of Wurtemburg to serve in the Lutheran ministry was the **Rev. William Edwin Traver** (January 24, 1847- January 31, 1930). He served in the Lutheran ministry for fifty-five years. Pastor Traver died in Rhinebeck, New York, in his home on East Market Street, on Friday, January 31, 1930. At the time of his death he was eighty-three years old. He had been sick for three months. The stated cause of death was "a complication of diseases."[1057]

The Rev. William Edwin Traver
Photo: Christ Lutheran Church in Germantown, New York.

The Rev. W. Edwin Traver lived in the village of Rhinebeck for the last three years of his life. He moved back to Rhinebeck when he retired from full-time ministry in 1928.

[1057] *The Rhinebeck Gazette*, "Rev. Wm. E. Traver Passes at Age of 83: Venerable Clergyman, Active in Lutheran Ministry for 55 years" February 8, 1930, p.1. Also, see interesting profile clipping in *Mrs. Samuel S. Frost's (1819-1912) Scrapbook,* (St. Paul's Archives), p.15.

Prior to his death, he had "displayed remarkable physical and mental vigor."[1058] He had served as Interim Pastor of Third Evangelical Lutheran Church in the village of Rhinebeck until they called the Rev. Lauren Henry Grandy (Hartwick, 1922, who served at Third Lutheran from 1929 to 1935, and died 1954) as their regular pastor.

Pastor Traver was born in the Town of Clinton, which was then known as "Zippleburg," in the Slate Quarry neighborhood. William E. Traver was the son of Martin (1818-1888) and Catharine Ann Traver (1813-1892).[1059] He was baptized on June 6, 1847,[1060] and confirmed in 1863 at St. Paul's (Wurtemburg). He grew up on a farm. As a youth he was known as "Bill Ed." Later in life he recalled that, after a long absence from Rhinebeck, old school acquaintances would meet him and inquire if he was the same "Bill Ed" from days gone by.[1061]

One of the most vivid memories of his childhood, which he often took pleasure in describing to younger listeners, was the procession that was held in Rhinebeck in connection with the first candidacy of Abraham Lincoln (i.e., the presidential election of 1860). He recalled that "a great crowd took part, two bands furnished music, and on an old wagon was carried a huge rail, which two stalwart men were busily splitting to the entertainment of all onlookers, in imitation of the great rail splitter of Illinois who headed the new Republican ticket."[1062] He added that, "never did he see so much enthusiasm shown over a Presidential election."[1063]

Traver began to study for the Lutheran ministry at the age of nineteen. During the next three years (1866 to 1870), he attended Hartwick Seminary. When the principal Timothy T. Titus, "became ill, lost his voice, and died early in 1873," the Seminary was forced to temporarily close for a year.[1064] At the time, Hartwick Seminary was also experiencing serious financial problems. Until 1872, there had been no formal ties between Hartwick and various Lutheran governing synods. In the reorganization that followed, each of the three synods in the region; i.e., the Franckean Synod, the Hartwick Synod, and the combined New York and New Jersey Synod, were assigned trustees on the board.[1065] As a result of these administrative difficulties at Hartwick, William E. Traver was forced to complete his theological education at the Gettysburg Lutheran Seminary. He graduated in June 1873.[1066]

[1058] Ibid.

[1059] See both Martin and Catharine's obituary clippings in *Mrs. Samuel S. Frost's (1819-1912) Scrapbook,* (St. Paul's Archives), p.33.

[1060] Baptized by the Rev. Charles Adam Smith, D.D. (1809-1879).

[1061] *The Rhinebeck Gazette*, February 8, 1930.

[1062] Ibid.

[1063] Ibid.

[1064] Bailey, *Hartwick College*, p.52.

[1065] Ibid., p.54.

[1066] Abdel Ross Wentz, *History of the Gettysburg Theological Seminary: 1826-1926* (Philadelphia: United Lutheran Publications House, 1926), p.445.

For three months following his graduation, he supplied St. Paul's Lutheran Church in West Camp. Afterwards he accepted a call to the Tribes Hill Lutheran Church, in West Amsterdam, Montgomery County, New York. He served here for four-and-one-half years (1873 to 1878). When he arrived "he found the church in a rather bad way."[1067] The church was heavily in debt, with a dwindling congregation. However, by the end of his tenure, the mortgage had been paid off, "and the church was flourishing in regards to both finances and enlarged membership."[1068]

The Rev. W. Edwin Traver "was a strong believer in the importance of Sunday School."[1069] After his retirement, the Rev. Traver enjoyed recalling his part in building up a thriving Sunday School at Zion Lutheran Church in Athens, New York. He served at Zion from 1878 to 1883. Historic Zion Lutheran Church in Athens was the congregation served by the Rev. Wilhelm Berkenmeyer until his death in 1751. On a certain Sunday, he made an announcement to his congregation that a Sunday School would start the following week. He added that it would be held if there were only himself present as the superintendent, his wife Melissa as a teacher, and his young daughter Gertrude as a scholar. The result of the undertaking was a success beyond expectation. And, he made an effort to have the poorer children from upper Athens attend, and interested himself in their welfare. "Undoubtedly… the new Sunday School had an important part in molding the character of these young people into the worthy and highly-honored citizens that many of them later became."[1070]

Reflecting on his years of experience, Rev. Traver stated that, "the most successful work I've done for the up building of the ministry has been through the Sunday School." "Sunday School," he added, "is not only important for the life of the church, but it is vital for the salvation of the country. People fail to realize that there is a generation coming right on behind them which some day is going to take their place."[1071]

From Athens, the Rev. Traver accepted a call to Orleans, Four Corners, New York (1883 to 1886). This church was located in northern New York State, in Jefferson County near the Thousand Islands. He remained there for only three years, "as the long winters were not to his liking."[1072]

His next charge was at St. John's Lutheran Church in Ancram, Columbia County, New York.[1073] He served in Ancram for eight-and-one-half years (1886 to 1894). He recalled that, when he first came to the church after seeing the shabby carpet that covered the floor and the bad condition of the building, "he almost fell over." Within three

---

[1067] *The Rhinebeck Gazette*, February 8, 1930.

[1068] Ibid.

[1069] Ibid., p.4.

[1070] Ibid., p.1.

[1071] Ibid., p.4.

[1072] Ibid.

[1073] St. John's Lutheran Church, 1277 County Route 7, Ancram, New York.

months, the task of renovation had been started, at a cost of $4,000 [adjusted for inflation $94,296.25 (2009)], and when he left, the entire debt had been paid off.[1074]

Pastor Traver's next pastorate was in Germantown, New York. Christ Evangelical Lutheran Church in Germantown [earlier known as "East Camp"] was the mother church of the Palatines in this region. This was his longest ministry. He remained there for twenty-four years (1894 to 1919).[1075] This church was also "in somewhat discouraging condition." When he arrived, more than $800 [adjusted for inflation $19,583.85 (2009)] was due on back salaries and there was some uncertainty as to whether he himself would be paid. Nevertheless, success again rewarded the pastor's efforts.[1076]

During his twenty-four year sojourn, the church, built in 1868, was remodeled at the cost of $10,000 (c.1900) [adjusted for inflation $254,467.94 (2009)], and other repairs were made to the property. The buildings were re-roofed with slate, not only was all this paid for, but the church treasury had $600 [adjusted for inflation, $15,268.08 (2009)] in the bank as savings. All other church organizations also had substantial bank accounts. Again, the Rev. Traver carried out the purpose which he felt lay behind his life mission. He explained that, during his career, "my work has been taking churches that were in a bad situation and building them up for someone else to carry on in the regular manner."[1077]

From Germantown, Pastor Traver went to St. Thomas Lutheran Church, Churchtown, New York, where he served for nine years (1919 to 1928). He retired from this call on May 1, 1928, and removed to Rhinebeck, New York, taking up a new residence on East Market Street in the village. Prior to his death Pastor Traver served as interim pastor during an extended vacancy at Third Lutheran Church in the village of Rhinebeck.

During his long career, Rev. Traver was sent three times as a delegate to the General Synod. Perhaps due to his experience as a student at Hartwick Seminary, he was one of the early advocates of the union between the three area Lutheran synods; i.e., The Hartwick Synod (1830), the Franckean Synod (1837), and the New York and New Jersey Synods (1872). In 1908, they were united to form the New York Synod which covered the entire state.[1078] While the New York Synod was being formed, Rev. Traver served on the committee that drafted the new constitution.[1079]

The Rev. Traver was married twice. His first wife, Melissa Adelaide Love, was a descendant of an old Dutch family from South Rondout [Kingston], New York. They were married in September 1879. The couple had one daughter, Gertrude [Mrs. Dewitt Moore, d. July 1928]. Melissa died on November 14, 1911. His second wife was Caroline Jane Niver (1875-1978). They were married on April 8, 1922. Caroline Niver

---

[1074] *The Rhinebeck Gazette*, February 8, 1930.

[1075] Ruth Decker, *275 Years of Lutheran Witness in the Central Hudson Valley* (Germantown, N.Y.: Christ Lutheran Church, 1985), p.37.

[1076] *The Rhinebeck Gazette*, February 8, 1930, p.4.

[1077] Ibid.

[1078] Abdel Ross Wentz, *The Lutheran Church in American History* (Philadelphia: United Lutheran Publications House, 1923, 1933), p.396.

[1079] *The Rhinebeck Gazette*, February 8, 1930.

was a school teacher in New York City. Caroline, her sister, and his daughter Gertrude (from his first wife) all graduated in 1894 in the last class to matriculate at Seymour Smith Academy at Pine Plains, New York.[1080]

Funeral services for Pastor Traver were held on Tuesday, February 11, 1930, at 2:30 PM at Third Evangelical Lutheran Church in the village of Rhinebeck. The church was filled to the doors and the coffin was borne by members of the Lutheran Brotherhood (men's group) and the Ladies Aid Society flanked the aisles.[1081]

The service was led by the Rev. H.E. Shimer, D.D., president of the Eastern Conference of the United Lutheran Synod. Dr. Shimer was assisted by the Rev. L.H. Grandy pastor of Third Lutheran Church—who preached the sermon—and the Rev. George E. Hipsley, D.D., pastor of St. Paul's Lutheran Church of Red Hook, New York. Dr. Hipsley paid tribute to Pastor Traver's long record of faithfulness in the Lutheran ministry. "A number of clergymen belonging to the Eastern Conference were present and the floral tributes were numerous and very beautiful."[1082]

He was buried between his two wives in Viewmonte; i.e., in the "new" cemetery near Christ Evangelical Lutheran Church in Germantown, New York.

The Rev. Chester Henry Traver, D.D.

A second son of Wurtemburg who entered the ministry was the **Rev. Chester Henry Traver, D.D.** He was born, the fourth of five brothers, in the town of Clinton in Dutchess County, New York, June 23, 1848, a son of Gideon Abram and Mary Caroline Teel Traver. Egbert G. Traver (1833-1900), an older brother, was an active member of St. Paul's and is buried in the Wurtemburg Cemetery.[1083] His younger brother was the Rev. Dr. John Gideon Traver (1863-1941).[1084]

According to area church historian Rev. William Hull, D.D. (1868-1939), Gideon A. Traver (1804-March 21, 1878),[1085] buried in the same plot at Wurtemburg Cemetery, was "one of the most esteemed laymen in the Lutheran Church in that section, frequently a delegate of his church to the Synod."[1086] Gideon A. Traver, a longtime trustee of the Church, was also one of the founding trustees of the Wurtemburg Cemetery Association.[1087]

[1080] Ibid., p.4.

[1081] Ibid.

[1082] Ibid.

[1083] See Egbert G. Traver's obituary in *Mrs. Samuel S. Frost's (1819-1912) Scrapbook,* (St. Paul's Archives), p. 39.

[1084] Heins, p.134.

[1085] See Gideon A. Traver's obituary in *Mrs. Samuel S. Frost's (1819-1912) Scrapbook,* (St. Paul's Archives), p.4.

[1086] William Hull, *History of the Lutheran Church in Dutchess County* (New York, J.E. Wible Printer: Gettysburg, PA, 1881), p.18.

[1087] *Brief History of Church with By-Laws, Rules and Regulations of the Wurtemburg Cemetery Association, Incorporated January 6th 1855* (Rhinebeck: Wurtemburg Cemetery Association, 1897), p.5.

As an infant, on July 11, 1848, Chester H. Traver was baptized by the Rev. Charles Adam Smith, D.D. (1809-1879), then pastor of St. Paul's Lutheran Church of Wurtemburg. He was confirmed on November 12, 1865, by the Rev. George Neff, D.D. (1813-1900). He was educated in area public schools and the DeGarmo Institute in Rhinebeck. In 1867, he entered Hartwick Seminary, in Otsego County, New York, and in 1870 he entered Pennsylvania College [now Gettysburg College], Gettysburg, Pennsylvania, from which he graduated in 1873.

The Rev. Chester Henry Traver, D.D.
Photo: Archives of St. Paul's Lutheran Church of Wurtemburg.

After leaving college, he took a theological course for three years, and was graduated at Gettysburg Lutheran Seminary in 1876. He was licensed by the New York and New Jersey Synod at Clarksville, New Jersey on October 18, 1875. He was ordained at Valatie, New York, September 11, 1876. He went to Chatham Village, New York, July, 1876, where he remained until 1878, and then went to Spruce Run, near Glen Gardner, New Jersey.

In 1885, he was called to the Evangelical Lutheran Church of St. Peter the Apostle [the Old Stone Church], Rhinebeck, New York, and after more than eleven years in charge there, came to St. Thomas' Lutheran Church in Churchtown, New York. Rev. Chester H. Traver's sixth pastorate in forty years was in Berne, New York.

The Rev. Traver was a trustee of Hartwick Seminary, and since his graduation from college had a deep interest in everything pertaining to education. During his long career, he did all that he could to advance the cause of education in the different places where he served. For his years of faithful service to the Lutheran Church he was awarded a Doctor of Divinity degree from Hartwick Seminary, in 1902.[1088]

He was especially interested in the history of the Lutheran Palatinate churches, and prepared sketches of all of the Lutheran churches located in Columbia and Dutchess counties, New York. For example, on September 18, 1915, his lengthy and detailed article, "Rev. Chester Traver's History of Wurttemburgh Church: Former Rhinebecker Writes Interesting Sketch About St. Paul's Lutheran Church," was published in the *The Rhinebeck Gazette*.[1089] This article was later re-edited and re-published in *The Lutheran Quarterly*.[1090] Both of these articles provided many useful and interesting historical details used in the preparation of this book.

Photo by the Rev. Mark D. Isaacs.

On September 20, 1876, he married Ida Jones (1850-1928), of Gettysburg, Pennsylvania. The couple had four children: Eulla J. (Traver) Rossman (1878-1961); Edna May Traver; Ethel Kent Traver (1882-1966); and Oliver Claggett Traver. He is buried next to his wife at the Wurtemburg Cemetery.

The Rev. John Gideon Traver, A.B., A.M., D.D.

The third son of St. Paul's (Wurtemburg) to enter the ministry was the **Rev. John Gideon Traver, A.B., A.M., D.D.** John Gideon Traver was born on December 24, 1863, the youngest of five brothers, at the family farm near Wurtemburg. He was a descendant of Sebastian Traver, one of the original settlers of Wurtemburg. His

---

[1088] Ibid., p.191.

[1089] Chester H. Traver, "Rev. Chester Traver's History of Wurttemburgh Church: Former Rhinebecker Writes Interesting Sketch About St. Paul's Lutheran Church" *The Rhinebeck Gazette*, September 18, 1915.

[1090] Chester H. Traver, D.D., "Historical Sketch of St. Paul's Lutheran Church, Rhinebeck, New York," *The Lutheran Quarterly*, July 1916, pp.382-398.

grandfather fought in the American Revolution.[1091]   His mother, Mary Caroline Teel Traver, died when he was only six years old. His father, Gideon A. Traver, died in 1878.[1092]

His eldest brother James lived near the village of Rhinebeck. After the death of his father, John Gideon Traver lived with his older brother. This enabled him to attend Rhinebeck High School. In the fall of 1880, he entered Hartwick Seminary. His course was interrupted by a life-threatening attack of pneumonia. At the time, "the physician gave little hope of his living to maturity."[1093] During his recovery, John Gideon Traver secured a teaching position in the one-room school house, "White School House, No.10," near Rhinebeck.[1094] During this time, according to his son the Rev. Amos John Traver, he went "outdoors every spare moment till returning health made possible resumption of his course at Hartwick Seminary."[1095]

John Gideon Traver's older brother, and lifelong mentor, was the Rev. Dr. Chester H. Traver. John Gideon Traver often turned to his older brother for pastoral advice and good counsel.

In 1883, he graduated as valedictorian of his class from his prep course at Hartwick Seminary. He then attended Gettysburg College and graduated in 1886.

In the fall of 1886, John Gideon Traver returned to teach at Hartwick Seminary. Thus, he began fifty-five years of uninterrupted service to the Seminary.

Dr. Traver grew up near Rhinebeck in the Rev. John Christopher Hartwick's old parish territory. He was married at St. Paul's on August 22, 1888, to Ettie Florence Tompkins (b. September 28, 1866), with the Rev. George W. Fortney presiding and Fred E. Traver as best man.[1096] He was associated for most of his career with Hartwick Seminary, as instructor, and as principal. In 1893, when he was not yet thirty years old, Dr. Traver was named Principal of Hartwick. He held this position for twenty-seven years, "longer than anyone."[1097]

As Hartwick Principal, Dr. Traver was a gentle disciplinarian with piercing eyes that, one student recalled, "would really look right through a person."[1098] While Dr. Traver was stern and unbending with the enforcement of Hartwick's rules prohibiting such student vices as drinking, dancing, and card playing, students enjoyed his enthusiastic

---

[1091] Henry Hardy Heins, editor, The Rev. Amos John Traver, D.D., "John Gideon Traver, A.M., D.D.," *Throughout all the Years: The Bicentennial Story of Hartwick in American: 1746-1946* (Oneonta, N.Y.: Hartwick College, 1946), p.135.

[1092] See Gideon A. Traver's obituary in *Mrs. Samuel S. Frost's (1819-1912) Scrapbook,* (St. Paul's Archives), p.4.

[1093] Henry Hardy Heins, p.135.

[1094] Ibid.

[1095] Ibid.

[1096] The brass Missal Stand, still in use on the altar of St. Paul's (Wurtemburg), was given in memory of Fred E. Traver and Minnie Frost Traver.

[1097] Ronald H. Bailey, *Hartwick College: A Bicentennial History: 1797-1997* (Oneonta, NY: Hartwick College), p.69.

[1098] Ibid.

238

approach to life. They called him "Uncle John" behind his back.   Dr. Traver rode his bicycle everywhere. He relished a good game of tennis, and liked to join in behind the plate when the baseball team practiced, and had a crooked finger to show for it.[1099]

The Rev. Dr. John Gideon Traver
Photo: Ronald H. Bailey,
Hartwick College: A Bicentennial History: 1797-1997.

Dr. Traver's duties would boggle the mind of a modern headmaster. He taught Greek, science, and other courses as needed. His great love was Latin. He loved to speak and read it, chuckling over the puns he found in Virgil. He taught Latin with such flair that vacationing students from Yale and Harvard often sought his tutelage.[1100]

In addition to teaching, Dr. Traver was also in charge of administration at Hartwick. The Principal had to provide for practically every need of his students and the institution. It was a family affair. The Travers lived in the Seminary, occupying an apartment in the north wing with the girls. The principal's study was strategically situated to block any unauthorized traffic between the separate wings housing boys and girls.

His wife, known fondly to the students as "Aunt Ettie," oversaw the kitchen and dining room.   Even his elderly mother-in-law, whom everyone called "Grandma Tompkins," helped out as chief cook. Mrs. Tompkins made savory soup in an old iron pot, baked bread and pies, and dispensed for the cure of all ailments copious doses of a patent medicine the students called "Dr. Dutton's Deadly Dope," which usually made them feel better, if for no other reason than its high alcoholic content.[1101]

Traver was responsible for providing board, maintenance and heat and light. He and any students he could enlist split and stacked the cords of delivered slab wood. To haul thirty to forty tons of coal from the railroad siding, he hitched up his old horse, Fanny, to

---

[1099] Ibid.

[1100] Ibid.

[1101] Ibid.

a wagon or recruited local farmers with their huskier teams. He dispensed the kerosene for all the lamps of school and church, and enforced a 10 PM lights out to make certain his charges did not burn the midnight oil.

More than a half century later, former students fondly recalled hearing the "flap, flap, flap" of Dr. Traver's house slippers as he made the rounds to enforce the curfew. He had to make sure that the icehouse was filled every winter with blocks from Goewey's Pond. His garden yielded potatoes, beans, and other produce for the Seminary tables. Poultry came from his own chicken yard, where the Rev. Louis Wagschal (class of 1909) recalled that the principal demonstrated lightning speed in plucking the birds, "a dip in the hot, then in the cold, and the feathers were off!" Wagschal, who later became a professor of Greek and Latin at Thiel College, and became pastor of Third Evangelical Lutheran Church in Rhinebeck, recalled that "in Dr. Traver lived and from him radiated love, honor and the spirit of the school."[1102]

His son, the Rev. Amos Traver [a well known Lutheran pastor and author], wrote that his father was "a Republican in politics, a militant dry, and had a hand in all the movements for the betterment of his section of the State for nearly half a century."[1103]

On August 20, 1941, while riding his bicycle to the Post Office to pick up the morning mail near the Hartwick Seminary, Dr. Traver was struck and killed by an automobile driven by a coal salesman named George Bower of Endicott, New York.[1104] He was buried at the Wurtemburg cemetery following a service led by Rev. William G. Boomhower (former pastor of St. Paul's and a Hartwick graduate) and the Rev. Elder Jay Himes.[1105]

The Rev. Philip E. Bierbauer

The fourth son of St. Paul's (Wurtemburg) to enter the ministry was the **Rev. Philip E. Bierbauer**. Philip was the son of W.H. Bierbauer and Annie Bierbauer. His grandfather and namesake Philip Bierbauer (1817-1898) was a longtime member of St. Paul's. He was born near Kircheim Bolanden in Rhenish Bavaria, Germany. He came to America "nearly sixty years ago," and is buried in the Wurtemburg Cemetery.[1106]

The Rev. Philip E. Bierbauer was born on January 18, 1879. According to Wurtemburg Church records he was baptized by the Rev. Joseph G. Griffith on January 14, 1881, with his sister Alma H. Bierbauer.

Philip E. Bierbauer graduated from Hartwick Seminary in 1896. He was licensed to preach the Gospel at Amsterdam, New York, in September 1897. His first charge was in Boulder, Colorado. After twelve years in Colorado, he was called to the Mühlenberg Memorial Church, Philadelphia, Pennsylvania. Philip E. Bierbauer, who appears to be the first regular pastor there, then served as pastor of Mühlenberg Memorial Church from

---

[1102] Ibid. p.70.

[1103] Heins, p.138.

[1104] *The Rhinebeck Gazette*, 1941.

[1105] "Many Memories of America's Past Alive in Wurtemburg Cemetery," *Hudson River Sampler*, Vol. IV, Number 7, November 2000.

[1106] See Philip Bierbauer's obituary in *Mrs. Samuel S. Frost's (1819-1912) Scrapbook,* (St. Paul's Archives), p.40.

about 1907 or 1908 to about 1913 or 1914. He then went to Saint Andrews Lutheran Church in Philadelphia, and served there until his death. The Rev. Philip E. Bierbauer died November 11, 1938, in Philadelphia.

The Rev. Henry Herbert Wahl, D.D.

To the list of the sons of St. Paul's (Wurtemburg) who entered the ministry we must add a fifth and a sixth name. The fifth name is the **Rev. Henry Herbert Wahl, D.D.,** (1891-1953), the husband of Verna Etta Traver (1893-1961). They were married on September 14, 1918. Verna Etta Traver Wahl was the daughter of Frederick Egbert Traver[1107] and Minnie L. Frost Traver [married February 6, 1889 at the home of Mandeville S. Frost[1108]].

Pastor Wahl was born in St. Agatha, Ontario, Canada. He graduated from the Hartwick Seminary in 1914, and from Waterloo College and Theological Seminary, Waterloo, Ontario, Canada. He was ordained at his home church of St. John's Lutheran of Waterloo, Ontario. His first call was to Conquerall Parish, Nova Scotia. He began his ministry there May 1, 1918. While in Nova Scotia, he also served Zion's Lutheran Church in Lunenberg. From here, on October 1, 1923, he was called to St. John's Lutheran Church in Hudson, New York.

In his obituary, *The Hudson Register* stated that, while serving at St. John's the church grew strong. Pastor Wahl, and St. John's Lutheran Church, took a leading position in the advancement of religion in the city of Hudson. During this time, "the Church's societies and missionary groups expanded and became more effective." Dr. Wahl was "a real shepherd and his flock, and no call went unheeded." He displayed a tremendous amount of energy and facility obligations he accepted when he became pastor. For example, in addition to being a dedicated pastor, he was also active in community affairs. Barbara Frost states that Pastor Wahl once took the lead in a public march of clergymen in Hudson to shut down the city's notorious "Diamond Street" district.[1109] The paper stated that, "His church, and his city, have suffered a staggering blow in the passing of Dr. Wahl."[1110]

For ten years, Dr. Wahl served as president of the Board of trustees of Hartwick Academy, New York. He also served, for many years, as a member of the Home Mission Committee of the United Synod of New York. Six times he served as a delegate to the convention of the United Lutheran Church in America. In Hudson he served as president of the Hudson Ministers Association and also serve various offices in the Columbia County Ministerial Association.

[1107] See Fred E. Traver's obituary in *Mrs. Samuel S. Frost's (1819-1912) Scrapbook,* (St. Paul's Archives), p.37.

[1108] See Traver-Frost wedding announcement in *Mrs. Samuel S. Frost's (1819-1912) Scrapbook,* (St. Paul's Archives), p.38.

[1109] Barbara Frost interview, November 23, 2007.

[1110] "Funeral of Dr. Wahl on Tuesday: Body of Beloved Pastor to Lie in State, Died in Columbia Memorial Saturday," *The Hudson Register,* June 1, 1953.

In June, 1952, Hartwick College conferred on Pastor Wahl the honorary degree of Doctor of Divinity, "being in recognition of his years of consecrated and fruitful service as pastor, religious leader, and teacher of youth."

The Rev. Henry Herbert Wahl, D.D.
Photo: Archives of St. Paul's Lutheran Church of Wurtemburg.

Dr. Wahl served as pastor of St. John's Lutheran Church in Hudson, New York, "faithfully and in a Christian-like manner for nearly thirty years,"[1111] i.e., from October 1, 1923 to May 30, 1953. Pastor Wahl is buried in the 1853 section of the Wurtemburg Cemetery.

Verna Etta Traver, Pastor Wahl's wife, was a graduate of Hartwick Seminary. Verna Wahl was tragically killed in an accident while exiting a bus near Ithaca on November 27, 1961. At the time she was on her way to do volunteer work in the community.

The Rev. Roy Steward, Jr.

The sixth son of St. Paul's (Wurtemburg) to enter the ministry is the **Rev. Roy Steward, Jr.,** President of the Evangelical Lutheran Conference and Ministerium [ELCM]. Pastor Roy is currently the pastor of three Lutheran churches in Altoona, Pennsylvania.

[1111] Ibid.

242

Roy Steward, Jr. grew up on a dairy farm on Wurtemburg Road. He was baptized at St. Paul's (Wurtemburg), and he graduated from Rhinebeck High School. He recalls that in high school he was known as "Wurtemburger."[1112]

Pastor Roy graduated from Hartwick College and the Lutheran Theological Seminary in Gettysburg in 1966.

In a recent interview, Pastor Roy fondly recalled attending Sunday School in the gallery, and pumping the old organ during worship services.

He also recalled that, "the first sermon that I ever preached was at the Wurtemburg Church on a Youth Sunday. At the time I was probably in junior high." The text was Joshua 24, "Choose Ye this Day whom ye will serve… but as for me and my house we will serve the Lord!"

Pastor Roy also recalled that "my Confirmation class met in the room with the second story left-front balcony window. Eventually, as an older teen, I taught a Sunday School Class for third-graders in the same space. I also taught Vacation Bible School and Sunday School classes on the opposite side right-front Balcony window and used the belfry to steeple stairway room as a craft room. I also taught Vacation Church School and Sunday School Classes in the basement kitchen area."

Also at Wurtemburg "I served on a variety of church committees, the Acolyte Guild and as Luther League president." During my high school years, Wurtemburg had "one of the most active Luther Leagues in New York State."

"On my way home from my dairy barn I would often stop at the Church when our organist Mary Traver Baas was practicing. She would sing over the hymns for the coming week that the pastor had selected and other hymns that were more singable."

As a young boy, "I served as a coffee pourer at the Turkey Suppers and Strawberry Festivals." These events were major social and community events. For example, in October 2010 St. Paul's (Wurtemburg) held its 149th Annual Turkey Supper. During the early 1960s, the Synod attempted to prohibit church suppers. The independent congregational members of the Wurtemburg Church staunchly resisted. In fact, stated Pastor Roy, "one pastor actually turned down a call to St. Paul's because the congregation continued to hold church suppers."

"Several years later," he added, "that same pastor turned out to be the ELCA Bishop that I would stand up to and whose actions would be a primary motivation for me to leave the ELCA. It is indeed amazing how paths of life cross and intersect."

He also recalled that, "In the Church Social Hall I became a member of 'Neighbors Gun Club.' In those days, prior to building their own building, the Gun Club met at St. Paul's for its monthly meetings. It was always so impressive to see so many men gathered at one time in the Church basement for the Gun Club meetings."

Pastor Roy recalled that, "many many hours of my youth and young adulthood were spent within and around these hallowed walls. Truly the Church was the center of my life in my youth, and young adulthood, as it continues to be to this day."

"During junior high and high school, I rented a farm for my cattle and for my farming endeavors. The land that I rented was owned by members of my home church, and the land that I rented encompassed the Church grounds on three sides. One day,

---

[1112] "Rev. Roy A. Stewart Biographical Materials," http://members.aol.com/revroyas/Bgrph.htm <August 7, 2006>

while he was away on vacation, my cows got out of the fences and made their way into the beautiful garden of our Pastor. Pastor Fred Dunn was originally from New York City. The pastor thought that the damage was done by raccoons until I confessed that it was in fact my cows. I made amends by giving him his pick of my sweet corn patch."

In January, and in May 2000, St. Paul's (Wurtemburg) voted unanimously in two separate votes to leave the Evangelical Lutheran Church in America [ELCA] and join the Evangelical Lutheran Conference and Ministerium [ELCM]. About this decision Pastor Roy stated that, "This beloved and historical Church, and the people who worshipped and taught the Word of God in it, was one of the most formative influences on my life. Here I was baptized! Here I was confirmed! Here I was first admitted to the Sacrament of Holy Communion." "I was absolutely honored and thrilled when my home church, St. Paul's (Wurtemburg), voted to become a part of our little mustard seed church."

About St. Paul's, Pastor Roy stated that, "I was privileged to have this beautiful historic setting in place, and to be touched by the history of what had transpired in this beautiful and sacred setting. I give thanks to God for the memories, and for the privilege, of being enabled to have my formative Christian understandings shaped in this setting."

Chapter Fourteen: Art and Architecture

St. Paul's Lutheran Church of Wurtemburg—the three cemeteries and the 1870 Parsonage—is located on about eight acres of land. The Church building is located on a high hill facing south. Thus, the altar is not located on the east wall—as Church tradition would dictate. The entrance faces south onto a large natural looking gravel parking lot and driveway surrounded by three cemeteries.

St. Paul's Lutheran Church of Wurtemburg was built in 1802
while Thomas Jefferson was serving his first term as President of the United States.
Photo by Nester Bryant.

St. Paul's churchyard-style colonial cemetery (c. 1800-1852) flanks the building to the immediate north and east. To the south is the 1853 "rural [style] cemetery." The new cemetery [c. 2000] is located just across Wurtemburg Road on the west side. The Church is surrounded by open land with a dramatic view of the Catskill Mountains to the west.

St. Paul's (Wurtemburg) is "in the [New England] meetinghouse tradition as adapted by Georgian craftsman."[1113] Reflecting Puritan austerity, these classic New England meetinghouses are deliberately less ornate than medieval and Renaissance churches. According to James F. White, the Puritans tended to have a "fear of art and music" because they regarded them "as dangerous distractions from hearing the Word of God."[1114]

The entrance doors feature quaint
ornamented "half-wagon wheel" windows.
Photo by the Rev. Mark D. Isaacs.

St. Paul's is beautiful because of its geometric simplicity and its chaste and simple style. Practical symmetry in design, combined with an ideal hilltop location, taking full advantage of the nearly constant breeze from the west, or the south, allows for cross

---

[1113] Landmarks of Dutchess County, p.168.

[1114] James F. White, *Protestant Worship and Church Architecture* (Eugene, OR: Wipf and Stock Publications, 2003), p.125.

ventilation. A 1980 *Building Structure Inventory Form,*[1115] compiled by the Rhinebeck Historical Society for the Division for Historic Preservation, New York State Parks and Recreation, describes St. Paul's as "a two-story clapboard structure[1116] with a broad gable roof and a three-bay facade with a pedimented gable. The building rests on a raised fieldstone foundation, typical of early nineteenth century area construction methods. The windows are twelve over twelve, six over six and two over two with plain sill and molded lintels. The facade is characterized by two-double paneled entrance doors and central tripartite windows with boldly molded tracery and central keystones."[1117]

Photo by the Rev. Mark D. Isaacs.

[1115] *Building Structure Inventory Form*—with a handwritten sheet—compiled by Connie Fowle, Rhinebeck Historical Society for the Division for Historic Preservation, New York State Parks and Recreation, August 27, 1980 (on file at the Quitman House, Rhinebeck New York).

[1116] Clapboard walls made of wooden planks layered like shingles.

[1117] Ibid.

Two sets of [red] double entry doors are framed with an impressive tympanum; i.e., New England style ornamental doorway with ornate trim. "The half-wheel windows at the front and the decorated cornices are particularly representative of the post-Colonial period."[1118] The portico is constructed of massive bluestones quarried from the area.

"The second floor windows are twelve-over twelve and fall just below a medallion cornice which extends across the gable. Above the cornice in the gable peak is a round window with lobare tracery. Slightly to the rear of the gable peak the square bell tower which supports an octagonal belfry caped with a bell cast roof and octagonal finial."[1119] Beneath the cornices a series of dentils [small rectangular blocks] have been added for decoration.

The Building Structure Inventory Form continues, "The interior dates to the mid-nineteenth century renovations of the building [i.e., 1831, 1861 and 1890], except that the gallery paneling and two Federal style doors [with original latches] in the balcony appear to be earlier."[1120]

"The interior of St. Paul's (Wurtemburg) shows the evidence of the resurgence of classicism noted at the mid-century through the Italianate taste. This is especially evident in the nave decoration, completed entablature and [cast iron] support columns [which support the gallery]."[1121]

A Note on Architectural Styles

In Dutchess County, New York, between 1786 and 1839, three distinctive architectural styles successively made their appearance; i.e., the Georgian, the Federal, and Greek Revival.[1122]

The earliest of these three high architectural styles, both public and domestic, is that of the Georgian. The origins of the Georgian style (1714-1840) can be traced to seventeenth-century England. In England, this style first arose during the reign of King George I, who ascended the throne in 1714, and continued until after the American Revolution (King George III).[1123] Like classical music, the classicism of the Georgian style was intended to convey the idea of clarity of expression, conservatism, tradition, stability, formal structure, geometric precision, culture, and a rational civilization and order.

Georgian style can be traced to a British reworking of Italian Palladian architecture, which exhibited strong interest in Greco-Roman features, such as the classical orders of architecture,[1124] pediments, porticos, cornices, a rigid symmetry and careful placement of architectural detail.[1125]

[1118] *Landmarks of Dutchess County*, p.168.

[1119] Ibid.

[1120] Ibid.

[1121] Building Structure Inventory Form.

[1122] Dutchess County Planning Board, p.115.

[1123] George I (1714-1727); George II (1727-1760); and George III (1760-1820).

[1124] i.e., "The Tuscan, the Doric, the Ionic, the Corinthian, and the Composite." See Asher Benjamin, *The American Builder's Companion: Or, A System of Architecture Particularly*

The octagon belfry with a bell cast roof and octagonal finial.
Photo by the Rev. Mark D. Isaacs.

"Colonial" Georgian architecture became the dominant style of eighteenth-century America. Georgian style replaced the functional vernacular Colonial styles of the early seventeenth and mid-eighteenth centuries. Typically, these early buildings, many constructed by early Dutch settlers, were one or one-and-a-half story structures built of

Adapted to the Present Style of Building (New York:: Dover Publications, 1827, 1969 reprint), pp.30-46.

[1125] Joyce C. Ghee, *Building in Dutchess: Reading the Landscape* (Poughkeepsie, New York: The Dutchess County Department of History, 1988), p.31.

fieldstones and mortar. Many examples of these "stark, no nonsense" old Dutch stone structures can still be seen in Dutchess and Ulster County.[1126]

Unlike earlier architectural styles, which were disseminated among craftsmen through the direct experience of the apprenticeship system, Georgian architecture was disseminated to builders through the new medium of inexpensive books of engravings. From the mid-eighteenth century, Georgian styles were assimilated into an architectural vernacular that became part and parcel of the training of every carpenter, mason, and plasterer.[1127]

Four Important Architects

Perhaps the best known—and most influential—architect of this period was Sir Christopher James Wren (1632-1723). He was a seventeenth-century English designer, astronomer, geometrician, scientist, and the greatest English architect of his time.

Sir Christopher Wren (1632-1723)

In 1662, a proposal was made for the formation of a society "for the promotion of Physico-Mathematical Experimental Learning." This organization received its royal charter from King Charles II, and "The Royal Society of London for the Promotion of Natural Knowledge" was formed. In addition to being a founding member of the Royal Society Christopher Wren also served as president from 1680 to 1682.

Wren's scientific interests ranged from astronomy, optics, the problem of determining longitude at sea, cosmology, mechanics, microscopy, surveying, medicine and meteorology. He observed, measured, dissected, built models, invented, employed

---

[1126] Ibid.

[1127] Ibid.

250

and improved a variety of new scientific instruments including the telescope and the microscope.[1128]

Perhaps no incident had more influence upon the modernizing of architecture in England than the Great Fire of London which occurred in 1666. This fire consumed more than 12,000 houses and destroyed eighty-seven churches.[1129] In addition to killing thousands of people, an estimated two-thirds of the city was reduced to ashes.

The Great Fire of 1666 was the second hammer blow that struck London. The first occurred in 1665, when the plague swept the city, and killed more than 100,000 Londoners—perhaps a quarter of the total population.[1130] Daniel Defoe (c.1660-1731) vividly retold long forgotten details of this horrific calamity in his classic *A Journal of the Plague Year* (1722).

After the plague, and the Great Fire, London was described by contemporaries as "a vast desert." The rebuilding of London called for architects. Christopher Wren was chosen as the chief architect for fifty-three London churches that were intended to replace those destroyed by the fire.[1131] And, since most of the medieval buildings that burned in London were wooden structures, the fire became an important stimulus for the wider use of brick in the reconstruction of both public buildings and private homes.

Wren's greatest architectural achievement was St. Paul's Cathedral in London. Wren, as the master of four professions; i.e., mathematics, astronomy, metrology, and architecture,[1132] incorporated "sacred geometry" into the cathedral's basic design. For example, St. Paul's, at five-hundred fifty-five feet long, is "all fiveness."[1133] The impressive dome, a distinctive London landmark that inspired the present U.S. Capitol dome, rises three-hundred and sixty-five feet [representing the days of the year].[1134] The Centrium rotunda is designed around seven radiating concentric circles, symbolic of the seven known planets.[1135]

However, his designs also had a practical function. Wren, a Protestant, once wrote that "in our Religion… [it is vital] that all who are present can both hear the Service and

---

[1128] Henry Wilson Coli, *Coil's Masonic Encyclopedia* (Richmond, VA: Macoy Publishing & Masonic Supply Co. 1961, 1995), pp.692-693.

[1129] Walter George Bell, *The Great Fire of London in 1666* (London: The Folio Society, 1920, 2003), p.147.

[1130] Walter George Bell, *The Great Plague in London: 1665* (London: The Folio Society, 1924, 2001), p.xi.

[1131] White, p.95.

[1132] Stephen Skinner, *Sacred Geometry: Deciphering the Code* (New York: Sterling Publishing, Co., 2006), p.136.

[1133] "The Pythagoreans had a special fondness for the number five." Mervin B. Hogan, "Pythagoras and the Number Five, *The Philalethes*, June 1986, p.10.

[1134] Skinner, p.137.

[1135] Ibid.

see the Preacher."[1136] Thus, he computed how close a person had to be in relation to the pulpit in order "to hear distinctly."[1137]

Due to the beauty of his designs—coupled with the sheer scale of the rebuilding of London—Sir Christopher Wren's "auditory design" on the inside, and staged towers on the outside, became the prototype for eighteenth-century American meetinghouses.[1138] Despite the fact that Wren and most of his followers never came to the colonies, his bold designs led to the development of an entire new school of architectural design, and eventually influenced the work done in the colonies.

Another important and influential architect from this period was **James Gibbs** (1682–1754).[1139] Gibbs was born in Scotland. He studied in Rome under Carlo Fontana. He returned to England in 1709. There he was appointed a member of the commission authorized to build fifty churches in London. Of these, only ten were completed— including two of Gibbs's most distinguished works, the churches of St. Mary-le-Strand (1714–1717) and St. Martin-in-the-Fields (1721–1726). The church of St. Martin-in-the-Fields formed the basic inspiration for many of the steepled churches of the colonial period in America—including St. Paul's (Wurtemburg).

Gibbs' work was heavily influenced by Sir Christopher Wren. The influence of James Gibbs, and the Georgian style, spread beyond England and into the colonies because he published a number of popular pattern books and builder's handbooks. He wrote a *Book of Architecture* (1728) and *Rules for Drawing the Several Parts of Architecture* (1732).[1140] These books, because they included lavish plates of his designs, were used by skilled craftsman to adapt and duplicate his designs in either stone or wood.

Charles Bulfinch (1763–1844) was America's first native architect.[1141] He was born in Boston, Massachusetts. He graduated from Harvard University, where he received a theoretical introduction to Neoclassicism and some training in mathematics and perspective. His son, Stephen Greenleaf Bulfinch (1809-1870), an author and Unitarian minister, wrote "that his father never studied with a master but that he was entirely self-taught."[1142]

As a member of the Boston Board of Selectmen in 1791, he was chosen Chairman in 1799—an office equivalent to mayor. Bulfinch held this important position for nineteen years. As Chairman, he also served as Police Superintendent. During this time, he worked to improve Boston's streets, drains, and lighting. Under his supervision, both the

---

[1136] White, p.95.

[1137] Ibid.

[1138] Ibid.

[1139] Bernd Evers, *Architectural Theory From the Renaissance to the Present* (Cologne: Taschen, 2006), p.260.

[1140] Ibid.

[1141] Harold Kirker, *The Architecture of Charles Bulfinch* (Cambridge: Harvard University Press, 1969, 1998), p.5.

[1142] Ibid. His older son was Thomas Bulfinch (1796-1867). He is the author of the classic *Bulfinch's Mythology,*

infrastructure and civic center of Boston were transformed into a dignified neoclassical style.

America's first native architect,
Charles Bulfinch (1763–1844)
was entirely self-taught.

Bullfinch's most monumental works include: the first theater in New England, the Federal Street Theater (1794); the famous Massachusetts Statehouse in Boston (1799); University Hall at Harvard (1815); Faneuil Hall (1805-1806); and the Massachusetts General Hospital (1820). His works are notable for their simplicity, balance, and good taste. His designs were the origin of a distinctive Federal style of classical domes, columns, and ornament that dominated early nineteenth-century American architecture.

In 1817, President James Monroe appointed Charles Bulfinch "Architect of the Capitol."[1143] Washington, D.C., because it had been burned by the British in 1814, was in need of rebuilding. From 1818 to 1830, Bulfinch designed and completed the U.S. Capitol building. His design of the west portico, with the terraces and steps forming the approach to it, can still be seen. Bullfinch's architectural work on the Capitol building, and on the Massachusetts Statehouse, set the basic pattern for state capitol buildings throughout the country.

He also designed a memorial column on Beacon Hill (1789); the Massachusetts State Prison (1803); a number of Massachusetts courthouses, and Franklin Crescent in Boston (1793). The First Church of Christ, Unitarian in Lancaster, Massachusetts (1816–1817), one of his finest works, is one of the few churches of the many that he designed that remain standing.

Bulfinch's works bear a distinctive stamp of their own. Their classic elegance, repose, and refinement of detail rank them among the best products of the nation's early

---

[1143] Ibid., p.6.

years.[1144] His style has been called "Federal Architecture." The Federal style is an adaptation of British-style Georgian architecture, but uniquely American. The Federal style of architecture, simpler than Georgian, was a later and more classic form of Georgian that also incorporated graceful, delicate interiors. The most characteristic Federal motif is the porticoed doorway, with its elliptical fanlight extending over narrow, flanking sidelights.

Many public buildings, as well as the majority of Hudson River estates built during this period, embody characteristics of both Georgian and Federal styles. Again, because of the popularity and wide distribution of design handbooks, even middle-class farmers in rural Dutchess County were building Georgian or Federal homes. With these buildings no architect was necessary; a skilled carpenter could easily adapt the classic principles underlying both styles to his own uses.

Asher Benjamin (1773-1845) was one of several young architects who were attracted to Boston during the early-nineteenth century. During this time Boston was experiencing unprecedented economic prosperity. And, during this time, Charles Bullfinch was at the height of his creative powers. Asher Benjamin was a disciple of Charles Bullfinch. Thus, structures built during this period are often called "Bullfinch-Benjamin style designs." Benjamin's designs transitioned between Federal style architecture and later Greek Revival style.

Benjamin was born in Greenfield, Massachusetts in 1773. He received his early training from a local builder. During his apprenticeship, he worked on the Old Connecticut State House, located in Hartford, Connecticut. This building had been designed by Charles Bulfinch. By 1800, Benjamin had designed a number of houses, public buildings, and churches throughout New England.

While his buildings were wonderful, Asher Benjamin's most lasting contribution to American architecture was the publication of seven handbooks, or builder's guides, on architecture. Benjamin's practical books served as a major source of architectural education for American carpenter-builders. His books contained basic designs and practical instruction on the construction of elementary structural and geometric forms. These important books served as templates for local craftsmen, who in turn interpreted his designs for a variety of building projects. These "pattern books," the first written by an American architect, brought architectural history, style, and geometry to ordinary builders in the field. These handbooks featured superb drawings and practical advice on not only full house plans, but also such details as circular staircases, doorways, mantlepieces, dormer windows, pilasters, balusters, and fences.[1145]

For example, Asher Benjamin's remarkable book, *The American Builder's Companion: Or A System of Architecture Particularly Adapted to the Present Style of Building* (1827), takes the reader through a series of developmental views and sophisticated geometric patterns that would enable a carpenter to replicate these designs. Benjamin's publications were reprinted throughout the early-nineteenth century.

[1144] Ibid.

[1145] Asher Benjamin, introduction by William Morgan, *The American Builder's Companion: Or, A System of Architecture Particularly Adapted to the Present Style of Building* (New York: Dover Publications, 1827, 1969), pp.v-ix.

the vernacular American interpretation of eighteenth-century
̣ the countryside beyond New England. Indeed, when we look
̣oth the interior and the exterior of St. Paul's (Wurtemburg), we
̣of Asher Benjamin's elegant designs.

Asher Benjamin (1773-1845),
a disciple of Charles Bullfinch,
transitioned between Federal style
architecture and the later Greek Revival style.

Benjamin's book, *The Practical House Carpenter*, published in 1830, had an enormous influence in changing American architectural taste towards the Greek Revival style from the Federal style, espoused by his previous handbooks. The Greek Revival, related to the Georgian and Federal styles, flourished in America from about 1820 to the Civil War. At this time, the Greek temple became the universal inspiration for public buildings, churches, and homes. The Pleasant Plains Presbyterian Church, located south of St. Paul's (Wurtemburg), is an outstanding example of pure Greek Revival style, particularly pure in that it eliminated the steeple in conformity with its temple prototype.[1146]

Tracking Architectural Changes at St. Paul's

From 1802 until sometime shortly after 1916 the worship space of St. Paul's was set up with a lecture-hall floor plan. The lecture-hall floor plan evolved in two stages. During the eighteenth century, reflecting "Wren's auditory church,"[1147] the Enlightenment, and Zwinglian-Reformed theology the pulpit was often of the massive "tub" type, often with a high sounding board. These huge pulpits "gave a note of authority to the preached word, which transcended the individual preacher."[1148] At this

---

[1146] *Dutchess County Planning Board*, p.116.

[1147] White, p.126.

[1148] Ibid., p.124.

time, congregations were thought of as passive audiences. Worship, centering on length edifying sermons, "was something done for them and to them by experts."[1149]

The Evangelical Lutheran Church of St. Peter the Apostle
(The Old Stone Church) was founded in 1715.
It was the mother church supplying pastors for area Lutheran congregations.
Prior to c.1910 St. Paul's had a similar arrangement
of the pulpit desk above the marble topped communion table.
Photo: The Rev. Dr. Mark D. Isaacs.

The second stage of the lecture-hall floor plan can still be seen at the Evangelical Lutheran Church of St. Peter the Apostle.[1150] This church, the mother church for Lutheran congregations in this area, was founded in 1715.[1151] This church was disbanded during the Great Depression and officially closed in 1938.

"The Old Stone Church," owned and maintained by the cemetery association, still stands frozen in time. Until about 2001, the building had been used for approximately ten years—with the worship space basically unaltered—by the Grace Bible Fellowship, a non-denominational fundamentalist church.[1152] For the past couple of years, after Grace

---

[1149] Ibid., p.125.

[1150] "The Old Stone Church," is located three miles north of the village of Rhinebeck on the Albany Post Road. This church was closed in 1938.

[1151] Hull, p.4. This church was closed in 1938.

[1152] That is, it is a Baptist Church!

Bible Fellowship built their own building just south of the cemetery, the Stone Church was rented out to a local Pentecostal group called "the Harvest Fellowship."

James F. White explains that this design is reflective of the influence of nineteenth-century Revivalism.[1153] The pulpit-desk, located on a raised pulpit platform, is placed front and center. This plan, a logical flowering of Zwinglian-Reformed theology, also stresses the preached Word. The pulpit-desk is located at the center, with the communion table below. Hence, the preached Word is given priority *over* the Sacrament.

With this Revivalist design, the preacher on the raised pulpit platform could "make sorties in all directions as they pleaded for conversions."[1154] This approach to worship was "emotional, subjective, and individualistic."[1155]

As the photo indicates, at St. Peter's, there are three chairs located behind the pulpit-desk. This arrangement is typical of this era. White explains that these large three chairs "had a much more practical use than representing the Trinity."[1156] They were used during the service by several different worship leaders. One chair might be for a song leader; the other for a visiting minister, a head elder or a deacon; and the larger central chair is for the preacher of the day. White adds that, "some of these chairs from pulpit platforms will be museum pieces in the twenty-first century, if not destroyed before then."[1157]

Here at St. Paul's (Wurtemburg), we still have three finely crafted black walnut chairs [c.1890]. Once, these chairs, like those shown at St. Peter the Apostle's, were positioned behind the centrally located pulpit-desk. These three chairs are still used at St. Paul's. However, they have been moved off to the east side, on the level of the congregation, and they now occupy a less central position.

The 1890 Re-opening of St. Paul's (Wurtemburg)

On July 20, 1890, following another series of repairs and improvements, St. Paul's held a special "Re-opening" service. A specially printed bulletin states, "The Church, having been closed for repairs since the first day of June will be reopened on the twentieth of July, 1890... All are cordially invited to attend not this occasion only, but all occasions of Public Worship."[1158]

The guest preacher for this event was the well known Pietist-Lutheran author, theologian and evangelist the Rev. Henry Ziegler, D.D. Dr. Ziegler, Rev. George W. Fortney's father-in-law, was visiting the 1870 Parsonage at the time. *The Rhinebeck Gazette,* reported that, "the sermon [text Romans 7:1-2] was a plain practical discourse such as the doctor is accustomed to deliver, and the new pulpit-desk gracing the platform for the first time, gave forth no uncertain sound."[1159]

[1153] White, pp.122-123.

[1154] Ibid., p.124.

[1155] Ibid.

[1156] Ibid., p.125.

[1157] Ibid.

[1158] Preserved in archives of the Rhinebeck Historical Society at the Quitman House.

[1159] *The Rhinebeck Gazette,* July 26, 1890.

According to *The Rhinebeck Gazette*, this renovation included "lowering the pulpit platform with the removal of columns and posts; transferring the choir [and the organ][1160] from the south gallery to the northwest corner of the main floor, where a comfortable and tasty platform was raised, carpeted and furnished with chairs. The whole interior of the church was papered and repainted pure white."[1161]

In addition to these improvements, "a full set of new pulpit furniture"[1162] was added. This included three chairs and "two stands."[1163] This set was made "of fine black walnut upholstered in dark crimson plush."*[1164]* The large preacher's chair was donated by Mrs. Barbara C. Rykert (1815-August 13, 1890),[1165] and the two smaller chairs were donated by Alfred L. Moore and Alfred Cookingham (March 31, 1817-April 4, 1898).[1166] Two chancel or "deacon chairs" were also donated by the Young Men's Association.

The Gazette adds, "The fine pulpit-desk [also still in use today] was the gift of Edward Cookingham and was made by Edward Grube of Rhinebeck. It is a handsome piece of furniture and is alike credible to the maker and donor." "The cost of these repairs, including the generous gifts... amounts to nearly $500 [in 2009 dollars, adjusted for inflation, this would be equivalent to $11,787.03]."[1167]

In 2005, using monies from the Memorial Fund, Church Council member Joseph Dahlem supervised a project to have these five 1890 chairs and tables refurbished, refinished, restored, and recovered. In this process original wood stains and fabric colors were matched. The final result was truly astonishing.

Oxford Movement Inspired Reforms

Between 1919 and 1924,[1168] the people of St. Paul's (Wurtemburg) abandoned their previous Zwinglian-Reformed/Revivalist inspired worship space and redesigned the building, reflecting the influence of the Oxford Movement, which tended to stress, "the authority of the clergy and the importance of the Sacraments."[1169] Up until this time, the

---

[1160] Chester A. Traver, 1915.

[1161] Ibid.

[1162] See also *1873 Wurtemburg Church Record Book*.

[1163] These "stands" were evidently free-standing credence tables. They were given by George H. Schultz and wife, and Joseph Arnett and wife. These stands are still in existence today and they have been repaired and refinished.

[1164] *The Rhinebeck Gazette*, July 26, 1890.

[1165] During the 1960s and 1970s, after this chair fell into disuse, it was reupholstered in a bright red-orange material and lent to the IBM Country Club for Santa's annual visit to the children. For the past six years it has also been used by the pastor for our annual Passover Seder held on Maundy Thursday.

[1166] Buried in the Wurtemburg Cemetery.

[1167] Ibid.

[1168] Probably after 1916 since the inscription on the wooden tomb-altar reads, "Edna Hermans Lown 1877-1916." However, in the church archives [folder #48], a handwritten note on a photo [photo #68] of the altar area bears the inscription; "altar changed 1913-1916."

[1169] White, p.132.

worship space at St. Paul's (Wurtemburg) "looked like the Dutch Reformed Church in the village;"[1170] i.e., with the pulpit at the center and a communion table below [Word *above* Sacrament].

Between 1919 and 1924, during the pastorate of the Rev. E.L. Davison, the chancel of the Church was remodeled, and the " Jesus The Good Shepherd" stained-glass window was installed. The "Jesus the Good Shepherd" stained glass window above the altar serves as a *reredos*.[1171] This window was installed in February 1921.[1172] Originally, the wood trim around the stained-glass window was dark-stained wood. In 1960, apparently in an effort to make the church look "more colonial," the trim was painted white. The stained-glass window bears the inscription "In memory of the Travers who were the pillars in this church." A small plaque on the sill reads, "Installed by Charles R. Traver." Church records indicate that Charles R. Traver died on September 6, 1928, at the age of sixty-five, and he is buried at the Wurtemburg Cemetery.[1173]

On December 20, 1920, Rev. E. L. Davison addressed the Lutheran Brotherhood men's group on "reasons for his desire to change the arrangement of the Altar."[1174] The congregation is separated from the chancel by a rail and three-steps. The pulpit [formerly the 1890 Revival pulpit-desk] was moved to the left, and a lectern was placed on the right. *The Minutes of Lutheran Brotherhood* for March 21, 1921, state that "The Committee in charge of remodeling the pulpit reported the work finished at the cost of $265.97 [adjusted for inflation this would equal $2,823.79 (2009)]."[1175]

At this time, when the old Zwinglian-Reformed style central pulpit was moved aside and replaced with three steps in the center leading up to a high altar, Barbara Frost tells an interesting story about her father's reaction to these changes. Benson Frost, Sr. was told by someone that the three steps represented the Holy Trinity. He was then asked, "don't you believe in worshipping the Trinity?" Benson replied, "Yes, but not with my feet!"[1176]

In church architecture, "The Oxford Movement" was inspired by the theology and a worldview that originated in Oxford and Cambridge. This influential movement was composed of thinkers who were "convinced that the Middle Ages represented the height

---

[1170] Barbara Frost, audio tape lecture on "The History of St. Paul's Lutheran Church of Wurtemburg" delivered to the Rhinebeck Historical Society, December 1990. The tape is preserved in the archives of St. Paul's.

[1171] A small plaque on the stained glass window reads, "Erected by Charles R. Traver." This "window in back of the altar" and the other changes mentioned here occurred during the tenure of Rev. E.L. Davison (July 20, 1919- November 30, 1924). See *1873 Wurtemburg Church Record Book* under "Pastors."

[1172] For some reason the exact date of the installation of this beautiful stained glass window was not recorded in the Wurtemburg Records. It took ten years of research in the extensive Wurtemburg Archives to discover the exact date that this window was installed. A firm date was established due to a passing reference in the *Minutes of the Lutheran Brotherhood* (1915-1927).

[1173] Ibid.

[1174] *Minutes of the Lutheran Brotherhood* (1915-1927), p.123. St. Paul's Archives.

[1175] Ibid., p.126.

[1176] Barbara Frost, audio tape lecture, December 1990.

of Christian piety and worship."[1177] White notes that, since its inception, the ideas of the Oxford-Cambridge Movement "have [ever since] dominated a large segment of Protestant building."[1178]

This is certainly true of the architecture of St. Paul's (Wurtemburg). Reflecting a powerful *domus dei* theology, the Oxford/Cambridge Movement sanctuary model[1179] replaced the old Zwinglian-Reformed style central pulpit—which was in place at Wurtemburg from 1802-1919—with a high-tomb altar with a retable[1180] and a throne holding a fine brass cross[1181] on the north wall.[1182] Two credence tables, on the left and on the right, were later attached to the wall.[1183] The candlesticks were presented by Mr. and Mrs. Austin S. Frost, Sr., in memory of Austin S. Frost, Jr.[1184] Solid brass flower vases were given in memory of Mandeville S. Frost (1845-1922) and Joseph Arnett (1940-1920).[1185]

It is interesting to note that, although these Oxford/Cambridge Movement changes were made, the Georgian box pews, reflecting Christopher Wren's "auditory style" with no central aisle, remain. Hence, if we read the architecture, we can see that the congregation worships in the meetinghouse *domus ecclesia* mode, while the clergy operate in the *domus dei* mode.

[1177] White, p.132.

[1178] Ibid., p.133.

[1179] Similar to Romanticism in literature and the arts, the Oxford Movement began in England between 1833 to 1841, as a reaction to the cold and sterile rationalism of the Enlightenment, to the anti-intellectualism and emotionalism of the Wesleyan and Evangelical revivals, and to the social upheaval caused by the Industrial Revolution (c.1750). Early Oxford Movement leaders "were reformers concerned with fundamentals." "Their doctrinal and historical studies led the movement into higher appreciation of the episcopal office and recognition of the unique values in corporate worship. There was a great revival of church life. Ancient church buildings were restored; new edifices were erected… daily services and frequent communions were encouraged… [Luther Reed, *The Lutheran Liturgy* (Philadelphia: Mühlenberg Press, 1947), p.158]."

[1180] The wooden tomb-altar bears the inscription, "Edna Hermans Lown 1877-1916." The altar was given in memory of Mary Traver Baas' mother who tragically died a few weeks after Mary's birth.

[1181] Given in memory of John Edward Schultz (July 24, 1819- November 12, 1900) and Wife [Sarah Margaret Allendorf Schultz (-1912)]. Both are buried at the Wurtemburg Cemetery. John Edward Schultz is the grandfather of Mary Traver Baas, our oldest living member.

[1182] The altar at St. Paul's [again, an 1802 building] is on the north wall not on the traditional the east wall.

[1183] These credence tables were given "In memory of Charles M. Frost, Jr., 1948-1961."

[1184] Killed in action in Belgium during World War Two. See Pvt. Austin Frost, Jr.'s obituary in *Mrs. Samuel S. Frost's (1819-1912) Scrapbook,* (St. Paul's Archives), p.68.

[1185] In the spring of 2006, the Altar Guild used monies from the Memorial Fund to have these vases replated and restored.

The 1919 Baptismal Font

The Neo-Gothic style Baptismal font, which has held the water for generations of St. Paul's Christians, was given in memory of Millard Boomhower (1902-1919). A brass plaque bears the inscription, *"Baptized and Confirmed in this Church, Buried in the Churchyard. Served in the World War May-December 1918."*

Millard Boomhower was only seventeen years old when he died on December 18, 1919. *The Rhinebeck Gazette* wrote that Millard was "one of the youngest lads in the country to enlist, and he overcame all sorts of obstacles to offer himself for duty."[1186] He served in the U.S. Naval Reserves. During his service he was stationed at the Brooklyn Navy Yard, New London, Connecticut, and Provincetown, Massachusetts. He also served on a "dangerous expedition on the *U.S.S. Allacuty* (sic?)[1187] to Portugal and Siberia from which many of his companions never returned."[1188]

While in service, Millard became ill with "an attack of influenza [i.e., the "Spanish flu" epidemic of 1918-1919 took the lives of an estimated 30 million people worldwide] and tonsillitis." He was discharged on December 18, 1918. Although he seemed to have recovered from the initial flu, Millard continued to suffer from respiratory complications. He had "inflammatory rheumatism from which heart trouble developed."[1189] He died one year to the day after his discharge.

His oldest brother, the Rev. William G. Boomhower served as pastor of St. Paul's (July 5, 1914-July 1, 1916). During this time, while his brother served as pastor, Millard lived in the 1870 Parsonage with his mother and older brother. *The Rhinebeck Gazette* wrote, "He was a lad remarkable for the promise of his manhood, striking personality, mental ability, daring love of adventure, hatred of shame and show and advocacy of all the ideals of true Americanism." They added, "He was buried close up by the Parsonage,[1190] which he had his happy boyhood home while his brother was Pastor of the Wurtemburg Church."[1191]

Liturgical Reform

In July 1996, following the influence of the liturgical reform movement, and the worship reforms of Post-Vatican Two, Rev. Mark D. Isaacs, after consulting the Church Council, relocated the altar. While retaining the 1916-era tomb-altar, this piece of furniture was pulled off the north wall. It now acts as a communion table enabling the presiding minister to face the congregation during weekly communion. The retable and a

---

[1186] "Recent Deaths, An Obituary Record of Those Who Have Recently Passed Away: Millard Boomhower," *The Rhinebeck Gazette*, December 27, 1919, p.1.

[1187] The *USS Alacrity* (SP-206) was an patrol boat [a converted private motor yacht] acquired by the U.S. Navy for the task of patrolling American coastal waters during the First World War. Assigned to the First Naval District section patrol, *Alacrity* spent the war conducting coastal patrols from the Boston and Provincetown, Massachusetts.

[1188] Ibid.

[1189] Ibid.

[1190] Young Millard Boomhower is buried within twenty-five feet from the southwest corner of the present 1870 Parsonage.

[1191] *The Rhinebeck Gazette*, December 27, 1919, p.1.

throne holding a brass cross, were retained by separating them from the altar and fixing them to the north wall.

Also at this time, two wall mounted credence bracket shelves were added to hold the brass altar vases.[1192] Previously, these vases were placed on the *retable*. Moving them off to the left and the right made the retable and the altar cleaner and simpler. The baptismal font was also moved to the center of the worship space at this time. One of the benefits of not having a central aisle is that the baptismal font can be placed in this central position.

The overall appearance of the worship space at St. Paul's is a healthy retention of the best of the Oxford/Cambridge Movement style worship space, with increased harmony and utility. Relocating the altar/communion table helped to change the dynamics of the worship experience at St. Paul's (Wurtemburg), reflecting more of a *domus ecclesia* spirit.

During weddings, when additional space is required for the ceremony, the altar can be moved back under the retable against the north wall.

Agony in the Garden

On the south wall of the church—high in the gallery—is a replica of the famous 1890 Heinrich Hoffmann painting of "The Agony in the Garden of Gethsemane." [1193] The original Hoffmann painting is displayed in a special side chapel at the Riverside Church in Manhattan.

The oversized replica, by Nina Radcliff Traver Young (1890-1972), was lovingly painted from the original in 1942. Nina reportedly made many trips to the Riverside Church to match the colors. This copy originally hung over the altar in St. Paul's Lutheran Church in Kingston, New York. In 1999, after the Kingston church had been disbanded, the sons of Nina, John Young and the Rev. Paul Young, Jr., presented the painting to St. Paul's (Wurtemburg). The painting currently graces the south wall of the balcony directly opposite from the altar. It is fitting that Nina Young's painting hangs here at St. Paul's (Wurtemburg). Nina Traver Young, the wife of the Rev. Paul Young, Sr. (1885-1976), is buried in the Wurtemburg Cemetery.

The Rev. Paul Young, Sr. was born in Richmond, Indiana, on April 20, 1885. He received his early education in the public schools of New York City. He graduated from Gettysburg College in 1906 and from Hartwick Seminary in 1913. He was ordained on October 2, 1913.

During his active career in the ministry, which covered a period of more than forty years, Pastor Young served the following churches: St. John's (Christopher Street, New

---

[1192] The heavy solid brass altar vases are dedicated "In the memory of Joseph Arnett, 1840-1920" and "In memory of Mandeville Frost, 1845-1922."

[1193] Heinrich Hofmann (1824-1902) was an internationally renowned German historical painter. He was born in Darmstadt. After studying in Dusseldorf and at the Antwerp Academy, he resided in Italy from 1854-1858. Hofmann settled in Dresden in 1862. There he became professor of art in the academy. While he chose his subjects from the whole field of literature and mythology, Hofmann is most widely known for his idealized scenes from the life of Jesus Christ. Several of these have been extensively reproduced in engravings, especially his "Christ in the Temple," painted in 1882.

York City), as assistant pastor 1912 to 1914; Emanuel Lutheran, Bronx, 1914 to 1927; St. Luke's, Farmingdale, Long Island, 1927 to 1933; St. Paul's, Kingston, New York, 1933 to 1940; and Zion Lutheran, Oldwick, New Jersey, 1947 to 1952. The ending of this last charge marked Pastor Young's retirement from full-time work in the ministry.

Heinrich Hoffman's "The Agony in the Garden of Gethsemane"
Photo: Riverside Church in Manhattan.

In the service of his country, Pastor Young spent the years 1906 to 1911 with the Medical Department and, under the auspices of the National Lutheran Council, served as chaplain at Sandy Hook, 1917 to 1918, and at Fort McClellan, Alabama, 1941 to 1947.[1194] While at Fort McClellan, because he was fluent in German, Pastor Young often conducted worship services for German prisoners of war.[1195]

After his retirement, between pastoral vacancies, the Rev. Paul Young, Sr. served as both a supply and as an interim pastor at St. Paul's (Wurtemburg). Older members of St. Paul's have fond memories of Pastor Young.

In an interview prior to his death, Warren T. Sigrist (1920-2007), a long-time member of Third Evangelical Lutheran Church, recalled that, "when Pastor Young would preach he would take an old pocket watch out of his pocket and lay it on the pulpit. He would talk for exactly twelve minutes and then sit down." Warren smiled and said, "Pastor Young was my kind of preacher!"

[1194] Miller, p.42.

[1195] Interview with John Young, Jr., c. 1994.

In 1963, to commemorate the fiftieth anniversary of his ordination, and as a thank you for his service to area Lutheran churches, the people of Third Evangelical Lutheran, Memorial (Rock City), and St. Paul's (Wurtemburg) held a special testimonial dinner to honor Pastor Young at the Grange Hall in Rhinebeck. The Rev. Paul Young, Sr. is buried in the Wurtemburg Cemetery. In the same family plot are buried the Rev. Paul Young, Jr. (1920-2002) and John Young, Jr. (1917-2006).

Other Improvements and Changes

In 1913, the basement of the Church was refitted with a new ceiling, painted, and beautified at the expense of about $300 [in 2009 dollars, adjusted for inflation, this would be equivalent to $6,430.27].[1196]

In addition, John Naisbitt's concept of "high tech and soft touch" helps to explain the aesthetic appeal of St. Paul's. Naisbitt teaches us that "we must learn to balance the material wonders of technology with the spiritual demands of our human nature."[1197] He is correct. The more cold high technology we have around us, the more we seem to need the human touch. St. Paul's is a traditional soft touch/human touch space. When one enters this ancient sacred space to worship, the weary post-modernist is instantly reconnected to something eternal and timeless. In the hard and fast post-modern age of flux, uncertainty, and sterile technology, we are fed by God's Word and Sacrament.

The Historic 1870 Parsonage

Up until 1870, pastors of St. Paul's lived in the village of Rhinebeck [four miles to the west]. In 1857, the Sexton's house [now the home of the late George Warner on Vliet Road] was remodeled and "the promise of a new parsonage soon" was made.[1198] The Civil War caused a delay in this plan until 1870. Another cause for the delay was the 1860 project of digging a basement under the Church and the extensive 1861 remodeling of the Church.

In his *Day Book*, Alvah G. Frost has an interesting note dated November 17, 1947. It reads:

> Mrs. John P. Hermans (b.1853) reported that a one and a half story parsonage building preceded the present parsonage built in 1870. When the latter building was being constructed, the pastor, the Rev. George Neff, D.D., lived in a part of the dwelling across the road to the north of what was known as the Henry Cookingham pond.[1199]

[1196] *1873 Wurtemburg Church Record Book.*

[1197] John Naisbitt, *Megatrends: Ten Directions Transforming Our Lives* (New York: Warner Books, 1982), p.40.

[1198] Chester A. Traver, 1915.

[1199] Alvah G. Frost's *Daybook* is in the archives of the Rhinebeck Historical Society in the Quitman House in Rhinebeck, New York.

In the Fall of 1870, the second parsonage—the present parsonage—was completed.[1200] At the time, the total cost to build the parsonage was $3,500 [in 2009 dollars, adjusted for inflation, this would be equivalent to $58,659.00]. Typically, during the nineteenth century, weddings were conducted in the Parsonage, or in people's homes. In the *1873 Church Record Book*, under the date of October 24, 1870, Rev. Dr. George Neff, while recording the marriage of Clemet Sweet and Henrietta Doyle of Milan, New York, noted, "first ceremonies in the new Parsonage."[1201]

The 1870 Wurtemburg Parsonage as it appeared c. 1913.
Note the "horse block" on the right designed to assist passengers onto horse drawn carriages.
Photo: Archives of St. Paul's Lutheran Church of Wurtemburg.

Over the years, many major improvements and repairs have been made to the Parsonage. The most recent, January 2006, was a major renovation of the kitchen. This renovation included removing a wall containing a long unused brick chimney that at one time had been used to vent smoke from the kitchen wood stove. During the renovation six or seven layers of kitchen floor and linoleum were removed. On one of these layers workers discovered a newspaper dated 1919, bearing the address of the Rev. Oscar A. Noran. When the floor boards were removed a crawl space under the kitchen was also revealed. In the crawl space we discovered the ancient mummified remains of three long dead cats! In addition, the renovation exposed ancient hand-hewn beams.

[1200] Alvah G. Frost, p.9.

[1201] *1873 Wurtemburg Church Record Book.*

Writing in 1881, Rev. William Hull reported that, "the whole church property, nearly free from debt, comprises a good Church building with basement, ample sheds, a fine Parsonage and a beautiful cemetery. It reports two-hundred-and-ten members and is a large and prosperous country congregation."[1202]

[1202] Hull, p.10.

Chapter Fifteen: Conclusion: St. Paul's (Wurtemburg) Today

What can we say about St. Paul's (Wurtemburg) today? It would be easy to dismiss this old building as hopelessly out of date and in need of replacement by a modern and efficient redesigned building.[1203] Or, it would be easy to call for St. Paul's merger with another area Lutheran congregation. However, to dismiss this historic old building—animated with the stories and memories of generations that enliven this sacred place—would be to miss the point. The walls and the grounds are saturated with generations of stories, with history, and with precious memories.

Two-hundred-and-fifty years after its founding, St. Paul's Lutheran Church of Wurtemburg is a vibrant, active, and growing congregation. The old Palatines have long since passed on, and their descendents have assimilated and dispersed. Occasionally, a Traver or a Cookingham descendent from Iowa or Idaho knocks on the door of the Parsonage, seeking genealogical information or a location of an ancestral grave in the cemetery. The vast majority of our current members are former Roman Catholics or other denominations. And, a majority of today's Church members hail from places far from Rhinebeck, or Red Hook, or Hyde Park. For better or for worse, in recent years, the Rhinebeck area has increasingly come into the demographic orbit of New York City.

As a result, while current members certainly cherish and respect our precious history, we tend to embrace the present and look toward the future. During the past decade, St. Paul's (Wurtemburg) has grown into a community and an area congregation with a diverse membership of many people from many different traditions. While we certainly honor and cherish the history and the tradition of the past two-hundred-and-fifty years, we look forward to continued faithful service and ministry to the people of this area. At the same time, we are truly blessed to have the honor and privilege of being stewards, members, and worshipers in this venerable old Church.

[1203] Richard Giles.

Appendix:

TABLE OF CLERGY WHO HAVE SERVED
ST. PAUL'S LUTHERAN CHURCH OF WURTEMBURG

Name, (Birth-Death), (*Seminary*), Tenure at St. Paul's

Rev. Johannes Christopher Hartwick [or Hartwig], (January 6, 1714-July 17, 1796), (*Halle University*), 1746-1758.

Rev. Johannes Fredrick Ries, (1722-1791), March 7, 1760-January 5, 1783.

Rev. George Heinrich Pfeiffer, (c.1747-October 26, 1827), May 17, 1784-1794.

Rev. Johann Friedrich Ernst, (1748-1805), 1794-1798.

Rev. Frederick Henry Quitman, D.D., (August 7, 1760 - June 26, 1832), (*Halle University, Doctor of Divinity degree from Harvard University,* 1811), February 18, 1798-August 23, 1825.

Rev. William J. Eyer, September 1825- September 1837.

Rev. Augustus Theodosius Geissenhainer, (July 11, 1814-March 3, 1882), June 8, 1838-1840.

Rev. Charles Adam Smith, D.D., (June 25, 1809 – February 15, 1879), (*Hartwick Seminary,* 1830), 1840-1850.

Rev. William Nace Scholl, D.D., (September 9, 1805-June 12, 1889), (*Gettysburg Seminary,* 1833), 1850-1855.

Rev. George Neff, D.D., (December 23, 1813-August 6, 1900), *(Gettysburg Seminary,* 1842), July 1855-July 1876.

Rev. Joseph G. Griffith, D.D., (February 11, 1839- December 11, 1907), (*Gettysburg Seminary,* 1867), September 1, 1876 -March 1, 1881.

Rev. John L. Kling, (July 1, 1838-February 2, 1923), (*Hartwick Seminary,* 1865), September 1, 1881-June 1, 1887.

Rev. George William Fortney, (December 27, 1845-August 30, 1909), (*Gettysburg Seminary,* 1873), January 1, 1888- May 26, 1895.

Rev. Chauncey W. Diefendorf, (February 1, 1838-November 19, 1909), (*Hartwick Seminary, c.* 1862, and Selinsgrove University in Pennsylvania, ordained in 1871), September 1, 1895-December 1, 1898.

Rev. Roscoe C. Wright, D.D., (*Gettysburg College, Hartwick Seminary, c.*1899), April 1, 1899-September 1, 1907.

Rev. John L. Kling, (July 1, 1838-February 2, 1923), (*Hartwick Seminary,* 1865), recalled February 1, 1908- December 1, 1913.

Rev. William Gibson Boomhower, D.D., (January 15, 1891-1974), *(Hartwick Seminary,* 1914), July 5, 1914- July 1, 1916.

Rev. Oscar B. Noran, (*Hartwick Seminary*), July 1917-March 30, 1919.

Rev. E. L. Davison, (*Hartwick Seminary,* 1913), July 20, 1919- November 30, 1924.

Rev. Elder Jay Himes, (1888-December 29, 1950), (*Theological School at Susquehanna University*), May 10, 1924-September 15, 1946.

Rev. Carl A. Romoser, September 1, 1947-1949.

Rev. Herbert Finch, (February 18, 1877-?), October 3, 1949-1954; (*Gettysburg College,* 1894, *Gettysburg Seminary,* 1902).

Rev. John L. de Papp, 1955-1958.

Rev. Rolf W. Eschke, (*Gettysburg Seminary*), 1959-1962.

Rev. Frederick Charles Dunn, (1924-1984), *(Wagner College, 1959, Philadelphia Seminary, 1963),* 1963-1967,

Rev. William Howard Beck, D.Min. (December 30, 1940-), *(Lutheran Theological Seminary-Gettysburg,* M.Div., 1966; D.Min., *Lancaster Theological Seminary,* D.Min., 1975), 1968-1970.

Rev. Sylvester Bader, (*Lutheran Theological Seminary-Philadelphia,* B.Div., 1938), 1970-1977.

Rev. Daniel M. Strobel, (*Lutheran Theological Seminary-Gettysburg,* M.Div., 1978), 1978-1984.

Rev. Richard Mowry, (*Lutheran Theological Seminary-Philadelphia,* M.Div., 1968), 1984-1996.

Rev. Mark D. Isaacs, (September 16, 1955-), (*Lutheran Theological Seminary-Gettysburg,* M.Div., 1992; S.T.M., 2005; *Trinity Theological Seminary,* 2006, Ph.D.; *Lutheran Theological Seminary-Philadelphia,* 2007, D.Min.; *Newburgh Theological Seminary,* 2008, Th.D.), June 29, 1996-present.

Bibliography:

Arndt, Johann. Translation and Introduction by Peter Erb. *True Christianity.* New York: Paulist Press, 1979.

Ashley, Maurice. *The Age of Absolutism: 1648-1775.* Springfield, MA: G. & C. Merriam Company, 1974.

Bachman, E. Theodore. *The United Lutheran Church in American: 1918-1962.* Minneapolis: Augsburg-Fortress, 1997.

Bailey, Ronald H. *Hartwick College: A Bicentennial History: 1797-1997.* Oneonta, NY: Hartwick College.

Barnes, Harry Elmer. *The History of Western Civilization.* New York: Harcourt, Brace and Company, 1935.

Bell, Walter George. *The Great Fire of London in 1666.* London: The Folio Society, 1920, 2003.

_____. *The Great Plague in London: 1665.* London: The Folio Society, 1924, 2001.

Bengel, Johann Albrecht. Translation by Charlton T. Lewis and Marvin R. Vincent (1860-1861). *Bengel's New Testament Commentary: Gnomon Novi Testamenti (1742).* Grand Rapids: Kregel Publications, 1981.

Benjamin, Asher. *The American Builder's Companion: Or A System of Architecture Particularly Adapted to the Present Style of Building.* New York: Dover Publications, reprint of the sixth (1827) edition, 1969.

_____. *The Country Builder's Assistant.* Reprint of the 1797 edition published in Greenfield, Massachusetts. Bedford, Massachusetts: Applewood Books, 1992.

Bergendoff, Conrad. *The Church of the Lutheran Reformation: A Historical Survey of Lutheranism.* St. Louis: Concordia Publishing House, 1967.

Berkenmeyer, Wilhelm Christoph. Translation by Simon Hart, translation initiated by Harry J. Kreider, and edited by John P. Dern. *The Albany Protocol: Wilhelm Christoph Berkenmeyer's Chronicle of Lutheran Affairs in New York Colony, 1731-1750.* Ann Arbor, MI, 1971.

Blanchard, Frank D., ["By The Minister, Elders, and Deacons"]. *History of the Reformed Dutch Church of Rhinebeck Flatts, New York.* Albany, New York: J.B. Lyon Company, 1921.

Blumenfeld, Samuel L. *N.E.A.: Trojan Horse in American Education.* Boise, ID: Paradigm Company, 1984.

_____. *Is Public Education Necessary?* Boise, ID: Paradigm Company, 1985.

Bonney, Richard. *Essential Histories: The Thirty Year's War: 1618-1648.* Oxford, U.K.: Osprey Publishing, 2002.

Book of Worship of the General Synod. Philadelphia: United Lutheran Publications House, 1899.

Bradshaw, Michael., et al. *Contemporary World Regional Geography: Global Connections, Local Voices.* New York: McGraw Hill, 2007.

Brant, Clare. *An American Aristocracy: The Livingstons.* New York: Doubleday & Co., 1986, 1990.

Brief History of Church with By-Laws, Rules and Regulations of Wurtemburg Cemetery Association. Rhinebeck, New York: 1897, p.5.

Burk, John Christian Frederic. *A Memoir of the Life and Writings of John Albert Bengel, Prelate of Wurtemberg, Compiled Principally from Original Manuscripts.* London: William Ball, 1837.

Cairns, Earle E. *Christianity Through the Centuries: A History of the Christian Church.* Grand Rapids: Zondervan Publishing House, 1996.

Calvin, John. *Institutes of the Christian Religion.* Translation by F. L. Battles, edited by J. T. McNeill. Philadelphia: Westminster Press, 1559, 1960.

Carson, Clarence B. *A Basic History of the United States: The Sections and the Civil War, 1826-1877.* Phenix, AL: American Textbook Committee, 1985, 2001.

_____. *A Basic History of the United States: The Growth of America: 1878-1928.* Phenix City, AL: American Textbook Committee, 1985, 2001.

Clarke, Marcella. *Diary of a Central School: The Story of Rhinebeck Central School.* Lowell, MA: King Publishing, 2004.

Clouse, Robert G. *The Church in the Age of Orthodoxy and the Enlightenment: Consolidation and Challenge from 1600 to 1800.* St. Louis: Concordia Press, 1980.

Coffin, Judith G. et al. *Western Civilizations: Their History and Their Culture.* New York: W.W. Norton, 2002.

Coil, Henry Wilson. *Coil's Masonic Encyclopedia.* Richmond, VA: Macoy Publishing & Masonic Supply Co. 1961, 1995.

Common Service Book and Hymnal. Philadelphia: The Board of Publication of the United Lutheran Church in America, 1917-1918.

Cross, Frank L., ed. *The Oxford Dictionary of the Christian Church.* New York: Oxford University Press, 1958, 1983.

Decker, Ruth. *275 Years of Lutheran Witness in the Central Hudson Valley: Christ Lutheran Church of Germantown, New York: 1710-1985.* Germantown, New York: Christ Lutheran Church, 1985.

Defoe, Daniel. *Robinson Crusoe.* New York: The Modern Library, 1719, 2001.

_____. *A Journal of the Plague Year.* 1722.

Diamond, Jared. *Guns, Germs and Steel: The Fate of Human Societies.* New York: W.W. Norton, 1997.

DiLorenzo, Thomas J. *How Capitalism Saved American: The Untold History of Our County from the Pilgrims to the Present.* New York: Crown Forum, 2004.

Douglas, J.D. *Who's Who in Christian History.* Wheaton, IL: Tyndale House, 1992.

Dowley, Tim. J. H. Y. Briggs, Robert Dean Linder, and David F. Wright. *Introduction to the History of Christianity.* Minneapolis: Fortress Press, 1995, 2002.

Durant, Will. *The Story of Civilization, Part VII, The Age of Reason Begins.* New York: Simon and Schuster, 1961.

Dutchess County Planning Board. *Landmarks of Dutchess County, 1683-1867: Architecture Worth Saving in New York State.* Albany, New York: New York State Council on the Arts, 1969.

Dyer, Frederick H. *A Compendium of the War of the Rebellion Compiled and Arranged from Official Records of the Federal and Confederate Armies, Reports of he Adjutant Generals of the Several States, the Army Registers, and Other Reliable Documents and Sources.* Des Moines, Iowa: The Dyer Publishing Company, 1908.

Ensign, Forest Chester. *Compulsory School Attendance and Child Labor.* Iowa City: Athens Press, 1921.

Erb, Peter C. *Pietists: Selected Writings.* New York: Paulist Press, 1983.

Evers, Bernd. *Architectural Theory From the Renaissance to the Present.* Cologne: Taschen, 2006.

Falckner, Justus. *Fundamental Instruction: Justus Faulkner's Catechism.* Translation and edited by Martin Kessler. Delhi, NY: American Lutheran Publicity Bureau, 2003.

Frost, Alvah G. *An Address Given to Commemorate the 175th Anniversary of the Founding of St. Paul's Lutheran Church, Wurtemburg, New York.* Pamphlet published in Rhinebeck, New York, 1935.

Frost, Elizabeth McR. *The Men of Wurtemburg and Their House of God: 1760-1960: A Short History of St. Paul's Lutheran Church of Wurtemburg.* Pamphlet published in Rhinebeck, New York, 1960.

Ghee, Joyce C. *Building in Dutchess: Reading the Landscape.* Poughkeepsie, New York: The Dutchess County Department of History, 1988.

Giles, Richard. *Re-Pitching the Tent: Reordering the Church Building for Worship and Mission.* Collegeville, Minnesota: The Liturgical Press, 1999.

Greaves, Percy L. *Mises Made Easier: A Glossary for Ludwig von Mises' "Human Action."* Irvington-on-Hudson, NY: Free Market Books, 1974.

Gritsch, Eric W. *Fortress Introduction to Lutheranism.* Minneapolis: Fortress Press, 1994.

Habenstein, Robert W., and William M. Lamers. *The History of American Funeral Directing.* Milwaukee, Wisconsin, 1955.

Hagglund, Bengt. *History of Theology.* St. Louis: Concordia Publishing House, 1968.

Hajo Holborn, *A History of Modern Germany: 1648-1840*, (Princeton: Princeton University Press, 1964, 1982.

Hanaburgh, D.H. *History of the 128th Regiment, New York Volunteers (U.S. Infantry) in the Late Civil War.* Poughkeepsie, N.Y.: The 128th Regimental Association, 1894.

Hart, Simon and Harry J. Kreider, translators. *Lutheranism Church in New York and New Jersey, 1722-1760: Lutheran Recorded in the Ministerial Archives of the Staatsarchiv, Hamburg, Germany.* United Lutheran Synod of New York and New England, 1962.

Hazellius, Ernest Lewis. *The Life of John Henry Stilling* [Johann Heinrich Jung-Stilling], *Doctor of Medicine and Philosophy, Court Counselor and Professor of Political Economy in the University of Marburg in Germany and Author of Many Religious Works.* Gettysburg: Press of the Theological Seminary, N.G. Neinstedt Printer, 1831.

Heidler, David S., and Jeanne T. Heidler, editors. *Encyclopedia of the American Civil War: A Political, Social, and Military History.* New York: W.W. Norton & Co., 2000.

Heins, Henry Hardy. *Throughout All The Years: The Bicentennial Story of Hartwick in America (1746-1946).* Oneonta: Board of Trustees of Hartwick College, 1946.

Hodge, Charles. *Systematic Theology.* Grand Rapids: William B. Eerdmans Publishing, 1872, 1982.

Hogan, Mervin B. "Pythagoras and the Number Five, *The Philalethes*, June 1986.

Hook, Sidney. *John Dewey: Philosopher of Science and Freedom.* New York: Barnes & Noble, 1959.

Horn, Edward T. *The Church at Worship.* Philadelphia: Mühlenberg Press, 1957.

Hull, Rev. William. *History of the Lutheran Church in Dutchess County, New York.* Gettysburg: J.E. Wible Printer, 1881. A reprinted booklet from *The Lutheran Quarterly*, July 1881.

Humphrey, Zephine. *A Book of New England.* Howell Sosken, 1947.

Isaacs, Mark D. *The 150th Anniversary of Third Evangelical Lutheran Church.* Rhinebeck, New York: 1842-1992.

_____. *THE END? Textual Criticism and Apocalyptic Speculation in Johann Albrecht Bengel (1687-1752).* Phoenix, AZ: Robert Welsh University Classical Press, 2010.

_____. *Centennial Rumination on Max Weber's "The Protestant Ethic and the Spirit of Capitalism."* Boca Raton, FL: Dissertation.com, 2005.

Jennson, J.C. *American Lutheran Biographies.* Milwaukee, 1890.

Johnson, Paul. *A History of the American People.* New York: HarperCollins, 1997.

Käsler, Dirk. *Max Weber: An Introduction to his Life and Work.* Chicago: University of Chicago Press, 1988.

Keels, Thomas H. *Images of America: Philadelphia Graveyard and Cemeteries.* Charleston, SC: Arcadia Publishing, 2003.

Kelly, Arthur C. *Records of Lutheran Churches of Rhinebeck, Dutchess County, New York Area: Members, Confirmands, and Family Lists: 1734-1889.* Rhinebeck, NY: Kinship Books, 2000.

Kelly, Arthur C. *Deaths, Marriages and Much Miscellaneous form Rhinebeck, New York Newspapers: 1846-1899.* Rhinebeck, NY: Kinship Books, 1978.

_____. *Baptismal Records of St. Peter's Lutheran Church, Rhinebeck, New York: 1733-1899.* Rhinebeck, NY: Kinship Books, 1968.

Kelly, Nancy. *A Brief History of Rhinebeck: The Living Past of a Hudson Valley Community.* New York: The Wise Family Trust, 2001.

Kirker, Harold. *The Architecture of Charles Bulfinch.* Cambridge, MA: Harvard University Press, 1969, 1998.

Kootz, Wolfgang. *Rothenburg ob der Tauber.* Kraichgau Verlag GmbH.

Krauth, Charles Porterfield. *The Conservative Reformation and Its Theology As Represented in the Augsburg Confession, And in the History and Literature of the Evangelical Lutheran Church.* Philadelphia, General Council Publication Board, 1913.

Kurtz, Michael J. *John Gottlieb Morris: Man of God, Man of Science.* The Maryland Historical Society, 1997.

Lawrence, Thea. *Unity Without Uniformity: The Rhinebeck Church Community, 1718-1918.* Monroe, NY: Library Research Association, 1992.

Lerner, Robert E., Standish Meacham, and Edward McNall Burns. *Western Civilizations: Their History and Their Culture.* New York, W.W. Norton, 1993.

Lewis, A.J. *Zinzendorf: The Ecumenical Pioneer: A Study in the Moravian Contribution to Christian Mission and Unity.* Philadelphia: The Westminster Press, 1962.

Lewis, Charlton T. *A History of Germany.* New York: Harper & Brothers, 1883.

Lueker, Erwin L., ed. *Lutheran Cyclopedia.* St. Louis: Concordia Publishing House, 1954, 1985.

Lunt, W.E. *History of England.* New York: Harper and Row, 1928, 1957.

Luther, Martin, ed. *The Theologia Germanica of Martin Luther.* Translation and commentary by Bengt Hoffman. New York: Paulist Press; The Classics of Western Spirituality, 1980.

MacCracken, Henry Noble. *Old Dutchess Forever! The Story of An American County.* New York: Hastings House, 1956.

McGrath, Alister E. *The Christian Theology Reader.* Malden, MA: Blackwell Publishers, 1995, 2001.

McGuffey, William Holmes, Stanley W. Lindberg, ed. *The Annotated McGuffey: Selections from the McGuffey Eclectic Readers, 1836-1920.* Florence, KT: Van Nostrand Reinhold, 1976.

_____. *McGuffey's Eclectic Readers.* John Wiley & Sons; 6th Rev. edition, 1989.

McKim, Donald K. *Handbook of Major Biblical Interpreters.* Downers Grove:, Illinois: InterVarsity Press, 2000.

McPherson, James M. *Battle Cry of Freedom.* New York: Oxford University Press, 1988.

Mallary, Peter T. *New England Churches & Meetinghouses: 1680-1830.* Secaucus, New Jersey: Chartell Books, Inc., 1985.

Mann, Charles. *1491: New Revelations of the Americas Before Columbus.* New York: Alfred A. Knopf, 2005.

Mann, William J. *The Life and Times of Henry Melchior Mühlenberg.* Philadelphia: G.W. Frederick, 1888.

May, Robert E. *DAB;* Claiborne, John Francis Hamtramck. *Life and Correspondence of John A. Quitman.* 2 vols. New York: Harper and Bros., 1860.

Miller, Allen O. and Eugene Osterhaven, translators. *The Heidelberg [or Palatine] Catechism.* Cleveland, OH: United Church Press, 1962.

Miller, Walter V. *Christ's Lutheran Church, Germantown, New York; 250th Anniversary.* Germantown, N.Y.: Christ Lutheran Church, 1960. A forty-eight page booklet published to commemorate *Christ Lutheran's* 250th anniversary in 1960.

Minutes of the 27th Synod of the Evangelical Lutheran Ministerium of New York and Adjacent Parts held in Albany, New York, October 15, 1832. Hudson, NY: Ashbol Stoddard, 1832.

Mitford, Jessica. *The American Way of Death.* New York: Simon and Schuster, 1963.

Mitford, Nancy. *The Sun King: Louis VIV at Versailles.* New York: Harper & Row Publishers, 1966.

Mommsen, Theodor. *The Provinces of the Roman Empire.* New York: Barnes & Noble, 1885, 1996.

Morison, Samuel Eliot, Henry Steele Commager, and William E. Leuchtenburg. *The Growth of the American Republic.* New York: Oxford University Press, 1969.

Morris, John G. *Fifty Years in the Lutheran Ministry.* Baltimore: James Young, 1878.

Morris, Robert. "Lew Wallace," *The Short Talk Bulletin.* Silver Spring, MD: The Masonic Service Association of North America, May 2005.

Morse, Howard H. *Historic Old Rhinebeck.* Rhinebeck, New York, 1908.

Mühlenberg, Henry Melchior. Translated by Theodore G. Tappert and John W. Doberstein. *The Journals of Henry Melchior Mühlenberg In Three Volumes.* Philadelphia: The Evangelical Lutheran Ministerium of Pennsylvania and Adjacent Parts and the Mühlenberg Press MCMXLII.

Murray, Charles. *Human Accomplishment: The Pursuit of Excellence in the Arts and Sciences, 800 B.C. to 1950.* New York: HarperCollins Publishers, 2003.

Naisbitt, John. *Megatrends: Ten Directions Transforming Our Lives.* New York: Warner Books, 1982.

Nash, Ronald. *The Closing of the American Heart.* Dallas, TX: Probe Books, 1990.

Nelson, E. Clifford. *Lutherans in North America.* Philadelphia: Fortress Press, 1975.

Nietzsche, Friedrich. *Thus Spake Zarathustra.* Translated by Alexander Tille. New York: The Macmillan Company, 1896, 1924.

Noebel, David A. *Understanding the Times: The Religious Worldviews of Our Day and the Search for Truth.* Eugene, OR: Harvest House Publishers, 1991.

Otterness, Philip. *Becoming German: The 1709 Palatine Migration to New York.* Ithaca, NY: Cornell University Press, 2004.

Otto, Rudolf. *The Idea of the Holy.* New York: Oxford University Press, 1923, 1969.

Ozment, Steven. *A Mighty Fortress: A New History of the German People.* New York: HarperCollins Publishers, 2004.

Plass, Ewald M. ed. *What Luther Says: A Practical In-Home Anthology for the Active Christian.* St. Louis: Concordia Publishing House, 1959.

Platt, Edmond. *The Eagle's History of Poughkeepsie" 1683-1905.* Poughkeepsie, NY: Poughkeepsie] Eagle, 1905. Poucher, J. Wilson, and Helen Wilkinson Reynolds. *Old Gravestones of Dutchess County, New York: Nineteen Thousand Inscriptions.* Poughkeepsie, New York: Dutchess County Historical Society, 1924.

Preus, Robert D. *The Theology of Post-Reformation Lutheranism.* St. Louis: Concordia Publishing House, 1970, 1999.

Pritchard, Evan. "The Major Algonquin Nations Throughout North America and What They Call Themselves." <www.wilkesweb.us/algonquin/nations.htm.> 7 August 2006.

Quitman, Frederick H. *A Treatise on Magic, Or, on the Intercourse between Spirits and Men.* Albany: Balance Press, 1810.

_____. *Evangelical catechism, or, A short exposition of the principal doctrines and precepts of the Christian religion: For the use of the churches belonging ...collection of prayers for parents and children.* William E. Norman, 1814.

_____. *Three sermons: The first preached before the Evangelical Lutheran Synod, convened in Christ's Church, in the town of Claverack, on Sunday the 7th of S ... rd on the Reformation by Doctor Martin Luther.* William E. Norman, 1817.

Rediger, G. Lloyd. *The Clergy Killers: Guidance for Pastors and Congregations Under Attack.* Louisville: Westminster John Knox Press, 1997.

Reed, Luther. *The Lutheran Liturgy.* Philadelphia: Mühlenberg Press, 1947.

_____. *The Worship: A Study of Corporate Devotion..* Philadelphia: Mühlenberg Press, 1959.

_____. *Philadelphia Seminary Biographical Record 1864-1923.*

Reid, Daniel G., ed. *Dictionary of Christianity in America.* Downers Grove, IL: 1990.

Reynolds, Helen W., editor. *The Records of Christ Church Poughkeepsie.* Poughkeepsie, NY: 1911.

A Rhinebeck Album: 1776-1876-1976. Rhinebeck: Rhinebeck Historical Society and Moran Printing, Inc., 1976.

Rothbard, Murray N. *Education Free & Compulsory.* Auburn, AL: Ludwig von Mises Institute, 1971, 1999.

Rugoff, Milton. *The Beechers: An American Family in the Nineteenth Century.* New York: Harper and Row, 1981.

Russell, Howard S. *Indian New England Before the Mayflower.* Hanover, NH: University Press of New England, 1980.

Ruttenber, Edward Manning. *Indian Tribes of Hudson's River: To 1700-1850.* Hope Farm Press, Country Books, 1872, facsimile reprint 1992. In two volumes.

Rushdoony, Rousas John. *The Messianic Character of American Education: Studies in the History of the Philosophy of Education.* Nutley, NJ: The Craig Press.

Sawyer, M. James. *Survivor's Guide to Theology.* Grand Rapids: Zondervan, 2006.

Schaff, Philip. *The Creeds of Christendom with A History and Critical Notes.* New York: Harper & Brothers, 1877.

_____ and David Schley Schaff. *History of the Christian Church.* Oak Harbor, WA: Logos Research Systems, Inc., 1997.

Schmucker, Simon Samuel. *Fraternal Appeal to the American Churches with a Plan for Catholic Union with Apostolic Principles.* Edited with an introduction by Frederick K. Wentz. Philadelphia: Fortress Press, 1838, 1965.

Schmucker, Beale M. *Memorial of Augustus Theodosius Geissenhainer.* Philadelphia: The Ministerium of Pennsylvania, 1883.

Scholz, Robert F. *Press Toward the Mark: History of the United Lutheran Synod of New York and New England: 1830-1930.* Metuchen, New Jersey: The Scarecrow Press, 1995.

ritage Association. *The 1743 Palatine House (The Old Lutheran) Years; 1743-1993: The Oldest Building in Schoharie County.* ~olished in Schoharie, New York: Schoharie Colonial Heritage ~on, 1993.

~ert F. *Press Toward the Mark: History of the United Lutheran Synod of New ork and New England: 1830-1930.* Metuchen, New Jersey: The Scarecrow Press, 1995.

~chmucker, Beale M. *Memorial of Augustus Theodosius Geissenhainer.* Philadelphia: The Ministerium of Pennsylvania, 1883.

Scott, Robert. *Letters to The Rev. Frederick H. Quitman, Occasioned by His Late Treatise on Magic.* Poughkeepsie: Adams, 1810.

Skinner, Stephen. *Sacred Geometry: Deciphering the Code.* New York: Sterling Publishing, Co., 2006.

Smith, Edward M. *Documentary History of Rhinebeck in Dutchess County.* Rhinebeck, N.Y. (1881), a 1974 Palatine Reprint.

Smith, James H. *History of Dutchess County, New York: 1683-1882.* Interlaken NY: Heart of the Lakes Publishing, 1882, 1980.

Sowell, Thomas. *Education: Assumptions verses History: Collected Papers.* Stanford, CA: Hoover Institution Press, 1986.

Spener, Philip Jacob. *Pia Desideria.* Philadelphia: Fortress Press, (1675), 1964.

Stürmer, Michael. *The German Empire: A Short History.* New York: The Modern Library, 2002.

Tapie, Victor L. *The Rise and Fall of the Habsburg Monarchy.* New York: Praeger Publishers, 1971.

Teachout, Terry. *The Skeptic: A Life of H.L. Mencken.* New York: HarperCollins, 2002.

Tiejen, Sari B. *Rhinebeck: Portrait of a Town.* Rhinebeck: Phanter Press, 1990.

Tillich, Paul. *A History of Christian Thought: From Its Judaic and Hellenistic Origins to Existentialism.* New York: Simon & Schuster, 1968.

Traver, William H. *Diary and Ledger of William H. Traver.* Rhinebeck: DAR Collection.

Urban, Wayne, and Jennings Wagoner, Jr., *American Education: A History.* New York: McGraw-Hill, 1996.

VanDeValk, Lori. *The Oliver Schoolhouse: An Exhibit at the Old Stone Fort Museum Complex, Schoharie, New York.* Schoharie, NY: Schoharie Historical Society, 2000.

Vamosh, Miriam Feinberg. *National Parks of Israel: Beit She'an: Capital of the Decapolis.* Israel: Eretz Ha-Tzvi, Inc, 1996.

Walvoord, John F. and Roy B. Zuck. *The Bible Knowledge Commentary: An Exposition of the Scriptures.* Wheaton, IL: Victor Books, 1983.

Waldman, Carl. *Atlas of the North American Indian.* New York: Checkmark Books, 2000.

Wallace, Lew. *Ben-Hur: A Tale of Christ .* Pleasantville, N.Y. The World's Best Reading Edition, 1880, 1992.

Weber, Max. *The Sociology of Religion,* Boston: Beacon Press, 1922.

_____. *The Protestant Ethic and the Spirit of Capitalism.* Translated by Stephen Kalberg. Los Angeles: Roxbury Publishing Company, 1904-1905, 2002.

Wedgwood, C.V. *The Thirty Years War.* London: The Folio Society, 1938, 1999.

Wenner, George U. *The Lutherans of New York (City): Their Story and Their Problems.* (New York: The Petersfield Press, 1918.

Wentz, Abdel Ross. *The Lutheran Church in American History.* Philadelphia: United Lutheran Publications House, 1923, 1933.

_____. *History of Gettysburg Seminary: 1826-1926.* Philadelphia: The United Lutheran Publication House, 1926.

_____. *A Basic History of Lutheranism in America.* Philadelphia: Mühlenberg Press, 1955.

White, James F. *Protestant Worship and Church Architecture: Theological and Historical Considerations.* Eugene, Oregon: Wipf and Stock Publishers, [previously published by Oxford University Press, 1964], 2003.

Williams, Kim-Eric. *The Journey of Justus Falckner.* Delhi, NY: ALPB Books, 2003.

Williams, Melvin G. *The Last Word: The Lure and Lore of Early New England Graveyards.* Boston: Oldstone Enterprises, 1973.

Wilson, James Grant, and John Fiske, ed. *Appleton's Cyclopedia of American Biography.* New York: D. Appleton and Company, 1887-1889.

Wolf, Edmund Jacob. *The Lutherans in America.* New York: J.A. Hill & Co., 1889.